Hitler and Spain

Hitler and Spain

The Nazi Role in the Spanish Civil War 1936-1939

ROBERT H. WHEALEY

THE UNIVERSITY PRESS OF KENTUCKY

To Lois

BURGESS
DP
269.47
G3
W46
1989
C.1

Library of Congress Cataloging-in Publication Data

Whealey, Robert H., 1930-
　　Hitler and Spain : the Nazi role in the Spanish Civil War,
　　1936-1939 / Robert H. Whealey.
　　　　p. cm.
　　Bibliography: p.
　　Includes index.
　　ISBN 0-8131-1621-X
　　1. Spain—History—Civil War, 1936-1939—Participation, German.
2. Germany—Foreign relations—Spain.　3. Spain—Foreign relations
—Germany.　4. Germany—Foreign relations—1933-1945.　5. Germans—
Spain—History—20th century.　6. World War, 1939-1945—Causes.
7. Hitler, Adolf, 1889-1945.　I. Title.
DP269.47.G3W46　1989
946.081—dc19　　　　　　　　　　　　　　　　　　88-2087

Contents

Tables

Figures

Maps

Preface

This book examines three basic questions. First, what role did Adolf Hitler play in bringing Francisco Franco to power in Spain? Second and third, during the years of the Spanish upheaval, what gains did the Führer of Nazi Germany make in the European balance of power generally, and in Franco's Spain specifically? In the decisive years of 1936-1939, Hitler made his Spanish decisions in four interrelated areas: political, military, ideological, and economic. This book traces the complex paths of development in each of these areas.

Franco and Hitler both won the Spanish Civil War. Generalissimo Franco's victory was a classic conquest. The Führer's victory proved more tenuous, although geographically broader. Despite, or perhaps because of, his lesser commitment than his Axis cohort, Benito Mussolini, Hitler's Spanish experiment succeeded spectacularly from July 1936 through March 1939.

Hitler was not a scientific experimenter; his mentality was essentially that of a daring gambler. But in a figurative sense he was experimenting with Spain, compared to his deep ideological commitments to territorial expansion in Eastern Europe. As the events unfolded on a day-to-day basis, the Nazis as a whole during 1936-39 were mostly adventurers in Spain, relative to the more serious demands they were making elsewhere. On the other hand, Hitler's Spanish venture was calculated in the sense that General Hermann Göring, Admiral Wilhelm Canaris, and merchant Johannes Bernhardt efficiently implemented Hitler's more limited commitments. They, like Hitler himself, had come out of World War I restless, venturesome. When other Great Powers shifted their attention to eastern Europe in March 1939, Hitler's use of Spain ran into increasing difficulties. That issue will be the focus of another work.

My archival research has concentrated on politics, economics, ideology, and military strategy. My understanding of military tactics, on the other hand, is based largely on secondary sources. Over the years I have tried to keep up with Spanish and German secondary accounts, as well as those in English. See the bibliographical note for more details.

My sincere thanks go to the many people who have aided me. Archivists who have helped with access to significant unpublished records include, at the National U.S. Archives, Patricia Dowling, Daniel Goggin, Meyer Fishbein, Milton Gustafson, Fred Pernell, James Primas, Gary Ryan, Howard Smyth, John Taylor, and Robert Wolf; of the Naval History staff, Dean Allard, F. Kent Loomis, Mildred Mayeax, and Harry E. Rilley; at the Freiburg Militärgeschichtliches Forschungsamt, Wilhelm Arenz, Gerd Brausch, Robert Endras, and Hans Maierhofer; of the staffs of the Archivo Histórico Nacional and the Servicio Histórico Militar, José Martínez Bande, in Madrid; and at the British Public Record Office, particularly Albert Harrington and C.P. Chalmers.

Thanks to the Library of Congress, especially Arnold Price; and the libraries of Columbia University, Harvard University (Widener), the University of Michigan, New York Public Library, Ohio State University, Ohio University, the University of Chicago, and the University of California at San Diego; the Hemeroteca Municipal and Hemeroteca Nacional in Madrid; the London School of Economics, the British Historical Institute and the British Museum; and the Kiel Weltwirtschaftsinstitut.

Thanks to the following people who aided my research in Spain: Miguel Santiago and María José Cosaga of the Ministry of Foreign Affairs; at the Joint American-Spanish Committee for Cultural and Educational Affairs, Ramón Bela, Thomas Middleton, and Ana María Mingote; Francisco Gadea-Oltra of the Ministry of Culture; and historians Víctor Morales Lezcano and Angel Viñas.

Two Germans who were active participants in the events described in this book granted oral interviews: Dr. Helmuth Wohlthat and State Secretary of the Air Force Erhard Milch (both now dead).

I acknowledge gratefully the chairman of my doctoral committee at the University of Michigan, Professor Howard Ehrmann, and Charles Chatfield at Wittenberg University (Ohio).

To Donald Detwiler of Southern Illinois University; Robert Koehl and Stanley G. Payne of the University of Wisconsin; the late Henry M. Pachter of the City University of New York; Bradley F. Smith of Cabrillo State University, California; and Harry R. Stevens of Ohio University, special thanks for reading the entire manuscript at different times and making interpretive comments. Thanks to Herbert R. Southworth for suggestions about the bibliographical note and for copies of German records unavailable in the archives. Willard C. Frank of Virginia Commonwealth University, Norfolk, read chapters 3 and 5; and Arno J. Mayer of Princeton read parts of chapters 1 and 2; to them, I am also indebted.

My sincere appreciation to my wife, Lois, and to Louise Allin, James Alsbrook, and John F. Cady of Ohio University, and Verbena Pastor and Anita Tuchrello for criticizing and proofreading. I acknowledge the financial aid of Ohio University's Research Committee and paid professional leave program, and the financial assistance of the Joint American-Spanish Committee for Cultural and Educational Affairs in 1977-78.

For language assistance, thanks to Martha Felstein; Tatiana Fotitch; Thomas Franz; Francisco Gadea and his wife, Maria; Helen Gawthrop; Paul Hehn; Joseph Ipacs; Barbara Kob; Joseph Roggenbauer; Kurt Rosenbaum; Franz Schwanauer; Karin Wright; and Julitta Young.

Finally, thanks to patient typists over the years: Betty Sue Empey, Paul T. Evans, Heather Evarts, Lisbeth Huntsman, Suzanne Prichard, David Whealey, and Jenifer Wohlwend.

Map 1
The Iberian
Peninsula 1936

0   50   100   150   200
MILES

1

Hitler's Diplomatic Policy toward Spain: July 1936

The outbreak of the Spanish Civil War marked a major turning point in the European balance of power. Adolf Hitler, the Führer of Germany, and Benito Mussolini, the Duce of Italy, aided the Spanish military rebellion in a cooperation that paved the way for their political understanding in October 1936—the Axis. On the other side of the barricades, the Soviet Union supported the Spanish Republicans, and substantial unofficial aid flowed from France to the Loyalists, though the French and British governments officially avoided confronting the Fascist and Nazi dictatorships.

The principal purpose of this volume is to document how Hitler used the Spanish crisis to strengthen the Third Reich. The civil war in Spain provided Hitler with a great opportunity. This "last great cause" drew all eyes to western Europe, divided the British and especially the French internally, and shifted the overall European balance of power. Thus Hitler could pursue territorial gains in eastern Europe.

The civil war that broke out in July 1936 had long roots in the troubled politics of Spain. Municipal elections in April 1931 repudiated King Alfonso XIII and the military dictatorship he had encouraged since 1923. Economic depression had further encouraged disillusionment with the old regime. Lawyers, journalists, and educators sympathetic to republicanism had for over a century complained of Spain's backwardness relative to France and Britain. They demanded a new democratic-republican constitution. Alfonso abdicated, and the royal family left Spain; thus was born the Second Spanish Republic.

The new government was a coalition of liberal-progressives and democratic socialists who immediately prepared a new constitution. They were supported in the streets and the countryside by labor unions and the heretofore illegal anarchist movement, the largest in Europe. Small groups of Stalinists and Trotskyites added their few, but loud, voices. The new constitution provided for proportional representation and a multiparty system modeled in spirit after the French Third Republic.

Among the goals of the first Republican leaders were to disestablish the Roman Catholic Church, cut down the overstaffed army officer corps, and recognize collective bargaining. Land reform was discussed, but little was actually accomplished. Regional autonomy was granted to the Basques and the Catalans, angering proponents of strong central government. Army officers attempted a coup in August 1932, but it was unsuccessful. The November 1933 elections brought a right-wing government to power.

The fundamental problem with Spanish politics from 1931 to 1936 was intolerance on all sides. This set the stage for partisan conflict, leading eventually to civil war. The Anarchists, Trotskyites, and some of the Socialists and Communists pressed for further peasant and working-class revolution. The church leaders, professional army officers, and landlords were bitter about their loss of privilege. Small property holders were frightened by the "red" rhetoric of the Left. Youth from the property-holding classes were drawn to fascist movements, the most important being the Falange Española, founded in 1933. Others supported the reactionary traditionalists known as Carlists, who called for the return of a monarchy, but not of Alfonso's house. Many business leaders backed the Alfonsoist monarchists, the army, and the church. Together with capitalists from Britain, America, and France, well-to-do Spaniards feared a revolution in Spain similar to the 1917 upheaval in Russia.

From November 1933 to the end of 1935, rightist coalitions of churchmen and monarchist sympathizers dominated the right-wing governments, after the first group of leftist reformers (1931-1933) was out of office. In the fall of 1934, a violent strike took place in Asturias. The conservative government finally collapsed in December 1935 over a question of taxes and gambling scandals.

On February 16, 1936, a close election brought to power a coalition of liberals, Socialists, Communists, Trotskyites, and Anarchists formed into a left-wing alliance of parties known as the Popular Front. The major issue uniting the group was amnesty for the strikers of 1934. Although antifascist in ideology, the Popular Front had little interest in foreign affairs because Spain for over a century had assumed a neutral stance toward the affairs of Europe.

The great failure of the newly elected leftist government was not coming together after the election and uniting behind a minimum program. The progressive liberals were divided into at least three parties on the basis of personality. The Socialists were divided between reformist and revolutionary wings. The Anarchists only voted for the Popular Front to avoid rule by the Right, but Anarchists were dedicated to further revolution. The Communists were too few to do much in parliament, but they influenced important socialist and liberal journalists. The Basques and Catalans were anxious to maintain their independence from Madrid.

From a foreign point of view, Britain, France, and the United States (in that order) had the most interest in Spain because of invested capital and markets. The Spanish parliamentary Left looked to those nations as models. Karl Marx had higher prestige with the revolutionary Left than Joseph Stalin had. Strategically, Spain was important to both the French and the Germans in their historic rivalry. Italy and Britain also had an interest in the gateway to the Mediterranean.

In the months following the February elections, confusion and sporadic violence escalated in Spain. The Spanish Civil War began on July 17, 1936, with an insurrection of army officers at Melilla in Spanish Morocco. Within hours, most of the right-wing officer corps throughout Spain had risen against the leftist Popular Front government of the Second Spanish Republic. Liberals, Socialists, Communists, leftists, Basques, and Catalans—a majority of the people in the major cities and more than half the countryside—rallied around the government, putting up stiffer resistance than the rebels had expected. Although the planned coup d'etat failed, it did succeed to the extent that the government found it impossible to suppress the insurgents, and Spain was engulfed in civil war. Each camp—Republican and Nationalist—consisted of a variety of classes, parties, and factions.

The rebel officers on the mainland needed the disciplined Moroccan forces commanded by General Francisco Franco to cross the Straits of Gibraltar and to give immediate help in conquering areas held by the Popular Front. This provided the opportunity for German and Italian leaders to intervene in Spain, thus helping turn the Spanish Civil War into a preliminary round of the great conflict known as World War II.[1]

Germany Expands Its Spanish Interests before July

When Adolf Hitler took power in 1933, Britain, France, and the United States were more important as traders and investors in Spain than was Germany.[2] To the relatively weak Spanish economy, however, considerable German economic and military pressure was applied in the early thirties.[3] Germany by 1935 was recovering from the depression faster than France was, and the Third Reich was beginning to assert itself economically. Spain purchased 120.3 million[4] gold pesetas (14.8 million gold dollars) worth of goods in Germany in 1935, particularly chemicals and electric appliances,[5] while Germans chiefly bought from Spain iron ore, pyrites, skins, fruits, and vegetables.

In addition to foreign trade and capital, numbers of foreign technical personnel help determine economic influence from abroad upon a relatively underdeveloped country.[6] In one sense the most important foreigners living in Spain were the Germans, because they formed the largest group of employed aliens. It is true that fewer Germans than Portuguese lived in Spain, and that total salaries and positions of Germans were lower than the French, the British, and the Americans; yet a much larger proportion of the resident Germans were employed.[7] Eight thousand of the total twelve to fifteen thousand[8] Germans living in Spain before the civil war resided in Barcelona, and about 260 German-owned or German-operated firms located their headquarters in the Catalan capital.[9]

Politically, many of the Germans in Spain were organized in the Nazi party's foreign branch, the Auslandsorganisation, or AO. During the course of the civil war, Nazi Germany would greatly increase its economic influence in Nationalist Spain and would participate generally in revolutionizing the Spanish picture.

As for military ambitions, since 1922 the Germans had been interested in building war vessels prohibited by the Treaty of Versailles. In 1925 King Alfonso XIII had offered the services of Spanish industry.[10] The Spaniards were interested in cash and in asserting some independence from French and British sea power; therefore, they agreed to tap German technical knowledge about submarines for the development of the Spanish arms industry and navy. In response, the German navy sent Captain Wilhelm Canaris, a career officer and a specialist on Spain, to arrange for submarine construction. As a young naval lieutenant during World War I, Canaris had served in Spain as an espionage agent against Britain and France.[11] Between 1915 and 1930 Canaris had traveled about a dozen times to Spain,[12] most of these trips arising out of the 1925 contract with private shipbuilder and arms manufacturer Horacio Echevarietta of Cádiz. The contract called for the building of twelve U-boats and one thousand torpedoes for Germany.[13] A key Canaris contact was Admiral Antonio Magaz, Alfonso's minister of navy in the 1920s who, during the civil war, was to become Nationalist ambassador in Berlin. The project ended after the fall of the Spanish monarchy in 1931,[14] although as late as 1933 the German navy still extended credits to the shipbuilder because Manuel Azaña, the Spanish prime minister, hesitated to repudiate the contract.[15]

The major objective of the German navy from 1919 to the outbreak of the civil war in Spain was preparation for a naval war with France and Poland.[16] The Germans assumed that, in any such war, the United States and Great Britain would remain neutral but potentially hostile. Spain's neutrality might be benevolent, so Canaris joined other planners in naval war games in which Spanish sea bases were scheduled to play a role against France.[17]

Between 1933 and June 1936, Canaris visited Spain at least twice.

Whom he saw and what he discussed remain matters of dispute, though in all likelihood he was working on setting up a secret organization to supply food and fuel to German vessels in the event of war with France. By the time Canaris became vice admiral and head of the German military intelligence (Abwehr) in January 1935, he knew more about Spanish affairs than any other high-ranking German official in Berlin.

In political terms, Spain had little place in Germany's plans before 1936. At least, Hitler's program for Europe as set forth in 1925 in *Mein Kampf* did not deal with it at all. But in "the secret book," written in 1928 and discovered after World War II, Hitler not only stated that Britain and Italy could serve Germany as allies but added that Spain and Hungary had the same aversion to France that Germany had.[18] Hitler, therefore, saw Spain as potentially weakening France, although he did not elaborate upon any possible Spanish-German alignment.

José Antonio Primo de Rivera, head of the fascist-inspired Spanish Falange, did visit Berlin in 1934,[19] where he discussed Nazi-Catholic relations with Nazi party ideologist Alfred Rosenberg. Subsequently Rosenberg forbade the translation of the Führer's anti-Catholic tracts into Spanish because avoidance of unnecessary offense to the dominant Spanish religion served Nazi political interests in Spain.[20] José Antonio spent only five minutes with the Führer,[21] and no follow-up seems to have succeeded the interview, because Spain was too remote from Hitler's more pressing problems. Hitler seems to have ignored Spain until the decisive days of July 1936.

Hitler Intervenes in the Civil War

When civil war broke out on July 17, 1936, the supreme authority in the rebel camp was in confusion. The acknowledged leader of the conspirators, General José Sanjurjo, died trying to return to Spain from Portuguese exile, and generals in the major cities of Madrid and Barcelona were overwhelmed by the Popular Front. The four most powerful insurgent commanders in the field were Emilio Mola in Burgos, Gonzalo Queipo de Llano in Andalusia, Antonio Aranda in Asturias, and Francisco Franco, who did not become Nationalist chief of state until October (see map 2).

From the beginning, the generals knew the rank-and-file Spanish infantry could not be counted on to support the uprising. Moreover, the adherence of most of the Spanish fleet and air force to the government isolated the insurgents in Morocco from those on the mainland. The rebels had to find a way for Franco's Spanish Foreign Legion to reach the Army of the North, headquartered at Burgos under Mola, the primary leader of the military conspiracy in mainland Spain. It was to foreign powers that the self-

Map 2. Nationalist Territory, July 1936

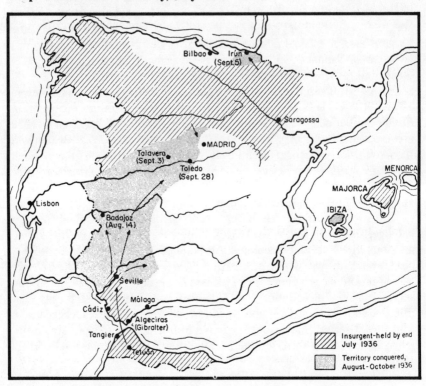

Bilbao · Irún
(Sept. 5)

Saragossa

Talavera
(Sept. 3)

· MADRID

Toledo
(Sept. 28)

MENORCA

MAJORCA

Lisbon

IBIZA

Badajoz
(Aug. 14)

Seville

Málaga

Cádiz

Algeciras
(Gibralter)

Tangier

Tetuán

▨ Insurgent-held by end
   July 1936

▦ Territory conquered,
   August - October 1936

Source: Gabriel Jackson, *The Spanish Republic and the Civil War, 1931-1939*
(Princeton, N.J., 1965), 270.

proclaimed nationalists turned for aid, and it was those foreign powers who
would help Franco emerge as chief of state.

Because of the divided leadership at the beginning of the rebellion,
Mola[22] and Franco[23] acted independently in seeking air support. Between
July 19 and 21, Franco sent two journalist agents to Rome in a bid for Italian
support; Mola asked the conservative monarchist landowner Antonio
Goicoechea to request Italian transport planes.

Franco also made a personal appeal to Hitler for planes and arms.
Having served as chief of the Spanish general staff in 1935, Franco was
better known in Germany than was Mola; Count Johannes von Welczeck,
who served for ten years as German ambassador in Madrid, had hoped in
1934-1935 that Franco would be appointed minister of war. Although
Franco was not officially the leader of the Nationalist movement in July
1936, Hitler chose from the start to deal exclusively with him.

The request for German aid was carried by four emissaries—two

Spanish officers and two Nazi-connected businessmen living in Spanish Morocco, Johannes Bernhardt and Adolf P. Langenheim.[24] They flew in a confiscated Lufthansa tri-motor Junkers transport plane that landed in Seville on July 23 and reached Berlin two days later.[25] Bernhardt and Langenheim talked first with Ernst Bohle, head of the AO, and with the Führer's deputy, Rudolf Hess.[26] From Berlin, the businessmen continued on to Bavaria to confer with Hitler, who was attending the Wagner festival at Bayreuth. When they met for three hours late in the evening of July 25, from about 10:30 P.M. to 1:30 A.M.,[27] the Führer asked them about Franco's chances of winning the war. Bernhardt apparently presented favorable prospects for victory, even convincing the Führer of the need to set up an economic organization in Spain to demonstrate that the Germans would not try to run the show from afar.[28] Hitler then decided to send Franco twenty tri-motor Junkers transports, together with six escort fighters.[29]

Among Hitler's advisors present in Bayreuth was General Hermann Göring, head of the Luftwaffe. On the afternoon of July 26, Göring ordered the creation of a special staff, the Sonderstab W[ilberg], borrowing officers from army, navy, and air, to administer the military aid sent to Franco.[30] The next day, Erhard Milch, state secretary for air, and General Hellmuth Wilberg began the formation of this interservice organization.[31] Wilberg, who had developed a reputation as one of the best pilots in Germany and who had been Milch's commanding officer in World War I, headed the Sonderstab W for almost two years.[32] Although it did keep track of supplies and services, its chief mission was to provide and command a secret German unit in Spain.[33] The complex duties of the staff required army, navy, and air force personnel to man the operations.

Wilberg immediately contacted German commercial and industrial organizations to secure goods for the Spanish operation. On the orders of Sonderstab W, the commander of the Naval Shipping Administration Section of the naval Oberkommando der Kriegsmarine (OKM) negotiated a contract with the Matthias Rohde freight-contracting company of Hamburg, to provide for secret shipment of supplies to Spain.[34]

Early in the morning of July 28, Franco's emissaries took off on the return flight to Tetuán, Spanish Morocco, Franco's base.[35] The following day, flights began by German planes transporting Moroccan troops between Africa and Spain.[36] Shortly thereafter, on the night of July 31, the S.S. *Usaramo*, chartered by the Rohde shippers, slipped out of Hamburg. Aboard were eighty-five Germans commanded by Major Alexander von Scheele, a World War I veteran who had fought in Africa and in the South American Chaco War in 1935; these men soon set up bases near Tetuán and Seville to service the Ju 52 planes.[37] Thus began Hitler's first Spanish military venture, Operation Feuerzauber,[38] named by the Führer for the Wagnerian operatic theme, the "Magic Fire."

Hitler's decision at Bayreuth set off a chain of events that led to continued German military intervention in Spain. After the expected speedy Nationalist victory failed to materialize, Hitler made a second basic commitment on August 28, when he authorized the German fighter pilots in the original contingent to engage in combat.[39] By late September, Hitler again expanded his intervention with Operation Otto, which supplied twenty-four tanks, flak, and radio equipment.[40] In addition, Scheele converted the Ju 52 transports into bombers, and Berlin transferred fifteen additional fighters to his command. By mid-October the Germans probably had 600 to 800 men in Spain.[41] Later that month Hitler decided on the biggest escalation of German participation in the war. The Legion Condor, with an initial strength of 3,786 men, 37 officers, and 92 all-new planes, joined the Spanish conflict in November 1936.[42] This legion, with replacements, was destined to fight for Franco until the surrender of Madrid and the end of the civil war. Not until May 26, 1939, would Hitler bring it home.

In summary, Hitler's military intervention escalated in at least three stages: Operation Feuerzauber in July 1936 providing air transportation to Franco; the August decision to join active combat against the Republicans, together with the subsequent expanded aid of Operation Otto,[43] decided on September 19; and the Legion Condor's dispatch in October-November 1936—called Luftübung Rügen by the air force and Winterübung Hansa by the navy.[44] For the following two and one-half years, Hitler basically maintained the troops he had already sent and did not further escalate German participation. He was, however, clearly violating the August 1936 Non-Intervention Agreement, designed by France and Britain to limit the Spanish Civil War.

Why did Hitler originally decide to intervene in Spain, even though seemingly he had only the slightest previous interest in the country? Or did the Führer of the Third Reich have a hand in the Spanish conspiracy before the civil war broke out?

Intriguing reports have been published that Sanjurjo, the original head of the military conspiracy, visited Hitler in Berlin early in 1936.[45] The Soviet paper *Pravda* stated on March 11, 1936, that Sanjurjo and a small entourage stayed at the Hotel Kaiserhof, the haunt of "big industrialists." *Pravda*'s Berlin correspondent speculated that a counterrevolution against the Popular Front government in Spain was being planned, and added that Sanjurjo had made an attempt to secure German military supplies.[46] Late in the civil war, one German general claimed that Sanjurjo had "conducted negotiations in Berlin," and that his death was a blow to Germany because Portugal drew closer to Britain.[47] However, unless further documentation on Sanjurjo's visit to Berlin is found, questions will remain about its significance. Nor did pre-rebellion contacts in 1934 between José Antonio and the

Germans cause the uprising or give the Falangists positions of influence in July 1936. Neither Spaniard held a decisive position when Hitler was called on for aid; Primo de Rivera was in jail and Sanjurjo was dead. Instead, Franco proved to be most crucial for German policy.

Similarly, although the long war did eventually provide the German military with an opportunity to train men and test equipment,[48] Hitler did not originally intervene for those reasons. In July, no one anticipated a long war because both rebels and Nazis hoped for a quick victory. Testing and training became important factors only at a later stage of Hitler's intervention, when a great variety of equipment was sent. Although some people were talking of a second world war emerging in 1937 and 1938, "Tryout in Spain" did not become a major theme in historiography and propaganda until after the outbreak of Anglo-German war in September 1939.

Hitler's gains from the Spanish Civil War were to be more diplomatic than military, and he intervened in Spain from the outset with his eyes focused on the reactions of Rome and Paris to the Spanish crisis.

Hitler Backs Mussolini's Intervention

Since the end of World War I, Hitler and Mussolini had been ideological twins in their detestation of democracy, liberalism, socialism, and communism. During the Weimar Republic in the twenties, Italy's Mussolini, the first fascist dictator to come to power, generally had supported Britain and France, the other two Versailles victors, against the possibility of a resurgent Germany. Hitler, for his part, in *Mein Kampf* projected a bilateral alliance between Italy and Germany.[49]

Despite their ideological similarities, Hitler and Mussolini did not ally quickly after the Führer took over in Germany in 1933; conflicting ambitions for Austria stood in their way. The Duce attempted to improve relations with the German dictator by a first meeting at Venice in June 1934, but Hitler spurned the overture by increasing German pressure on Austria. The attempted coup of Austrian Nazis against pro-Italian Chancellor Engelbert Dollfuss brought Italian troops to the Brenner Pass in July 1934. At that time, Mussolini's territorial interest in maintaining a buffer state on the Alps outweighed his ideological predilections.

Nevertheless, the Duce soon began reorienting his foreign policy away from Britain and France and toward Germany, mainly because Hitler cautiously supported Mussolini's fight to conquer Ethiopia from October 1935 to May 1936.[50] Similarities of domestic ideology also exerted a powerful pull. Beginning in 1935 the Duce once again took the initiative and approached the Führer several times, seeking closer cooperation.[51] Again Hitler did not commit himself to any major agreement with a weak Italy, then in trouble with France and Britain over Abyssinia.[52] However, Hitler did offer Italy benevolent neutrality,[53] economic cooperation, words of assurance that he respected Austrian independence,[54] and an agreement that attacks on each other in their controlled presses would cease.[55] In the following months, Italian and German fascism increasingly joined in denouncing both democracy and communism. Hitler's gradual rapprochement with the profascist Austrian government culminated in the German-Austrian Treaty of Friendship of July 11, 1936, a move that had Mussolini's blessing.

This diplomatic about-face was, in part, a result of the firm stand that Britain and France took against Italy in the Ethiopian War. The Anglo-French-sponsored League of Nations sanctions against Italian aggression, and the collapse of the pro-Italian Laval government in France further alienated the Duce from Britain and France. Mussolini, therefore, assured Hitler at the end of February 1936 that Italy would not fight for the enforcement of the Locarno Treaties of 1925 or the Versailles Treaty of 1919, both of which guaranteed the German-French border if Germany were to march into the demilitarized Rhineland.[56] The Duce's assurance came as welcome news inasmuch as Hitler had already resolved to take this action against France. The Führer naturally encouraged the Italian dictator to maintain his belligerent stand against France and Britain.

At this time, Hitler informed Mussolini of his concern about the weakening of "anti-communist forces" in Romania, Czechoslovakia, France, and Spain. Later in the spring of 1936, Mussolini let Hitler know that he too was deeply concerned about the future of Spain.[57] Meanwhile, for both political and ideological reasons, the two fascist dictators, acting independently, were verbally attacking the Popular Front governments that came to power in the Spanish elections of February and the French elections of May.

The growing strength of fascism in the mid 1930s had frightened the Soviet Union into the "popular front" strategy. Soviet propaganda services sometimes supported, sometimes led, and frequently attempted to control the diverse associations and committees that comprised the various national popular front movements. Fascist exaggeration of the role of the Communist element in the Popular Front distorted both French and Spanish realities. Actually, the general fascist attack on "communism" extended to liberals and socialists as well as to partisans of the Communist Third International, or Comintern, founded in 1919.

In any case, foreign policy alignments in 1936 served to intensify the ideological agreement that Hitler and Mussolini had long shared. Although Hitler and Mussolini made no specific deal concerning Spain, they followed parallel foreign policies for nearly six months preceding the outbreak of the civil war, especially toward the Spanish Popular Front and the Ethiopian War.

Aside from his "anti-communist" stand, Hitler had little stake in internal Spanish politics; but, as a factor in Italo-French diplomatic rivalry, Spain became important to him. With Mussolini, matters were different. The Duce had long entertained ambitious plans for the western end of what he called "our Mediterranean." For at least ten years he had been supporting conspiracies against various Spanish governments that were friendly toward France. In 1926, for example, the Duce had aided the separatist movement of Colonel Francisco Macià—a prominent leader of Catalan nationalism and somewhat of a leftist—against the monarchist dictatorship of General Miguel Primo de Rivera, the father of Falange chief José Antonio.[58] In 1932 the Duce, ever the ideological opportunist, had supported the reactionary monarchist Lieutenant General Emilio Barrera, along with the Jesuits and other right-wing Spaniards, against the leftist Republican government.[59] In March 1934, Mussolini had promised to supply Barrera and his confederates with weapons.[60] Among the signers of this agreement was monarchist conspirator Antonio Goicoechea, later to play a role in Italian intervention in the civil war. The Carlist group again visited Mussolini in April 1935.[61] By early 1935, the Duce had a branch office of the Italian military intelligence agency, the Servizio Informazione Militare (SIM), in Barcelona gathering information.[62] As of June 1936, Italian submarines were visiting Spanish waters.[63]

On the ideological front, Mussolini had met in 1928 with one of the founders of the Spanish Falange,[64] the party often regarded as the Spanish version of fascism.[65] To advance the Fascist cause, Mussolini subsidized the Falangist press for at least a year prior to the 1936 uprising.[66] From June 1935 to February 1936, the Italians gave the Falange chief, José Antonio Primo de Rivera, 50,000 lire (more than $4,000) monthly. The Duce reduced the payment to $2,000 per month between February and July 1936,[67] perhaps because the Italians were short of foreign currency following economic sanctions imposed by the League of Nations against Italian aggression in Ethiopia. This subsidy did Mussolini little good, however, because José Antonio was imprisoned by the Popular Front in March. He continued to be held through the early stage of the rebellion and was executed in November.

Mussolini certainly had maintained more serious contacts with Spanish rightists before the civil war than had Hitler; yet, in spite of the intelligence missions and involvement in earlier plots, the sequence of events in July caught Mussolini unprepared. From March 1934 to July 1936, Mussolini's main contact in Spain was Goicoechea, the banker, landowner, and reactionary member of Renovación Española, the major monarchist party advocating the return of Alfonso XIII. On June 23, 1936, Goicoechea contacted the Italian army and the Italian foreign minister, to inform them of Spanish rightist plans for a counterrevolution. The Duce was alerted, but he was preoccupied with cleaning up in Ethiopia. The Alfonsoist made a second appeal to the Italian army and minister of foreign affairs on July 12 and 13, and again his plea met with a negative reply.[68]

On July 13, Goicoechea also tried to send word to Mussolini through an Italian agent in Barcelona that the date for the uprising would be the eighteenth.[69] But revolutionaries in a labor union militia killed the Italian agent, and the message never got through. Goicoechea left Madrid on the night of the seventeenth and escaped to Burgos, where he made contact with Mola on July 22.[70] Goicoechea and educator/historian Pedro Sáinz Rodríquez flew to Rome the next day to plead for aid on Mola's behalf.

Meanwhile, a member of the Spanish army representing Franco informed an Italian air attaché on July 15 in Madrid that the plot was set for 8:00 A.M. on the eighteenth in Morocco, but the Italian ambassador quashed the attaché's enthusiasm for Italian involvement.[71] Despite all the advance information given to the Italians on the Spanish officers' plotting against the Popular Front,[72] Mussolini hesitated to back the coup when it did occur. Later, Franco sent his own messengers, journalists Luis Bolín and Marqués Luca de Tena, to Rome on July 21.[73]

Mussolini, who did not know Franco personally, was confused about the relative authority and strengths of Generals Mola and Franco. Mola had been planning the conspiracy since early spring 1936, while Franco had remained noncommittal until at least June and possibly as late as July 13.[74] However, the death of Sanjurjo and the course of military events from July 19 to 21 gave Franco new importance. He was the man with the disciplined Spanish troops in Morocco, ready for airlift to the mainland. After sending his personal emissaries to the Duce, Franco made a second appeal through the Italian military attaché in Tangier.[75] He notified Mussolini that he had appealed to Hitler and implied that if Hitler answered the appeal, the Germans rather than the Italians would gain greater influence in Nationalist Spain. This possibility the Duce could prevent by sending a dozen planes. Franco also told Mussolini that the French were sending planes to the Republicans.

Still, the Duce hesitated because of opposition from his war and foreign ministries[76]—and because of money. Unlike Hitler, Mussolini was demanding hard foreign currency for war supplies. Here, Spanish millionaire Juan March, already in exile in Rome, played a key role. As the chief financial backer of the revolt, March put up one million pounds ($4.9 million) for the first twelve planes, Savoia 81s and Caproni bomber-transports.[77] Even so, Mussolini received at least five separate appeals from Spain before he finally agreed to send planes, presumably on July 25 or 26.[78]

Did the Führer and the Duce confer by telephone or courier about sending aid? Milch, the Luftwaffe general, says they did;[79] and, in the

Führer's later speech on the occasion of the 1939 return of the Legion Condor, Hitler said that his decision to aid Franco had been made "in complete agreement with Italy."[80] The diplomatic climate was right for close cooperation. On July 25, just hours before Hitler met Franco's emissaries in Bayreuth, Germany's ambassador, Ulrich von Hassell, called on Count Galeazzo Ciano, Italy's foreign minister.[81] After extending German de facto recognition of the Italian empire in Abyssinia, Hassell mentioned his concern about French Popular Front assistance to the Spanish Popular Front. Ciano replied that this also worried him, and he offered to have Italian ships protect German nationals in Spain until the German fleet arrived. The two promised to keep each other informed about future developments.

It should be remembered, however, that Hitler and Mussolini sent planes to Franco not only because the planes were needed to transport troops to the mainland but also because Franco's base in North Africa was easier to reach than Mola's. Nine of the twelve Italian planes and the first of the twenty-six German planes arrived in Spanish Morocco almost simultaneously on July 30.[82] But, from surviving flight records of the Franco forces, the Junkers initially aided the rebel movement more than did the Italian planes.[83] Three of the Savoias actually crash-landed in French North Africa after running out of gasoline, an event that caused an immediate international incident.

The German navy also was first to make its presence felt in Nationalist waters. The Italians, like the Americans and the British, sent vessels to rescue their refugee nationals from Republican territory. The Germans, however, sent a different kind of naval mission. On August 2, the pocket battleship *Deutschland* made a widely publicized visit to Ceuta, Spanish Morocco. Admiral Rolf Carls met there with Franco, Colonel Juan Beigbeder (one of the first leaders of the uprising in Morocco and a former military attaché in Berlin), and Nazi leaders Langenheim and Bernhardt, who had just returned by air from Berlin and Bayreuth.[84]

Following the symbolic importance of the *Deutschland* mission, Italian arms deliveries to Spain and the Balearics during the month of August surpassed those made by Germany. The Duce had no desire to see the Führer really get ahead of him; he had done too much talking about the Mediterranean being a "Roman sea" to allow that. By September 23, Italy had sent 200 men, 68 planes, and several hundred small arms.[85] In contrast, by the end of August the Germans had dispatched only their 26-plane group, 86 men, and oil and replacement supplies.[86]

Despite the possibility of a Hitler-Mussolini consultation on July 25, there is no documentary evidence of their coordination on Spanish policy before early August. Between August 3 and 7, Italy's propaganda chief (minister of popular culture) Dino Alfieri traveled to Germany. There he discussed with his German counterpart, Joseph Paul Goebbels, a mutually approved German-Italian press policy against "the bolshevik danger."[87] Alfieri also brought a personal message from the Duce, and he conferred with Hitler for some twenty-five minutes.[88] Joint Italian-German military cooperation in Spain definitely began on August 4 with a meeting in northern Italy between the heads of the German and Italian secret services, Admiral Wilhelm Canaris and Colonel Mario Roatta.[89]

The decisions in Berlin and Rome to send military supplies to Franco rather than to Mola quickly proved decisive in Franco's rise to power. Mola had taken the initiative in Spain from February to July 1936, but he had counted on a quick coup, and its failure made him feel politically more uncertain by August.[90] On the other hand, Franco's past experience of long campaigns in Morocco better prepared him from the beginning for a long war. On August 3, Mola agreed that Franco should have priority and manage relations with the Germans and the Italians.[91] Any military supplies that Mola needed for northern Spain would be handled in the future through Franco.[92]

Seen from the international point of view, Germany and Italy continued to follow independent, but parallel, policies after the civil war started. Because of their common antipathy to the League of Nations, to Britain and France, to the Popular Front and to communism, Hitler and Mussolini had been coming closer before the civil war. The appeal of Franco to both of them reinforced their ties. The bonds forged by Italian-German cooperation in Spain would have the gravest consequences for the traditional position of France as a Great Power.

Anglo-French "Nonintervention" Aids Hitler

In 1936 French officials were worried less about Mussolini than about Hitler, who in March had reoccupied the Rhineland. However, the Duce's attempts to have Italy recognized as the foremost power in the Mediterranean bothered both the British and the French. On the eve of the Spanish Civil War, French-Italian relations were near an all-time low, partly because of Italian resentment toward the Anglo-French League of Nations policy during the Ethiopian War. (League sanctions were not lifted until May 1936.) Italian-French relations were further strained by the French electoral victory of the anti-fascist coalition that created the Popular Front government headed by Léon Blum, who was both a Jew and a democratic socialist.

On the one hand, the emerging Popular Front movement in France of Communists, Socialists, and liberals challenged the ideological foundations of fascism and nazism. On the other hand, the offensive of the Spanish army officer corps, with their Falangist and reactionary monarchist allies, presented the French with the threat of a possibly pro-fascist, pro-Italian, and pro-German government on their southern border. The Popular Front government headed by Blum thus had both ideological and diplomatic reasons to oppose the victory of the Spanish Right.

On July 21, 1936, the liberal Madrid government of Prime Minister José Giral asked the French government for permission to purchase twenty planes, plus arms and ammunition. With Blum's approval, the French air minister at first agreed to dispatch the requested French aircraft.[93] But on the evening of July 25, after Blum had visited London, the French cabinet vetoed that decision, and further arms shipments to the Republicans were officially prohibited by the French government.[94] Ironically, this was the same night that Hitler and Mussolini were deciding upon sending planes to Franco. What caused this reversal by the French?

As chance would have it, before the eruption of the Spanish crisis Blum and his foreign minister, Yvon Delbos, had already been scheduled for meetings in London. On July 22-24, they met with Prime Minister Stanley Baldwin, Foreign Minister Anthony Eden, Chancellor of the Exchequer Neville Chamberlain, and Under State Secretary in the War Office Duff Cooper.[95] Officially, these discussions covered only the violation of the Locarno pact by Hitler the previous March and the possibility of a new Western Five-Power agreement with Germany on the Rhine.[96] Unofficially, however, the Spanish situation came up for discussion, and the British hinted that if the French got themselves entangled with the Spanish Popular Front government, British support would not be forthcoming. According to Blum, the foreign minister urged prudence but did not make a specific threat,[97] while the prime minister told Blum not to expect any English help on Spanish involvement.[98]

Meanwhile, British authorities also were having to deal with the question of aid to the Spanish insurgents. The British Foreign Office was informed on July 23 that private British interests had sold four Fokker planes to the rebels, to be sent via Portugal. Eden personally disapproved of the sale, but he concluded he had no legal power to prevent it. However, the British Foreign Office drew up a general memorandum for an international nonintervention policy in the Spanish strife. This was approved by Eden on the twenty-fourth.[99]

British Tory leaders generally were not as opposed to the Spanish insurgents as the French Popular Front leaders were. Early in the war Eden told the German chargé, Prince Otto von Bismarck, that Franco was pro-British, that a Nationalist victory would not in any way weaken British dominance in Spanish waters, and that the British accepted in good faith Italy's disclaimer of territorial designs on Spain or the Balearics.[100] During July, the British foreign secretary apparently paid no attention to the arrival of German and

Italian planes in Spain, nor did he object to the prospect of a Nationalist victory.

Other members to the British government seem to have been even more sympathetic to the rebel cause. Baldwin supposedly told Eden on July 26 that "on no account, France or other, must [you] bring us in to fight on the side of the Russians."[101] This comment, if accurately quoted, indicates that Baldwin was both disturbed and misinformed. The Russians were not yet in Spain, and Prime Minister José Giral's Madrid government was not even socialist, much less communist. But the British Conservative party's ideological bias tended to throw it on Franco's side out of fear of a spreading social crisis in Europe.

Back in France, a bitter debate had raged in the press between the Right and the Left from July 22 to July 25 on the question of exporting arms to the Spanish Republic. This did not pass unnoticed by the Germans. On July 23, the German Foreign Ministry voiced concern in London and Paris that the French Popular Front government was planning to send planes to the legitimate government in Madrid.[102] Consequently, the chief of the Spanish desk in the German Foreign Ministry asked his London embassy to take up with the British Foreign Office the French rightist press reports about deliveries of French planes to the Spanish government. Meeting with Eden, Bismarck mentioned the reports and affirmed that Germany had "absolutely reliable information" that the stories were true. Eden's dry response was that he, too, read a pro-German and right-wing paper, the *Daily Mail*.[103]

The Germans also closely watched the British-French talks. The German embassy in London obtained a secret report written by an anonymous high official in the British government (or press) who had spoken to both foreign ministers at the time of the July meeting in London. According to this report, Eden said that the conference was held only at the insistence of France, and he definitely urged Delbos to exercise strict nonalignment between the two Spanish factions.[104]

The crucial French decision not to send military aid to the Republic may have resulted, in part, from fear that the class war then going on in Spain would spread to France.[105] However, a second and more significant explanation rests on British coolness toward French support for the Spanish government.[106] Remember that it was immediately after the French delegation returned to Paris that the cabinet, on the evening of July 25, decided against export of arms officially to the Republic. The cabinet did, however, permit the export to Spain of the promised twenty Potez-54s through private channels.[107] The French cabinet also agreed to send a top naval officer to London to try to persuade the British navy to do nothing that might aid the rebel faction.

In London in early August, Admiral François Darlan met with the first sea lord, Admiral A.E.M. Chatfield, a Franco sympathizer and anti-Soviet.[108] Darlan voiced France's concern that Italy might take the Balearics and Germany the Canary Islands. Chatfield voiced some skepticism, but he agreed with Darlan that the two fleets should jointly watch the islands for German and Italian activity. Both men reaffirmed that the traditional principle of nonintervention should be maintained in Spanish politics.[109] In contrast, Sir Samuel Hoare, first lord of the admiralty, concluded that French fears did not warrant action, and that the British navy would withdraw from Spanish waters after refugee rescue was completed. Although this viewpoint did not prevail, it indicates the strength of British detachment from the concerns of France. He added that Germany and Italy did not want a confrontation in Spain; rather, they wanted a new "Locarno," or Western Power Pact, and "that we should do nothing to help Communism in Spain," since "communism" (in other words, social and national revolution) threatened the British Empire.[110] Only on August 8, after the completion of Darlan's mission, did the Paris government take definite legal steps to suspend permanently the export of private arms to Spain.[111]

The British government, meanwhile, had already moved more vigorously against further export of weapons to Spain. Reversing the earlier decision to permit the four privately sold Fokkers to fly to Portugal, Eden on July 29 also turned down an official Portuguese government request for arms. The Foreign Office suspected that they were actually intended for Spain and began to press Portugal not to take sides in the Spanish conflict.[112]

By the end of July, the British government unilaterally was opposing the export of arms to any party in Spain. The Foreign Office justified the new policy with the argument that the Spanish battleground could grow into a struggle of "world fascism against world communism." Acceptance of this formula turned out to be a defeat for liberals everywhere, because it ignored the political center and oversimplified the complexities of the Spanish situation, forcing at least sixteen party viewpoints into starkly "red" or "black" molds. "World fascism against world communism" also became a self-fulfilling prophecy that, for almost three years, was to guide the policy of the British government and the fluctuating majorities of the badly divided French government.

On August 2 came the official birth of the nonintervention policy when a French-sponsored circular note was sent to other European governments, requesting them to agree to an international arms embargo against both sides in Spain.[113] Until the agreement was firm, the French reserved the right to send arms to the Republic.[114] There was never any question of getting British adherence, because the note reflected British policy, but those most tempted to intervene—Italy, Germany, the Soviet Union, and Portugal—

delayed their answers. On August 28, when Italy, the last holdout, finally agreed to the French proposal, an international Non-Intervention Agreement came into effect, and a Non-Intervention Committee (NIC)—including ambassadors of Germany, France, Italy, the USSR, and Portugal—was set up in London.

The NIC aimed originally at applying an international arms embargo against both sides of Spain. Ostensibly the committee was trying to prevent the civil war in Spain from expanding into a Great Power war in Europe. After first working to prohibit the export of weapons, the NIC later took up the transportation of men to fight for opposing sides in Spain. Although it was France that officially began the worldwide arms embargo effort in August, Great Britain mainly kept the idea alive from September 1936 to the end of the war. Germany, Italy, Portugal, and the USSR had no intention of following the formula, and they secretly violated both the letter and the spirit of the nonintervention obligation.

The French governments that went in and out of power during this period were badly torn between their pro-British and pro-Soviet factions and enforced the agreement sporadically. The French ambassador in London reported in January 1937 that the British government believed itself especially authorized to make proposals because the NIC was sitting in London.[115] Delbos, the French foreign minister, also told the Spanish republican ambassador that, at the beginning of the war, "the French government was obliged by England to take the initiative on Non-Intervention" and that the British government wanted the triumph of Franco.[116] Recent researchers have concentrated their attention on the legal maneuvers of August 1936 and have not looked much beyond that month. Therefore, these historians tend to put maximum responsibility for the nonintervention policy on the French government, although it was the British who most strongly championed the cause. Be that as it may, the French decisions of July 25, August 2, and August 8 (which became firm policy during the next month) had considerable effect on the eventual outcome of the civil war. While the German and Italian governments financed, recruited, and secretly dispatched organized units to Spain, the French volunteers and arms merchants, in cooperation with the Soviets, had to buck the official policy of their government.

Although the Germans thought the French government was insincere in its declaration of nonintervention, they were glad to see the French cabinet on July 25 prohibit governmental exports of war material to the Loyalists. Hitler may have reacted to the French indecision and squabbling about Spain by determining on his own military intervention and by influencing the Duce on July 25-26 toward deciding to send planes. However, the French Popular Front cabinet of July 1936 held its own during the first phase of the interventionist game. Into August, informal French supplies probably matched the German aid. In order to weaken the French tie with Britain, Hitler increasingly denounced the "red" tendencies of the Popular Front government in France and its links to the continuation of the Spanish Civil War.[117] The unified German and Italian dictatorial governments were thus willing to risk more than the various French cabinets from 1936 to 1939.

The Soviets Step in for the Republic

Early Soviet influence in Spain had been primarily ideological.[118] Communist Russia had developed little economic or strategic interest in the western Mediterranean before the civil war. Yet, the Communist Third International (Comintern) and the Russian Revolution of 1917 had strongly attracted parts of the Spanish Left. Russian influence in Spain did not have to be subsidized in order to flourish because the initiative for Marxist and Leninist propaganda had been taken on by many Spaniards themselves.[119]

Since 1934 the Soviet Union had been urging socialists and liberals in Spain—like those in Britain, France, and the United States—to create a united "popular front" against the fascists.[120] Stalin had for the most part abandoned the exportation of revolution in 1928 after the Chinese fiasco and his repudiation of Trotsky, the prime Soviet proponent of world revolution. The period 1928-1934 saw Stalin stressing a "united front from below," meaning destruction of the independent leftist, social democratic, and Trotskyist groups in favor of a tightly controlled, conspiratorial party, available to serve Soviet national interests. From 1934, after Hitler's Non-Aggression Pact with Poland, to the 1936 outbreak of the civil war in Spain, the Soviet dictator was interested mainly in protecting Soviet frontiers from a feared Japanese or German armed invasion. Under these circumstances, stimulating social revolution in other countries would have been of little help to the Soviet Union. The Foreign Ministry, consequently, under the direction of Maxim Litvinov, assumed a conservative, defensive reaction against Hitler's *Drang nach Osten*. Georgi Dimitroff, secretary of the Comintern, encouraged the development of a popular front in every country to stand up to Hitler and to Mussolini as well.[121]

The Spanish Communist party, from 1935 to July 17, 1936, was trying to attract proletarian voters from the other parties. Therefore, the old Leninist revolutionary rhetoric was maintained to some extent. At the same time, the Communists made new appeals to the conservative petit bourgeoisie and salariat to stand united in a Popular Front against a possible coup by pro-fascist, reactionary, and nationalistic officers. The Soviet Union worked hard with propaganda, and probably money,[122] to help get popular front governments elected in both France and Spain in the spring of 1936. The Spanish Communist party received only 3 percent of the vote in the election, which translated into fifteen deputies in the Cortes.[123]

The Spanish insurgent officers, nevertheless, charged that the Soviet Union deliberately precipitated the civil war by planning a social revolution to occur between February and July 1936. These vague charges have since been discounted by the major students of the subject.[124]

Spain may or may not have been on the verge of social revolution in the months prior to July.[125] After the February Popular Front electoral victory brought liberals to power, the Left continued agitation for social reform, the president was impeached, many peasants squatted on large estates, strikes were called, and churches were burned. On the Right, the Falangists and the Carlists expanded their private militias.[126] Like Lenin from April to October 1917, Francisco Largo Caballero, leader of the socialist labor union, Unión General de Trabajadores (UGT), and the anarchist leaders were advocating more radical revolution in their speeches. What was different from Russia of November 1917, however, was a lack of specific plans by either the revolutionary socialists or the Anarchists to carry out an armed coup. The Spanish Left was too divided: into bickering liberals, Anarchists, revolutionary Socialists, the small authoritarian Stalinist Communist party, and a group of "Leninist-Trotskyites," the revolutionary Partido Obrero Unificación Marxista (POUM). How widespread the arson and murders were and who was responsible are still controversial.[127] At the other end of the political spectrum, the reactionary Carlists, the Alfonsoists, and the fascist Falangists must share a measure of responsibility for the unrest and polarization of Spanish society during those crucial months.

The major charge advanced after 1937 by liberals, Socialists, Anarchists, and the so-called Trotskyites was not that Stalin provoked revolution in July 1936, but rather that he sabotaged a potentially revolutionary situation for the diplomatic and domestic interests of his own reactionary power in the USSR.[128]

Actually, Russian military intervention in Spain, like that of the Germans, developed in stages. Following the outbreak of the civil war, the USSR encouraged maximum aid to the Spanish Popular Front by rousing up popular front activists throughout western Europe. Stalin presumably acquiesced in the moves made by French Communists and by the Italian and German exiles in Paris. At their head stood Willi Münzenberg, the leading popular front propagandist during the early 1930s and the founder of many international communist front groups that sprang up in France, Belgium, and elsewhere following the naming of Hitler as chancellor in 1933. Münzenberg took more interest in the fate of Spanish proletarian revolution than did Stalin.[129] He helped spur western European popular front organizations to purchase secondhand weapons of various types from private sources and to recruit volunteers to fight for the Spanish "democratic cause."[130]

Although it is not clear exactly how and when the Soviet decision to intervene militarily in Spain was made, it may have occurred at a Moscow meeting held as early as July 21. According to the conservative French press, the Moscow discussion of Spain that day led to a joint meeting of leaders of the Comintern and the Profintern (the Communist-led federation of labor unions) held in Prague on July 26.[131] At that meeting, the leadership allegedly planned to send aid indirectly to the Spanish Republicans. Moscow would supply the money, while liberal and socialist groups in the West would supply the arms and the men. A five-man committee selected to administer the funds consisted of French Communist Maurice Thorez, Italian Communist Palmiro Togliatti ("Ercoli"), and three Spaniards—two of them Communists—plus Largo Caballero, the Socialist. After the meeting Ercoli allegedly proceeded to Paris to confer with the French Communist party.[132]

However, this whole conservative scenario seems dubious. The Germans seem to have known nothing about these alleged moves. The date of July 21, when Moscow supposedly held its first discussion about intervention, corresponded with the date when Giral, the Spanish prime minister, appealed for military aid from Blum's Paris government. The key meeting in which Soviet aid was supposedly agreed upon (July 26) came after the French government decided officially to go along with the British Foreign Office and the French conservatives in limiting military aid shipments to the Popular Front in Spain. The supposed Soviet decision of July 26 also corresponds with the dates when Hitler decided at Bayreuth to send the Junkers transports to Franco, and when Mussolini sent the Savoia bombers.

From the incomplete evidence available, it seems more likely that either the USSR made no decision on July 21 or, at best, the Comintern may have sent agents to find out what was going on in Spain. Actually, the Russians were probably waiting to see what the French, Italians, and Germans were going to do. World-renowned writer André Malraux, president of the French branch of a Communist-front organization called the Committee against War and Fascism, flew to Madrid about July 21 to serve as a private volunteer.[133] He later returned to France to recruit some twenty planes and pilots, which arrived on August 13 at Barajas, near Madrid, and began operations a few days later.[134] Similarly, the Italian Communist Nino Nanetti arrived in Barcelona from Toulouse[135] on July 20. As early as August 1, the French Communist party began collecting arms for shipment to Spain.[136] On August 3, the Comintern quietly initiated a worldwide call for communists to join the other international volunteers who were flocking to Spain.[137] Foreign anarchists, socialists, and liberals, along with communists, had already been volunteering in small numbers in Barcelona.[138] The Soviet newspapers *Pravda* and *Izvestia* reported on August 6 that Moscow's trade unions had collected 12.1 million rubles (two million dollars), ostensibly for relief of the Spanish workers' militia.[139]

As the war developed, in early September the Madrid government shifted further to the left. During that month Socialist Largo Caballero replaced the liberal Giral as premier, and for the first time Communists entered the Spanish cabinet. Also during September, the British and French governments decided to enforce the nonintervention policy sponsored by the London committee against the shipment of arms to the Republican government of Spain. At the same time, Franco's forces were making important military gains, marching east from Cáceres to Toledo and Madrid.

The Soviets thereupon made a second crucial decision to send their own arms and military advisors to direct the international volunteers. The Communist International issued an invitation for noncommunist volunteers to utilize its well-organized underground railway system to Spain. In executing this project, the Soviet Union had the cooperation not only of the French Communist party but of some French officials as well.[140] As of September 12-14, it became official Soviet policy to send military aid to the Republican government of Spain.[141] Shortly thereafter, on September 25—in violation of the spirit of the Non-Intervention Agreement—the first of five Russian ships, the *Neva*, arrived in Republican Spain with food, secret arms, and munitions.[142] According to Italian intelligence reporting from Alicante, the *Neva* unloaded 3,000 cases of rifles, 4,000 cases of munitions, and various boxes of aviation equipment on September 29.[143]

In September, as the Soviets gradually dispatched weapons, the Republicans organized their gold reserves for shipment to the USSR. In mid-September the Bank of Spain prepared to ship to Moscow some 510 tons of gold, amounting to 72.6 percent of the country's large holdings of monetary gold.[144] Throughout the war, the Republic was to spend a total of some $775 million in gold abroad, of which the Republicans spent $237 million directly in capitalist markets.[145] Although gold worth $518 million was sent to Moscow in the fall of 1936, most of that amount—at least $340 million— was re-exported to the Banque Commerciale pour l'Europe du Nord of Paris.[146] The latter was spent gradually on International Brigades, by the Republican war ministries, and by CAMPSA-Gentibus, a new Soviet-model monopoly trading company that was supposed to centralize Republican purchasing activities abroad.[147] Thus, private companies, French cooperation, and the Communist International actually were more important than the USSR in the day-to-day foreign economic operations that sustained the Republican war effort from September 1936 to the war's end. Also, it appears that only $131.5 million of the $178 million in Spanish gold spent in Moscow during 1937 went for weapons, with perhaps an additional $85 million in Soviet-provided credit spent in 1938.[148] This relatively low figure for direct Soviet participation reflects the indirect operations employed by Comintern activities in western Europe.[149]

One good way of measuring foreign intervention over the course of the Spanish Civil War is to compare the money spent or loaned on both sides for military aid. As noted, the Soviets utilized some $518 million in Spanish gold to pay what Russia charged the Republic for the services of the International Brigades, plus an $85 million Soviet loan. Axis credit included 540 million German reichsmarks ($215 million) plus 6.8 billion Italian lire ($354 million),[150]—totaling $569 million. Actually, the Republic spent about $237 million of the $518 million in France, while there was some $76 million in cash sales from the western democracies to the Nationalists.[151] Probably not included in these figures were the private contributions to the Republicans from leftists in the democracies, and the Nationalists' payments to the Moroccan mercenaries.

After the Soviets secretly decided on September 14 to dispatch military supplies on a cash basis, they continued their less obvious intervention by recruiting international volunteers from other parts of the world. Russian personnel as such did not, therefore, bulk large as a military factor on the side of the Spanish Republic. An estimated total of 600 to 800 Russian military advisors served in Loyalist Spain at any given time, while throughout the war the total number of Russians never exceeded 2,000.[152] This was about one-eighth of the number of German "advisors" whom Hitler sent to Franco. Russian planes did not take to the air over Spain until the first week of October 1936[153]—after Hitler's original Feuerzauber and Otto operations, but before his sending of the Legion Condor. A French historian says that five Soviet pilots came at the end of August to Madrid in a French fighter Dewoitine 371 as part of an advanced planning group.[154] Between mid-September and October 23, the main body of 183 Soviet pilots was flown to Albacete through France, utilizing a four-engined Fokker XXXVI.

The Soviet Union was more active in enlisting volunteers, mostly through the NKVD (People's Commission for Internal Affairs) secret police and the Communist parties of western Europe. From July to mid-October, foreign Communist volunteers and other popular front personnel traveled to Spain individually. The resulting International Brigades, volunteers from some fifty-odd countries who fought for the Republic, were officially recognized by the Spanish government after October 23. They were supplied by Moscow and its friends in Paris. The headquarters for recruits at Albacete was directed by the French Communist André Marty, and the enlistees from Germany, France, Italy, and Poland numbered more than 60 percent Communist in membership.[155] Following a month or more of preparation, the initial brigade charged into battle for the first time on October 23.[156] During the course of the Spanish Civil War, perhaps as many as 59,400 men were to serve as brigaders.[157] Because of the increased Comintern activity in September and October, Hitler and Mussolini felt justified in escalating their own military units in November.

Thus, while the role of Soviet troops throughout the war was small, the role of the Communist International, if one includes all the volunteers more or less under Moscow's influence, was large. The brigaders totaled about two-thirds as many men as the combined German and Italian troops. Compare the estimated maximum of 59,400 International Brigaders (only 35,000 if one accepts a liberal's figure)[158] plus the 2,000 Russians, with the overall figures of 16,800 Germans and 80,000 Italians.[159] If one also counts the 53,000 Moroccans[160] who fought for Franco, then the foreign troops on the rightist side constituted an overwhelming majority. In August 1937 the International Brigades had an effective strength of 16,000[161] who faced 5,000 Germans and 45,000 Italians.[162] Furthermore, technologically speaking, the weaponry of the regular German and Italian military was more than a match for the varied weapons and disorganized supply sources of the Comintern.

Not only did the Nationalists get more aid on credit, but the Republicans also spent more money on obsolete equipment and on indirect charges to middlemen in their delivery system. Shipping rates to Popular Front ports, for instance, were three times the rates to Nationalist ports. A second advantage for the Nationalists was that, in contrast with the upstarts who were necessary for Republican procurement, powerful and established British and American businessmen dealt directly with Franco's purchasing agents.[163]

Moreover, in time the Soviets cut down on their aid to the Republic, while the Axis continued to extend strong support to Franco. After June 1938, the Soviet Union quietly retreated from its Spanish venture, partly because the French put heavy restrictions on the transit of Soviet supplies from France to Spain.[164] By September 1938, the Republican prime minister officially called for the withdrawal of the International Brigades. Additionally, the hopes of international support for the beleaguered Spanish Republic were dashed by the Munich Conference. In September 1938, France and Britain coerced Czechoslovakia to cede the Sudetenland to Germany without offering resistance. Stalin, who already suspected Chamberlain and the French foreign minister, Georges Bonnet, could have no doubt that he had been isolated from the European concert.

By July 1938, the official press organ of the Wehrmacht had already concluded that the USSR had written Spain off as lost,[165] and that it continued to support the Republicans only to save face. The Republic's chargé in Moscow concluded in April 1938 that "many Russians believe we have lost the war," and he requested recall to Spain before the Soviets made any declaration of withdrawal.[166] Mussolini and Hitler, on the other hand, stuck closer to their Spanish nationalist allies until the end of the war.

One would have to be overimaginative to see the crisis of 1936 as a consciously planned fulfillment of Hitler's 1928 dreams of using Spain against France. When opportunity knocked in 1936, however, Hitler seized upon the Spanish generals' "movement" as an anti-French factor to help tip the European balance of power in his favor.

The civil war in Spain was to have a profound effect upon European diplomatic history. The war would strengthen Germany by weakening any would-be alliance of its traditional enemy, France, with Britain and Soviet Russia. France would move carefully to preserve its limited entente with Britain, which would help to alienate the Soviet Union, thus turning the 1935 Soviet-French mutual assistance pact into a mere paper agreement. The civil war also would bitterly divide opinion inside France; hence, it would weaken the French at home and abroad. On the other side, Italy, which recently had been isolated by the Ethiopian crisis, would be encouraged by war in Spain to continue its budding rapprochement with Germany. Germany, whose relative diplomatic isolation since World War I had not decreased substantially since Hitler's accession to power, would be able to consolidate ties with Italy and Japan by invoking an "anticommunist crusade."

With the intent of weakening France and the Soviet Union in early 1936, Hitler was already beginning to perform in two rings—Rome and Tokyo—to get others to dance to his tune. The Spanish arena was now added as a third ring to provide even further distraction for London and Paris. In addition to Franco, who would eventually win in Spain, Hitler would emerge as the major European beneficiary of the civil war.

2

The Ideology of Anticommunism: July 1936–March 1939

Hitler's Anticommunist Faith and Opportunism

Political propagandists of all persuasions utilize religion and ideology by manipulating words and images that incite people to kill. Favorite techniques appeal to patriotism and seek to dehumanize the enemy. In the twentieth century people have fought over such abstractions as Christianity, Islam, Huns, communists, fascists, aggressors, "the nation," and "the enemy." Anticommunism, like the anti-Christ from the Book of Revelation, arises from a Manichean concept of a dualistic world where people suppose that good and evil can be clearly and readily differentiated. Nationalism and anticommunism were two concepts that united Franco and Hitler.

Adolf Hitler exploited the slogan "anticommunism" to facilitate his relations not only with other governments but also with corporate, ecclesiastical, and press leaders. He teamed up with and manipulated those who were outspoken in their opposition to Soviet foreign policy, to the activities of the Communist International, to national liberation movements, to social revolution, and even to social reform. He appointed as his special negotiator a tireless advocate for an anticommunist foreign policy, the Nazi party's foreign policy advisor, Joachim von Ribbentrop.

Hitler's anticommunist stand in Spain clearly affected Germany's relations not only in Europe but with Japan, a future ally on the other side of the globe. Ribbentrop had approached the Japanese army about concluding an anti-Comintern pact in 1935. At the beginning of July 1936, before the civil war in Spain started, the German ambassador in Tokyo discussed the alliance project in a visit with Hitler and Luftwaffe Chief Hermann Göring at Berchtesgaden.[1] On July 22, Hitler included both Ribbentrop and his assistant, Hans von Raumer, who ran the Nazi party's foreign office (Dienststelle Ribbentrop), in a meeting with the Japanese military attaché, General Hiroshi Oshima. Under discussion was a proposed anti-Comintern pact.[2] Hitler and Ribbentrop formulated the first draft between July 22 and 24,[3] just before Nazi comrade Johannes Bernhardt delivered Franco's appeal for airplanes. Thus, the Führer clearly had anti-Soviet moves on his mind when Franco brought the Spanish upheaval forcefully to his attention.

Ribbentrop continued talks with Oshima and with Japan's ambassador, Viscount Kintomo Mushakoji, for the next three weeks, and the hesitant Japanese eventually agreed upon a text on August 16.[4] The purpose of the pact was both diplomatic and propagandistic. It was a traditional entente, or loose political understanding, between two imperialistic states, and it was primarily directed against the Soviet Union. Yet, Hitler and Ribbentrop phrased the treaty against the global Communist International (not synonymous with the USSR) in such vague fashion that the terms gave the Nazis and the Japanese military a pretext to intervene in the domestic affairs of any nation that had a communist party or that experienced any kind of revolution or disorder. From the international perspective, the aggressive language threatened the status quo; yet, at the same time, the draft treaty incorporated a conservative overtone. Its language was designed to appeal to conservative and reactionary parties and bureaucracies throughout the world, because it was not overtly directed against them. They, too, were anticommunist in sentiment, and sometimes not able to tell the difference between traditional conservativism and Hitler's brand of fascist rhetoric. The pact could and would provide a cover for the military adventures of Japan in China and Germany in Spain.

The formal timing of the signature of the treaty and the question of whether to publish the text were major items still left undecided in mid-August. The problem was that the Japanese objected to making their signature public. Because Germany had no frontier with the USSR, an anti-Soviet pact would place most of any actual military burden on the borders of Japan's recently established protectorate of Manchukuo.

The onset of civil war in Spain provided Hitler with a handy propaganda asset for bargaining with Japan. Within a few months civil war headlines in Spain helped to persuade Japanese army leaders that Hitler was indeed taking an active military stand against bolshevism.[5] The final, secret text of the German-Japanese Anti-Comintern Pact was signed on October 23, 1936,[6] the very day on which the communist-supported International Brigades took their first public action in Spain; also on that same day Hitler and the Italian foreign minister concluded a protocol establishing a Rome-Berlin entente that, before long, would be dubbed the Axis. The next week, Hitler prepared the dispatch of the Legion Condor, thus escalating his Spanish intervention. It was on November 19, the day after Hitler recognized the new government of Franco in Burgos, that the Japanese ambassador finally authorized the Germans to make the Anti-Comintern Pact public. The text, published six days later, opposed "communism" in general terms, while secret military clauses were cautiously directed against the USSR.[7] Hitler thus achieved a major diplomatic victory with Japan, in part owing to German activities in Spain.

In July 1936, Hitler was faced with much more pressing foreign problems than any "Russian threat." Whatever the German dictator may have meant by "the communist danger," the term did not imply any direct military threat from the USSR. Poland, as a buffer state, protected the USSR and Germany from any direct confrontation with each other. At the time, Hitler regarded Soviet military and industrial capacity with contempt[8] and as a justification of the policy of *Lebensraum*, or living space. Hitler, since the early 1920s, had dreamed of conquering the Ukraine and resettling the area with Germans, creating an empire he hoped would dominate the Eurasian land mass. In Hitler's eyes, bolshevism under Stalin's leadership was mismanaging the natural resources of the Soviet Union. The poor performance of Russian-led brigades in Spain only increased his disrespect for the Soviet military.[9] However, neighboring France, Czechoslovakia, Poland, and Austria were Hitler's immediate targets at the time when the civil war in Spain suddenly presented an unforeseen opportunity for the Führer.

Hitler and Mussolini viewed Franco's repression of Spanish social revolution in different contexts. As early as August 1936, the Duce undertook to justify his intervention in the civil war in terms of preventing a communist takeover of Spain.[10] He reiterated repeatedly a standard defensive diplomatic formula that sounded good in conservative Britain and in the French Foreign Office: namely, that he was forced to send military aid in order to prevent communist advances (i.e., another 1917 Bolshevik revolution) in western Europe. Hitler, for various reasons, postponed open boasting that German units were aiding the Spanish Nationalists until near the end of the war.[11]

Despite his violent anticommunist speeches throughout the civil war, there is no hard evidence that Hitler sent planes to Franco in July 1936 because of fear and hatred of either Spanish social revolution or the alleged designs of Russian foreign policy. His instructions to Göring and to Bernhardt, who returned to Spain to carry out the Führer's mission, were to keep out of Spanish politics and to pursue economic ends.[12]

In fact, Hitler came to believe that "during the civil war, the idealism was not on Franco's side; it was to be found among the Reds." He then argued that the Catholic church was the main enemy oppressing the Spanish people, that a reactionary crew surrounded Franco, and that, in the next civil war, he, the Führer, would support the Spanish "reds."[13] This later comment sheds light on the distinction between Hitler's convictions and his use of opportunistic slogans, and it also reflects his bitterness toward an ungrateful postwar Franco.

Since the 1920s, Hitler had frequently proclaimed to both German and foreign conservatives that he was a bulwark of European civilization against communism. Whenever Hitler was looking for concessions from people who believed in the social status quo, he emphasized his role as an anticommunist.[14] In September 1932, for example, he told one of his earliest followers in the Nazi party, "I have got to play ball with capitalism and keep the Versailles power[s] in line by holding aloft the bogy of Bolshevism— make them believe that Nazi Germany is the last bulwark against the Red flood. That's the only way to come through the danger period to get rid of Versailles and rearm. I can talk peace and mean war. . . . [It is] easier to overthrow Moscow with Capitalists on my side. . . . Capitalism would rather have me than Stalin and will accept my terms. . . . We could force John Bull to his knees."[15]

Hitler repeatedly used fear of communism as a political formula for diplomatic maneuvering. Three instances from 1935 and early 1936 include his conversation with the British foreign minister in March 1935,[16] his public speech on the occasion of German reoccupation of the Rhineland on March 7, 1936,[17] and his talks with the Japanese ambassador, Mushakoji, on June 9, 1936.[18]

Early in the civil war in Spain, Hitler effectively played the anticommunist card at least eight times.[19] Later, in November 1937, came his conversation with the British privy seal, Lord Halifax, that helped to convince a confused Halifax that Hitler was sincere in keeping communism out of Germany and blocking its passage west.[20] Even more pertinent, Hitler told the British prime minister, Neville Chamberlain, at the Munich Conference on September 30, 1938, that he had supported Generalissimo Franco only because of his abhorrence of bolshevism. If he, the Führer, had failed to stop bolshevism in Spain, it could have spread (as if it were a disease) to France, Holland, and Belgium.[21] Chamberlain replied that if a second Spanish revolution were to break out, the four capitalist Great Powers (Britain, France, Germany, and Italy) should respond jointly. Hitler then backed away, replying that he would have to think about that.[22]

Ribbentrop followed the standard Hitler line in late 1938 when he asserted to Bonnet, the French foreign minister, that the Third Reich was fighting in Spain against bolshevism and that France would not regret the German action. The line had limited effect, however; Bonnet retorted that the Spanish problem was solved, that he was hostile to disorder, and that France was not complacent in the face of bolshevism.[23]

A different Hitler—that of *Mein Kampf*—revealed himself in a Reichstag speech on January 30, 1937. Promoting the concept of National Socialism, he described its main plank as the abolition both of the liberal concept of the individual and of the Marxist concept of humanity. These were to be superseded by the *Volk* community that was "rooted in the soil by common blood." He reminded his audience sneeringly that Spain was a "democratic model" of revolution in which 170,000 people had already been slaughtered. For the benefit of conservative listeners, he characterized bolshevism as a pestilence that had caused commerce to decline and was turning Spain into a desert. Then Hitler claimed that bolshevism was only the front for an (imaginary) anti-German "Jewish International." Unlike Anthony Eden, who had decried the division of Europe into blocs, the Führer insisted that Europe had already been divided between the Jewish Communists and the National Socialists. His own National Socialism was the German concept of a universal biological theory of race which all countries should follow.[24]

Hitler's anticommunist propaganda pulled the wool over the eyes of many conservatives in Britain and France. He was truly both a madman and a genius: mad in his objectives, a genius in his propaganda effectiveness. The slow way in which the Spanish Civil War was fought and the intentional propaganda evoked about its outcome contributed greatly to Hitler's public relations machine by exploiting the widespread fear—shared by business, government, and the clergy—of social revolution, atheism, loss of property, and loss of nationhood.[25]

Still, Hitler's anticommunist professions were more than mere diplomatic tactics. In 1936 he was indeed concerned about the German Communist party groups in exile in France, Czechoslovakia, the Lowlands, and Denmark.[26] The long struggle against the German Communist party (KPD) in the German streets from 1919 to the accession of the Führer of the Nazi party to the chancellorship in January 1933 created scars that Hitler could never forget. The German Communists exiled in Paris and the French Communist party could be conceived as being a threat to the Nazis, but only a minor one. In no way did the Popular Front government in Spain, with its small Communist party receiving only 3 percent of the vote, threaten German interests or even Hitler's nationalist dreams. Spain was for Hitler a question of experimental *Realpolitik*. His sincere fear and hatred of communism focused mainly on Jews and on the suspected secret activities of the KPD and leftist émigrés. Hitler hated the Soviet government in 1936, and, as a young war veteran coached in nationalist propaganda in 1919, he had loathed the pro-international German Spartakists and Social Democrats. Ideology is a sincere faith of youth; most politicians learn the art of propaganda and let their ideological convictions mellow. Although the mature Führer had developed his persuasive skills over the years, throughout his life he remained a dedicated anti-Semite. By 1936 he could, however, subordinate on occasion his anticommunist sentiments to larger diplomatic and economic objectives.

Hitler in 1936 reflected his youthful resentments and, at the same time, exploited the symbolic "communism" in many ways: (1) to voice his personal racial bias—"Communism is Jewish"; (2) to quiet German domestic opposition to his rule by invoking the images of revolutionary Communist Karl Liebknecht or Ernst Thaelmann, and of the social, economic, ideological, and constitutional unrest of 1919 and 1932; (3) to persuade Christian churches to tolerate his claims, for he was denouncing atheistic and godless Marxists; (4) to win alliances with Japan and Italy; (5) to "blacken" (or "redden") the French in the eyes of rightists in eastern Europe and Britain; (6) to get conservatives and reactionaries in France to abandon their inactive alliance of 1935 with the USSR; (7) to subvert Czechoslovakia and Austria; (8) to mislead fearful British conservatives into thinking that he could aid in halting social revolution in Spain and thereby also discourage revolution in the British Empire; (9) to cover his own military and economic expansion in Spain; and (10) to denigrate the government of the USSR and thereby prepare for eventual attack. The Führer was determined to provide the Germans with more *Lebensraum*.

Not all Germans maintained Hitler's flexible view of Spanish communism. German Foreign Ministry officials serving in Spain entertained genuine fear of a prospective social revolution from which they assumed the Communist party would reap major benefits,[27] but they were vague on details. The former ambassador, Count Johannes Welczeck, had worried about communist takeover as a threat to German property in Spain. Lack of knowledge was reflected in a Madrid report to Berlin shortly after the Popular Front victory: in April 1936, the German chargé confessed that he had no way of assessing the Spanish right-wing claim that the well-known Hungarian revolutionary agent, Bela Kun, had arrived in Spain.[28] The two Comintern agents giving instructions to the Spanish Communist party at that time apparently were an Argentine and a Pole,[29] yet the German intelligence-gathering apparatus mentioned neither one. Another indication of official ignorance of Communist party activities appears in a counselor's report of the July 19 workers' revolution in Madrid. Describing this leftist response to the Spanish officers' uprising, he labeled as "communist" the well-known anarchist trade union, the CNT.[30]

In the mid-1930s at least three German agencies were involved in systematic anticommunist activity. One was the Internal Section, a special branch of the Nazi Foreign Ministry created in September 1933 to study ideological questions abroad.[31] Headed by Vico von Bülow-Schwante, the Internal Section had been partly responsible for inviting the leader of the Spanish Falangists to visit Germany in 1934.[32] Bülow-Schwante's office, however, concerned itself primarily with assisting the National Socialists and the Propaganda Ministry to project Nazi ideas outside Germany's borders. In this connection the section studied foreign ideologies. It advertised German "unity" for the benefit of foreigners; kept tabs on German Communists, Social Democrats, and liberals; and tried to keep informed on all foreign party movements. The amount of National Socialist propaganda directed toward Spain was small in comparison with the propaganda aimed at French and British right-wingers. Unlike the Soviet Communists, the National Socialists had little interest in enlisting foreign converts to a universal Nazi program. Anticommunist and pronationalist statements that obscured Nazi expansionist designs at the time of the outbreak of the Spanish war were considered sufficient. The Nazi party in 1936 could ally with the native fascists or reactionaries in other countries because they shared the belief that each nation could develop its own unique concepts of fascism, although Nazi "leadership" was stressed by 1937.

A second systematically anticommunist unit was created in 1935, when the German Propaganda Ministry initiated a special Anti-Comintern Section to direct a war of words toward "fighting bolshevism." Its indirect approach was to induce the world press to accept National Socialist and anti-bolshevik publicity.[33] Not until the spring of 1936 did the Anti-Comintern Section become concerned with Spain. The first published article in German on the Spanish communist movement was just one among the many attacks on communism published in an anti-Comintern organ secretly subsidized by Goebbels's Propaganda Ministry.[34] Illustrating a new German Spanish cultural concern in June 1936, the Spanish editor of a pro-clerical weekly, *Trabajo*, visited the anti-Comintern propaganda section.[35]

Nazi-inspired anticommunist journalistic ventures in Spain before the civil war were few, primarily because Berlin regarded Spanish politics with relative indifference. Even after Spain's civil war began, the German Propaganda Ministry utilized stories of Spanish leftist atrocities mainly to frighten conservatives in London and Paris. The periodical *Anti-Comintern* published far more articles written by English, French, and American anticommunist fanatics than by reactionary or fascist Spaniards. The chief of the Ministry, Joseph Goebbels, personally preferred socialistic to capitalistic principles,[36] but because of Hitler's concern with diplomatic ends, the agency subsidized and humored a variety of foreign anticommunists. Hitler's major object was to isolate France from its friends and allies—the Russians, the British, the Czechs—and anticommunist propaganda provided a major weapon for his arsenal.

In addition to the Internal Section and the Anti-Comintern Section, a third German government office involved in anticommunist activity was the Abwehr, or military intelligence, which assembled much secret information on foreign Communists. It was headed after 1935 by Spanish expert Vice Admiral Canaris. As far back as 1928, the Abwehr had received a Spanish offer for a bilateral German-Spanish police agreement against the travel of Communist agents,[37] but that particular project had been stillborn. In the summer of 1933, Ambassador Welczeck had conferred with his new Führer about "the bolshevik danger" in Spain and had advocated increasing German espionage activities against radical movements.[38] According to Welczeck, Hitler met his proposals "only halfway" by agreeing to send Abwehr agents, disguised as businessmen, to Spanish cities to observe communist-anarchist activity. Unfortunately, these spies' reports have not been found.[39]

In 1934 the German secret police, the Gestapo, had agreed with the Hungarian and Polish police to share information concerning the activities of Communists.[40] However, the German Foreign Ministry, in the spring of 1935, had rejected as premature the offer of the right-wing Spanish Republican government to a similar information exchange.[41] The Germans gave first priority to reaching an agreement with the Italian police, which was concluded in April 1936. Then the Gestapo assigned agent Paul Winzer to the Madrid embassy as an official "criminal commissar" to observe communist methods under the newly elected Popular Front.[42] Arriving in Spain only in May, Winzer had little time in June and July[43] to discover anything specific about the alleged communist takeover conspiracy.[44] Nonetheless, the Gestapo was not so ill-informed as the Foreign Ministry about Spanish Communists in mid-1936. Keeping tabs on the Spanish Communist party was not the same task as discovering broad information on the possibility of a social revolution. Winzer accurately reported that the Spanish Socialists were deeply split between a revolutionary faction and a more moderate parliamentary faction, and he asserted that the situation afforded possibilities for Moscow to influence Spain.[45] Actually, the information about the socialist split could have been gleaned from the daily press.

From the German records it appears that Winzer's main concern was the activities of emigré German Marxists in Spain.[46] On July 18, when the army uprising occurred in mainland Spain, Winzer was in Barcelona watching German emigré leftists participate in a counter-Olympic Games.[47] (The official worldwide Olympic events were being held in Germany, and the Barcelona games amounted to an anti-German protest.) After viewing the civil strife in Barcelona for a week, the Gestapo agent sailed on an Italian steamship for Germany.[48] After the civil war broke out, conservatives, reactionaries, and fascists everywhere were looking for evidence of a great communist plot in Spain. Winzer did not uncover such a plot; indeed, it was never found.

Mussolini's Intensifying Anticommunism

Among the many people whom Hitler approached about communism in 1936, none was more important than Italy's Mussolini. Hitler's speeches on communism and the history of German anticommunist activity from 1933 to 1936 provided a series of stepping stones to a German foreign policy that more and more cooperated with Italy.

Italian fascism had preceded German nazism by a decade as an answer to social revolution, both Leninist and other. Benito Mussolini, an ex-socialist, prided himself on founding fascism, a system he believed superior to communism, socialism, liberalism, or conservatism. Fascism, a reaction to World War I, appealed both to the radicals in the streets and to conservatives with property. Fascists appealed to patriotism, country, authority, military glory, imperialist tradition, and a career open to talents. What happened in Italy could best be called a manifestation of the radical right, something that Germany in 1933 and Spain in 1936 were also to experience.

In 1936 the Duce had a certain authority with conservatives in the democracies. To the American and British ambassadors, he often asserted in 1936-1937 that he had to fight in Spain to prevent a communist takeover.[49] The two ambassadors, both conservative sympathizers with Italian fascism, gained the impression that Mussolini wanted a conservative, capitalist, and Catholic Spain. Privately, Mussolini was telling his son-in-law confidant, Count Ciano, that British and French capitalists and their jackal press annoyed him more than did Stalin's government in the Soviet Union.[50]

The fact is that Mussolini resented and coveted the wealth, power, and empires of Britain and France in the Mediterranean and Africa. As a leader of a have-not nation, Mussolini thought of himself as a revolutionary. The Duce sought military victories in Spain as a means of gaining the respect of the British and French for Italian fighting ability. In short, Mussolini's fascism manifested the contradictions inherent in his philosophy of the "radical right"—radical demands made for reactionary goals. In his mind, a communist Spain meant less a Spain manipulated by the USSR than a Spain dominated by the leftist French Popular Front.

Insofar as nazism was anti-French, anti-liberal, anti-Marxist, and anti-internationalist, the Nazis made good allies for the Duce. Both the Nazis and the Fascists had a common interest in eliminating political opposition in their own countries, especially that of the communist parties. The main question facing the foreign policies of the two countries was how far the Fascists and the Nazis would unite to work as an imperial force to operate in other countries. From the general ideological positions of Hitler and Mussolini, they might have allied against international communism immediately after Hitler came to power,[51] but practical politics, particularly on the question of Austria, kept them apart at first.

Fascist-Nazi collaboration required agreement on their geographic spheres of interest and on specific techniques of cooperation. Therefore, the Nazi party, the Gestapo, the Internal Section of the Foreign Ministry, the

Propaganda Ministry, and Military Intelligence had met on several occasions with their Italian counterparts before the general Axis accord emerged in 1936.

The process began in April 1933 when Göring visited Rome to proclaim to Mussolini the "affinity of thought and sentiments existing between Fascism and National Socialism."[52] The next month, Goebbels visited the Duce to discuss ideological issues.[53] Mussolini responded by creating, in June 1933, a new section in his Ministry of Culture that preceded Goebbels's Anti-Comintern Section and was also dedicated to voicing anticommunism as part of the fascist campaign. Mussolini called his propaganda institute the Comitato di Azione per Universalita di Roma (Action Committee for the Universality of Rome).[54]

Although both Hitler and Mussolini preached anticommunism, a difference in tone was evident in their propaganda. The Duce publicized the fascist idea positively, rather than using the more generally negative anticommunist approach of Goebbels. The proud Mussolini appeared more interested in exporting his aggressive philosophy than in counteracting liberal and Marxist-Leninist thinking.

Italian journalist Enrico Insabato went in May 1934 to Germany to see Hitler's foreign policy advisor, prominent during the 1920s, Alfred Rosenberg, and his assistant, Georg Leibbrandt. He followed this trip with two further visits in the spring and in November 1935.[55] These initiatives bore little fruit because the Führer relegated Rosenberg to the sidelines of general European foreign policy and told him to concentrate on the USSR as an academic subject in May 1936.[56] Specifically, he vetoed any role for Rosenberg in dealing with Italians.

More important to Hitler was Ribbentrop. At the Nürnberg Party Day in September 1935, Rudolf Likus of the semiprivate Nazi foreign office Dienststelle Ribbentrop, and Luigi Barzini, a journalist representing Mussolini's newspaper the Popolo d'Italia, proclaimed a united front against bolshevism.[57] Italian propaganda thereafter moved toward the German line; anticommunism was easier to sell than profascism.

Despite their ideological similarities, the question of Austria prevented greater cooperation for at least the first three years of Hitler's rule in Germany. The Austrian question remained so sensitive that—from July 11, 1936, when the Führer concluded a friendship treaty with Vienna, to March 1938, when he took it over—Austria would seldom be mentioned by the two dictators. Rather, Hitler and Mussolini worked on other issues—particularly Spain—so that by March 1938 the Duce was in no position to protest Hitler's takeover.

The process of reconciliation had first begun over Ethiopia. During the course of the crisis (which began brewing in the fall of 1934, and ended with defeat of the Ethiopians in May 1936), Mussolini shifted to working out a broader agreement with Germany.[58] Hence, the German and Italian chiefs of military intelligence, Admiral Canaris and Colonel Mario Roatta, met near Verona on September 16-17, 1935. Roatta suggested that Italy and Germany work together in the field of military intelligence "against bolshevism."[59] Acting upon Gestapo suggestions in November 1935, the chief of the Internal Section in the Nazi Foreign Ministry invited the Italians to conclude a police agreement with Germany, aimed against communist and masonic subversion.[60] The following spring the Duce authorized his police chief and six others to go to Germany, where they visited Dachau. Between March 29 and April 2, 1936, they were received by officials of the foreign ministry: Heinrich Himmler, chief of the SS and German police; his assistant, Reinhard Heydrich, head of the Gestapo; and Göring, the Reich air minister.[61] The discussions eventually led to the formulation of detailed bilateral police agreements regarding codes, travel, exchange of information, etc.—all of which were drawn up between October 15 and 22, 1936, when Himmler, Heydrich, and others visited Rome.[62] These agreements were aimed at all political opponents of the two regimes, whether communist or not. The two parties agreed to nothing specific in regard to either Spain or the Soviet Union.

Although Hitler and Mussolini were concerned about Soviet activities in Spain, their anticommunist relations also developed as a cover for their own imperialism. Anticommunism served as a catalyst, bringing Mussolini to support Hitler's ambitions on the Rhine, and bringing Hitler to support Mussolini's grab of Ethiopia. As they worked together with parallel diplomatic policies, Hitler and Mussolini used the slogan of anticommunism to create the Rome-Berlin entente. Cooperation toward this end had begun in late 1935, had been nourished by the joint military units sent to assist Franco in July 1936, and had been legalized by the protocol of October 23.[63] Christened "the Axis" by Mussolini's Milan speech of November 1, 1936, news of the entente was coincidental with Hitler's secret dispatch of the Legion Condor to Spain. After expanding Italian operations in Spain, Mussolini reorganized his Ministry of Culture in February 1937, replacing the older section for exporting fascist ideology with a new but more limited Center of Anti-Communist Studies. The new organization paralleled more closely Goebbels's Anti-Comintern Section.[64]

In general, Hitler's decision to make a modest military intervention in Spain proved helpful in his general anticommunist propaganda[65] offensive throughout the civil war. It enabled him to cite social crisis in Spain when talking to Mussolini, Franco, Japanese military men, and conservatives in Britain, France, and eastern Europe. The Spanish Civil War helped spawn the Axis entente.

Franco Proclaims the Anticommunist Faith

Historians know far more about Hitler's understanding of communism than they do about Franco's.[66] Before the outbreak of the civil war, Franco had risen as a professional military man whose theory of politics was to remain silent. Franco clearly held a conservative-reactionary position; he never voted for the republic, and he never said "Viva la Republica!"[67] Yet Franco had served various Spanish Republican ministers of war from 1931 to February 1936, ending as chief of staff. Before being "exiled" to the Canary Islands, he apparently believed that monarchy was not worth spilling blood for. Although some other officers had begun talking secretly about a coup from May 1931 on, Franco resisted committing himself until June or July 1936.[68] Why did he then join the conspiracy? Franco's motives remain so obscure that one of his capitalist and monarchist supporters frankly concluded, "Franco doesn't know why he rebelled."[69]

What is clear is that after February 1936, Generals Mola and Sanjurjo began secret talks with disgruntled leaders of the Falange, the Carlists, the Alfonsists, the political Catholics (José Gil Robles, chief of the CEDA party), and the church hierarchy, to plan a rebellion against the legally elected Popular Front government.[70] Between February and the first week in July, various confusing plots and prospective juntas were being privately discussed. Mola nominated himself as chief coordinator, while the cautious Franco held back from any commitment. Mola's attitude toward Communists was clear. He regarded the Spanish Communist party as an instrument of a foreign power, the Soviet Union, intent on weakening the Spanish army. Mola had been against the Spanish Communist party, the PCE, since 1930 on practical grounds, for it sponsored antimilitary and anticolonial propaganda.[71]

Members of Franco's family provide conflicting clues to his political viewpoint before early 1936. His younger brother, aviator Ramón—as famous in Spain as Charles Lindbergh in America—was at one time an anarchist with possible contacts with the Soviet secret police, the GPU.[72] An enigmatic hint of Franco's attitude toward the Soviets was given in January 1936 during his visit to London as chief of staff during the funeral of King George V. On that occasion his cousin and private secretary commented that the "Spanish military delegation" noticed that their uniforms were shabby in comparison to those of the Soviet officers (probably the first ones they had ever seen, for the Second Spanish Republic did not have diplomatic relations with the USSR until after the civil war began); and that the Russians "seemed more like representatives of a bourgeois state than a proletarian state. . . ."[73]

Just after the election of the Popular Front, Franco told the conservative

Franco a traditional reaction, not Facist - who collaborates with Fasc.

38   Hitler and Spain

prime minister of the old government that the major problem of Spain was public order.[74] As Franco came closer toward making a decision to join the plotters, he gave the liberal minister of war a last warning to heed dissatisfaction among the officer corps. In a list of three grievances sent on June 23,[75] Franco called for the reinstatement of army officers who had been court-martialed for the repression of the Catalan rebellion of 1934, and he objected to the arbitrary promotion of certain officers and the demotion or exile of others (including, by implication, his own posting to the Canary Islands). No specific charges were leveled at parties, not even the Communists. Writing later, his cousin says Franco referred to the spring and summer of 1936 as the "hour of the communists,"[76] but what he meant by this is not clear. Did he fear danger merely from the small Communist party, or from all the "reds" of the political Left? At the time Spain had the largest anarchist party in Europe, and Franco had commanded the army operation that suppressed the Asturian coal miners' rebellion (Socialists, Communists, and Anarchists) in the fall of 1934.

One of the civilian conspirators of the July coup attempt, Catholic historian and ideologue Pedro Sáinz Rodríguez, sized up Franco in the period April to July 17 as having no higher ambition than to become high commissioner for Spanish Morocco. Writing after breaking with the generalissimo, Sáinz portrayed Franco as a short, insecure officer who was fearful of assassination, surrounded by a ceremonially attired Moroccan body-guard, and with a weak voice and a dislike of crowds. Sáinz noted, however, that Franco had absolutely no fear of death on the battlefield.[77]

Psychologically, Franco's personality was secretive—more like Stalin than like the flamboyant Hitler or Mussolini. Certainly, Franco was neither an ideologue nor a propagandist, like the two Axis dictators, and it was only after July 1936 that he put on many demonstrations of Catholic piety.[78] Noteworthy is how relatively late, April 1937, Franco and the church hierarchy came to an agreement on the church's future.

In sum, Franco's anticommunism differed in character from Hitler's. Their different social and national origins help explain the political differences that would come to light in 1939-1940. While the civil war lasted, however, their similar anticommunist propaganda misled many people.

The most important keys to Franco's thinking were the need for public order and opposition to revolution—not Catholicism or opposition to Stalinism and the Soviet Union. In a strong, handwritten message of July 21, 1936, to a commander of the Civil Guards, Franco wrote that the enemy, "the forces of revolution," lacked discipline, while true Spaniards could win with confident troops. He signed it, "Viva España!"[79] Franco believed that the liberal parties, which he assumed were controlled by the Masons, shared responsibility for "the spirit of revolution." They had weakened the army by crushing the first Sanjurjo rebellion in August 1932,[80] and they had exiled Franco to the Canary Islands in March 1936. One of Franco's first acts of repression as commander of the expeditionary colonial army was to outlaw the Masons,[81] perceived by him as anti-Catholic, pro-liberal, and internationalist in the Enlightenment tradition. Franco trusted neither Masons nor Communists because they supposedly followed foreign masters—in the masonic case, English and French.

Ironically, in July 1936 tactical needs brought Franco to rely on foreigners. To gain that support in his war against the Spanish Popular Front, Franco labeled his Spanish enemies as Communists. His first appeals for aircraft to Hitler and Mussolini were made on the basis of anticommunism,[82] and because Hitler and Mussolini were noted throughout Europe as anti-red, couching these pleas this way made sense.

After securing aid from Mussolini and Hitler on the basis of anticommunism, Franco began to think about Britain. The half-English journalist Luís Bolín, a longtime reporter in London for the monarchist newspaper *ABC*, had already served the conspiracy in England. From July 5 to 11 Bolín helped the mission of Juan March that procured a DeHaviland *Dragon Rapide*, which flew Franco from the Canary Islands to Tetuán on July 19. Upon returning from his mission to Rome with the first flight of Savoias on July 30, Bolín became Franco's first press chief.[83] It may well have been he who educated Franco on the use of the word communism to appeal to foreign conservatives.[84] While there is no direct evidence of this, it is possible because of Bolín's many contacts in England, especially with the press. In an interview on July 29 with an English press agency Reuters representative in Tangier, Franco linked together Britain, Germany, and Italy, appealing to them to sympathize with his cause in order to drive out communism.[85]

In mid-August, the Marqués Antonio Portago, who wanted to serve the Nationalist cause in London, wrote to Franco's press advisor Bolín, suggesting that more propaganda was needed. Portago drew up a sweeping press release, claiming that Spain was the "stepping stone of World Revolution." Spain could be "the Waterloo of World Bolshevism advocated by Moscow. . . . Spain today is actually in the hands of the Communists . . . [and unless defeated] Moscow will open other branch offices abroad."[86] The draft editorial sent to Bolín was approved by Franco later that month for the Hearst Press and the International News Service.

The reference to Moscow, however, was pure rhetoric. The main headquarters of the Nationalist foreign intelligence was in Biarritz. From there, they sent agents to London, The Hague, Rotterdam, Brussels, Antwerp, Paris, Lyons, Marseilles, Toulouse, Zurich, and Geneva—but not to Moscow.[87] The insurgents knew Moscow was too remote geographically from the military regime fighting to overthrow the Popular Front. Loyalist Spain would survive or die depending more on French decisions than on Soviet ones. The Spanish Right feared nearby Western leftists more than distant Russians.

Franco himself tried his hand at anticommunist propaganda. He had a friend in France, World War I hero Marshal Henri Philippe Pétain, whom Franco had met in the Rif Wars. Franco wrote in late July or early August to Pétain, and this is perhaps the earliest personal text historians have in which Franco himself (as distinguished from hired journalists) defined his concept of communism. In this private message, Franco appealed to military honor and comradeship in arms while affirming that "the Spanish Army was engaged in a decisive struggle for all of Europe and for civilization." His enemy was "international communism headed by Russia," which was currently recruiting aid in France. He asked the marshal to ensure that the French army would avoid supporting "Communist criminals." Franco contrasted militarily held cities in Spain, supposedly ruled with "order and quiet," with the rival "Communist" government in Spain, spreading "anarchy, fire, and theft."[88] As far as is known, Pétain did not respond; Franco thereafter concentrated on military and governmental matters, leaving propaganda to others.

It is easy to underestimate the political sophistication of the supposedly strictly military Franco. However, from the general's prior contacts with Englishmen and Frenchmen, particularly the French in Morocco, Franco knew that anti-Russian, anticommunist views were widely held. In his first speech after the July coup, Franco appealed for order and for the unity of the Spanish nation. He also specifically claimed that the spirit of revolution was being exploited by Soviet agents.[89] Whether he actually had evidence of Comintern activities remains to be shown, but denouncing Soviet subversion without specific evidence of their activities had long been a favorite technique of the Right. On October 10, when Franco learned that five Russian ships with fifty tanks were proceeding to Spain, he said, "I not only face a Red Spain, but also Russia."[90] The Soviet Union indeed was now one of Franco's real enemies.

The question of leadership was a pressing internal problem in the early weeks of the rebellion. Key to the destiny of Franco and Spain was the insurgent generals' decision to proclaim Franco officially as chief of state and generalissimo on October 1, 1936. Bernhardt, the major Nazi liaison between Hitler and Franco, who had successfully carried Franco's request for aid to Hitler the previous July, and Colonel Walter Warlimont of the German Ministry of War encouraged the cautious, supposedly nonpolitical Franco to take the vital step of becoming chief of state.[91] The Nazi ideologues, Hitler and Göring, were delighted at the news because they thought Franco's victory would assure future benefits to the Third Reich, stemming from their investment in Nationalist Spain.

Franco's elevation to prime leadership in the rebel camp had been made possible partly by his success in gaining foreign support by citing the Communist menace. The Nationalist intelligence section clarified its attitude toward communism relatively late. This was on April 19, 1937, when Franco forcibly unified the Carlists and the Falange parties into one totalitarian party (the Falange Española y Tradicionalista, or FET) headed by himself as El Caudillo. He created an Office of Investigation, composed of three individuals, to collect all anti- and procommunist propaganda in collaboration with Goebbels's anti-Comintern effort. The Spanish office particularly suspected people who had connections with the Masons, the League for the Rights of Man (Paris), the Friends of the Soviet Union, the Red Aid International (a creation of Willi Münzenberg, a leading German Communist propagandist who had been in exile in Paris since 1933), the League against Fascism, the League against War and Imperialism, and four other leftist groups.[92]

For purposes of foreign propaganda, it was profitable for Franco to lump his assorted opposition under the labels "Communist" or "red." Fanaticism bred by war always polarizes ideologies; it is no surprise that Franco began to shout about "Russian wolves" even before the Soviets dispatched military aid to the Republicans. As we have seen, for Franco the Spanish "reds" included not only Communists but also Masons, Anarchists, "Spanish Marxists" (Leninists or Trotskyites), both revolutionary and reform Socialists, the three liberal or Republican parties, and the separatists, both Basque and Catalan.[93] They were all what he called "anti-Spain," and Franco's conception of his country as a Great Power was an ideal abstraction like Philip II's glorious golden Spain.

Clearly a counterrevolutionary who longed for Spain's past glories, Franco was also a professional military man who ventured into politics cautiously, and he was more interested in social order than in the promotion of political propaganda for expansionist purposes—unlike Hitler and Mussolini. Franco saw a more immediate red threat to the army in "the Spanish Lenin," Socialist Largo Caballero, than in the Spanish Communist party or the Soviet Union. Republican President Manuel Azaña, although himself hostile to the Anarchists and to Largo Caballero's revolutionary rhetoric, was in Franco's eyes synonymous with the rest of the "reds," because Azaña was a Mason who threatened the army.

Historically, Franco saw Paris, where Azaña had been educated, as a more important center of Spain's problem than Moscow; the election in May 1936 of the French Popular Front government had intensified fears among the Spanish Right. Then, despite his differences in outlook from Hitler and

Mussolini, Franco was pushed into closer ties with nazism and fascism by events in Spain, while after September and October 1936 the Soviets became real enemies because of their concrete military aid to the Republic. Likewise, events in Spain led the Popular Front in France to increase its antifascist propaganda, identifying Franco with Hitler and Mussolini as just another fascist. Thus the Spanish Civil War's dynamism quickly polarized the political and diplomatic chessboard in Europe.

Indeed, with the establishment of a single party, the FET, in Burgos, the reactionary general moved closer to the fascist concepts of Hitler and Mussolini. The Falange chief, José Antonio Primo de Rivera, who had been shot by Republicans in November 1936 after months of imprisonment, attained the status of martyred saint of the Falangist party. Falangists, whose original members called themselves the national syndicalists, were rapidly gaining in numbers among the Nationalists, partly because of recruitment of frightened anticommunists, in the same way the Nazis had grown in Germany in the crises of 1923 and 1929. In 1937 the effective leader of the Falange became Ramón Serrano Suñer, Franco's brother-in-law. Serrano Suñer, educated in law in Italy, had belonged to the Catholic CEDA and had served in the Spanish parliament in the early 1930s. Imprisoned by the Republicans in Madrid on July 18, 1936, he had managed to escape to Burgos by late February 1937. By April, Franco had turned much of the responsibility for anticommunist propaganda and party organization over to Serrano Suñer. If fascism were to win in Spain, Serrano Suñer appeared to be in a key position for the future.[94]

The Spanish Civil War, as a whole, was a tactical measure for Hitler— Spain was a pawn in his struggle with the Great Powers. Military aid was given in such amounts as to ensure that Mussolini stayed in Spain while incidentally providing Franco with an eventual victory over social revolution in Spain. Hitler, however, wanted every penny to be repaid. This economic policy calls in question the conservatives' praises for the "sincere saviors of Western Civilization from the menace of communism."

Despite Hitler's indifference to the Spanish social structure, there were some Nazis who truly promoted a "new" Spain, run by the Falange, that would help the workers oust the old regime. Actually, the leftist Strasser wing of National Socialism (1921-1934) had wanted not to defeat social revolution but to control it, after stamping out the other parties. A similar program attracted some Falangists in Spain. In 1936, however, Hitler was not interested in replaying this old ideological type of 1920s politics in Spain. Like any traditional conservative diplomat, he was anxious to keep his military aid limited while pushing his ally Mussolini forward. After some hesitation, Mussolini answered the call.

At the time, conservatives in Britain and the rest of the capitalist world misunderstood Hitler's anticommunism as some fixed ideology. Actually, Franco, Mussolini, and particularly Hitler often used the term flexibly to deceive opponents in a diplomatic struggle. Hitler's anticommunism in Spain was part of a larger European experiment that allowed him to play in the Italian, Japanese, and Spanish arenas. It kept Britain, France, and the Soviet Union divided as well as splitting the popular fronts in Spain and France. Ex-Socialist Mussolini's manipulation of the term was even more conscious than that of Hitler. For Franco, anticommunism was a vital counterrevolutionary program, but he also used the term to solidify alliances with conservatives and fascists.

3

The Diplomacy of the Anti-Comintern Bloc

Hitler Permits the Duce to Take the Lead

The 1936 Spanish generals' coup attempt stimulated further cooperation between Italy and Germany on several fronts. During the first week of August 1936, propaganda ministers Goebbels and Alfieri worked out a joint German-Italian stand against the "bolshevik danger" in Spain. At the same time Admiral Canaris, the German military intelligence chief, met at Bolzano with his Italian counterpart, Roatta, to discuss secret military aspects of the Spanish question.[1] Colonel Roatta confirmed that Mussolini had sent nine planes, and that a shipload of ammunition and military personnel was on the way. They also discussed Italian and German cooperation on the issue of supplying oil to the Spanish military. The two agreed that Roatta would fly in a German plane to meet Franco and afterwards would inform Canaris of his observations in Spain.

Spanish rebel forces made swift strides during August. Transfer of Franco's Spanish Foreign Legionnaires from Morocco to the mainland went well, and the vital frontier with Portugal was secured by the fall of Badajoz on the fourteenth. News and rumors about intervention were daily rocking Europe, and warships still hovered about Spain even though most foreign nationals had been evacuated.

About August 22 Hitler cast the die for further German cooperation with Italy by sending Prince Phillip of Hesse as special liaison to Rome.[2] There Hesse began what would be a series of assurances to Mussolini that the Führer had no ambitions in the Mediterranean. Both dictators agreed at the end of August to pursue a negative goal: prevention of a bolshevik regime in Spain.[3]

Meanwhile, concerned because most of his country's fleet was patrolling Spanish waters, the German naval commander-in-chief, Admiral Erich Raeder, insisted upon an urgent meeting with the foreign minister to discuss the political and military implications of extended German involvement in Spain.[4] Raeder recommended to the Führer on August 22 that the Germans either pull out of Spain altogether, or, if they really wanted a Nationalist victory, dispatch substantial forces. Two days later Hitler decided to send a military mission to Franco's headquarters to measure the rebels' supply needs; additional military supplies for Franco's expanding war followed in September, in Operation Otto.[5]

On August 25 Germany's war minister, Werner von Blomberg, told Lieutenant Colonel Walter Warlimont (code name "Guido")—a mineral expert then working on the army Economic Warfare staff—that the German war in Spain was expanding.[6] Hitler was determined to give Franco additional support in German weapons, if necessary, but he wanted to check to see whether Italy was prepared to do the same. Warlimont and Admiral Canaris accordingly flew to Rome to confer with the Italians before proceeding on to Spain.[7]

A series of cooperative efforts was proposed in Rome. On August 26, Ciano, the Italian foreign minister, informed Roatta about the Mussolini-Hitler agreement to send the joint mission to General Franco.[8] The Italians and Germans were to survey the possibilities and proposals for supplying the Spanish nationalists with war material and personnel, keep the Spanish supreme command advised about carrying out military operations against the "reds," and arrange guaranteed payment in Spanish raw materials to the two aiding countries. On August 28 Canaris and Roatta worked out the details of the several objectives. Three days later, a party of three Germans and three Italians left for Spain via Tangier.[9]

On September 6 the contingent conferred with Franco at his headquarters in Cáceres.[10] Although the rebel general had no previous knowledge of the mission, he displayed no surprise and promptly asked for tanks, anti-tank guns, anti-aircraft guns, and communications equipment. Roatta and Canaris meanwhile agreed that Italy and Germany would, in the future, exchange military technical data through their respective military attachés.[11] Although the mission took over a month to draw up a plan, by mid-October Operation Otto was demonstrating a degree of consensus between Italy and Germany about their roles in guaranteeing Franco's victory.[12]

After the completion of Otto, Warlimont stayed on in Spain and did not return to Germany until December. In Cáceres he began by reorganizing German personnel and building a general staff;[13] by October 13 he commanded at least seven officers. Twice a week Warlimont, in civilian dress or sometimes in an Italian uniform, accompanied Franco to observe the combat performance of German, Italian, and Spanish tanks, planes, and men in action. It was Franco who recommended that Germany expand its intervention, and by mid-October there may have been as many as 600 to 800 Germans fighting in Spain.[14] This laid the groundwork for Hitler's third military decision—made at the end of October—to send the Legion Condor to Spain.

Aside from the dispatch of the joint German-Italian mission to Franco and the formulation of the Canaris-Roatta technical agreement, Mussolini was pursuing his own independent Spanish policy, particularly in the Balearics. His Balearic Island venture apparently began on August 13, when a local Falangist chief made a proposition for further Italian support to Sáinz Rodríguez, then Franco's informal envoy in Rome. The Falangist had deposited money with the Italian consul to pay for planes and had flatteringly signed his letter "Long live Italy! and long live the Duce!"[15] Mussolini responded by sending him three Savoia seaplanes on August 15,[16] which happened to be the same day the Germans landed four anti-aircraft guns.[17] Four days later Italian fighters and an anti-aircraft battery arrived in Mallorca, the largest island of the Balearics, and the original Italian seaplanes began bombing Republican positions. Between August 29 and September 4,[18] some 4,000 Spanish Falangists were reported to have landed on the island. According to one Spanish socialist source, 500 Italian pilots disguised in Spanish Nationalist uniforms accompanied them.[19] However, the Duce's files indicate this group actually consisted of only 50 Italians.[20] Although the Germans maintained a small presence on Mallorca, the Italians built their own major base there. At Roatta's request, the Italian Ministry of Marine, which exercised jurisdiction over Italian activities in the Balearics, secretly sent Captain Count Giovanni Remedio Ferretti to develop an Italian naval base on the island. He used the pseudonym "Count Rossi,"[21] a name also employed by the highly public leader of the Fascist militia of the Balearic operation, General Arconovaldo Bonaccorsi.[22] The latter, a red-headed lawyer from Bologna,[23] landed on August 27.

As indicated by this confusing use of such pseudonyms,[24] there was much secrecy and mystery connected with the Italian invasion of the Balearics, and the Italians left their German associates in the dark about many of their actions. Roatta's mission also resulted in the dispatch to Spain of an additional 176 Italians with 32 pieces of artillery, 10 tanks, and listening devices on September 23.[25] In contrast, the Germans during September sent only four men and one supply shipment. These were to replenish the stocks consumed by the Junkers squadron sent as Operation Feuerzauber, Hitler's first military venture into Spain.[26]

Germany and Italy were cooperating in Spain, but underneath the air of cooperation the Italians were jealous. The Italian ambassador in Spain (still officially accredited to the Spanish Republic) explicitly recommended to Foreign Minister Ciano that, if he wished to upstage the Germans, Italy should be the more active party in aiding the rebels.[27]

Meanwhile, Hitler and Mussolini were taking further strides toward general political consultation. On September 23, 1936, the day the Italian reinforcements began steaming toward Spain, an important German-Italian meeting took place in Rome. Hitler's private attorney, Hans Frank, a Reich minister without portfolio, visited Mussolini and his son-in-law, Ciano. Frank, an ex-Freikorps man and early Nazi party member, was a Munich lawyer who had admired Italian fascism during the 1920s.[28] Speaking as Hitler's representative, he told the Duce and the count that "the Führer regards the Mediterranean as a purely Italian sea," and that the Baltic was Germany's Mediterranean.[29] Frank added that Hitler had no interest in Spanish territory, and that his only motive in Spain was to maintain the common fascist front against bolshevism. Taking up suggestions Mussolini had made during the Ethiopian War, Hitler now recommended that he and the Duce forge closer ideological ties between the Fascist and National Socialist parties. Ciano agreed wholeheartedly and added that Spain would constitute the first trench against the Anglo-French entente, and that the "tactical field on which we must execute the maneuver is that of anti-Bolshevism."[30]

The details of Frank's Rome mission were probably concealed from Hitler's foreign minister, the conservative Constantin von Neurath. As was his practice, Hitler kept the strings of foreign policy in his hands by sending his own negotiators—Hermann Göring, Wilhelm Canaris, Joachim von Ribbentrop, and others—to confer with top-level foreign leaders. On this occasion Frank brought a key personal message from the Führer inviting the Duce to Berlin.[31] The wary Duce, however, delayed his trip for almost a year.

Instead of going himself, Mussolini immediately sent Ciano. Along the way, Ciano held an important conversation with Göring in Budapest on October 10.[32] There the Italian reaffirmed the understanding derived from the Hesse and Frank talks in Rome, that Italy could have a free hand in the Mediterranean in exchange for Germany's free hand in the Baltic. Ciano denied that Italy desired territory in Spain except for the Balearic Islands and Ceuta. Göring thereupon disavowed any German desire for additional territory whatsoever, and added that Germany's interest in Spain was economic. Ciano noted that he was concerned about the attitude of Britain, which he described as acting mainly against Germany—an allegation Göring denied. During the conversation, each seemed to be using Britain as a threatening club to prove to the other that his own country would be needed as an ally.

After the meeting with Ciano in Budapest, Göring flew on to Rome accompanied by his state secretary for the Luftwaffe, General Milch, and six other officers. There they conferred with the Duce and Italian aviation leaders from October 15 to 18.[33]

Meanwhile, Ciano arrived in Germany to conclude with Hitler the series of political understandings that soon became known as the "Rome-

Berlin Axis." They discussed almost a dozen topics, and they agreed on a formal protocol to oppose the League of Nations and the Anglo-French-sponsored revival of the Five-Power Pact of Locarno of 1925, reaffirming the inviolability of the French-German frontier, which London was promoting to unite the West and to perpetuate the status quo. Again the two fascist dictators agreed that Italians and Germans would form a common front against bolshevism.[34] On Spanish policy they reached three agreements: to carry out German-Italian military efforts jointly; to recognize Franco as head of the government of Spain as soon as he captured Madrid (which they expected to happen in a few days); and to prevent the creation of any rival Catalan state by the French.

Perhaps the most significant provision of this Axis entente was an accompanying oral agreement in which Hitler once again recognized that "the Mediterranean is an Italian sea," and that "any future modification of the Mediterranean balance of power must be in Italy's favor." In exchange, the Axis agreement declared that "Germany must have liberty of action toward the East and the Baltic."[35] The vagueness of the term "East" left room for some later misunderstanding as to whether or not this included Austria or was limited to the Baltic, as Frank had mentioned in September. One year later, in September 1937, when the Duce visited Berlin for the first time, the formula, although still vague, would become a little clearer. Hitler and Mussolini then would agree that "the interests and potentialities of Italy will have due preference here [Spain] and, quite generally, Italy will not be impeded by Germany in the Mediterranean, whereas, on the other hand, the special German interests in Austria will not be impaired by Italy."[36] According to Ciano, this meant that the Duce favored "a thorough-going nazification" of Austria,[37] but that it did not accord Hitler a free hand.[38]

When the Axis protocol was concluded in late October 1936, Hitler and Blomberg, his minister of war, were pressing Franco for an early military conclusion of the civil war,[39] and Franco's prospects looked good. Hitler promised Ciano that more air units would be sent to aid Franco's victory.[40] Plans for helping Franco's forces—including the joint operations Luftübung Rügen (air) and Winterübung Hansa (naval) to establish a new German unit—were drawn up at the end of the month to take effect on November 4.[41] General Hugo Sperrle, first commander of the newly created unit, left Germany for Spain via Rome on October 31.[42]

Sperrle had no Nazi political affiliations but had a record of military experience in Russia in 1934.[43] His chief of staff was Baron Wolfram von Richthofen, cousin of the "Red Baron" who had commanded the famous World War I Richthofen Squadron in which Göring had served. Moreover, Wolfram von Richthofen had served in Rome in 1929-1931 as an "informal" air attaché in violation of the disarmament clauses of the Versailles treaty.[44]

Not only did he know Italy, but he had a good understanding of the Spanish language and of Franco's needs. This aggressive chief of staff eventually succeeded Sperrle, a relatively lazy infantryman, as commander.[45] Even during Sperrle's command, however, Göring regarded Richthofen as his man for military affairs in Spain.

As Germany expanded its military aid, some dispute arose about what nation commanded the military personnel in the newly designated unit. Spain's Moroccan army had its own foreign legion, similar to the French. The few hundred Italians and Germans who had arrived before mid-October were, as a legal cover, part of the Spanish Foreign Legion from Franco's point of view.[46] These included the eighty-six men in Operation Feuerzauber, plus the four or five tank instructors[47] who arrived with twenty-four to thirty tanks[48] under Operation Otto.[49]

During the push to take the capital in late October and early November, Franco put out a call to Rome and Berlin for additional volunteers. Having rolled to the very gates of Madrid, Franco's forces were being held off by the Loyalists, now strengthened by the communist-supported International Brigades and Soviet military aid. Franco's original idea had been to expand the Spanish Foreign Legion under his command, with its composition to be one-quarter each Italians, Germans, Spaniards, and Portuguese.[50] Hitler and Canaris, however, preferred to arrange for a separate German regiment,[51] and accordingly they sent two intelligence officers to Franco's headquarters to discuss the matter.[52] These officers refused Franco's suggestion of placing additional Germans in the Spanish legion: so, in order to receive more German aid, Franco had to allow establishment of the independent unit.

This Legion Condor, as it soon came to be called by the Spaniards, served directly under the command of Sperrle and of General Wilberg from Berlin, not under Franco. It was in no way connected to the Spanish Foreign Legion, as the German legionnaires had been before the arrival of Sperrle's men.[53]

The name Condor for the unit also connected the past with the present. For some time the German Lufthansa A.G. had been flying civilian transport planes from Spain to the Canary Islands and on to South America. These Ju 52 planes were called the Condor Lufthansa after the giant birds of the South American Andes.[54]

Somebody in the Legion Condor wrote a song for the regiment as early as November 11:[55]

Die Jungfrau Maria ist unsere Legion	(The Virgin Mary is our Legion.
Franco über Azaña.	Franco over Azaña.
Arriba España. . . .	Upward Spain. . . .

Figure 1. The Emblem of the Legion Condor

Source: Raymond L. Proctor, *Hitler's
Luftwaffe in the Spanish Civil War* (Westport, Conn., 1982).

Es ist so schoen	It is so beautiful
in der Condor A.G.	in the Condor Company.
Jetze sind wir Legionäre	Now we are Legionnaires
RLM ade ("good-bye"). . . .	Reich Air Ministry Goodbye. . . .
Es kommt kein Feind uns in die Quer	We will meet no enemy on the square
Wo unser Banner weht	where our banner flies.
Wir sind die Condor Legion	We are the Condor Legion
Der niemand wiedersteht.	that no man can hold back.)

Between November 6 and November 18, 92 planes and more than 3,800 men and officers on 6 vessels were dispatched to Spain. Thus began Operation Winterübung Hansa, the code name for the delivery of the main force of the Legion Condor by the navy.[56] Several artillery units, signal battalions, and units for the training of Spaniards joined the air squadrons that formed the bulk of the German troops. Thirty-three of the multi-engine aircraft were flown in via Italy as part of the air Operation Luftübung Rügen.[57]

U-boat warfare also became a consideration for both Italy and Germany in October. Under pressure from Franco, Italy sent two submarines to Spanish waters about October 21, and in November came two more.[58] On October 24 Hitler informed the Duce that the Germans would also send two submarines to Spanish waters. This Operation Ursula was part of a plan to attack Republican vessels.

Soon a joint German-Italian policy on submarines was needed, and on

November 17 Lieutenant Commander Hellmuth Heye of the OKM Operations Section and Commander Werner Lange, naval attaché in Rome, signed for the Third Reich a naval agreement with Italy, dividing responsibility in Spanish waters. The Italians who signed this accord were Admiral Vladimiro Pini and Rear Admiral Oscar Giamberardino.[59] The Axis wanted to avoid confusion since Spanish republican submarines were in the area. The Italians, suspicious also of German submarines in the Mediterranean, put in the requirement that the area north and east of Cabo de Gata (near Almería) would be reserved for Italian submarines, while Germans were accorded supremacy over the waters west of that point.[60] (See Map 1.)

This Heye-Pini agreement meant that Italy took jurisdiction over the sea near the ports where the heaviest shipping to the Republic occurred. After briefly considering competing with the Italians, the Germans suddenly canceled Operation Ursula;[61] the Duce, on the other hand, soon increased his patrols to seven submarines.[62] During the rest of the war the Germans limited their submarine action largely to observing merchantmen and assisting with minelaying. While at the outset the Italian and German submarine efforts were nearly equal, the Italians soon took the lead; in 1937 they were to sink many merchantmen bound for Loyalist ports.

On land, the Duce at first had not been eager to expand his Spanish commitment. When Madrid did not fall as hoped in October, the two fascist states decided to recognize Franco anyway. On November 18, 1936, at Hitler's insistence and probably to impress the Japanese, Germany and Italy both assigned chargés d'affaires to Franco's headquarters, by then moved to Salamanca. Hitler selected as his choice retired Lieutenant General Wilhelm Faupel, head of the Ibero-Amerikanisches Institut (and formerly a member of a Freikorps) and possessor of ten years' experience in Argentina and Peru.[63]

Any prestige conferred by overt Axis recognition could not, however, turn the tide of battle by itself. The Nationalists needed more trained men equipped with modern weapons. Perhaps because the Duce was surprised to see how large the German Legion Condor actually was, and certainly because of the growing size of the International Brigades, he decided upon a larger Italian venture in Spain.

Compared to the speedy and thorough planning that led to the creation of the Legion Condor, Mussolini's technical plans were slower to mature. His first move, after watching the Germans, had been to escalate naval operations. It was apparently not until November 20 that he conceived the idea of sending an independent Italian division, rather than more individual Italians, to join Franco's legions.[64] This idea developed concurrently with key political and diplomatic maneuvers.

Conscious to some extent of Italy's technological weakness, the Duce

was making overtures to Japan and Britain as well as to Germany. On
November 28 Mussolini hinted to the Japanese that he was ready to join the
German-Japanese Anti-Comintern Pact.[65] The Japanese, however, delayed
accepting the Italian proposal until 1937, when they felt the need for support
because of their invasion of China.

In any case, Britain was more important to the Duce than was Japan. On
November 1, when Mussolini made his famous speech in Milan announcing
the formation of the pro-German Axis, he had also included phrases to open
the door for an understanding with Britain at the expense of France. The
activity of the Italian military and naval forces in the Balearics had increased
concern in London. In September and October, Foreign Minister Eden had
proposed a mild protest to the Italians, and, after considerable discussion,
the British cabinet had approved this mild warning that turned into a treaty
offer: "Any alteration of the *status quo* in the Western Mediterranean must
be a matter of closest concern to His Majesty's Government."[66] Afterward,
following lengthy negotiations, the British and Italians signed and announced publicly a gentlemen's agreement to maintain Spain's territorial
integrity,[67] and to recognize the territorial status quo in the Mediterranean
generally. This was proclaimed to the world on January 2, 1937.[68] Most
members of the Tory party, the Foreign Office, and the cabinet took the
agreement seriously as a pressure that would maintain European peace.
Privately, however, the ambitious Duce not only was thinking of staying in
the Balearics but already was speculating about a sudden attack on British
Malta.[69]

From November 1936, when Mussolini made offers to deal with both
Berlin and London, to March 1939, the end of the Spanish Civil War, the
four Great Powers of western Europe would experiment with various types of
alliances, alignments, and ententes.[70] The largely secret Rome-Berlin Axis
proved in the end to be the strongest, and the public London-Rome gentlemen's agreement was one of the frailest.

While London and Rome were negotiating the gentlemen's agreement,
the Duce sent Fillipo Anfuso, Ciano's chef de cabinet, to Spain. Anfuso
returned to Rome from his visit with Franco at the end of November 1936
with a draft treaty[71] against communism that also granted the Italians
political and economic concessions in Spain. This document provided more
concrete gains to the Duce than did his vague agreement with the British.

On November 28 Franco signed with Italy the "anticommunist treaty."
The document abandoned Article Sixteen, the enforcement and sanctions
clause of the League of Nations Covenant; it prohibited transit of French
troops across Spain in the event of an Italian-French war; and it also
guaranteed Spanish benevolent neutrality toward Italy in case of general war.
Spain further agreed "to assure it [Italy] all the supplies which it might need,

as well as all facilities for the use of harbors, airlines, railroads, transit routes, and trans-shipment."[72] Mussolini in turn promised orally to provide three to four thousand infantrymen to help Franco's land army achieve victory.[73]

Nationalist Spain's unofficial ambassador to Italy and to the Vatican, Admiral Antonio Magaz, had been in Rome since late July or early August 1936;[74] in November, he sought permission to recruit Italians for the Spanish Foreign Legion.[75] At first Mussolini agreed.[76] Then, in light of Hitler's dispatch of the Legion Condor and of Anfuso's anticommunist agreement, the Duce set out on a new strategy. General Roatta was sent back to Franco to discuss the formation of two Italian tank companies and the sending of a section of anti-tank guns, flak, and mortars.[77] On December 7 Roatta was appointed by Mussolini as commander of all Italians in Spain for both the newly planned all-Italian units and the mixed brigades.[78] Militarily at this point, the Duce was still second to the Führer; but politically and ideologically he had already put himself out in front, and further military commitment was soon to follow.

In contrast to the new Italian-Spanish anticommunist treaty providing rewards for Italy to be paid by Franco's Spain, the Germans had asked relatively little in political concessions from the insurgent generals. Hitler's political fruits were to be reaped not in the Iberian Peninsula per se but from the deterioration of the general European situation, caused in part by the Spanish Civil War. After expanding the civil war by sending the Legion Condor, the Führer came to realize by December that it was better not to escalate the war further. For one thing, under the Axis agreements, Hitler gave Mussolini priority in Spain, once the Duce had sent in his own troops.

For another, the War Ministry and the commander in chief, Colonel General Werner von Fritsch, were particularly opposed to increasing German participation in the war because it worsened Germany's relations with Britain and France.[79] Caution also was recommended by the Foreign Ministry, especially Ernst von Weizsäcker, the political director,[80] and to a lesser extent by the conservative foreign minister, Constantin von Neurath.[81] They argued that the Anfuso-Franco agreement of late November gave Italy such substantial new political gains that it would be useless for Germany to make further military escalation in Spain, even if Hitler should desire it. The Foreign Ministry also argued that Germany's goal in Spain should in the future be confined to obtaining greater economic concessions. The Führer was swayed by the views of the old Weimar conservatives still left in the regime, who contended that, since Italy's stake in the Nationalist victory in Spain was greater, Italy should also supply the bulk of the military forces.

Mussolini soon was to learn of the German reluctance to escalate military aid. When he wanted larger German ground troop support for

Franco, he appealed to Hitler to assign a military man to attend a highly important conference in Rome on December 6.[82] Before the conference met, however, Hitler decided that henceforth the Italians should take the principal role.[83] Abwehr Chief Canaris was dispatched to Rome, where he informed the resident German ambassador that Hitler intended to reduce German military participation in Spain as compared with Italian participation.[84] At the December 6 conference with Italian military leaders, Canaris assumed an observer role, which understandably displeased Mussolini.[85] The Abwehr chief also indicated Germany's unwillingness to send divisions to Spain, an attitude that made the Duce briefly postpone his own decision on sending expanded aid to Franco.

Another appeal for more German forces came from Faupel, Hitler's new chargé in Salamanca, who had arrived in Spain on November 28. Faupel owed his appointment to the influence of Nazi Reichsleiters Rudolf Hess and Ernst Bohle,[86] who had originally arranged for Franco's appeal to reach Hitler in July. Faupel had been designated over the objections of Foreign Ministry leaders and the commander-in-chief of the army, none of whom had a high opinion of him, despite his years as a Latin American military advisor. A week after first meeting with Franco (whom the chargé thought unprepared to rule an army and a nation), Faupel appealed directly to Hitler for a German division to be sent in support of the Spanish crusade.[87] The anti-bolshevik Faupel also immediately thought of including Spain in the Anti-Comintern Pact, just after Germany and Japan had signed.

Following initial talks in Spain, General Faupel returned to Berlin to report on December 17 concerning the Spanish situation. On the morning of December 22, Hitler held a very important meeting for German policy. Present in the Reich Chancellery were Göring, Blomberg, General Werner von Fritsch (head of the Wehrmacht), Faupel, Colonel Warlimont (returned from helping to organize Operation Otto and the Legion Condor), and Colonel Friedrich Hossbach, Hitler's adjutant for military affairs. The opinions of all except Faupel were to limit aid. In response, Hitler decided that Germany would send no more men to Spain except as replacements for Legion Condor personnel and a small SS unit to train Spanish police officers.[88] This meeting and its outcome leaked out and were discussed in the world press, giving Faupel his only page-one coverage in the *New York Times* (December 24, 1936).

Hitler explained to his entourage his ideas on the Spanish Civil War in these terms: "If the attention of the European powers could further be directed to Spain, this would entail considerable advantages for German policy in Europe. . . . Germany's interests, which alone should be considered, were therefore not so deeply involved in an early conclusion of the Spanish Civil War as to risk a limitation of its own rearmament. On the contrary, German policy would be advanced if the Spanish question continued for a time to occupy Europe's attention and therefore diverted it from Germany."[89]

These ideas were hardly original with Hitler. They are also found in a dispatch written by Ambassador Hassell in Rome covering the long-term development of German-Italian relations. In it, Hassell argued that Mussolini had warmed up to Hitler's Reich in January 1936 as a result of the Abyssinian crisis. Currently the Spanish Civil War was having the same effect, namely, preventing Italy from being drawn into the Anglo-French net. Italy, consequently, would have no choice but to turn to Germany.[90]

A few days before Hitler's Reich Chancellery conference, Italy had begun a major escalation of forces in Spain. Thousands of regular army units and Black Shirt militia were embarking for the Spanish arena.[91] The new Corpo Truppe Volontarie (CTV) was born between December 7, when Mussolini appointed Roatta, and December 18, when the first three thousand men embarked for Cádiz. Mussolini kept the form of his military organization secret from Franco, who had been expecting Italian troops to join his legion rather than independent units.[92] Mussolini was confident that Britain would not object, because their gentlemen's agreement, then ready for final signatures, provided that the territorial status quo in Spain would not be altered, regardless of the outcome of the civil war.

Thus, by the end of the autumn of 1936, divergent policies toward Spain had developed on the parts of Hitler and Mussolini. Italian intervention had expanded, beginning with the decision in late August to increase arms deliveries to the Balearics. In early November the Germans had begun sending the Legion Condor. By mid-December, after the Anfuso-Franco "anticommunist treaty" of November 28, large numbers of Italian regular army troops were being dispatched to fight in Spain.

His commitment to Franco going far beyond that of Hitler, Mussolini once again asked Berlin in January to send more military aid to the Nationalists. This time the reply came via General Göring, who visited Italy on January 15: Germany would only maintain the current strength of the Legion Condor in Spain,[93] and the Duce should provide any additional foreign troops needed to ensure Franco's victory. It was also agreed that Franco would choose the proportion of German and Italian supplies for his campaign.[94] Göring and Mussolini covered a broad agenda for the future of the Axis operations in Spain, including propaganda, a joint blockade, intelligence, and a renewed invitation to the Duce to visit Hitler in Berlin.[95]

From November 1936 to January 1937, the ad hoc decisions of the two Axis dictators had definitely shifted the German-Italian balance in Spain to Italy. The Führer gave up military parity and, later, superiority to the Italians, despite the dispatch of the Legion Condor. Hitler's basic policy became one of limited commitment, concentrating on extracting economic returns and maximum political benefits from the exertions of others.

Mussolini Expands and Withdraws from Spain, 1937-1939

Following Mussolini's decision of December 1936 to expand Italian military forces in Spain beyond Germany's commitments, he became the victim of his own propaganda. On January 18, 1937, the Duce had 17,422 ground troops fighting in Spain, and by January 30 there were 28,700.[96] The number escalated to a maximum of 44,648 by May 1937.[97] By August 1938, Hitler had 5,600 troops secretly fighting in Spain, while Mussolini maintained 37,400-45,000 fighting men there, "gloriously" visible.[98] By the end of the war, Hitler was to spend $215 million on Franco, compared to Mussolini's $354 million.[99] By sending more men and war materiel to Spain, the Duce lost the diplomatic flexibility he had once enjoyed. In the eyes of the world, the Italian divisions in Spain confirmed Mussolini's role as Franco's major supporter. Fascist newspapers boasted openly of the Duce's anticommunist military campaigns.[100]

Hitler, in contrast, maintained strict secrecy on German military activities in Spain; the Gestapo and the Abwehr saw to that. Thus, morale became a major problem of the Legion Condor. The German troops and many Nazis, especially Ambassador Faupel,[101] could not understand the limited war, and they objected behind the scenes. Complaints were heard that the Legion Condor—with its bombers, fighters, tanks, and signal units—sat passively outside Madrid for six weeks during November and December 1936. Military information from Spain was sent back to Berlin in a leisurely manner, with no publicity given to the deeds of the unknown legion, and with no reinforcements forthcoming.[102] Furthermore, in Faupel's view, the troops were rotated too infrequently in early 1936.

This tactic, incidentally, indicates that training and testing in Spain were not Hitler's original motive. He did not at first exact the maximum military experience for his armed services, because too much turnover in personnel would have led to security leaks. Later, in 1937 and 1938 when the Führer felt more confident in face of the irresolution of Britain and France, rotation became frequent. By the end of 1937, 9,278 men had been sent, and 3,615 had been rotated home. In 1938 the numbers returning equalled the numbers sent.[103]

Not until November 5, 1937, did Hitler clearly enunciate to his subordinates his Mediterranean policy in the now famous Reich Chancellery speech reported by adjutant Hossbach.[104] With the dream of *Lebensraum* lurking in the back of his mind, the Führer pointed out that Germany would strengthen Italy's rear; if Italy got into a war with Britain and France, the Germans could support the Italians with raw materials. It would, therefore, be wise for Germany to let the Spanish war drag on and to encourage Italy to hang onto Mallorca. Meanwhile, Germany would make use of the persistence of the war to "settle" the Austrian and Czech problems. The fanatic German nationalists would not be satisfied until the German-speaking Austrians and Sudentenlanders (and even those "inferior" Bohemians and Moravians) were incorporated into a Greater Reich; Hitler then could put pressure on Poland and Russia. Mussolini's navy helped in these great ambitions by opposing France and Britain in Spanish waters.

In contrast to Hitler's Machiavellian view of Spain, Mussolini boldly vowed to Franco, the British, the French, and the Germans that he would continue to supply the Nationalists until their victory had been won.[105] The Italian military rout suffered at Guadalajara in March 1937—when thousands of Italians surrendered to the Spanish "reds"—was a blow to Mussolini's military prestige, and it stiffened his resolve to commit more men and material to the war. This defeat enraged the Duce, while the Führer only laughed in private.[106]

On occasion Mussolini resented Hitler's "brutal friendship." In June 1937 he complained to one of Chamberlain's confidants that the Führer egged him on in Spain while using the civil war as a smoke screen to obscure Nazi moves. The dictator privately told the British diplomats that, as a result, his own relations with the Germans had worsened, and that he actually wanted his troops out of the civil war.[107] But the imperalist Mussolini could not bring himself to abandon Franco publicly, partly because Italy's fighting men would lose more face in light of the Guadalajara humiliation. He would be ridiculed in the major capitals of the world as the man who ran away. So, despite occasional doubts, the Duce pushed himself further into the Spanish imbroglio, while repeatedly asserting that he was fighting in Spain only to "stop communism."

In July 1937, the Sonderstab W convinced the Spanish military to redeploy the German reconnaissance squadron, AS/88, a 110-man unit of the Legion Condor, from Cádiz to Pollensa on the island of Mallorca.[108] From their respective bases on Mallorca, the Italian air force bombed the area from Cartagena to Tarragona, and the Germans bombed from Tarragona to the French frontier.[109] Thus, the Legion Condor and the CTV worked out an air jurisdiction similar to the Heye-Pini naval agreement of November 1936.

Mussolini also continued to expand naval operations throughout the Mediterranean. A personal appeal from Franco in August 1937 led Mussolini to commit a larger portion of his navy to the Spanish cause.[110] Ignoring the spirit and the letter of the 1936 Non-Intervention Agreement, four Italian submarines were stationed outside the Republican ports of Barcelona, Tarragona, Valencia, and Cartagena, with orders to fire on all

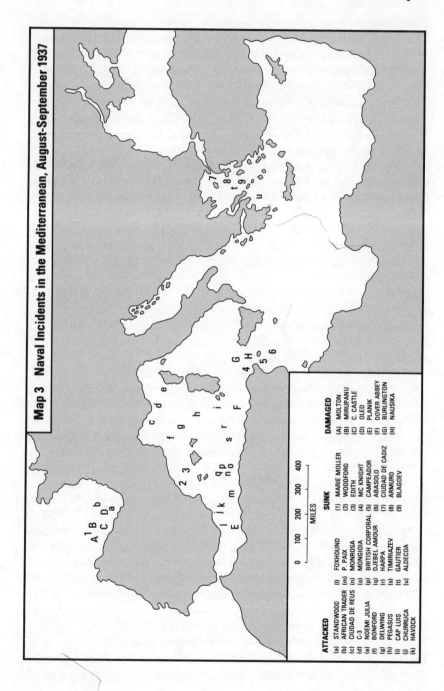

Map 3   Naval Incidents in the Mediterranean, August-September 1937

ATTACKED

(a) STANDWOOD
(b) AFRICAN TRADER
(c) CIUDAD DE REUS
(d) C-3
(e) NOEMI JULIA
(f) BONFORD
(g) DELWING
(h) CAP LUIS
(i) CHURRUCA
(j) HAVOCK

(l) FOXHOUND
(m) P. PAIX
(n) MONROSA
(o) MONGIOIA
(p) BRITISH CORPORAL
(q) DJEBEL AMOUR
(r) HARPA
(s) TIMIRIAZEV
(t) GAUTIER
(u) ALDECOA

SUNK

(1) MARIE MOLLER
(2) WOODFORD
(3) EDITH
(4) MC KNIGHT
(5) CAMPEADOR
(6) ABASOLO
(7) CIUDAD DE CADIZ
(8) ARMURO
(9) BLAGOEV

DAMAGED

(A) MOLTON
(B) MIRUPANU
(C) C. CASTLE
(D) OLED
(E) PLANIK
(F) DOVER ABBEY
(G) BURLINGTON
(H) NAUSIKA

MILES

0   100   200   300   400

Soviet and Spanish Republican flags by day as well as on British and French flags by night.[111] Two additional submarines watched the Dardanelles, while two destroyers watched over the Straits of Messina. Other submarines and destroyers patrolled the Sicilian Channel; friendly German, Japanese, and Portuguese merchantmen were warned not to use this passageway. In the western Mediterranean, the so-called Spanish white fleet was stationed between Melilla and the Balearics, while Italian ships watched the area from the Balearics to Sardinia (see map 3).

In total, the Italians used fifty-two submarines and forty-one cruisers and destroyers in their Mediterranean force.[112] A dozen vessels were attacked between August 11 and 31.[113] The Non-Intervention Committee, acting at the insistence of Britain and France, labeled this illegal maritime warfare "piracy." London and Paris sought to maintain the traditional principle of the freedom of the seas; but, because Chamberlain did not want to alienate Mussolini, Italy was not specifically condemned. The Anglo-French entente nevertheless protested strongly and called a conference at Nyon, September 10-12, 1937, to take measures against the "pirate" subs in the Mediterranean.[114] Mussolini called off his submarines but launched a quieter operation. In this one, submarines under the command of Nationalist Spaniards confined operations to the Balearic Island region from September 17 to February 5, 1938.[115]

The Duce finally visited Berlin in September 1937, where the Führer dazzled him with exhibitions of teutonic efficiency and flattered him as the founder of international fascism. The Duce's Berlin speech identified the Italian Fascist revolution and the German National Socialist revolution as a joint crusade against the Comintern, the League of Nations, and senile democratic capitalism; thus, Italian "volunteers" in Spain were saving European culture.[116] Hitler mocked the Duce in private but flattered him in public, and the Führer concluded after the visit that Mussolini had bound himself to Germany forever.[117]

Following his Berlin visit, Mussolini finally acceded to the Anti-Comintern Pact.[118] Negotiations had begun in February to convince Italy to join the ideological-political pact.[119] Negotiator Ribbentrop, who at this point officially held the post of ambassador in London, flew to Rome on November 6, 1937, to obtain the Duce's signature. A few weeks later Italy withdrew from the League of Nations. On November 25 the Anti-Comintern Pact became trilateral, and military talks followed, directed mainly against the Anglo-French "entente." Ostensibly the Soviet Union was the prime target of the pact, but the defensive democracies, especially France, became the more important objects of fascist contempt. Indeed, Mussolini maintained correct relations with the Soviet Union, and an Italian construction firm assisted the Soviets in building warships.[120] On the other hand, the

Duce denounced Blum, the French Popular Front leader, as backed by international Jewry.[121] On October 31, 1937, the Italian ambassador was withdrawn from Paris as a protest against relations that had been worsening for more than a year. The old career diplomat, trying to paint a realistic picture of the Parisian situation, told Mussolini that France regarded Italy as its number-one enemy. Mussolini retorted: "A great honor. I want to be feared and hated rather than tolerated or protected."[122]

To the chief of staff of the Sonderstab W, which was administering aid to the Spanish insurgents, Hitler put his Machiavellian objectives graphically. The Führer surprised Colonel Erwin Jaenecke by commenting, just after a Franco victory at Teruel in the winter of 1937-1938, that he, Hitler, would like to see a "red" Catalonia. Since a "red" Catalonia would have to be protected by France, Franco and France would then become rivals. Besides, Franco would tend to blame Britain for the situation. Moreover, industrial Catalonia would be cut off from the rest of Spain's cheap raw materials, which then would be available to aid German industry. As for Mussolini, "a red Catalonia would be like a thick, fat bone before the Italian dog kennel, and Mussolini could stand around gnawing at it, while he does not trouble himself worrying about other things in Europe, which he couldn't do anything about anyway."[123]

Hitler followed his words by making one of his rare interventions into the Spanish tactical situation. He told the shocked Jaenecke to encourage Franco to move south toward the Almadén mercury mines and to leave Catalonia alone. Apparently Franco accepted for a while the advice about turning south. Having reached the Mediterranean in April 1938 at Vinaroz, the next logical move would have been to press north toward Barcelona. Instead, on April 20 the generalissimo turned west toward Teruel and south toward Valencia.[124] Franco did, however, concentrate on Catalonia in the summer and fall of 1938.

In the course of 1938 two token Anglo-Italian agreements were pressed upon the Duce by the appeasing Chamberlain in an effort to get withdrawal of Italian troops from Spain. The Italian dictator finally agreed on November 16, 1938, to withdraw 10,000 of his 40,000 fighting men, but Chamberlain's hope of weaning Mussolini from Hitler and turning him toward France and a stable Europe run by the four Great Powers was an illusion. In describing his contempt for the "bourgeoisie," Mussolini told his son-in-law, Foreign Minister Ciano: "When Spain is finished I will think of something else. The character of the Italian people must be moulded by fighting."[125] For the time being, the Spanish military situation attracted his attention. But the passion for glory, which prompted him to demand victory for Franco, also welded him to Hitler and to the ideology of anticommunism.

During the course of 1937 and 1938 the civil war dragged on, with the Nationalists gradually gaining territory. Franco's men, with Axis support, took Málaga in January, the Basque country in midyear, and Asturias in the fall of 1937. In the spring of 1938 they broke out to the Mediterranean, splitting Valencia from Catalonia. In July-August 1938 the Nationalists opened the offensive on the Ebro to wipe out the leftists of Catalonia. After the Anglo-French retreat of September 1938 at Munich, when a democratic Czechoslovakia was forced to surrender the Sudetenland (a process in which Stalin was excluded from Chamberlain's four-power concert), Mussolini felt so confident that in November his Fascist party began demanding that France make concessions to Italy in Corsica and Tunis.[126]

Thus, the Duce continued to follow perfectly the Hitler-backed strategy of "Italian leadership in the Mediterranean." Only after Franco's victory at Barcelona on January 26, 1939, achieved with the assistance of the CTV, (Corpo Truppe Volontarie), did the Duce feel satisfied. Proclaiming that "Spain is now completely liberated from the infamy of the Reds,"[127] he thereby regained his flexibility in dealing with Germans on questions of anticommunist propaganda. Commenting in January on the German text for a new Anti-Comintern Pact, foreign minister Ciano noted, "In one paragraph was mentioned 'the threat of Bolshevist dissolution' as the aim of the pact. In reality, where is this threat? And even if such a threat existed, though not to our countries, why should we be concerned about it? We should not. Every possibility of dissolution and breakdown of other peoples should be encouraged and favored by us at the proper moment."[128]

Not until Hitler decided to march on Prague in March 1939 did the Duce suddenly grasp that he had been acting as a cat's-paw for Hitler's eastern aims. By this time Hitler's Italian-Mediterranean strategy seemed about to die a natural death. By March 15, the Spanish flames had died down to mere embers; everybody expected that the Spanish war would be over in a few days.

The Duce's March 14 reaction to the message that Germany would soon incorporate Bohemia was not unfavorable.[129] When the event actually occurred the next day, however, Mussolini shouted out his annoyance. He resented not so much the extinction of Czechoslovakia as the fact that Hitler accomplished it in one day, while his own Black Shirts had been bogged down in Spain for two and a half years and had gained little or no tangible reward. In his own words, "The Italians would laugh at me; every time Hitler occupies a country he sends me a message!"[130]

After agonizing hours, even days, of reevaluation, the Duce designed a trick to rival those of Hitler. On April 7 Italy swooped down on Albania without giving the Germans more than a few hours' notice.[131] After the collapse of Albania, the rapidity of which surprised even Mussolini, the

Duce gave the word on April 11 or 12 to withdraw his troops from Spain.[132] The Italian dictator felt satisfied that Albania compensated for Bohemia. He had expected more outcry from Anglo-French circles, and the small Italian contingents sent to Spain in the last week of March had served as reassurance and a decoy. Mussolini, for the first time in two years, saw Spain the way Hitler had seen it: as a diversionary tactic to cover his ambitions elsewhere in the eastern Mediterranean and the Balkans.

Germany Works to Develop Direct Ties with Spain

After July 1936, through the National Socialist party and the foreign ministry, Hitler persistently instructed German civilians in Spain to avoid political questions and to concentrate on economic relations.[133] Although Hitler rejected the notion of direct political ties with Spain during the early months of the intervention, this picture underwent gradual change as civil war continued. Because of the war's length and the growing tension in Germany's relations with other Great Powers, a second strand of complex events evolved in Spanish-German relations.

During the early days of the war, Franco had striven for solidarity with Hitler. In November 1936, for instance, Franco's chief of police, General Severiano Martínez Anido, requested that the SS send a German delegation to Spain to help build up the Spanish police force.[134] The Sonderstab W sent as advisor Hermann Göring's cousin, Count Wolf von Helldorf.[135]

Pressure came from another quarter. In January 1937, a representative of the Polish military asked the Spanish Nationalists for permission to examine captured Russian equipment. Franco refused the request on the basis that the Germans would not like it: Poland was allied to France, and the French government would inform the USSR.[136] On the other hand, when the Japanese military attaché asked for the same privilege at about the same time, he was recommended by the Germans, and permission was granted.[137]

Propaganda also helped solidify Burgos-Berlin relations. On November 18, 1936, the day Hitler recognized the Burgos regime, he met with his foreign minister, Neurath, and the newly appointed chargé d'affaires to Spain, Faupel, who had strong links to the Nazi party *Auslandsorganisation*. Earlier, while heading the Ibero-Amerikanisches Institut, Faupel had thought and written on the positive role of the AO in protecting German interests abroad and strengthening German expatriate ties with the Fatherland.[138] Hitler subsequently wanted Faupel to take with him to Spain a specialist on propaganda and another for organization of the Falange; Hess, the Führer's deputy, was to be consulted in the naming of these men. While Faupel was not to concern himself with military matters, it was expected he would need to be informed about everything by the military. His task was defined as advising the generalissimo upon request, representing German interests with Franco, and reporting to Berlin about Spanish developments. [139]

Even without adding an economic expert (commercial attaché Richard Enge was already in Spain), Faupel traveled with a large entourage. The group included Hans Kroeger, delegate of the Nazi party and the Ministry of Propaganda; Willi Köhn of the SS, later consul general; Hans Stille, later secretary of the legation; and Gestapo agent Paul Winzer, who had been in Barcelona when the uprising failed there in July. [140]

The War Ministry had reservations about Faupel from the first. Ambassador von Ribbentrop's "spy" in Berlin, Rudolf Likus, reported to his chief in London that Faupel had terrible relations with the War Ministry, and that his appointment was opposed by Fritsch, the ministry's chief of staff. [141] Once in Spain, Faupel's relations with the military were to go from bad to worse, for he delivered opinions and recommendations the Legion Condor command did not like.

It has been noted that Faupel's December call for greatly increased numbers of German troops was denied. He also immediately turned his attention to the training of the military and the Falange. In his first report from Spain, Faupel specifically requested sending as trainers three Spanish-speaking retired military men, like himself veterans of South America. By late winter this training was under way. In mid-April he heard with satisfaction Franco's account that the first group of Spaniards trained by a man recommended by Faupel was ready for action. [142]

Faupel also requested the naming of a certain officer of the brown-shirted stormtroops (Sturmabteilung or SA) to the post of liaison officer in the field. [143] The war minister, Blomberg, to say nothing of the Legion Condor commander, Sperrle, must have been affronted by Faupel's assessment: "There is urgent need of a senior officer who gets along well with Spaniards and can speak the language, to function as liaison officer with the divisions at the front." Faupel ingenuously added: "I may perhaps be accused of meddling in things which are outside of my present sphere of activity. . . . Whenever and wherever I intervene, it is done in such a way that the work of Sperrle, Funck, [military attaché] etc., is not interfered with, but rather supported. . . . Any friction between us is out of the question." [144]

In early January 1937, Faupel was looking forward to the arrival in Spain of some fifty German instructors within six weeks. Many of them were German businessmen with military experience who formerly had been active in Spain. By the end of January, Faupel was backing as "absolutely necessary" a plan for a joint German-Italian general staff. Ignoring the Germans currently serving with Franco, Faupel suggested as the German head of this joint staff one Colonel Hans Knauer (retired). A veteran of

World War I, Knauer had advised Chileans until 1935 and was the father of a flier for Franco.[145] This plan was rejected in Berlin. As a result of such meddling, Faupel soon was barely on speaking terms with Sperrle.

Despite difficulties with the Legion Condor, however, Faupel had some success in the diplomatic field. On February 8, after the Nationalists succeeded in taking Málaga, Hitler and Mussolini announced the naming of ambassadors to Salamanca, thereby increasing Faupel's status. The Wilhelmstrasse took its first important political step toward tying Spain to itself when it secured Franco's pledge of neutrality in any future war by the secret protocol of March 20, 1937, which Faupel signed.[146] By its terms, Franco agreed not to participate in treaties with third powers directed against Germany and to avoid "everything that might serve to the advantage of the attacker or to the disadvantage of the attacked." This bilateral agreement notably obtained less for the Third Reich on paper than the Anfuso-Franco agreement had accorded to Italy four months earlier. For example, the League of Nations, the Balearic Islands, and the transshipment of foreign troops were not specifically mentioned in the German treaty. The Germans were informed of the existence of the Anfuso agreement, and they quoted it to Mussolini when the question arose of further supplying Franco's military needs. The Duce, however, seems to have been uninformed of the German-Spanish neutrality protocol of March 1937.

Faupel's modest success with the protocol did not assure good relations with Franco. In March, when Faupel presented his credentials as ambassador to the generalissimo, Ramón Serrano Suñer, Franco's brother-in-law, thought it curious that the old general showed up in academic robes and mortarboard.[147] More than questions of style were involved, however. The retired general's attempted interference in Spanish military matters and domestic politics eventually made him persona non grata with the Spanish chief of state.

According to Serrano Suñer—Franco's adviser on Falangist party matters and subsequently his minister of the interior—Faupel encouraged radical elements in the Falange. Like many Nazis, Faupel's notions of the need for social reform in Spain were more revolutionary than were the views held by Franco and most of his military associates. Whereas Franco's crusade was a counterrevolution, the arrogant Faupel associated the Falange with the "revolutionary" doctrines of National Socialism. He sought to provide Spain's poor with an alternative to "Jewish internationlist Marxist-Leninism." Although, in the eyes of liberals or democratic socialists, the Falangists and the Nazis were reactionary and counterrevolutionary, the old-fashioned Alfonsists and Carlists who surrounded Franco viewed the Falangists as classless troublemakers.

In April 1937, when the Spanish chief of state forced the unification of the reactionary *tradicionalistas* and the radical Falangists into a single party, the FET, he ousted Manuel Hedilla as Falange chief. Faupel spoke up for Hedilla in early June, possibly saving him from execution, but not doing the German ambassador any good with Franco. Still, Faupel pressed on and personally arranged for visits of Spaniards to Germany—such as the leaders of the feminine section of the Falange in July 1937, including Pilar Primo de Rivera, sister of the martyred José Antonio. [148] Faupel also annoyed Franco by taking up the economic causes of certain Germans who were already a source of irritation. [149]

Meanwhile, Faupel's relations with the Legion Condor were worsening. The party leader (*Gauleiter*) for Schleswig-Holstein visited Spain in May and noted later that the German military hated Faupel so much they would not fill his car with army gasoline. [150] Commander Sperrle spoke no Spanish—a black mark against him in Faupel's eyes—and Sperrle grumbled pessimistically in the hearing of German-speaking Spanish officers about the stalemated military situation. (Although they despised each other, Sperrle and Faupel did agree in disliking Franco's slow and cautious campaigning.) After the fall of the last of the Basque provinces in June, the smoldering dispute between the two flared into the open. Sperrle snubbed an attempt by Faupel to make up and complained about Faupel's behavior to his superiors. [151] For his part, Faupel told of Sperrle's defeatism and of his opposition to the economic maneuverings by other Germans in Spain, who passed the complaints on to Berlin. [152]

In July, Sperrle and Faupel brought their disagreements before Hitler, but the Führer refused to heed complaints about the slow war in Spain. [153] As a rigid Nazi and a hispanophile, Faupel took the crusade against bolshevism seriously. He just could not understand Hitler's Europeanwide diplomatic strategy of allowing Italy to assume the political leadership and military burdens of Spain. Looking for glory on the Spanish battlefields, and oblivious to Franco's opposition to much foreign intervention, Faupel wanted a speedy military victory. Because the old general either did not, or could not, understand the Führer's use of Spain to further Hitler's ambitions in the East, he was forced to resign as ambassador in late August 1937. "Ill health" was cited for his resignation.

Faupel was replaced by Eberhard von Stohrer, the Foreign Ministry's original choice for chargé d'affaires in Spain in the fall of 1936. He had been bypassed in favor of Faupel, the Nazi party's nominee. Stohrer was an aristocratic career diplomat who had served in Spain during World War I. [154] Originally he had been named ambassador to the Spanish Republic in July 1936, but he had not proceeded to the post because of the civil war's outbreak. [155] In contrast to Faupel, Stohrer got along far better in Spain; according to Franco's minister of interior, Serrano Suñer, Stohrer better understood the problems facing the Franco government.[156] Despite his non-Nazi background, the old, patriotic, aristocratic Stohrer, as a careerist, spoke up vigorously in Spain for the German Foreign Ministry—even after Hitler's echo, the upstart Ribbentrop, became foreign minister in February 1938. Since 1933, Stohrer, like most career men, had resented the Nazi foreign policy advisor, but new foreign opportunities provided by Hitler dragged those with private reservations along in the New Reich.

While overcoming Faupel's reputation for meddling, Stohrer continued to encourage political ties between Spain and Germany as originally sponsored by Faupel. On the Spanish side, Dionisio Ridruejo, one of the leading pro-German propagandists within the Falange, went to Germany in June 1937 to observe an international congress of Kraft durch Freude; there he met Hitler.[157] Serrano Suñer, who had assured Faupel that he admired Germany, though from afar, went to the 1937 fall Nazi party rally at Nürnberg along with Franco's brother Nicolás, Franco's adjutant general, José Varela, and four others. The chief Falangists saw Hitler only from a distance.[158] In an extended return visit, eight members of the Hitler Youth, invited by the Falange, entered Spain via Lisbon. They toured the major Nationalist cities—Badajoz, Seville, Málaga, Jerez, León, Oviedo, Santander, Bilbao, Irún, Zaragoza, Burgos, Valladolid, Salamanca, Toledo—and the Madrid front between October 28 and November 17.[159] In 1938 the Franco government spent 150,000 RM ($60,000) to import seventy German films.[160] According to Ridruejo, Franco and most of the Spanish army leaders increasingly came to admire Germany over the course of the war.[161] Thus, Hitler had plenty of opportunities to exploit closer relations with the Spaniards, had he chosen to do so.

By 1938 Foreign Minister Ribbentrop was ready to push for a formal Hispano-German treaty despite Hitler's lack of interest. Ribbentrop's chief ambition, from 1935 to May 1937, had been to get British adherence to an anti-Comintern pact (the intent being to weaken the French-Soviet-Czechoslovak pacts of 1935), but Britain had failed to fulfill his hopes.[162] The German-Japanese Anti-Comintern Pact of November 1936, however, had been expanded by the accession of Italy in the fall of 1937. Inclusion of Franco's government in the anticommunist agreement would provide Ribbentrop with an additional possibility for developing closer political ties between Germany and Spain, at the expense of Britain and France. Indeed, Ciano, the Italian foreign minister, after discussing the treaty with Ribbentrop, soon began to think of a place for Spain in the expanded multilateral anti-Comintern bloc. Just after Italy's November 1937 decision to adhere to the pact, Ciano made the following notation: "We must not go about asking little states to join—it must remain a pact of giants. But three countries interest me: Spain, representing the prolongation of the Axis to the Atlantic;

Brazil, in order to shake the whole democratic system in South America; and Poland, as a line of defense against Russia. For Spain we must wait."[163]

Once Italy had been officially included in the Anti-Comintern Pact, Ambassador Stohrer revived Faupel's and Ribbentrop's suggestion of signing up Spain as well.[164] Stohrer also concluded a secret German-Spanish police agreement on November 25, 1937, whereby Franco's chief of police would send Spaniards to Berlin in order to learn from the Gestapo.[165]

On the basis of Faupel's experience with Hitler, Stohrer knew he had to wait for a suitable moment to suggest a broader public Spanish adhesion to the Anti-Comintern Pact. The problem was how to interest a basically disinterested Hitler in closer political ties with Spain. Inasmuch as the Foreign Ministry assumed that Franco was going to win the war, it wanted to use the "New Spain" along with Italy as factors antagonistic to the Anglo-French entente. In contrast, Hitler saw little need to tie Spain to the Axis because he still entertained the hope that Britain would remain neutral in continental affairs. Hitler still thought Britain could be separated from France, especially on eastern European matters, and he also did not want to infringe on Mussolini's right to take such initiatives with Spain.

In December 1937 Stohrer promised Ernst von Weizsäcker, the state secretary and chief assistant of the German foreign minister, that he would propose long-term plans for future German relations with Spain.[166] Stohrer sent his proposal, which was finished in mid-February 1938, to Berlin on March 1.[167] The German ambassador claimed that the March 1937 secret proposal guaranteeing Spain's neutrality was not sufficient compensation to justify continued sacrifices of German troops in the civil war. Stohrer suggested that Germany not only get Spain to join the Anti-Comintern Pact but also that Germany enter more actively into Spanish officer training. The two measures would act as master counterweights to French and British Mediterranean and North African interests.

The now anti-British Ribbentrop had become foreign minister on February 4, 1938, and he brought the Stohrer-Weizsäcker proposals for a Spanish-German political tie to the forefront. Ribbentrop also had learned of plans for Italy to lead Spain into the Anti-Comintern Pact as a check against the democratic bloc, which included the United States.[168] With this information from Spain and Italy, the new foreign minister prepared a case for Hitler; the center of anti-Comintern initiatives, he argued, must remain in Berlin, not Rome.

Early in April 1938, when it appeared that Franco would soon win the war, the Wilhelmstrasse drew up a draft treaty,[169] based largely on the year-old secret protocol and on Stohrer's recent suggestions. Inasmuch as Hitler had executed the Austrian *Anschluss* in March without the Duce balking, Ribbentrop recommended to Hitler a new bilateral Treaty of Friendship as a way of assuring the benefits of a Spanish-German military alliance without assuming its obligations. Significantly, the foreign minister felt that the treaty would "bind Franco closely to the Berlin-Rome Axis and assure us that Spain would not be used by France and England as an area for military operations or transit of troops."[170]

Future political relations between Spain and Germany, and the place of Italy in those relations, were outlined in the first four of nine articles in the draft treaty. Articles One and Two provided that Germany and Spain would "constantly maintain contact and consult" with each other on problems arising out of the Communist International. Article Three provided that if either were threatened by a third power, the other would grant it "political and diplomatic support" to eliminate such a threat. Article Four sought to assure the collaboration of the Italians.

On April 6 Ribbentrop submitted his draft to Hitler, who put a question mark on the word "political" in Article Three and another question mark beside Article Seven, which incorporated Stohrer's suggestions on officer training.[171] After Hitler and Ribbentrop met, the only change made in the text was to leave out the word political in Article Three. The Führer also declared that he considered a commercial treaty better than this project, which was of little practical value (although Article Nine did provide for the "intensification of economic relations"). He thought articles Five and Six were useful, but they merely reinforced the benevolent neutrality obligations of Spain under the March 1937 protocol. Hitler's verbal objections must not have been strenuous, however, because the Foreign Ministry draft, including Article Seven on officer training, remained basically unchanged.

In May 1938 the German embassy in San Sebastián presented the Ribbentrop-Stohrer friendship treaty to Franco. He responded by approving the treaty in principle but saying he had to wait until the end of the civil war to avoid arousing British suspicions.[172] Ribbentrop did not wish to appear eager—particularly since the Nationalist military situation had deteriorated again—and he agreed to the delay,[173] which turned out to last almost a year.

While the deal hung fire, Hitler's preoccupation with eastern European policy and his tendency to ignore Spain created suspicion in the Nationalist camp. As early as March 12, 1938, after Hitler annexed Austria, the Nationalist Foreign Ministry at Burgos drew up a policy statement on the necessity of strict neutrality if general war broke out between the Axis and the Anglo-French entente.[174]

Hitler affronted Franco by failing to consider the dangers posed to the Nationalists as the Czech crisis deepened.[175] From April to September, as the matter of the Sudentenland was increasingly preoccupying Europe, Hitler was planning Operation Green, a military conquest of Czechoslovakia. At the same time, the British intervened to see if Prague's voluntary cession of the Sudetenland might not satisfy Hitler. The French stalled, and Stalin vociferously recommended resistance, although militarily he hid behind the French. A German-French war could reverse the French government's nonintervention policy and lead to all-out backing of the Spanish Republicans. The generalissimo claimed he had absolute knowledge of French general staff planning, and that, in the event of all-out war, the French planned to attack Spanish Morocco and perhaps Cádiz. Franco assumed that the French would use Czechoslovakia as a pretext to take the offensive in the Mediterranean, while the British could put pressure on Portugal and cut off his oil.[176]

Led by these considerations, Franco in turn annoyed Hitler by declaring to French diplomats in September 1938 that Spain would be neutral if Germany were involved in war with Britain and France.[177] This brief Franco-Hitler rift soon disappeared, however. Both dictators won by the September Munich Conference because it completed the isolation of the Soviet Union. Already in the process of withdrawing its support of the Spanish Republicans, Moscow had little further motive after Munich for delaying Franco's victory.

Two months after the Munich meeting, Stohrer again reminded the Spanish foreign minister, Gómez-Jordana, that Spain's adherence to the two draft treaties—the Anti-Comintern Pact and the bilateral Treaty of Friendship—would be desirable.[178] At the time, the German embassy had nearly completed three more documents: a treaty formalizing cultural ties between Germany and Spain; a more extensive police agreement; and, finally, a work permit agreement for German nationals in Spain.[179] On the day of the opening of a new offensive by Franco against Catalonia, December 23, 1938, the Spanish ambassador in Berlin informed Weizsäcker, the state secretary, that the Spanish government "was prepared to go beyond" the March 1937 secret neutrality protocol.[180]

January 1939 was the decisive month for the end of the Spanish Civil War. The success of Franco's all-out invasion of Catalonia, his last major offensive, caused Barcelona to fall on January 26. The time was ripe for El Caudillo to honor his earlier pledge to sign the two major draft treaties, in addition to the neutrality treaty already in effect.

In anticipation of the ultimate victory, Hitler began to contemplate bringing home the Legion Condor, and officials at the Wilhelmstrasse held a policy meeting on January 4 with Ambassador Stohrer, who was in Berlin for political consultations.[181] In it, the Foreign Ministry decided to endorse Stohrer's view that the Ribbentrop-Stohrer draft of the Treaty of Friendship should be taken out of the files, where it had remained since May 1938, and presented anew to the Spaniards.

During the next two months, while the Germans pressured the hesitant

Spaniards to sign the bilateral friendship treaty, efforts also were made to get Franco's signature to the multilateral Anti-Comintern Pact. Although it had originally been designed by Germany, the Foreign Ministry now let the Italians take the initiative on the multilateral treaty. On January 31, the Italian diplomatic representative San Sebastián received instructions to proceed with getting Spain's adherence.[182] The next day Berlin authorized Stohrer to back his Italian colleague in a joint *démarche* with the foot-dragging Franco.[183]

At the close of the war, on March 27, Gómez-Jordana, the Spanish foreign minister, finally signed the Anti-Comintern Pact.[184] Four days later in Burgos he also signed the German-Spanish Treaty of Friendship.[185] The article in the friendship treaty aimed against "international communism" presumably reassured Franco.[186] As it turned out, it was a past fear for Spain, not a future threat, but Franco's "red" phobia seemed to give Hitler a promising diplomatic lever.

This chapter has detailed the development of Hitler's interest in the outcome of the Spanish Civil War and the turning of a liberal-capitalist Spain—a potential friend of France and Britain—into a reactionary-fascist Spain, a potential enemy. In part, the Spanish people, whose actions were limited by geography and lack of economic development, served Hitler as pawns on a bigger board. Hitler skillfully babied an egotistical Mussolini from July 1936 to the end of the civil war to solidify the vague Axis agreements. The Anglo-French entente, intended to counter Hitler, might be regarded as another experiment. The term entente is a shorthand designation for British-French relations as seen by the Axis from November 1936 to 1939. Mussolini and Hitler assumed the existence of a London-Paris tie, and both worked to split the democracies. Yet after June 1937[187] Hitler gradually relinquished hope of winning Britain to the Anti-Comintern Pact or of splitting Paris and London.

The civil war in Spain was solidifying a divided Europe into blocs, yet Britain resisted the trend and pressed for a renewed Western pact dubbed the "second Locarno."[188] Mussolini in November 1936 probably saw himself as balancing between London and Berlin while trying to isolate Paris. In reality, Mussolini's own commitment to Franco's victory in Spain and London's tie to Paris throughout the next two years pushed the Duce further toward Hitler.

In Europe as a whole, the effect of the war in Spain on the balance of power was to tip the scale more and more toward the Third Reich. Despite limited military effort and political attention in Spain, Hitler had gained much in Europe since July 1936. While the Spanish Civil War dragged on, German foreign policy was able to achieve new successes in Austria and

Czechoslovakia. Hitler's power increased in part due to political-ideological confusion on the parts of the other Great Powers, whose politicians were distracted by Spain's war of classes and ideologies. The British and French governments also were paralyzed by the "communist specter," while the Soviet Union suspected Anglo-French complicity with Axis expansion. Hence, five Great Powers were fundamentally divided on what to do about this diplomatic sore spot. During the Spanish Civil War, German solidarity grew with Italy and Japan, while basic German relations with Britain gradually deteriorated, despite British Prime Minister Chamberlain's efforts to avoid the coming showdown. After the fall of Prague to the Nazis in the spring of 1939, all eyes focused on Poland, where Hitler announced new demands, and where Chamberlain and Edouard Daladier, the French prime minister, promised new support.

For player Hitler, Rome remained his first ring throughout the civil war, while Tokyo and Spain functioned as secondary rings. By adhesion to the Anti-Comintern Pact on March 27, 1939, and by the signed (but not yet ratified) bilateral friendship treaty with Germany, Franco's Spain had seemingly thrown her lot in with the Axis.

4

The Development of German
Economic Interests

German Influence Builds with HISMA, ROWAK, and SOFINDUS

In July 1936, at the start of German aid to Franco, Hitler expressly ordered Göring to secure economic rewards. Thus, economic, rather than political or ideological, means were used to create institutions in Spain that could, in the long run, help Germany. The Germans immediately established a civilian economic agency in Spain to serve as a cover-up for the German military intervention and to begin arranging for payments by the rebels. These tasks were undertaken by Johannes Bernhardt, one of the two German businessmen in Morocco who had carried Franco's original appeal to Hitler.

Bernhardt owed his sudden rise to prominence primarily to the ascendancy of the Nazis. Since 1933, Bernhardt had been active in the Nazi party's foreign branch, the *Auslandsorganisation,* in Spanish Morocco. After meeting with Hitler in Bayreuth, Bernhardt, who then had a modest economic status, became in effect an employee of Göring's in Spain.[1] In July 1936, Göring held top economic and military posts in Germany; besides being air force chief, he was commissioner for raw materials and foreign exchange. Bernhardt returned immediately via plane to Spanish Morocco to set up the business end of the Moroccan transportation enterprise.

Not only did Bernhardt have good contacts with the Nazis in Berlin; he also had good relations with the rebels. In 1929 Bernhardt, with earlier business experience in Hamburg and South America, had become a salesman in the firm of H. & O. Wilmer, a trading agency in Tetuán for German-made telephones, radios, and arms, including Junkers aircraft.[2] Apparently Bernhardt met Franco for the first time on July 21, 1936, when Franco decided to send a personal emissary to appeal for help from Hitler.[3] Although no Bernhardt-Franco ties seem to have existed prior to the revolt, the relatively obscure salesman did know some of Franco's rebel military associates who had served in Africa—especially, Generals Queipo de Llano and Aranda, and Colonel Juan Yagüe.[4] Bernhardt also may have had knowledge of the conspiracy in the spring. In any case, his access to top-level German and Spanish military, political, and economic circles was to serve him well in the development of a new Spanish-German trading company.

On July 31, 1936, Bernhardt, then thirty-nine years old, and Fernando Carranza, age sixty-three, organized in Tetuán the Sociedad Hispano-Marroquí de Transportes (HISMA), a trust incorporated under Spanish law and controlled by the two men on a fifty-fifty basis.[5] Carranza's role was to give the firm "owning" the troop transport planes legality in the eyes of the rebels. Carranza—a retired naval officer born in El Ferrol (Franco's birthplace), but whose family home before the war was located in Cádiz—had been devoting his leisure years to writing about Moroccans when the civil war broke out. As an old friend, he was selected by Franco in July to be the silent Spanish partner of the new joint Spanish-German company.[6] The liaison was to be a tense one, however. Eight months later, in March 1937, the Carlist Carranza would send a protest to Franco, disassociating himself from Bernhardt, whom he labeled as beneath his class. Carranza accused his Nazi upstart partner of taking pesetas out of Carranza's original share of the investment.[7] From the overall standpoint of the war this personal quarrel meant little, and the elderly Carranza was later noted as one of the big three caciques of Cádiz and the owner of a fishing fleet.[8] However, the protest suggests one reason the Spaniards would come to keep Nazis at arm's length. Carranza was not replaced, and, since he did not contribute capital or management skills to the company, he remained a straw man in any case.

During the civil war Bernhardt built an economic empire for himself and Nazi Germany. HISMA was originally a transportation company exercising legal control over the Luftwaffe's Junker transports; under Bernhardt's active management, however, the company also immediately began arranging for shipments of Spanish goods to Germany in partial payment for the planes and the German services.

The whole question of payment for German arms by the rebel Spaniards was a complicated one. At the time Franco requested aid, the insurgents were embarrassed for funds; they had the backing of millionaires, yet the Republican government in Madrid controlled Spain's gold reserves. Then, as the speedy victory anticipated by Franco and the Germans failed to materialize and the Francoists increased their demands for more German economic and military aid, the problem of mounting debts became pressing. Credit and loans could postpone the day of payment. The alternative was "pay as you go" by maximizing exports from Nationalist territory to Germany, or by paying the Germans in "blocked" pesetas. The latter could be spent only in Spain and thus would commit Germany to invest in Spain's future.[9]

The Germans, however, were particular about what they would accept. Under Hjalmar Schacht, the economics minister, they had been drastically limiting their imports for some time. Germany also lacked gold reserves, and the mark, fixed at an artificial value by Schacht, had little value in the international markets dominated by the Versailles victors.

Bernhardt hoped to convince Franco to pay with some of Spain's small amount of foreign exchange ("hard currency"—dollars and pounds sterling), which could be used by Berlin to import vital commodities such as petroleum from the dollar-sterling bloc.[10] This method of payment was used to some extent. For instance, Bernhardt received a cheque for £500 ($2,485), which he paid to a German account in the Midland Bank of London as early as August 14, as partial payment for the first Ju 52s.[11] Later an employee of HISMA negotiated in Zaragoza a contract to sell nine He 51 fighters on October 17, 1936.[12] Ten percent of the purchase price was to be paid in pounds sterling to a London bank.

From Spain itself, Göring and the Reich War Ministry mainly desired raw materials to strengthen the Third Reich's war potential. For example, Germany's mushrooming armed forces had to be clothed and shod; so wool, skins, and hides were soon traveling to Germany from Spain under the auspices of HISMA. But developed and undeveloped mines and their ores proved to be the Spanish assets that most interested the Germans. Bernhardt quickly made contracts with Spanish and British mining companies operating in territory held by the Spanish generals. The earliest contracts provided for the sale of ore to HISMA in exchange for transport services for Franco's armies. Thus, the SS *Usaramo*—the very ship that had carried Major Alexander von Scheele's contingent to Spain to service the first German planes—returned to Germany in August 1936 with a cargo of Spanish or Moroccan copper ore.[13]

With the nationalists interested in utilizing all possible means for payment, even marginal mining operations took on a new importance. On the July trip to Bayreuth, Bernhardt had been accompanied by the Nazi AO chief in Spanish Morocco, a mining engineer named Adolf P. Langenheim. The AO chief had made his home in Morocco for over thirty years and had fruitlessly attempted in the past to get certain iron mining claims recognized by the German and Spanish governments.[14] Apparently small claims such as Langenheim's helped account for some of the ore export from Spain to Germany that suddenly began flourishing after July 1936.

However, the bulk of the shipments stemmed from larger and longer-established mining complexes. The Junta de Defensa Nacional seized all minerals in Spain as of August 28, 1936.[15] The four biggest assets possessed thereafter by Franco's armed forces were the Compañía Española de Minas del Rif—iron mines in Morocco—and three British companies on the peninsula which mined iron and copper pyrites. On October 31, 1936, HISMA signed a contract with Rif iron mines, agreeing to take 840,000 tons through December 31, 1937. HISMA also took over the rights of the old contract between Altos Hornos, an Urquijo company equivalent to Spain's United States Steel Company, Bilbao, and Germany's Rohstoffhandel der Vereinigten Stahlwerke of Dortmund.[16]

Germany was very much interested in pyrite ores because they furnished not only iron or copper but also a raw material fundamental to the nation's vital chemical industry. This is especially significant in that German chemists were one of the key explanations for the rise of Germany as a military and commercial power from the nineteenth century. Pyrites are the main commercial source of sulfur dioxide, the basic ingredient of sulfuric acid. Sulfuric acid is to the chemical industry what iron is to metallurgy, because chemists use this acid in making all other acids and a great variety of other chemical compounds. Thus, pyrites were vitally important to the German synthetic, munition, and fertilizer industries.

In the late 1930s, nearly 90 percent of the mines producing Spanish pyrites were in the hands of British firms. The three biggest were Rio Tinto, employing 7,000 to 8,500 workers[17] and representing an investment of £5.5 million,[18] and the Tharsis and Orconera mining companies, with pyrite mines located mostly in Huelva Province. During the civil war, the British management of the three pyrite complexes continued production of the ore as usual, but the companies' earnings could not be taken out of Nationalist Spain.[19] In May 1937, as part of its economic war against its enemies, the Franco regime prohibited the sale of pyrites to France.[20] Rio Tinto sold instead to HISMA, because Bernhardt was behind this decree against France. He pointed out to Franco that prewar contracts should be cancelled, and he reminded the generalissimo that the French government was aiding the Spanish Left, and that the French mining companies were under Jewish influence.[21] HISMA provided the Nationalist regime with statistics showing Rio Tinto deliveries to chemical plants in France, Belgium, and Czechoslovakia.[22] Franco, heavily dependent on HISMA's provision of German arms, was not in a position to argue the point. British interests could not repatriate profits to London and had to wait until after the war for repayment. Current production was redirected to Germany. Thus Franco's decrees, in effect, forced the British companies to grant credits enabling the Nationalist government to buy German arms. From July 1936 to July 1938, Rio Tinto furnished ore worth £2 million ($9.9 million) to the Nationalist authorities, and in 1937 the company lost £300,000 ($1.5 million) on its Spanish branch.[23]

For his part, Bernhardt offered the three major British pyrite companies "friendly" contracts and blamed their Spanish troubles on the Franco government.[24] HISMA even tried to persuade Rio Tinto to take German surplus coal, instead of that which normally came from Britain, as payment for pyrites.[25]

This pyrite ore and some other Spanish raw materials were purchased by Bernhardt with notes that were then sent to the Sonderstab W account section in Berlin for cancellation against shipments of arms and additional goods and services.[26] Lieutenant Colonel Warlimont, who headed the military mission to Franco from September to December 1936, originally came from the economic staff of the Reich War Ministry. After observing the military situation, Warlimont decided within two weeks to abandon any economic role of the ministry, turning the economic functions of his mission over to Bernhardt.[27] According to Bernhardt, the war ministry dropped its economic interest after he and Warlimont went on a special mission on September 28 to Göring's hunting lodge in East Prussia.[28] Hitler and Göring were delighted at the news of Franco becoming chief of state; they thought Franco's victory would assure future benefits to the Third Reich stemming from their investment in Nationalist Spain.

Because German chemical firms could use all the pyrites HISMA could procure, Bernhardt's profits grew. He enjoyed the middle position of supplying both raw materials to German industry and Franco's needs for German military and civilian goods.

By September and October 1936, Franco was calling for more German credits to support the civilian economy.[29] The Nationalists needed coal because the Asturian coal fields were controlled by the Popular Front. Moreover, factory machinery in the insurgent zone needed replacing, and Franco wanted more arms supplied directly to him.

There were some attempts to bypass Bernhardt. On October 9, former monarchist and Republican ambassador in Berlin Francisco Agramonte, a career man, approached Hans Clodius of the economic department in the German Foreign Ministry. Without mentioning Bernhardt, Agramonte stated that the junta, now headquartered at Burgos, was concluding pyrites contracts with Germany's number-one chemical manufacturer, I.G. Farben at Frankfurt, and the ambassador requested that the Germans send an economic delegation to the Nationalist Headquarters. Clodius, on behalf of the legalistic Foreign Ministry, declined to make any agreement with a man who represented a rebel government still not officially recognized by Hitler. He told Agramonte that the Wilhelmstrasse first required a basic political decision by the Führer about the recognition of the junta.[30] That nod came on November 18, partly because of the economic pressure exerted by Bernhardt, Göring, and Franco, but the normalization of economic relations brought up by Agramonte did not take place.

Göring had been pushing forward the economic planning for Spain, even before Hitler decided upon the political recognition of Burgos. Conferences in October among Göring, the war minister, and the Finance Ministry determined that the war and foreign ministries would avoid further involvement in the Spanish project. Because of his political clout, the problem of organizing the administration of additional Nazi economic and military aid to Spain was handed over to Göring.[31]

About this time Göring, because of German economic conditions in general, was increasing his responsibilities in the whole field of economics. In April 1936 he had presided over a conference of about twenty top Germans in the economic sphere, including Schacht, the economics minister and Reichsbank president, Lutz Schwerin von Krosigk, the finance minister, and Colonel Georg Thomas of the Economic Warfare staff, among others. These meetings continued, and out of them had come the Reich marshal's appointment as commissioner for foreign exchange and raw materials.[32]

During July and August, Hitler himself had been thinking about broadening central economic planning. He had in mind both his ideological preference for autarky (economic self-sufficiency) and his general foreign policy goals.[33] Richard Walther Darré, minister of food and agriculture, also pressed for expansion of Göring's jurisdiction. After a long dispute with Schacht, backer of big industry and traditional private capitalism, Darré wrote Hitler on September 5 that Germany could no longer tolerate liberal economic principles. Darré argued that Hitler should create a disciplined "general staff" under party leader Göring in order to make Germany self-sufficient and to establish comprehensive priorities in the economic sector.[34] Schacht, Reichsbank president since 1925, had, from Darré's point of view, too many ties with Anglo-American finance. Hitler's solution was labeled the Four-Year Plan, and Göring was named as its commissioner. Ironically enough, the plan was announced publicly during an energetic denunciation of bolshevism at the Nürnberg Party Day on September 9. Formal implementation of the anti-liberal plan came on October 18, 1936, as the culmination of a lengthy economic debate in Nazi inner circles.

Economically, nazism meant a partially planned economy with the maintenance of private ownership of industry. That industry, however, was compelled to serve party ends by preparing to fight. Commenting on Germany's shortages of raw materials and foreign exchange, and the meaning of the Four-Year Plan, Hitler said, "We are already in a state of war, although the guns have not gone off."[35] Thus Hitler's Four-Year Plan intensified the development of a war economy. Partly as a result of Hitler's intervention in Spain, Germany mobilized its economy before the laissez-faire advocates in Britain and France. The civil war in Spain speeded up the gradual move toward autarky inherent in Hitler's economic philosophy.

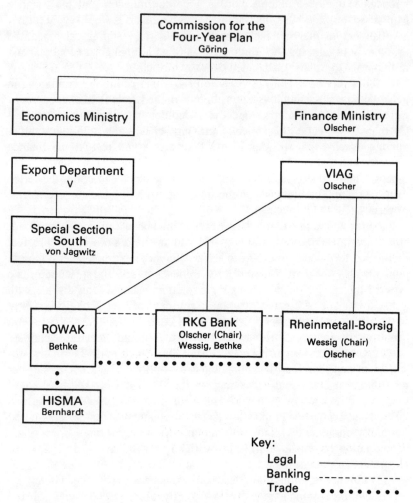

FIGURE 2

The Relation of HISMA and ROWAK to the German Economic System

With his key positions, Göring had the ability to step into either a "private" deal, a party operation, a military situation, or a traditional interstate fiscal clearing problem. The fluid state of the Third Reich's military-industrial complex, however, was causing repercussions in Spain. The military Operation Otto, conceived first in the war ministry, took from August 24 to September 29 to implement, apparently because the German economy was in a state of flux. Meanwhile, Göring's comrade in Spain,

Johannes Bernhardt, raised additional economic problems for the Berlin party men. When Bernhardt presented Franco's demands for more military and economic aid on credit, Göring answered the call by expanding the infant Four-Year Plan offices.[36]

To find personnel for the Spanish economic operation, he sought the aid of Paul Körner, state secretary in the Ministry of Economics, who suggested the creation in Germany of a new trading corporation to receive Spanish raw materials.[37] According to Körner, setting it up would take four weeks. Bernhardt claimed that, with the aid of party chief Rudolf Hess and the AO, the corporation could be created in three days. Indeed, Hess did nominate Nazi AO members with business experience in South America. Among them were Eberhard von Jagwitz and Friedrich Bethke. Jagwitz, a major in World War I, had lived in Argentina, was an old friend of Bernhardt, and had worked in the AO office in Berlin for Ernst Bohle since 1934.[38] Bethke was working for a drug company in Chile and was in Berlin on vacation when he was recruited in October for the German-Spanish operation.[39]

As a result of Bernhardt's conference with Göring, on October 2, 1936, a new government corporation was initiated under the chairmanship of Jagwitz.[40] It was given a credit of three-million reichsmarks ($1.2 million) and the name Rohstoffe-und-Waren-Einkaufsgesellschaft G.m.b.H. (ROWAK).[41]

To provide credit to Franco and ROWAK, Göring applied to Alfred Olscher, ministerial director of the finance ministry. In addition to his finance post, Olscher also held a seat on the board[42] of Vereinigte Industrie Unternehmung A.G. (VIAG), a large stockholding company owned by the finance ministry. VIAG, then the largest government-owned corporation in Germany, held its assets in the Reichskredit Gesellschaft (RKG), the fourth-largest banking chain in Germany, whose chairman was none other than Olscher.[43] ROWAK thus became a financial subsidiary of VIAG. Olscher, a man who wore three hats—those of the finance ministry, VIAG, and RKG—acquired a vital link to Bernhardt's system for extending arms on credit to Franco (see figure 2).

ROWAK's first function was to be sole purchasing agent for the Spanish raw materials supplied through HISMA. An administrative order (November 9, 1936), by the foreign exchange division of the Reich Economic Ministry prohibited private sales or purchases in any part of Spain, except through ROWAK.[44] This laid the foundation for ROWAK's economic power, and the monopoly company then charged all German importers purchasing Spanish goods a commission of 2 to 3 percent. In addition, the ROWAK director, Jagwitz, acted as sole sales agent for any German firm exporting to Spain, and charged a commission of 3 to 5 percent on such exports.[45] Jagwitz seems to have set his fees at levels that discouraged

German civilian sales to Spain. In this way the German military aid was given top priority, and German activities in Spain could be controlled and kept more secret.[46]

In contrast to the roadblocks put in the way of private German firms, the ROWAK system clearly benefitted government contracts with such quasi-private firms as Rheinmetall-Borsig, one of the biggest arms suppliers to Spain[47] and the manufacturer of the famous "eighty-eight" anti-aircraft gun. This pattern of interlocking directorates sheds further light on the powers of ROWAK in relation to Spain. Max Wessig headed Rheinmetall-Borsig, a subsidiary of VIAG, and he kept the company accounts at RKG, a bank of which he was a board member; in addition, Olscher of VIAG and RKG was on the Rheinmetall-Borsig board. Bethke replaced Jagwitz as chairman of ROWAK in 1938 when Jagwitz became a special ministerial director for foreign trade in the Economics Ministry. This ministry was increasingly being nazified from below and from above as the ambitious Göring curtailed Reichsbank president Schacht's power. By the spring of 1938, ROWAK was integrated within the nazified Economics Ministry.[48] The relationship of Göring and his subordinates was more feudal than military, however, so Figure 2 is a mere snapshot from a moving scene.[49] Although HISMA, ROWAK, and Rheinmetall were different in kind from purely government or purely private organizations, the Third Reich had, by 1936-1938, developed what today could be called a military-industrial complex.

In Spain, HISMA developed monopoly rights similar to those exercised by ROWAK in Germany. Had Franco been able, he probably would have cancelled the charter of the monopoly buyer company, sold his raw materials for the best price on the international market, and bought arms and supplies as cheaply as possible. Instead, the generalissimo, with the exception of one Italian tie, was forced to do his main purchasing from Bernhardt's monopolistic HISMA. To administer the chief of state's nonmilitary political and economic affairs, Franco made his brother Nicolás general secretary of the Junta Técnica del Estado, the Nationalist organ of government set up in October 1936. Nicolás Franco had the primary duty of maintaining contact with Bernhardt and Italian arms suppliers. During 1936 and the first part of 1937, Nicolás chose the military items that needed to be ordered from HISMA. Bernhardt then sent Franco's requests to ROWAK, which handled the German end of the business.[50]

Italy used a prewar Chilean nitrate import firm, SAFNI (Società Fertilizzanti Naturali Italiani), incorporated in Rome, for its trade to Spain.[51] One of the great differences between the German and Italian economic policies, however, was that the Italians had no real parallel to HISMA in Spain itself. Nicolás Franco did his bargaining with the Italians in Rome.[52]

The Spanish Nationalists were restive with the HISMA-ROWAK trading system, especially when Bernhardt pressed Franco for payment in scarce foreign exchange.[53] About February 10, 1937, the Spanish junta asked for an intergovernmental clearing and commodity agreement that would regularize trade.[54] Bernhardt and Bethke were prepared to put up a good fight for their one-sided monopoly. A key conference was held in Berlin with Göring presiding, and the HISMA-ROWAK exchange system emerged victorious: Göring refused the Spanish request for an official clearing agreement between two equal governments.[55] Despite the rejection, Nicolás Franco continued promoting a clearing agreement as a step toward free trade. In mid-May, Ambassador Faupel told Franco that German aid might not be forthcoming if the Spaniards did not continue trade through Bernhardt's system.[56] The generalissimo reluctantly agreed.[57]

The one German exception to the monopoly rights of HISMA-ROWAK was the mysterious, semi-illegal activity of Colonel Josef Veltjens. Before the outbreak of the civil war, Veltjens had become interested in selling German arms to the Spaniards. In fact, it is possible that some of the right-wing conspirators contacted his agents in Spain twice—on June 17, 1936,[58] and several weeks later, on July 6.[59] The evidence is too fragmentary to prove the sweeping thesis held by some on the Left that Germans played a secret role in starting the Spanish Civil War. If any German did provide pre-uprising aid, however, Veltjens is a major contender for the role.

Veltjens, a World War I ace and friend of Göring from those days,[60] joined a Freikorps in the early 1920s and the Nazi party and the Brownshirts in 1929.[61] Hitler had him expelled from the party in 1931 for corruption and Veltjens was still on the Nazi party blacklist when the rebel coup was attempted in 1936.[62] In June, when the Spanish army conspirators were hatching their preliminary plans, Veltjens was making his living in Berlin by exporting arms. Possibly before, but definitely shortly after the outbreak of the generals' coup, Veltjens developed a new personal contact with Göring, who then protected the colonel's career against hostile elements in the Nazi party until his death in World War II.[63]

On July 22, 1936, before Bernhardt completed his famous flight to Hitler, the German steamship *Girgenti* was docked in the Spanish port of Valencia when a dozen leftist militiamen boarded her, looking for arms. The ship's captain repelled them by force, and the German Foreign Ministry protested the militia action to the Madrid government.[64] Soon thereafter, the vessel was definitely chartered by Veltjens, for on August 22 it left Hamburg loaded with weapons from the Sonderstab W and the OKM and bound for the Nationalist port of La Coruña.[65] The question arises whether Veltjens had chartered the *Girgenti* prior to the Spanish generals' rising for the voyage to Valencia.[66] In any case, Veltjens also dispatched a half dozen He 51 fighters for General Mola, which were delivered at La Coruña on August 14.[67]

In September, Veltjens sent Mola a second load of ten million rounds of

7.92 caliber cartridges specially made to fit Spanish weapons.[68] Then in late 1936, Veltjens joined with Henry Aschpuvis of Hamburg to form a new shipping company managing three vessels and called the Hansagesellschaft Aschpuvis & Veltjens.[69] Aschpuvis had a small operation before the civil war, and the new firm's first ships were chartered. In November 1936 the firm's steamship *Urundi* transported a brigade of six hundred Irish Catholic fascist Blueshirts, headed by General Eoin O'Duffy, to Franco Spain.[70] By 1938 Aschpuvis & Veltjens was building a one-million-reichsmarks office in Hamburg.[71]

The main business activity of Veltjens, however, was to perform special transport services for HISMA, ROWAK, and the OKM.[72] Veltjens specialized in the shipment of high explosives,[73] and throughout the war he continued to contract with the Nationalist government to procure the special cartridges needed to fit Spanish weapons.[74] The bills that he charged Franco's army were assigned to Bernhardt's HISMA for collection in Spain, but Veltjens received for his special service valuable convertible pounds sterling, rather than the frozen paper reichsmarks or blocked pesetas that HISMA was piling up in Spanish banks. Veltjens apparently had this extra power because some of his specialized arms exports required the previous import of nickel, tungsten, and other items that required German allocation of scarce foreign exchange.

In early 1937, Aschpuvis & Veltjens, to disguise its activities from the Non-Intervention Committee and from the rest of the German government, bought a French freighter, a Danish freighter, and a Swedish freighter to ship munitions to *Republican* Spain.[75] In the summer of 1937, Veltjens added two more vessels to his secret fleet (which flew Panamanian flags) to continue violating the Non-Intervention Agreement by supplying both Spanish warring factions. By November 1938, the Reich Economics Ministry recorded a monthly turnover of £60,000 in foreign exchange from Veltjens's clandestine Spanish shipping activities.[76]

Still, from the standpoint of the overall magnitude of economic-military development of the Spanish Civil War, Veltjens was a secondary character in the story. Franco's postwar debt to Veltjens, according to the German government, was 14.2 million RM ($5.7 million) out of a total German claim of 538 million RM ($215 million).[77] For all practical purposes, Bernhardt's HISMA remained a monopoly. The sinister episodes linked with Veltjens simply provided a minor break in the overwhelming rise of the ROWAK-HISMA complex.

It can be seen, then, that HISMA's monopoly rights rested mainly on Franco's desperate need for arms and his unrecognized international position. International diplomacy forced Franco to give way to the monopoly's continued existence, because only Germany and Italy were willing secretly to sell the Nationalists arms contrary to the embargo imposed by the Non-Intervention Agreement.

Despite Hitler's rescue of Franco at a crucial stage of the war, the Spanish aristocrats who surrounded Franco objected to the lowly social origins and corrupt behavior that characterized the band of adventurers who worked for Bernhardt. It has been noted that Carranza became totally alienated from the company he nominally founded. Others have testified that Bernhardt apparently had four passports,[78] and a very close associate charged him with embezzlement.[79] One of HISMA's high officials had been a street photographer a few years before the war, and others peddled gold watches and silks to wealthy Spaniards in defiance of the exchange regulations of the Franco government. A high Spanish military source told the American consul at Seville: "As soon as the war is over we shall not be slow in getting rid of the Germans: but when one's house is on fire a bucket of water will be appreciated from anyone even if he has halitosis."[80]

For some of its employees, ROWAK recruited Spanish residents in Germany. Mostly produce and wine merchants, they had been cut out of the middleman business by ROWAK, which now marketed all Spanish products.[81]

In hopes of Nationalist victory, the Germans were working through their monopoly setup to enhance Germany's eventual postwar economic position in Spain. On February 18, 1937, Göring, as commissioner of the Four-Year Plan, gave Bernhardt a third mission. Not only was he ordered to expand Spanish exports to Germany and to collect foreign exchange, but also—with an eye to the future—to increase German investment in Spain, particularly in mining.[82] Consequently, under the terms of a July 16, 1937, secret protocol,[83] the German Foreign Ministry arranged legally that part of the Spanish war debt would be liquidated by "German commercial" activities; in other words, HISMA's increased investment in Spain. During the civil war Franco did pay HISMA at least 25 million RM ($10 million), which the German company used primarily to buy up Spanish mines.[84]

A HISMA subsidiary concentrating on mining investments, Montaña S.A., began operations in 1937. Assisted by geologists sent out to Spain by another Göring subordinate, Wilhelm Keppler, state secretary for mining under the Four-Year Plan, Montaña obtained two hundred-odd claims[85] on old mines of the major minerals found in Spain, from wolfram to copper. The property rights and mining concessions of Montaña S.A. caused a long-lasting dispute, engaging the energies of Bernhardt and Ambassador Stohrer for nearly a year. After numerous legal skirmishes with the Franco authorities, who were reluctant to allow Spanish mines in which the Spaniards had certain legal claims to come under predominantly German control, Montaña achieved a more settled status late in 1938.[86]

As Bernhardt found enterprising ways by which the Francoists could pay for the arms and civilian necessities sold on credit, HISMA's original function as an air transport company faded into the background. During 1937 he formed about ten subsidiary companies,[87] and small-time promoters went to work for them. This complex of Spanish corporations, all organized under the banner of HISMA (a term used rather loosely), had its original management headquarters in Seville but later moved to Salamanca to keep in touch with the generalissimo.[88] In addition to Montaña, one of the more important subsidiaries created by Bernhardt and his associates was called Nova S.A. Nova had a monopoly on sales of German communications and transportation equipment—and on arms imported from ROWAK.

HISMA and his other companies continued to grow, so Bernhardt reorganized them into a holding company called SOFINDUS (Sociedad Financiera Industrial Ltda.), incorporated in November 1938 in Lisbon and valued at 2.5 million pesetas ($250,000).[89] The old name stuck, however, and for this reason much of the literature continued from 1939 to 1945 to refer to HISMA, or to speak of "HISMA-SOFINDUS." As the Nationalist troops expanded throughout the peninsula, the German monopoly operations also expanded: in 1939 they employed 260 persons, half of whom were Spaniards, in fourteen companies engaged in fourteen types of activities—transport, hides, mines, machinery, wine, and fruit.[90] This was not a very large contribution to the total Spanish national output, but it was significant in the international trading position of Spain.[91] Despite occasional strained relations between Bernhardt and the Spanish chief of state, Franco gave the SOFINDUS director a personal gift at the end of the war of 1.4 million pesetas ($140,000).[92]

SOFINDUS maintained offices in eight Spanish cities in 1939, and, in contrast to the other fourteen companies, confined its activities to acting as a central foreign trade broker for German-Spanish trade.[93] Bernhardt remained titular head, but he had to organize a complicated interlocking directorate. For instance, Christopher Fiessler, a resident of Seville and friend of Bernhardt, was appointed president of HISMA (overseas transport), president of PRODAG (agricultural export), member of the board of directors of Minerales de España (ore export), and attorney for SOFINDUS (finance and central organization).

In late 1938 Göring made another change when he promoted the former ROWAK chief, Jagwitz, to the post of state secretary in the Economics Ministry. The promotion came as part of a general shake-up involving the gradual decline in power of Schacht as minister of economics and his replacement by a Göring appointee. Party man Jagwitz was placed in charge of foreign trade, and his assistant, Bethke, also a former director of ROWAK, became ministerial director under him in a special section. ROWAK was

Table 1. Effect of Spanish Civil War on Exports of Pyrites and Iron Ore (in Thousands of Tons)

To	1935	1936	1937	1938
		Iron Ore[a]		
Germany	1,321.0	1,067.0	302.0[b]	1,083.0[b]
Great Britain	1,129.0	1,186.0	938.0	510.0
		Pyrites		
Germany	563.0	404.0	836.0	896.0
Great Britain	205.0	198.0	290.0	326.0
France	342.0	99.0	1.5	—

Source: I.G. Farben Vo. Wi. Abt, "Der spanische Aussenhandel," Frankfurt a.M. to OKW/WI Rü Amt, 18 Apr. 1940 (Misc. Germ. Rec., 243/1958110-58, frames 26-27, 53-54.

[a]Iron ore from Spanish Morocco not included.

[b]The change between 1937 and 1938 reflects the fall of Viscaya Province, the largest iron-ore-producing province in Spain, to Franco in June 1937.

nominally taken over by another minor party man from South America by the name of Anton Wahle,[94] but Bethke retained in the special section the real decision-making power of ROWAK.

By early 1939, various Germans were expressing a good deal of discontent with HISMA-SOFINDUS. The old prewar German companies with business in Spain accused Bernhardt of mismanagement, since many of the mining claims had proved unworkable and a number of subsidiaries were operating at a loss.[95] The fact remained, however, that German economic interests as a whole had greatly expanded their proportion of Spain's trade in certain vital products. At the end of 1935, 35 percent of Spanish exports of iron ore, pyrites, wool, and skins had gone to Germany. By the end of 1939, 80 percent of these products went to Germany.[96] The gain in Germany's position as a Spanish importer was particularly significant when measured in terms of pyrite sales. Although total exports from Spain to the industrial powers had decreased, Germany had gained a larger share of those exports still available, as compared to Britain and France. Furthermore, much of the increased importance of German-Spanish trade was achieved at the expense of Germany's major international rival, France (see table 1).

HISMA obtained ore not only from the mainland of Spain but also, as previously noted, from the protectorate of Spanish Morocco. The major iron ore mines there were the Rif mines. Bernhardt had complained in early 1937 that the company's finance had Jewish and British strings attached to it;[97] yet, despite his suspicions, the company had exported most of its ore to

Table 2. Annual Export of Iron Ore from Spanish Morocco, 1936-1938 (in Kilograms)

To	1936	1937	1938
Germany	592,281,950	802,343,572	742,401,536
Great Britain	191,180,250	182,735,525	163,895,775
Holland[a]	96,379,860	245,291,070	7,551,600
France	64,983,125	—	—
Italy	6,191,500	146,703,025	397,495,975

Source: Spain, Ministerio de Industria y Comercio, *Estadística Minera y Metalúrgica de España*, 1942, 860.
[a]Much of this ore was reexported to Germany.

Germany before the war. In 1936, the Third Reich bought 503,000 tons of Rif iron ore out of a total of 986,000 tons exported.[98] Bernhardt negotiated a new contract between Rif mines and himself in October 1936 so as to raise the German share of the exports to 840,000 tons for the following year.[99] Bernhardt's overall success in obtaining iron ore from Morocco can be seen in table 2.

In Tables 3 and 4, the reader can observe the general ascent of HISMA during the whole civil war period. The total value of exports from Nationalist Spain to ROWAK was 224.million RM ($90 million). The total value of German manufactures and coal imported for Spain's civilian and war needs was 125.1 million RM ($50 million). The difference went to pay for arms in the state account. Besides this $40 million, the Germans held additional bills for arms sold in blocked pesetas. In all, they claimed a grand total of $215 million of Nationalist war debts owed to them.

The economic role of the Italians in Spain differed markedly from the German role—there were few gains in Spain for Italy, other than Moroccan iron ore (table 2). Before the civil war, Spanish exports to Italy were relatively small. Temporarily, at least, Spain increased its exports to Italy from 44.4 million lire ($3.2 million) in 1936 to 177 million lire ($9.2 million) in 1938.[100] In the long run, economic relations were to remain poor, however, because these exports repaid little of the Italian military effort. The Italian and Spanish economies were too similar. Both countries exported citrus fruits, pyrites, sulfur, and mercury, and both needed wheat, coal, and oil.

The Spanish Civil War proved a tremendous drain on the Italian economy, for the Duce's country was no great economic power.[101] From July 1936 to the end of November, the British-owned mine Rio Tinto sent Italy only one small cargo vessel of pyrites.[102] It was not until May 1938, after

Germany obtained an amortization agreement with Franco, that Italy obtained a similar agreement. [103] Although Italy sent more arms to the Nationalist Spaniards than Germany did, the Burgos government continued to export more to Germany than to Italy. Spain exported to the two Axis powers in ratios that favored the Reich 3 to 1 for 1936, 9 to 1 for 1937, and 2.7 to 1 for 1938. [104] The real economic significance of the Spanish Civil War for Mussolini was that Italy had somewhat exhausted itself by 1939, which probably helped delay the Duce's entry into the Anglo-French war with Germany for another nine months. [105]

The prewar situation in which Britain, America, and France predominated in the Spanish economy altered considerably as a result of the civil war. France had supported the loser by permitting International Brigaders and supplies to cross French territory on the way to Loyalist Spain. Britain and the United States remained largely neutral, while Germany had backed the winner—Nationalist Spain. These political and military facts made their impact economically. Though all countries lost absolutely because of the destruction wrought by war, the Germans gained a larger share of the fewer products Spain had for export, relative to Britain and France. [106]

In the peacetime year of 1935, every country had tried to maximize its own exports, but, by the time of growing international tension in 1938, Britain and Germany were more and more interested in planning for blockades and blockade-breaking. Under the new conditions, the Axis and the Anglo-French entente increased their interest in obtaining the raw materials of Spain. By 1939 Nazi Germany was Nationalist Spain's primary trading partner in both exports and imports, having overtaken both the United States and Britain in relative importance of trade with Spain, compared to 1935. Meanwhile, the "New Spain" had imposed a near embargo against France.

Comparing table 5 with the situation in 1935, one notes that the total for Spanish exports to the four most significant economic powers actually increased, from 40 million gold dollars to 46 million. [107] But a significant amount of exports available shifted from France to Germany. In 1935 France obtained 8.5 million gold dollars in Spanish exports; in 1938, only 3 million. Germany in 1935 obtained $9.2 million, compared to $22 million in 1938, when the Third Reich obtained almost half of the Spanish exports available.

Whether Germany's gain in percentage of Spain's available exports would be permanent, however, remained in question. The Germans were not satisfied with current gains alone. The rise of the Reich as the number-one foreign trading influence in Spain resulted from the temporary condition of civil war, and the Germans in March 1939 wanted long-term legal protection of this increased trade by treaty rights. [108] They also wanted Spain to cut back Anglo-French investment and to increase the German investment.

Table 3. Total Value of HISMA Exports, September 1936 to 31 December 1939 (in Reichsmarks)

Products	1936[a]	1937	1938	1939	Total
Ores & Metals	5,233,409	19,901,210	34,453,888	19,211,042	78,799,549
Raw materials vegetable origin	787,000	12,314,996	7,827,800	5,980,727	26,910,523
Raw materials animal origin	767,851	20,802,059	6,874,828	7,487,125	35,931,863
Vegetables	1,570,000	31,733,634	26,072,284	34,816,056	94,191,974
Fruit		12,082,785	14,026,208	28,151,926	54,260,919
Finished goods		5,839	5,869	5,036	16,744
Total	8,358,260	96,840,523	89,260,877	95,651,912 [Jan.-March: 30,196,302]	290,111,572 [Civil War Period (September 1936-March 1939): 224,655,962]
Total (Pesetas)	28,752,414	333,131,399	307,472,571	331,487,544	1,000,843,928

Sources: HISMA, Ltd., "Statistical Report" (Madrid, Dec. 1939), pp. 10–12; unpublished set of tables, original c/o Herbert R. Southworth, Ruedo Ibérico, Paris; photocopy in author's possession.
[a]Statistics begin in September.

Germany Pushes Trading Concessions and Damage Claims

At the outbreak of the Spanish Civil War, German and Spanish traders were guided by a comprehensive commercial treaty concluded between their two countries on May 7, 1926.[109] When the full extent of the Italian military aid to Franco became apparent in the first half of January 1937, the chargé, Faupel, suggested to Berlin that it would be in the German interest to conclude economic negotiations before German political influence fell to second place.[110] Hitler directed that this suggestion be acted on as soon as possible.[111]

In February 1937 the Germans, taking advantage of their military aid to Franco, submitted a draft agreement of six articles amending the 1926 treaty. The German Foreign Ministry hoped to reduce the existing discriminations by obtaining from Spain most-favored-nation tariffs toward Germany, as well as most-favored-nation treatment for German ships and citizens visiting Spanish ports.[112] The Spaniards did not hurry to conclude the agreement. On July 8, 1937, Faupel protested the delay in signing his proposed economic agreement, which he claimed had been "long since worked out."[113] The German ambassador also complained of Spanish intrigues against the HISMA-ROWAK barter system.

Within a week, the public economic treaty and three secret protocols were signed in Burgos.[114] By the secret protocol of July 12, the Spaniards and Germans postponed comprehensive economic negotiations until the end of the war, while, in a second protocol of July 15, they merely agreed to maximize current trade.[115] In actuality, these agreements were simply Spanish promises to extend better terms of trade to German merchants after the war ended.

Later, ROWAK concluded a semi-private contract with Spanish merchants in Guinea for okume wood, used in making plywood for building planes. The Germans wanted to buy all the wood the colony could supply, while the Spaniards wanted to reserve some for Italy. The Germans also were interested in obtaining a three-year contract in the spring of 1938.[116] After long negotiations, on December 6, 1938, the Spanish ambassador, Antonio Magaz, signed a special okume protocol with ROWAK, providing sixty-thousand tons for the German market for 1939, and another sixty-thousand tons for 1940; included was an agreement that, if for "technical reasons" the Spaniards could not deliver the wood, they were not to deliver it to third countries but only to Spain itself.[117] This treaty indicates that the Germans were thinking of the post-civil-war economic situation in Spain in relation to a wider European conflict.

In addition to difficulties on trade and tariffs, there was a problem of prewar commercial debts. By 1936 Spain had accumulated a balance-of-payments surplus of $12 million against Germany through the expenditures

Table 4. Total Value of HISMA Imports, October 1936 to 31 December 1939

	1936[a]	1937	1938	1939	Total
Reichsmarks	2,668,488	43,028,219	62,906,060	59,465,400 [Jan.-March 16,535,966]	168,068,167 [Civil War total (Jan. 1936-March 1939): 125,138,733]
Pesetas	9,179,600	148,017,074	216,573,555	205,777,914	579,548,143

Sources: HISMA, Ltd., "Statistical Report" (Madrid, Dec. 1939), pp. 10-12; unpublished set of tables, original c/o Herbert R. Southworth, Ruedo Ibérico, Paris; photocopy in author's possession.

[a]Statistics begin in October.

Table 5. Volume of Foreign Trade with Spain in 1938 (Value of Gold Dollars in Millions)

Nation	Imports	Exports
Germany	19	22
Great Britain	12	16
United States	7	5
France	6	3
Total	44	46

Source: Marion Einhorn: *"Die ökonomischen Hintergründe der faschistischen Intervention in Spanien 1936-1937* (Berlin, 1962), citing *Nachrichten für Aussenhandel,* 9 July 1940.

of German tourists in Spain and Spanish loans to the Weimar Republic.[118] Normal operation of the Spanish Foreign Exchange Office became impossible after July 1936, owing to wartime disruptions. After Hitler recognized the Burgos government in November 1936, Franco attempted to spend Spain's accumulated prewar bank balance in Germany. Officials of the Banco de España who had fled to Nationalist territory approached the Reichsbank, suggesting the possibility of drawing out one million RM ($400,000) in Spanish credits for the rebel war effort. On December 3, 1936, however, all funds in both countries were officially frozen.[119] The German bank postponed the question of the prewar accounts until the end of the civil war and the signing of a comprehensive commercial treaty.[120]

This move was linked with another important economic question between Germany and Spain: the claims of German private citizens who lost property in the Spanish Civil War. These claims explain why the Reichsbank would not hand over to Franco the surplus accumulated in Spain's "invisible" capital account since the 1920s. The Germans wanted to see how the overall economic costs of the war would fall, because, if the republic won, they did not want to be liable twice. Some thirteen thousand expatriate Germans in Spain had been forced to flee their homes and businesses in Republican territory because of anti-German feeling aroused by Hitler's aid to Franco and by the general anti-fascist and anti-Nazi propaganda put out by the Left since Hitler's coming to power in 1933. Most of the investment of the Third Reich was located in the Republican-held industrial centers of Barcelona, Madrid, Bilbao, and Valencia. Assuming 100-percent loss, these claims amounted to 160 million RM ($64 million) as tabulated by the AO of the Nazi party in August 1937; of this, 90 million RM ($36 million) assumed a total write-off for property of the Germans who had fled. The remaining 70 million RM ($28 million) covered inventories that had been delivered in 1935 and early 1936 by German exporters on normal short-term business credit but that was still unpaid because of wartime disruption.[121]

Early in the civil war, Olscher, ministerial director in the Finance Ministry, held the view that the Reich must avoid accepting responsibility for bringing suit against the Franco government on behalf of German citizens.[122] He cited the precedent of the Russian Revolution and said claims for property damage should be postponed. It will be recalled that Olscher had been instrumental in the creation of ROWAK, which was dependent upon the Finance Ministry for credits, and that he held an interest in Rheinmetall-Borsig, the firm supplying much of Franco's artillery. For Olscher, of course, the interests of ROWAK and Rheinmetall-Borsig could only be jeopardized if bringing petty claims from prewar commerce against Franco's government created "bad blood."

On the other hand, the AO leadership in Berlin, while agreeing with Olscher that claims should be postponed until the end of the war, busied themselves collecting information about German losses in Spain. Alfred Hess (brother of the celebrated Rudolf)—who acted as an assistant of the AO chief, Ernst Bohle—pressed for this action.[123] In mid-1937, therefore, the AO created the Hilfsausschuss für die Spanien-Deutschen, a committee that handled relief and listened to and recorded the complaints and claims of German refugees from Spain.[124] Rudolf Hess, deputy to the Führer and head of Nazi party administration and patronage, told the newly appointed Ambassador Stohrer to take up these claims with Franco.[125] On October 24, 1937, Franco declared to Stohrer that he was willing to accept responsibility for damages in principle, and he suggested establishment of a mixed claims commission.

At the beginning of 1938 an agent of the German Relief Committee, a unit of the AO, went to Spain to gather further information on the commercial claims.[126] Somebody in the Finance Ministry, possibly Olscher, conferred with the Nazi claims investigator before his departure, warning him not to support the business claims at that time. The Finance Ministry argued that this would only ruin the Reich's reconstruction opportunities, while, if German businessmen were permitted to return to Spain, they would have nothing to import or sell anyway.[127] The Relief Committee thought, at least temporarily, that the advice was sound; hence, it did little to support the German refugees after its agent got to Spain.

Still, some four thousand claims that had been filed with the Relief Committee in the summer of 1937 were rigorously investigated by cross-checking with party personnel in Spain.[128] After the German union with Austria in March 1938, the claims of a few Austrians were also considered,[129] but the AO automatically excluded German Jews living in Spain because of "their responsibility for the outbreak of war."[130] Because of Nazi race theory, Jews were not considered worthy of ordinary German legal protection. Goebbels promoted the line by delivering inflammatory speeches at Nürnberg rallies in the autumn of 1937, blaming the entire Spanish Civil War on "Jewish bolshevism."

Because of tariffs, shipping rebates, frozen prewar capital accounts, war damages, and HISMA-ROWAK's growing war debt, the Germans, early in the civil war, had accepted the Spanish Nationalist argument that no comprehensive economic negotiations could take place under wartime conditions. The Wilhelmstrasse had decided to postpone pressing for a new treaty to replace the one of May 1926 until after the war. The July 1937 agreements[131] merely gave Nazi Germany first option on contracts (as opposed to Britain, France, and the United States) to reconstruct New Spain's economy. When Nationalist forces split the Republican territory and reached the Mediterranean in April 1938, Berlin assumed that Franco was bringing the Spanish war to a close. Hitler thought immediately that the time was right to conclude an economic treaty.[132] Shortly afterwards, however, he learned that Republican resistance was still strong and shelved the idea of negotiations. It did not arise again until January 1939, when Franco was overrunning Catalonia.[133]

As a result of Hitler's intervention and military aid to Franco, Nazi party people were able to secure new economic influence in Spain through the rise of Bernhardt's HISMA-SOFINDUS. For example, the Nazi military-industrial complex invested $8 million in five mining companies,[134] and Spanish pyrites exports to Germany increased from 563,000 tons in 1935 to 896,000 tons in 1938. By January 1939, almost 50 percent of Franco's foreign trade went to and from Germany. Moreover, the destructive nature and long duration of the war, as well as Franco's political outlook, seemingly portended a revolution in Spain's foreign economic policy. The Nationalist government spoke vaguely of autarky[135] and denounced the traditional liberal capitalistic Anglo-French influence in Spain.

The Nazis entertained great hopes that a Falangist Spain would cement close ties with them after the civil war. The problem for the Third Reich in 1939 was whether the recently won trading position in Spain would prove to be truly permanent, or whether American, British, and French capitalists would recover their former influence. Even with the increased investments of SOFINDUS, the prewar British ($194 million), French ($135 million), and American ($80 million)[136] capital could be more important in the Spanish economy if Franco chose to recognize their claims, because the new German total was only $46 million—$36 million in old investments plus $10 million for SOFINDUS.

If ROWAK were to claim the entire $215 million that Spain[137] owed for the services of the Legion Condor and the Sonderstab W, however, that would be a formidable investment in relation to the traditional economic power of the liberal capitalist bloc prior to the civil war.

In 1936, Hitler assumed that German economic gains in Spain would be valuable for their own sake. When he dispatched his first planes, he believed their cost would be paid for by the Nationalist movement. During the war, he granted Spain as an economic fief to Göring through the Four-Year Plan, HISMA, and ROWAK. That fief, Hitler believed, could play a real role in his evolving plans for expansion in eastern Europe.

5

The Place of Spain
in German War Plans

The Mysterious Admiral Canaris Deals with Spain

Responsibility for Hitler's actions in the Spanish Civil War has sometimes been laid upon Admiral Wilhelm Canaris, Hitler's chief of military intelligence.[1] Through his twenty-year history of activity in Spain, Canaris was the officer in the German War Ministry with the best contacts in that country when the civil war began.

Canaris remains one of the controversial figures of recent German history, not only because of his "cloak and dagger" operations, but because of his eventual opposition to Hitler. Jailed shortly after the failure of an attempt to assassinate Hitler in July 1944, the admiral was executed by the Nazis in April 1945.

The best-known biographers of the Abwehr chief have not satisfactorily explained the beginnings nor the extent of his opposition to Hitler. The first unambiguous evidence of Canaris's opposition to Hitler's foreign policy does not occur until August 27, 1938, when Canaris recommended that Konrad Henlein, leader of the Sudentenland Nazis, inform the Führer of his inclinations against war with Britain.[2] Almost a year later, on July 22, 1939, Canaris warned the Italians—who at that point were also reluctant to fight Britain and France—that Hitler was determined to bring on a general war, despite the unpreparedness of the German armed forces.[3] Here the documentation is even clearer, because Canaris told an Italian military intelligence officer that he opposed a German war with Britain.

On the other hand, in 1935, according to all documents, the master spy seems to have been devoted to Hitler.[4] In the 1920s and early 1930s, Canaris had welcomed nazism as an answer to communism[5]—communism probably meaning social revolution or socialization of property. After his promotion in January 1935 to Abwehr chief, he definitely supported the effort to conclude the Anti-Comintern Pact with Japan.6

In the context of Hitler's Spanish gambit, an important question arises—whether Canaris played a key role in German decisions concerning the Spanish Civil War. When Canaris's name appears in the documents during the 1936-1939 period, he is collecting information or carrying out orders, not making policy. Nonetheless, his influence on German policy cannot be dismissed. Regardless of the conflicting interpretations of his behavior, the head of German military intelligence had strong ties to a conservative-reactionary Spain. Canaris thought like a conservative-reactionary Prussian of the 1920s, a group that showed its latent power again in the July 1944 assassination attempt against Hitler.

Shortly after the July 1936 Spanish uprising, Canaris's old friends in Spain held important offices: General Severiano Martínez Anido became Franco's police chief, and Colonel Alfredo Kindelán headed the air force. From Canaris's viewpoint, therefore, the 1936 rebellion was simply to restore the old order in Spain, after the leftist politicians from 1931 to July 1936 had placed obstacles in the path of German long-range naval planning.7

The historian must ask whether the admiral actively encouraged the July 1936 uprising,8 as three of his hagiographers claim.9 A British Marxist journalist, for whom Canaris was a villain, believed in 1938 that Hitler's military intelligence chief had taken the initiative in advising Spanish intervention.10 Some circumstantial evidence suggests that this interpretation may be correct, because as early as 1933 the Abwehr had "businessmen spies" observing "communist" activities in Spain.11 But what do these terms spies and Communists really mean?

Actually, Canaris organized three types of agents. First, there were regular personnel in the army and navy who did espionage work. Second, there were the part-time spy-patriots—Germans living abroad who worked in business, industry, or shipping (sometimes with reserve commissions), and who volunteered part-time information. Third, Canaris had lined up the Etappendienst, a clandestine service to supply German vessels, especially submarines, with oil, ship's stores, and docking facilities in the event of war with France.12 Altogether, Canaris had perhaps fifty full-time or part-time agents in Spain on the eve of the war in 1936.13

As to communism, Canaris personally had a fanatical hatred and fear of social revolution, dating at least from Germany's troubles following World War I. In fact, he had served on the court martial that exonerated the murderers of Karl Liebknecht and Rosa Luxemburg,14 for which he was much maligned by the German Communist party in the public press. Further strengthening his ultra-conservative views on social questions was his family background and marriage into great wealth.[15] He thought more like Franco than like Hitler, Göring, or Faupel.

The extent of Abwehr involvement in events during the decisive first three weeks of the civil war poses a complex question. According to the testimony of an Abwehr officer captured by the Soviets at the end of World War II, Canaris had an agent named Edmond Niemann in the Canary Islands on July 17, 1936, who made contact with Franco from the very beginning. Niemann supposedly flew with Franco to Tetuán and brought in veteran Nazis Langenheim and Bernhardt to see Franco, then to carry the decisive messages for Hitler and Göring. After the German businessmen's triumphant return, Langenheim became the head Abwehr agent for Spanish Morocco.[16]

On the basis of surviving documentation and Bernhardt's testimony, however, Spanish historian Angel Viñas and German historian Hans-Henning Abendroth have discounted this story.[17] At least Bernhardt, who made the flight, stated that he never saw Canaris at Bayreuth on July 25-26. Neither Bernhardt nor his biographers mention Niemann, and Bernhardt claimed Langenheim was too old to play an active role in espionage.[18] Bernhardt said his real objection was that, unlike himself, Langenheim was not as enthusiastic for nazism or for Franco's rebellion.[19] Nevertheless, Langenheim did have three sons, two of whom worked with him in Morocco for the Abwehr, with the third on Ribbentrop's staff.[20] Furthermore, ignoring his age, both British and French intelligence reported as late as 1940 that Langenheim was one of the top three German agents in Spanish Morocco,[21] while the French had suspected him for years. Given the Abwehr's extensive network of "businessmen spies," it is possible, although not proven, that Langenheim and even Bernhardt were reporting to Canaris in July 1936.

The three biographers of the Right seem to base their belief that Canaris was present when Hitler decided to intervene in Spain on a Foreign Ministry document stating that "an admiral" was at Bayreuth along with Göring and Blomberg.[22] A naval document, however, names Rear Admiral Eugen Lindau of the Kriegsmarine Dienststelle (naval coordinator of merchant shipping) as present at Bayreuth and says nothing about Canaris.[23]

Yet there is still further evidence that Canaris could have known all about the Bernhardt mission. Bernhardt, before going to Bayreuth, asked Ernst Bohle, his party chief in Berlin, to present Franco's letter to Hitler. Bohle had never met Bernhardt, and he regarded Franco as an uncertainty. He communicated the story to SS Obergruppenführer (General) Wilhelm Brückner, Hitler's SS adjutant, who gave permission for Bernhardt to go on to Bayreuth.[24] Brückner may very well have consulted the Abwehr. In any case, when Bernhardt spoke to Hitler, Brückner brought in a detailed dossier on Spain, so that a well-prepared Hitler had already been thinking of the Spanish question before Bernhardt's arrival.[25]

In any event, it is likely that Hitler got advice from Canaris on Spain, even if the elusive admiral did not attend the Bayreuth conference in person. General Rudolf Bamler, who worked as chief of Abwehr Department III (counterespionage), testified after World War II that Canaris persuaded Hitler to aid Franco primarily through Göring and, secondarily, through Ribbentrop and Himmler.[26] Göring, in part, confirmed this testimony at the Nürnberg Trials.[27]

Erhard Milch, the state secretary, has said that the Bernhardt party (possibly including Spanish officers and Langenheim) first went to Canaris in Berlin on July 24-25,[28] before Bernhardt and the Franco messengers went on to Bayreuth. In Milch's opinion, the Abwehr chief was too cautious to make any decision, but it is certain that Blomberg and Milch then appealed through Bohle and Hess to authorize the Spanish party to see Hitler in Bayreuth. Göring later contacted Milch on Sunday, July 26, after Hitler decided to send Franco aid.[29] Milch's story confirms Bamler's and Göring's estimates of Canaris's character—namely, that he worked very indirectly, and that he was not likely to give Hitler advice that the Führer did not want to hear.

Nevertheless, Milch's account supports some kind of role for Canaris in Hitler's original decision to intervene in Spain. Recent historians have "over-revised" the exaggerated role assigned to Canaris by earlier writers of the Right. The newer works dismiss Canaris as unimportant in initiating German intervention, but they have ignored the question of just exactly what the intelligence chief was doing during the vital days July 17 to July 25.

Our knowledge of the events from July 17 to the end of the month depends, in large measure, on the sketchy memoirs recorded by Nazis and Spanish Nationalists, mostly after April 1939. One memoir implies that General Mola, conspirator in Navarre, had made contact with Canaris by July 12 or 13.[30] If Canaris had been in touch with rightist leaders such as Mola, José Sanjurjo, or José Gil Robles, between February and July 1936, then the admiral was well aware of a possible army revolt in Spain. Because of the death of Sanjurjo on July 20, however, it may be that Canaris had bet on the wrong man. According to Bamler, Canaris had long known Franco but had a poor opinion of the general at the outbreak of the civil war. Canaris hoped that General Martínez Anido, his acquaintance since the 1920s, would take over after the death of Sanjurjo.[31] Martínez Anido had achieved considerable notoriety for his bloody suppression of the Barcelona unions in 1920 and later in his position as minister of interior in charge of the repressive Civil Guards under General Miguel Primo de Rivera. If the reports about Canaris's contacts with the Spanish rightists other than Franco before July 1936 are correct,[32] this may explain why arms salesman Bernhardt and the Nazi party became so involved. It was Franco who nominated Bernhardt.

In conclusion, Canaris did advise Hitler somehow in July 1936. He undoubtedly counseled tactical caution, but he may have backed Hitler's own resolve. Messages from Spain, July 17-25, reached the Abwehr in Germany through the German military attaché in Paris.[33] Also, on about July 25 or 26, the self-appointed rebel "ambassador" in Paris, Count José Quiñones de León, sent his secretary to Berlin to appeal for arms for Mola. In Berlin, Mola's messenger was joined by another Mola agent on July 28, just after Hitler had already agreed to send planes to Franco. Both of Mola's representatives met with Canaris in Berlin, and they regarded him as their principal advocate. However, Count Welczeck—at that time ambassador to Paris after ten years' service in Madrid—was well informed about these two Mola emissaries and opposed their going to Berlin. He feared that any German aid to the Spanish rebels could complicate relations with France, while the disunited rebels probably would not win.[34] Welczeck may have warned Canaris to be cautious, but—with the French cabinet's reversal, on the night of July 25, of their earlier decision to back the Republicans—both Welczeck and Canaris had less reason for worry that France would fully back the Spanish Republic.

To Bernhardt, late on the night of July 25, Hitler appeared to have the latest information on the Spanish crisis and to be well informed, despite the very confused unfolding of the plots. The Führer already was consulting a dossier on Spain, and by this date the general lines of the Spanish events certainly did not pose much of a mystery to Canaris.[35]

The most likely explanation of Canaris's behavior during the first week of the civil war is that he was concentrating on reactions in Paris[36] and Rome. In any case, Canaris definitely discussed Spain with top Italians on August 4 and August 26-28. Like his Italian counterpart, General Roatta, Canaris went immediately to Spain; unlike Roatta, his stay was brief. During August, he received news of Spanish events mostly through insurgent agents in Paris and Lisbon, in addition to his own brief trip to Seville.[37] He apparently met with Franco and German military advisor Colonel Warlimont once or twice in September.[38] Certainly Canaris traveled to Spain in late October with the news that the Legion Condor was being sent.[39] It is also documented that he attended the December 6 conference in Rome on stepping-up ground support for Franco;[40] the Abwehr chief, like Hitler at that time, wanted Mussolini to maximize Italian participation, while German aid was being minimized.

In 1937 Canaris made at least three trips to Spain.[41] He reported on

Franco's disagreement with General Sperrle[42] over the slow pace of the war, and probably on the feud between Sperrle and Ambassador Faupel as well. In July 1937 Canaris told Franco's operations chief that Göring's group wanted to win the war, and that he was working in Berlin to obtain more material for Franco. Canaris also assured the Spanish Caudillo of his heartfelt sympathy for the Nationalist cause, his appreciation of Franco's performance, and that his report to Berlin would make more aid forthcoming. The German intelligence chief then requested that the Russian prisoners whom the rebel armies had captured be turned over to the Germans; Franco agreed. Next, Canaris asked that the Nationalists send all the information they had on French Morocco. Lastly, the intelligence chief recommended that the Caudillo employ in the Nationalist movement his old friend in Spain, an associate of shipbuilder Horacio Echevarietta, Naval Captain Daniel Araoz, the Barón de Sacro Lirio.[43] The baron became a personal advisor to Franco on aviation matters and a director of civil aviation.[44]

Canaris made at least three trips to Spain in 1938, one of which resulted in diplomatic activity to tie Spain politically to Germany.[45] The Abwehr chief also inspected the military situation in Spain; as a result, reinforcements were sent to the Legion Condor after a long halt in aid. At the end of the war, in April 1939, Canaris pressed Franco to publicize Spain's attachment to the Axis through the signature of the Anti-Comintern Pact.[46] Then in July 1939 he was in Spain preparing the ground for Abwehr operations during a possible future war with the West.[47]

Despite the Abwehr chief's obvious activity and personal influence, his aims still remain somewhat mysterious. Apparently Hitler trusted Canaris. The Führer was a born talker and Canaris, a born listener.[48] Canaris's reactionary social philosophy could easily explain his support for Hitler's experiment in Spain. But Canaris's philosophy could also militate against Hitler once it became clear that the Führer was willing to risk war with a conservative British Empire. He differed with Hitler by August 1938 on the eve of the Sudentenland crisis, and again in the summer of 1939, simply because Canaris feared that Germany would lose a naval war with Britain.

Canaris's opposition to France was more important than either his long-standing connections and romantic affinity with the Spanish Right or his desire to crush a suspected social revolution, Communist or otherwise. As an intelligence officer, Canaris had 35 agents in France in 1935, 153 by 1937, and 274 by 1938.[49] As a naval officer, he had joined in planning war games in which Spanish sea bases were to play a role against France.[50] In fact, the major objective of the German navy from 1919 to the outbreak of the civil war in Spain was preparation for a naval war with France and Poland. Canaris believed that, to win such a war, the United States and Great Britain would have to remain neutral. In 1935 the German navy, like Hitler, wanted an Italian alliance, or at least benevolent neutrality, to weaken French naval power in the Mediterranean. Therefore, when Hitler received Franco's appeal at Bayreuth, neither Hitler nor the navy needed great persuasion to aid Franco; they had the same interest—to weaken French seapower by backing the ambitions of Mussolini and Franco, assuming a quick rebel military victory.

In addition, Spain could prove useful for German strategy in the event of a land war with France. The U.S. military attaché in Berlin reported, in the first weeks of the civil war, that the threat posed by a fascist Spain could mean the removal of six French divisions from the German frontier.[51] To Canaris, then, as to Hitler and others, Spain was a means to a larger end, just as it had been in World War I.

According to a conservative confidant of Canaris, the Abwehr chief supported Hitler's Spanish policy throughout the civil war on military and conservative social grounds; but, at the same time he opposed Hitler at home on moral grounds.[52] Yet Canaris's moral reservations led to no overt action, as, for example during the Blomberg-Fritsch crisis of February 1938, when Hitler purged the Prussian army leadership and installed his minion, General Wilhelm Keitel. Further, opposition to the possibility of a British war was not equivalent to sabotage of the Nazi regime. The master spy's prime resistance to Hitler, from 1939 to 1944, consisted in tolerating one of Hitler's real opponents, Major General Hans Oster, within the Abwehr organization—but Oster played no role in Spain. Canaris, a fascinating and enigmatic figure who flitted in and out of the Spanish story, remains in the end as mysterious as ever. The admiral's influence on the Spanish issue may have been his greatest role.

The Legion Condor Performs in Spain

Military history and the way battles are won or lost influence diplomats and politicians in guessing about the future balance of power. Military victories create a bandwagon effect politically. Hitler directly contributed to Franco's military victory on land, sea, and air. Hitler's first aid, Operation Feuerzauber, flew 13,523 Spanish and Moroccan infantrymen[53] across the Straits of Gibraltar to Seville when they were most needed by the rebels—between July 29 and October 11, 1936. This was the first successful large-scale airlift in history. Because Franco had only five signal officers at the beginning of the war, the initial aid of German communications equipment and technicians was also important.[54] These were mostly sent during Hitler's second stage of military intervention, Operation Otto.

By November Hitler was dispatching to Spain the Legion Condor, which attained a maximum strength of 5,600 men and from 140 to 150 planes[55] that were vital to a Nationalist victory. Over the course of the war, Germany shipped at least 16,846 and possibly as many as 19,000 men to Spain, losing about 355,[56] while 232 planes of the legion were also lost.[57] During the period November 1, 1937, to October 31, 1938, the Sonderstab W, which administered aid to Franco, reported 96 Republican planes destroyed in Spain; by comparison, only 35 Nationalist planes had been destroyed.[58]

Organizationally, the Legion Condor consisted of five major aviation units: S/88, the command station; J/88, four squadrons of fighters (36-48 machines); K/88, four squadrons of bombers with 9 to 12 planes each; A/88, one squadron of land observation planes; and AS/88, eventually two squadrons of sea scout planes. The four fighting units comprised 99 to 132 planes in all.[59] In addition, the German aviation command created two units for experiments (VK/88), six batteries of flak gunnery, F/88,[60] and a field artillery group known as Lucht.[61] The Legion Condor also included two radio decoding and communications groups known as Wolm[62] and an original 30- to 48-tank corps organized under the name of Drohne.[63] These fighting units were supported by LN/88, ammunitions group; B/88, traffic control; P/88, telegraph and telephone; and SAN/88, parts and sanitation.[64]

In addition to this direct support, another major contribution made by the Germans to Franco's victory consisted of training 56,000 Spanish officers, known as group Imker.[65] Finally, German equipment generally was superior to that of all other powers, except for Russian heavy tanks, because the German War Ministry improved its equipment by testing in Spain. The German 8.8 cm anti-aircraft gun proved to be the best in the conflict. Early in the war the Italian CR 32 proved to be the best fighter aircraft, and the German He 51, an inferior machine. By early 1937 the Me 109B appeared, and by early 1939 the Me 109E was the fastest fighter plane of the war.[66] All told, the Luftwaffe tried out some twenty-seven types of aircraft in Spain.[67]

The German bombing technique developed over Madrid in late October 1936 consisted of bombing in three waves. First came the 2,000-pound bombs, which smashed concrete buildings; then the 220-pound bombs to break up the rubble in smaller pieces; then the incendiary and antipersonnel 22-pound bombs to kill the men who came to put out the fires. In total, the Germans dropped more than 21 million tons of bombs on Spain in the course of the war.[68] The top German ace in Spain was Captain Werner Mölders, who shot down fourteen planes; the war as a whole produced fifteen German aces.[69]

Compared to the Italians, the Germans sent more technical services for their $215 million, while the Italians with their $354 million contributed much more in the form of infantry to the Nationalists. The combined Italian and German money nearly equalled the amount of gold that the Republicans spent in Paris and Moscow. The Italians sent 80,000 men, reaching a maximum operational strength of 44,700 to 48,000,[70] of whom they lost 3,819.[71] However, they also sent Franco 729 aircraft;[72] the Germans sent at least 593 aircraft, and possibly as many as 708.[73] In February 1939, the total Nationalist air strength had reached 491 planes, which included 126 German-manned and 192 Italian-manned craft. Spanish personnel piloted 173 planes, about two-thirds of them Italian and one-third German.[74]

Better equipment and training were major reasons for the Axis victory in Spain over the technically and logistically weaker "private" aid from France and the semiofficial, Soviet-dominated Comintern. British Military Intelligence concluded that the Nationalists gained permanent superiority in the air by October 1936, and that the Russian pilots had disappeared from the Spanish skies by late November 1937.[75] The regular Italian and German forces together lost 4,170 men, compared with the 11,876—Frenchmen, Germans, Italians, Americans, and eastern Europeans—who sacrificed their lives volunteering for the International Brigades.[76]

The combat history of the Legion Condor is difficult to evaluate on an independent tactical basis, since the legion was cooperating daily with the Italians and Spaniards. Who received the credit if an He 111 shot down a French plane? Condor planes included Spanish observers and trainees on their missions. In early 1937, Sperrle was put in charge of a combined air operation of 150 planes—his own legion, the Italians, and Spaniards—over the northern front in Franco's war against the Basques.[77] Although Franco had on his staff five Germans and five Italian advisors, he apparently listened most closely to Sperrle, then to his two successors, Generals Helmuth Volkmann and Richthofen.

Besides the Gibraltar airlift from July to October 1936, German units fought in thirty battles, from bombing the Battleship *Jaime I* on August 12, through two battles of Teruel in the winter of 1937-38 (probably the bloodiest of the fighting on both sides), to the last offensive, sprung in Toledo Province toward Madrid on March 27, 1939.[78]

In July through October 1936, Franco marched from Seville to Badajoz to Cáceres to Toledo to Madrid. Mola wiped out pockets of resistance from Pamplona to the outskirts of Madrid during the same period. The International Brigades probably saved Madrid in late October. The ensuing stalemate at Madrid from October 1936 to January 1937 convinced Sperrle and Franco that they should turn their attention to the northern front—the Basque country and Asturias.

On April 26, 1937, the Luftwaffe bombed the Basque village of Guernica. A few days later Franco's forces captured the town and tried to deny the fact of the bombing for the sake of international public opinion. This led to a series of charges and countercharges, so that the story of this relatively minor military event became a study in morality, international law, and propaganda.[79]

The Spanish Republic lost control of the sea coasts in September 1936 when Franco and Mussolini won the battle of Mallorca.[80] This island was lost not for lack of sea power but because the Republican minister of the navy cautiously decided to evacuate Loyalist forces for political and strategic reasons. Later that same month, the Republican navy lost control of the Straits of Gibraltar. During the war British private merchant vessels supplying the Republic were frequently attacked by Italian and Nationalist blockade vessels and aircraft. According to British private shipping company statistics, they suffered 125 attacks and 14 sinkings; 40 men were killed and 68 wounded.[81] The British government claimed 162 attacks on private merchantmen in which the Axis and the Nationalists sank 20 vessels, killed 20 men, and injured 26.[82] The Legion Condor, the Italian "corps," and the Nationalist air force using Mallorca were responsible for more sinkings in 1938 than the Italian submarines in 1937.[83]

Throughout the war, the commander of the Legion Condor met with Franco on almost a daily basis. The Axis chargés, Anfuso and Faupel, had agreed to the joint Italian-German staff in the generalissimo's headquarters. The only problem with that formula was that Faupel tried to add his own voice, to the annoyance of Franco and the Italians.[84] A subject of continuing debate among the generalissimo and Sperrle, Volkmann, and Richthofen was the choice of targets. According to the Germans, Franco had a stubborn tendency to lose sight of grand strategy for the sake of minor tactical or psychological victories. For example, the battles of Toledo in September 1936 and Teruel (December 1937 to February 1938) were senseless wastes of time from the German point of view.[85] The German task was to keep Franco on the main target of Madrid. Ironically, while Hitler wanted a slow war for the sake of his European strategy, Franco wanted an even slower war for tactical reasons. The chief of state dallied in order to capture valuable war plants, consolidate his disloyal rear, and humor the British. The German military claimed that only through General Antonio Aranda's chief of staff, General Juan Vigón, did the whole strategy of the war become successful.[86] Aranda, one of Franco's major corps commanders, was the conqueror of Oviedo, Teruel, and Valencia, among others. Vigón took German advice, so that a most significant contribution of Germany to the Franco crusade may have been to provide it with a strategy. Spanish military historians and future research may, however, repudiate that claim.

The German military came to recognize that the Spanish war had more to teach them than World War I, while the French conservatives, with minds riveted on World War I and the Bolshevik Revolution, learned the wrong lessons from Spain. The Germans learned nine major military lessons from the Spanish Civil War on land, sea, and in the air. These lessons included, first, to concentrate their armor in a spearhead;[87] and second, to spread their modern fighter planes[88] because, with greater speed, World War I's close aerial formations no longer worked.[89] Captain Werner Mölders revolutionized aerial tactics. He later demonstrated for the British and Americans the "Finger Four" formation, based on his Spanish experience.[90]

The third lesson, which deserves some elaboration, was to coordinate armor and bombing to create panic—the famous *Blitzkrieg.* Colonel Wilhelm Ritter von Thoma, commander of the tank corps Dróhne (containing sixty tanks by December 1936),[91] developed this tactic and became the mentor of General Heinz Guderian of World War II fame. Because of the secrecy of Hitler, the pride of Franco, and the conservatism of the Italians and French (as well as exaggerated propaganda by the air forces of the world), the story of Spain's tank units is still obscure.[92]

From November 1936 to July 1937, the Russian T-26 tank proved superior to the German light tank (the Mark I) and the Italian Fiat.[93] Thoma experimented with the Mark II and III in Spain.[94] During the battle of Brunete, July 6-28, 1937, the Republic still had more and better Russian machines, but the Russian advisors lost the battle because they did not follow up their tanks with Republican infantry. General José Varela, with the advice of the German Drohne personnel, developed better coordinated tactics combining artillery, aircraft, and tanks. The tactic was then known as the *Schwerpunkt,* spearhead or breakthrough.[95] The first official German historian of the Spanish war, Werner von Beumelburg, recognized the success of "close cooperation of air force and ground troops" not at Brunete but rather in the later battle of Santander in August 1937.[96] As chief instructor, Thoma had trained a Spanish unit of 180 tanks by 1938.[97] General Juan Yagüe and the Legion Condor used the *Schwerpunkt* maneuver in July and August on the Ebro; some days the Germans gained twenty-five miles.[98] In the Catalan campaign the Germans doubled their previous pace to fifty miles a day.

The air side of the *Blitzkrieg* was developed by General von Richthofen,[99] who took his dive bombers to Poland and France after the Spanish war. For political reasons, Hitler was content that the civil war, for a while, bear the appearance of a stationary siege, a *Sitzkrieg,* like World War I. From Thoma's and Richthofen's vantage points, the coordinated attacks of dive bombers and tanks were winning in 1938. Spain, not Poland, thus saw the first *Blitzkrieg.*[100] The earliest mention of the word *Blitzkrieg* comes in May 1939 from General Georg Thomas of the OKW economic staff.[101]

The Italians never got over their defeat at Guadalajara, in which their light tanks got bogged down in the mud,[102] and never learned the lessons of Drohne. French military intelligence came to the conclusion in June 1938 that the German light tank had proved inferior, so the French concentrated on the heavy tank thereafter.[103] In France in 1940, the secret of the Thoma-Guderian success was to have regiments composed of two-thirds medium tanks and one-third fast tanks, coordinated with modern fighter-bombers. As part of the German general staff, Thoma fought in twenty-four battles in Poland, France, Russia, and Africa, while he had participated in 192 tank actions with the Legion Condor in Spain.[104]

The joint Nationalist-German mass bombing of Guernica, coordinated by Germany's Sperrle and Richthofen and Spain's Mola and Vigón, led to such an international outcry that the massive bombing experiment was not continued, at least not on towns.[105] The bombing of Guernica produced at least a thousand victims.[106] From a technical point of view, the mixed high explosive and incendiary raid was made to destroy a strategic bridge and a weapons factory. It was probably an "accidental" side effect that Guernica's wooden houses burned quickly. In any case, the Sonderstab W concluded that the raid was a complete success,[107] although the target factory and bridge were not hit. Guernica served as a foretaste of the brutal inefficiency of so-called "strategic bombing," or rather the indiscriminate bombing of civilians, that marked World War II and the Korean and American-Indochina wars.

More important to the history of bombing, although given less publicity, was the systematic bombing of the Catalan coast. From January 19 to March 31, 1938, the combined operations of German, Italian, and Nationalist aircraft killed at least 1,349 persons in 88 attacks.[108] Those air raids continued on into the following year. Their purpose was allegedly to stop Republican sea deliveries of materials, so it was a form of economic war—although it was also a kind of "terror bombing" employed to demoralize the Catalans.

The fourth, fifth, and sixth lessons of the Spanish Civil War affected the Luftwaffe and enabled the Germans to improve their air fighting equipment as the months rolled by. The Me 109 was superior to Russian and French planes. On the other hand, the Stuka dive bomber was effective against enemy fortifications but was generally vulnerable.[109] As a result of their Spanish experience, the long-range strategic bomber units learned to avoid anti-aircraft artillery by adopting night bombing. Navigational techniques for flying at night and in bad weather were also developed, so that in these areas the Luftwaffe was superior to Britain's RAF in 1939.[110] The Nationalist troops appreciated the morale boost that German air superiority provided.

The German air force decided in January 1937 to modify the entire production schedule of military aircraft. They increased production of the heavy fighter plane and the light bomber, but these changes forced them to

drop development of the heavy bomber. [111] The consequences of this decision were to help Hitler win the Battle of Poland and the Battle of France, but
they also may have contributed to the loss of the Battle of Britain. In addition, the Germans developed a torpedo plane that might have been effective
against the British fleet in World War II had Hitler not rejected the Legion
Condor experience. [112] The Japanese proved the effectiveness of the torpedo
plane at Pearl Harbor.

A seventh lesson was learned by the supply sections of the Legion
Condor. When Operation Winterübung began, the legion had one hundred
different types of motor vehicles. Eventually a simplified parts department
and supply train were developed to help keep the infantry mobile. [113] These
were used later in France. Eighth, the Germans had a chance to test captured
Russian equipment, with one result being Germany's rapid development of a
heavier tank. [114] Finally, it was in Spain that the Germans, who originally
viewed the 8.8 cm gun (the "eighty-eight") as an anti-aircraft weapon,
learned that it could be mobilized as field artillery and as an antitank
weapon. [115]

There were other general benefits to the German military from the
Spanish war. Needless to say, some of the 16,800 to 19,000 who served in
Spain entered Poland in the fall of 1939 as combat veterans. Twenty-nine top
German World War II aces had Spanish experience. [116] More specifically,
the Legion Condor veterans organized a training team in Germany upon
their return and trained 200 air crews for the Polish campaign. [117] Man for
man, the German army was the best in the world in 1939 (excluding possibly
the Japanese), in part due to Spanish experience.

The prime lesson of the Spanish Civil War for Keitel—stationed in
Berlin throughout that war but later Hitler's "chief of staff" for the Wehrmacht—was mobilization planning and the need for closer coordination
between the services, the Foreign Ministry and the propaganda ministry. [118]
In fact, the Sonderstab W was a precursor to the Oberkommando der
Wehrmacht, announced in February 1938. Warlimont was an architect of
both organizations. Hitler applied Keitel's and Warlimont's ideas of coordinated propaganda and military might by having Sperrle, former commander
of the Legion Condor, present at Berchtesgaden on February 12, 1938,
when Hitler terrorized the Austrian chancellor, Kurt von Schuschnigg. At
one point in the meeting, Hitler reinforced his "persuasion" for Anschluss
by calling on Sperrle to speak about the Spanish experience. [119]

Sperrle in May 1940 cooperated with Generals Albert Kesselring, Karl
von Runstadt, and Fedor von Boch in Operation Yellow, which decisively
defeated France. [120] Richthofen in 1941 commanded the VIII Air Corps and
contributed to Hitler's conquest of Crete. [121]

The western hemisphere was also affected by the German military intervention in Spain. The Legion Condor proved to be a practical training ground for the Spanish-speaking German agents who infiltrated Latin America in 1939 and 1940.[122]

The lessons of Spain should not, of course, be exaggerated. Some of the German military experience proved valuable in World War II, while other "lessons" were misapplied by the successors of the Legion Condor or were shown to be misleading. Göring and Thoma also learned negative lessons from Spain, namely a contempt for the Italian military.[123] Despite Hitler's personal flattery of the Duce, the Axis relationship remained strained at lower echelons throughout its short history. Experiences during the Spanish war were one source of this strain.

Although given worldwide publicity, the raid on Guernica had little effect on the military or diplomatic outcome of the war, except that the incident intensified the mutual hostility of the British and the Axis press.[124] Throughout the civil war, despite the efforts of the British government and the Tory party to maintain "the spirit of Locarno" and "appeasement," the events in Spain—the Guernica incident in particular—helped create anti-German feeling in Britain. Ironically, many conservatives who would later suffer in the Battle of Britain chose to believe in 1937 that the Guernica holocaust was a propaganda stunt trumped up by "the reds."

Except for Guernica, the extent of military victories attributable to the Germans became apparent only after Franco's triumph on March 31, 1939. The slow way in which Franco conquered territory at the time obscured the importance of the lessons of the drawn-out war in Spain. Further, the British and French military deduced some wrong lessons from the civil war because they failed to gauge German diplomatic and military power accurately.

Perhaps the greatest tribute to the Legion Condor was made by General Franco in July 1938 when he told the German ambassador that the services of the "Legion Condor could not be dispensed with."[125] This judgment should be balanced by the comment that, despite the achievements of Thoma and Richthofen, the lessons of the Spanish experiment were incompletely absorbed by the Luftwaffe chief, Göring. He remained too much of an individualistic World War I ace, essentially ignorant of supply, logistics, strategy, tactics and technology.[126] But whatever Göring's shortcomings may have been, the Nationalists respected the technical efficiency and comprehensiveness of the Germans more than they did the larger numbers of the Italians.

Naval Strategy Shifts against Britain

Because of their strategic interests in the Balearic Islands, the Canary Islands, and Gibraltar, the French and British probably viewed the German navy's assistance to Nationalist Spain as even more important than Hitler's aviation, tank, artillery, and communications services. The Oberkommando der Kriegsmarine (OKM) did not take an active part in naval warfare, however. The German navy instead concentrated on delivery of war material and on gathering intelligence. In August 1936, a special team of German naval officers reconditioned the Spanish heavy cruiser *Canarias* and trained replacements for officers killed by leftist sailors. In October, the *Canarias* and the cruiser *Almirante Cervera* took control of the Straits of Gibraltar away from the Republican navy. The Germans also assisted the Nationalists to lay mines around the Republican ports of Almería and Valencia, resulting in the loss of nineteen Loyalist vessels.[127] German advisors helped sweep mines from northern coasts after Franco's armies took the Basque country in June 1937; each Nationalist minesweeper had a German officer on board.

The OKM also aided the Legion Condor by creating a section known as the Gruppe Nordsee, consisting of about seventy-five communications and supply personnel.[128] Nordsee had two radio men in Salamanca with the code name "Anker," fourteen men in Cádiz ("Partner"), three at El Ferrol ("Peter"), one at Seville ("Witan"), and twelve in the observation sea plane squadron AS/88, stationed at Melilla[129] and later in the Balearics. Altogether, 2,200 German sailors served on German warships in Spanish waters.[130]

During the civil war the radio men of Gruppe Nordsee for the most part limited their work to reporting the activities of the Spanish Loyalists and the movement of British, Soviet, and French merchant vessels aiding those forces. The deliveries to the Republicans included both food and other consumer goods not prohibited by the NIC, but also contraband arms. For example, between January 1 and March 31, 1938, Nordsee reported that twenty-two British, three Greek, two American, one French, and one Russian vessel had brought supplies from the USSR to various Republican ports.[131] Such information helped the Nationalist navy's efforts to maintain their blockade, while the Germans avoided confronting the superior British navy. At the same time, Hitler deployed an intelligence unit that, in the event of a wider war, could have functioned beyond Spain.

Germany had fought France twice in the past two generations; thus Berlin's military elite had been thinking of another war against France since 1919. Geographic considerations and World War I experience led Berlin's naval planners to expect more help from Spain than the German army could hope for in such an event. The navy could weaken France's southern front by operations in Spanish waters, while the army would have to concentrate on going for Paris directly. During the first year and a half of the civil war, Hitler subordinated his ambitions for German military action to his prime diplomatic aim of manipulating the other Great Powers because he was not yet ready for a showdown with France. Although the navy had a stake in Spanish waters, in 1936 Hitler at first did not expect that the Abwehr agents in Spain could be used openly against Britain, the world's foremost sea power. By April 1938, however, his viewpoint would change, and Spain would be seen as useful for his overall strategy.

Despite Hitler's interest in building a large German navy, he had confused ideas about how to employ it. In *Mein Kampf,* the Führer had written of making Britain an ally. The Anglo-German naval arms limitation agreement of June 1935 was supposed to reaffirm the hopes of both London and Berlin that another 1914 would never happen. Ribbentrop was sent to London as ambassador in August 1936 to get an agreement on the basis of anticommunism, but the ex-champagne salesman did not impress the aristocratic British. Ribbentrop's disillusionment with England increased gradually, beginning in May 1937 and becoming complete by December.[132] Nonetheless, the German War Ministry assumed, until June 1937, that Britain would be neutral in its war plans against France.[133]

Into 1937 the Tory cabinet was still hoping that Hitler would sign another "Western Locarno Pact," even though Nazi Germany had violated the Locarno treaty by occupying the Rhineland the year before. British officialdom—particularly Foreign Secretary Anthony Eden—showed more hostility toward Mussolini's Mediterranean ambitions than toward Hitler's activity in Spanish waters. Upon the dispatch of Italian troops to the Balearic Islands in September 1936 and further large-scale landings of the Black Shirts in December and January, Eden argued to a hesitant British cabinet that the aggressiveness of the Duce should be stopped. The major British concern was not the small German navy but fear that the large Italian navy would stay in the islands.[134] Eden's famous resignation of February 1938 protested his prime minister's Italian, rather than German, policy.

The first incident emerging out of the civil war that had much effect on the overall Anglo-German relationship involved the pocket battleship *Deutschland.* In fact, the most sensational events during the entire war involving the German navy were the bombing of the *Deutschland* by Loyalist aircraft and the retaliatory shelling by the German navy of the city of Almería on May 29-30, 1937.[135] Afterwards, Ribbentrop shocked the British at an NIC meeting by announcing Hitler's decision to withdraw from the committee.[136] The incident briefly raised the possibility that the Spanish Civil War might expand into a general war.[137] Almería proved to be the exception to the rule, however, and the incident had more of an impact on London and Paris than it had on the eventual success of the Nationalist blockade. The Left in the liberal democracies used the incident to publicize the German danger, while the Right, indignant at the attack on the *Deutschland,* continued its compromises in the NIC.

As a result of the *Deutschland*-Almería incident, the Anglo-French entente powers and the Axis temporarily drew further apart. In June 1937,

Blomberg, the minister of war, visited Rome for military consultation with the Italians,[138] while Hitler cancelled a planned visit by Germany's foreign minister, Neurath, to London. The bombing of the *Deutschland* was cited as an excuse.[139] Furthermore, the Germans alleged that about two weeks after the "Soviet" bombing, a "Russian" submarine fired a torpedo at the German cruiser *Leipzig* while it was near Oran, Algeria.[140] No damage was done, no submarine was seen, and the German commander of the fleet observed later that the listening equipment was defective.[141] The commander of the *Leipzig* saw no torpedo wake and also reported that the original report of torpedoing had been a false alarm.[142]

Hitler thereafter became increasingly anti-British for the sake of maintaining a united front with Mussolini.[143] For their part, the British were disappointed that Neurath did not make the London trip, and they blamed Ribbentrop for Hitler's snub.[144] The Germans agreed to return to the NIC on June 15,[145] but they continued to boycott the four-power naval patrol commission[146] that, since April, had been attempting to control (by doing little more than reporting on) merchant vessels trading with the two Spanish factions.

Meanwhile, Hitler's eastern policy forced the OKM to make new war plans. On June 18, 1937, the German naval operations chief, Admiral Wilhelm Marschall, drew up a proposal for the commander in chief, Admiral Erich Raeder; it assumed, for the first time since the Versailles treaty, that Great Britain might back a Soviet-French war against Germany. But the OKM concluded that British sea power was too strong for Germany, so Germany must avoid a war.[147] Nevertheless, Marschall included a naval war with Britain as part of Hitler's war plans against Czechoslovakia.

Blomberg also drew up a series of war possibilities involving France and Britain in June 1937. Case Green envisioned a two-front war with German concentration on Czechoslovakia; Case Red, a two-front war with France; and Extension Green/Red, a war in which Britain would intervene. Case Richard foresaw the extension of the Spanish Civil War into world war by a "provoked incident."[148] The four plans hypothesized war with Britain as well as France. In all four the Iberian Peninsula could be involved sooner or later, if the fluid Axis and the fluid entente crystallized into two hard, rival alliance systems.

Nonetheless, Hitler was unwilling to back these plans with increased appropriations for the navy at home or with greater material aid to Spain. Inasmuch as the navy was just contemplating theoretical problems, it still hoped to avoid war with Britain, as well as with France, because the OKM just did not have enough firepower. Planning against France alone, as had been traditional since the 1920s, continued simultaneously with the Red, Green, Extension Green/Red, and Richard contingencies until as late as

November 1937.[149] Hitler himself still worked to keep the civil war localized while continuing to hope that Britain would not back France if French-German warfare erupted over some eastern European question.

In contrast to Hitler, Mussolini expanded his commitment to Franco's anticommunist war through "piracy" on the Mediterranean in August and September 1937. Italian submarines' torpedoing of merchant vessels led to new difficulties with the Anglo-French entente, resulting in the Nyon Conference, held September 10-13,[150] which Germany refused to attend. After much British pressure on Italy to participate, which they technically refused, the Italians later endorsed the pact in principle. Mussolini did send a naval representative to a subsequent Paris meeting on September 30, which modified the Nyon texts of September 13 to suit Mussolini's sensibilities.[151] For Chamberlain some kind of agreement with Italy and France was a *sine qua non*.

From a naval standpoint, both the Nyon texts and Paris texts were of a symbolic nature, since Mussolini subsequently concentrated more on bombing than on naval action. Earlier in August the Italian navy secretly invited Germany to take part in the "pirate activities," asking that a German operations officer come to Rome. Furthermore, in outlining Italy's proposals to the German naval attaché, Rear Admiral Eduardo Somigli referred to his monologue as our "common discussions." The Germans remained cool; the attaché merely thanked Somigli for the information and said he would inform Berlin.[152] Although the German navy gladly accepted the right to use the ports of Cagliari, Naples, and Genoa,[153] Hitler mainly reacted to Mussolini's difficulties with the entente by advising him to hang on to Mallorca.[154]

After the Anglo-French resolve to take action against submarines in the future, proclaimed at the Nyon Conference, Mussolini visited the Führer in Berlin during the last week of September. The two fascist imperialists secretly divided Europe into two spheres of influence: Germany would get the East, while Italy would control the Mediterranean. In early November the Duce made the decisive move of signing the German-Japanese Anti-Comintern Pact, further splitting Europe and its global empires into blocs. Hitler welcomed Italy's pressure on Anglo-French interests in the Mediterranean. The Führer observed that the British and French had done relatively little at Nyon and invited the Italians to participate in the proceedings against their own "pirates" while the entente excluded the USSR. Weakness only encouraged Hitler's own claims in the East.[155] The Italian foreign minister, Ciano, referred to the pact as "a military alliance forcing England to reconsider her position everywhere."[156] Likewise, the Duce thought he was "in the centre of the most formidable political and military combination which has ever existed."[157]

It is certainly true that the Axis support overwhelmed Soviet aid in the naval sphere. The Soviets sent the Republicans four motor torpedo boats, while the combined Axis sent Franco directly four destroyers, two submarines, and ten motor torpedo boats. The German contribution to the Nationalists was six motor torpedo boats, two more than the Soviet Union sent the Republic, but minor compared to Italian aid. During August and September 1937, when Mussolini went on the naval offensive throughout the Mediterranean, he indirectly assisted Franco's war effort with fifty-two Italian submarines, forty-one cruisers and destroyers, and two naval auxiliaries masquerading as Spanish cruisers.[158]

The Duce and Ciano were fond of heroic talk. Nevertheless, in their more sober moments, the Italians realized that militarily they needed the assistance of German forces in Spain. At one point Mussolini asked the Germans for a unification of the Legion Condor and the CTV under a single command, but the Germans politely refused.[159] Because of Spain, the Italians sought a general military understanding with Germany that the OKW delayed giving. Ciano by February 1938 advised General Alberto Pariani, under secretary for war, that military staff talks with the OKW should soon begin.[160] The Italians were talking of an Axis war against both Britain and France, but the Germans postponed military discussions until April 1939.[161]

Hitler set aside his war minister's fear of a two-front war involving Czechoslovakia by his famous November 5, 1937, speech to his military advisers. In it he confidently excluded the possibility of British intervention against his designs for aggressive war against Czechoslovakia. According to Hitler, the Spanish Civil War was capturing all of Europe's attention; Britain was weak, owing to trouble with Spain, Ireland, Italy, and Japan, and in "all probability England and perhaps also France have already silently written off Czechoslovakia."[162]

Later that November Göring boasted to the American ambassador in Paris that "the British Fleet cannot operate anywhere at the present time. It is completely pinned down by ourselves in the North Sea and by the Italians in the Mediterranean."[163]

Boasts aside, it should be remembered that active German planning with Spain to weaken the Versailles powers did not develop from a premeditated plan by Hitler. The outbreak and development of the civil war resulted from a complex series of unforeseen events, and Hitler made his immediate decisions about Spain with an eye on Italy and France. Only gradually did European events encourage Hitler to think about postwar military opportunities in Franco's Spain in connection with war against Britain.

In the fall of 1937, however, at least one ambitious German was already thinking about expanded postwar military-economic opportunities. This was

Friedrich von Lupin, general secretary of the Ausfuhrgemeinschaft für Kriegsgerät (AGK), a cartel that had monopolized German arms exports, and that Lupin had been instrumental in creating in 1935.[164] He had also been active before the civil war in selling arms to Spain. In September 1937 he pointed out to the Foreign Ministry that Britain and the Franco government might soon begin economic discussions.[165] Thus, Lupin suggested that Germany usurp the pre-civil-war position of the British firm of Vickers, Ltd., in the field of Spanish naval construction. At the time, nothing came of the suggestion; both the navy and Hitler still had hopes of avoiding conflict with Britain by focusing British attention on the communist danger within Spain.

Naval Ambitions Grow to the End of Civil War

By March and April 1938, the somewhat passive and divided Anglo-French entente was confronted by developments in the civil war and shifts in the general international balance. Hitler's march into Vienna led to the creation of a second Blum Popular Front cabinet that opened the French-Spanish frontier for the freer delivery of weapons to the Spanish Republicans. In April 1938 Nationalist troops were driving a wedge into the Republican front, cutting off the Levante from Catalonia and giving Franco access to the Mediterranean coast. Ribbentrop temporarily persuaded Hitler that El Caudillo's victory was at hand. Even though the new foreign minister turned out to be wrong, the April 1938 preparations made by Germany for Franco's victory shed light on Germany's future naval strategy.

What role could Spain then play in the new pressure Hitler was placing on European peace? Did the Germans have designs on Gibraltar or the Canaries?

Admiral Canaris visited Spain to assess Franco's Mediterranean offensive and subsequently sent a warning to Berlin that El Caudillo was trying to secure a free hand for himself. Immediately, Ribbentrop drafted a postwar friendship treaty for Hitler's approval.[166] Hitler, Ribbentrop, and Ambassador Stohrer had prepared the draft treaty for Franco by April 6, 1938. They planned to use it as a device to tie Spain to the Axis. Article Seven, for instance, was drawn up "to promote the fostering of comradely relations and the exchange of practical military experience between their armed forces."[167] The Germans interpreted this to mean that French and British military technology would be excluded from Spain. At the same time, in April 1938, Hitler again modified his war plan against Czechoslovakia. Now, the Extended Green Plan, Fall Grün, concentrated exclusively on Czechoslovakia, assuming that there would be no British or French intervention.

Hitler waved Britain and France aside with the comment that the British navy would not be prepared for two years, and its air force was out of date.[168] Still, lower-ranking officers in the OKM continued to worry about Britain, with some reason. On March 6, the British cruiser *Arethusa* had helped to ward off an attack by Legion Condor planes on the port of Barcelona. This annoyed Keitel, the OKW chief.[169]

Even though Hitler told his conservative army advisors that he would carry out war against Czechoslovakia only if England and France would not intervene, Hitler had no way of guaranteeing the future. Despite his confidence, the German armed forces were still maintaining attack plans against Britain and France, in case the West "started" war after the invasion of Czechoslovakia.[170] In pursuance of the provisions of the draft German-Spanish Treaty of Friendship and the Green Plan for Czechoslovakia, the OKM sketched out a specific role for Spain.

On April 7, a representative of the Hamburg-Amerika shipping line had a conversation with Lieutenant Commander Hellmuth Heye of Naval Operations, in which the use of Spanish docks to construct some commercial shipping for Germany was discussed.[171] Bernhardt, whose HISMA enjoyed profits from a monopoly of trade in German weapons and Spanish raw materials,[172] had already informed both parties of his interest in postwar construction possibilities in Spain. In addition, the German naval attaché in Spain, Commander Kurt Meyer-Döhner, informed the OKM that Bernhardt had proposed joint postwar construction to Göring, who had endorsed the idea. Consequently, Bernhardt came to Berlin on April 21, 1938, to ask the OKM for its cooperation. Bernhardt wanted German commercial shipbuilding interests to join with his company to help Nationalist Spanish industry reconstruct merchant shipping.[173] In the course of the conversation, Bernhardt mentioned that he had been interested for at least four months in obtaining Spanish docking facilities for Germany. Taking up where arms merchant Lupin of the AGK had left off in his September 1937 visit, Bernhardt had been negotiating with four private Spanish firms, including Canaris's old 1920s contact, Echevarietta.[174] Although Bernhardt knew Spanish market conditions, he needed credits and technical assistance from German shipbuilders. Unfortunately for Bernhardt, the German builders showed no interest in his projects, so Bernhardt was now appealing to the OKM for support. Both Bernhardt and Meyer-Döhner saw possibilities in a joint German-Spanish construction proposal, using Spanish docks to support Germany in the event of war with Britain and France. It also would afford an opportunity to oust Britain's influential Vickers Ltd. from Spain.

More important than Bernhardt's pressure, however, were strategic decisions in Berlin. The chief of the Operations Section of the OKM, after receiving Ribbentrop's draft treaty for Spain and Hitler's Extended Green

Plan, drew up a more specific plan for even broader German-Spanish naval cooperation.[175]

In a possible war with France and Britain, the Straits of Gibraltar and the Balearic Islands would play, according to Vice Admiral Günther Guse, a significant role. Although benevolently neutral, Spain would have a duty to cooperate with Germany on all questions concerning international and maritime law. Guse, the operations chief, believed that benevolent neutrality favoring the Axis would be better than a Spanish declaration of war because the raw materials of Spain would be safer during a British blockade under the Spanish flag than if a weak Spain were an ineffective war partner. Yet Spain could supply German war vessels and aircraft, and would cooperate in the field of intelligence. Moreover, Spain could exert political influence on Portugal and the Latin American states to take up pro-German positions, and Spain could leave "the pro-British" League of Nations. The Germans would undertake to reconstruct the Spanish commercial and fishing fleets, particularly in the strategically located Canary Islands. Expanding upon Bernhardt's and Lupin's suggestions to construct vessels for Germany, Guse's plan envisioned Germany aiding in the construction of war vessels. The chief of naval operations also suggested the training of Spanish sailors (which Canaris had just discussed with Franco).[176]

Guse sent his proposals to the German National Defense Office on April 26, 1938, and there they remained in the dead file for months. Hitler was still optimistic that Britain and France would not deter his plans for Czechoslovakia. In addition, Franco's situation had deteriorated because of the heavy aid France sent to the Republicans during the brief tenure of Blum's second Popular Front premiership.[177] The Germans had ceased delivery of replacements for the Legion Condor about three months before, possibly in an attempt to implement Hitler's Machiavellian, but half-hearted, hope for a French-oriented Catalonia.[178] Therefore, Franco and Ribbentrop agreed to postpone the planned friendship treaty until the end of the civil war.

Meanwhile, in May 1938 at a lower level in the bureaucracy, Canaris's representative, Lieutenant Eberhard Messerschmidt, who had had experience in Spain since the twenties, was lending support to Bernhardt's Spanish naval construction proposal. Messerschmidt proposed that four German companies (including Rheinmetall-Borsig where Göring had influence) form a consortium to create a Spanish firm that would replace Vickers in Spanish naval construction. Both commercial and war shipping could be built for Spain, and aviation and trucking equipment could be manufactured later.[179] The proposal received Guse's endorsement, and further talks with Bernhardt and German industrialists were held in early June 1938 at the Naval Ministry.[180]

Shortly thereafter, Heye made a secret trip to Iberia and Morocco on behalf of Naval Operations, visiting Burgos, Seville, Cádiz, Gibraltar, Tetuán, Melilla, Mallorca, and Lisbon. At his ports of call he discussed the varied interests of the OKM with the Spaniards, the Italians, and the Legion Condor officers in the field.[181] Heye visited the Echevarietta docks, then being rebuilt with German money at San Fernando near Cádiz; discussed with Vice Admiral Francisco Bastarreche, commander of the Cádiz base, the possibility of Germany lending Spain torpedo equipment; and talked with the Spanish operations chief and with the commander of the Legion Condor seaplane observation squadron about information gained concerning the British base at Gibraltar. Leaving no prospect to chance, he examined possible U-boat sites in Spanish Morocco and the Balearics, and explored with the Italian naval command the possibility of Italian naval aid to the Spaniards in the Balearics. Because the purpose of the extensive talks was mainly to look into Spanish opportunities, no definite agreements were concluded. Indeed, this thorough survey of Spanish conditions convinced Heye that it was absolutely necessary for the Italian navy, not the German, to take the lead in any postwar naval reconstruction aid to Spain. German naval production was limited; and consistent with the spirit of the Axis, Italy should maintain the burden of Spain.

As of December 1937 the Spaniards already had begun to work on a contract with Italy to build eight destroyers.[182] Admiral Francisco Moreno—the operations chief whose attention was focused on fighting the current war in Spanish waters rather than planning for postwar expansion—had suggested that Spanish naval officers be sent to Germany for immediate training. The unenthusiastic Heye thought the idea could be useful to Germany if it did not cause competition with Italy. At the time, however, the OKM did nothing about Moreno's request, inasmuch as the presence of Spanish cadets in Germany had little short-range value in strengthening anti-British influence in Spain.

In any case, the growing Czechoslovakian crisis in the summer of 1938 caused German military planners once again to speed up their thinking about the need for direct German-Spanish ties. As the Sudetenland crisis worsened in August, the German navy again had to face the possibility of general war. It seemed that France and Britain, hitherto divided over Ethiopia, Spain, and the role of the USSR, were gradually coming together. If, therefore, the Western powers declared war on behalf of Czechoslovakia, it would be handy for the German navy, which was totally unprepared for a protracted world conflict, to have the assistance not only of the Italian and Japanese navies but even of Franco's modest naval facilities.

As far as Spain was concerned, more important to the Germans than the fleet was the possibility of acquiring naval supplies by virtue of Spain's strategic location. Captain Kurt Fricke, who had replaced Guse as chief of the OKM Operations Section, on August 18 revived the suggestions that his predecessor had made the previous April. Fricke proposed that talks—for the exchange of intelligence; cooperation in supporting each other's fleets with oil, ammunition, and supplies; and common definitions of international laws, such as the meaning of belligerent rights—be taken up by the German naval attachés in Rome, Tokyo, and San Sebastián.[183] Although Hitler approved Fricke's suggestion on August 31,[184] little was done immediately to implement the plan; the Führer was still confident that the British and French navies could be discounted. Nevertheless, the OKM decided on September 1 to act on the matter of officer training. The Spanish admiralty had suggested in April and again in June that Spanish officers be sent to Germany for refresher courses.[185] In September the Germans countered with a proposal to send one German officer and twelve noncommissioned officers to Spain in exchange for a single Spanish officer to be sent to a German naval school. In the event of war with Britain and France, the navy of the Third Reich would at least have additional observers stationed in the strategic Iberian Peninsula.

As further evidence of the German navy's general interest in Spain during this time of international tension over Czechoslovakia, Admiral Canaris brought Don Juan, son of ex-King Alfonso, to tour naval installations in Germany from August 21 to 28. Canaris showed Don Juan the Hitler *Sportsfest,* the shipyards, the Siemens naval arms plants, the naval base at Wilhelmshafen, and U-boat maneuvers in the North Sea.[186] Because of dissension within the Spanish Right about restoring the monarchy, Prince Juan's trip had Franco's prior approval on the condition that it be considered only a "private visit."[187]

The passionate discussion within Franco's camp about a return of the monarchy may have meant that the elusive, cautious, but patriotic Canaris was preparing the ground for a possible turn of events. Or did a Machiavellian, anti-Hitler Canaris—knowing that Don Juan was persona non grata—deliberately invite the heir-apparent to Berlin, hoping it would cause an embarrassment between Hitler and Franco? In any case, despite Hitler's confidence that he was not risking general war over Czechoslovakia, the German navy kept in mind both short- and long-range plans involving Spain.

By late August, when the Czech crisis had become acute, Hitler decided to modify his overall military plans again.[188] Now he expected more backing from his Italian ally than he thought France would receive from Britain. When questioned about the hastened Green Plan, as amended on August 25, 1938, for taking over Czechoslovakia, Göring later said that Hitler and he had thought the entire French navy would be necessary to contain the

Italians in the Mediterranean.[189] Hitler still did not expect Britain to intervene in any case, so the Italian navy was expected to ensure that the French would not be available for action in the North Sea.

The optimistic Nationalist Spanish leaders generally ignored the problems of eastern Europe and focused instead on a long-range postwar naval program—the enlargement of the Spanish fleet. Franco—a naval officer's son who had been raised in the naval academy town of El Ferrol,[190] and who had originally planned on a naval career rather than one in the army—had ambitions for the future power of the Spanish navy now that victory seemed within his grasp.[191] His minister of industry and commerce, Juan Suanzes, and Suanzes's right-hand man, Lieutenant Jesús Alfaro, were both naval officers. Rebuilding the Spanish fleet was one of the prime interests—if not the prime interest—of Suanzes, whose ministry was to be in charge of reconstructing war-torn Spain. In 1939 Suanzes proposed to his Caudillo and former classmate a ten-year construction program that would include four battleships of 38,000 tons with 38 cm guns, twelve cruisers, sixty destroyers, and an unspecified number of submarines.[192] In contrast, relative to the Great Powers, Spain's token navy before the war had consisted of two battleships, three active cruisers (plus two fitting out and one under repair), and twelve active destroyers (plus five in fitting out).[193] The question still remained: who would construct the projected, extravagant fleet.

Since April 1938, Guse, Heye, Messerschmidt, and Bernhardt had all made general suggestions that Germany give technical aid to oust British naval influence from Spain. A major problem facing both Spaniards and Germans, however, was the shortage of docking and engineering facilities, so German proposals would be difficult to implement economically.

During late August 1938, when so much other German naval activity vis-à-vis Spain was under way, a key German arms salesman went to Spain to do further scouting. Hans Eltze, director of Rheinmetall-Borsig, Düsseldorf (one of the more active members of the AGK cartel), had been vitally interested in the Canaris-Echevarietta deal of 1925. In order to sell German arms, he had traveled to Spain in November and December 1935, to Spain and Portugal in August 1936, and again to Portugal that December.[194] Then in August 1938, during the general European crisis, he was making at least a fourth Spanish visit to survey Franco's naval needs. The AGK interests were economic and technical, and Eltze made his trip at the invitation of Bernhardt, Göring's arms salesman. As far as is known, the activities of Eltze were kept completely separate from combat activities of the Sonderstab W and the Legion Condor. From Franco's standpoint, Eltze was officially discussing only Spanish post–civil war naval needs. But if world war broke out in Czechoslovakia, and if the two Spanish camps were drawn in, then Eltze would be available for immediate military supply requests.

In Burgos and Bilbao, Eltze talked with Spanish naval officers, including Lieutenant Alfaro of the industry and commerce ministry.[195] Alfaro limited his part of the talks to Spanish postwar needs, yet he told the AGK representative that Spain was anxious to cut its ties with Vickers.[196] The British company had hitherto controlled Spanish naval construction through a monopoly of patents and a 140-million peseta loan ($20 million).[197] Alfaro pointed out to Eltze, however, that just because the Nationalist regime would be happy to see the British company go, that did not mean it wanted Germany to replace the British.

The AGK director returned to Germany even before the Sudetenland crisis was "solved" at Munich with a temporary papering-over of the growing Anglo-German breach. In Berlin, Eltze reaffirmed the conclusions of Lupin and Heye, as well as the general Axis guideline of not interfering with Italian-Spanish contracts, that in the future Spain would work primarily with Italy in the field of postwar naval construction. He, too, foresaw no future in Spain for increased German naval arms exports and joint construction contracts.

On September 4, Admiral Bastarreche, of the naval base near Cádiz, informed German naval attaché Meyer-Döhner that Italy would build the first four battleships in Suanzes's program.[198] The Italians would add to their already existing agreement with Spain to construct eight destroyers at El Ferrol.

In September 1938, however, the building of a large postwar Spanish fleet was still only a gleam in Suanzes's eye. The Republicans had to be defeated, and Franco had to avoid getting involved in an Anglo-German war over the Sudetenland. As the crisis developed, Franco's government indicated to Germany its lack of interest in eastern European affairs, its inability to support Germany, and even a belated fear and hostility toward the effect the crisis might have on Franco's possibility of victory.[199] Although Franco had wanted to remain neutral in any larger war, he still needed Hitler's military equipment for his own counterrevolution and therefore wanted to keep Hitler's good will. Thus, Admiral Cervera, chief of the Spanish naval staff, spoke in cautious tones to the German naval attaché about the kind of aid Germany could expect from Nationalist Spain if a general war broke out. Cervera's deputy chief of staff, Rear Admiral Salvador Moreno (brother of the operations chief, Francisco Moreno), assured Meyer-Döhner that Spain would "spontaneously" support Germany with "all means without compromising its neutrality," in the event of a war with the western democracies.[200]

The exact meaning of this vague formula did not come to a test because of the Anglo-French retreat at Munich in September. After the Four Power

Agreement on Czechoslovakia was signed, the German navy temporarily dropped its interest in developing Spain's naval possibilities.

Military planning followed politics. Between September 1937 and September 1938, German arms dealers and naval officers showed interest in Spain in ten different respects: (1) encouraging Franco's dream of building a large navy; (2) ousting British influence from the Spanish naval construction industry; (3) preferably accomplishing these two steps with Italian capital; (4) gathering intelligence from Gibraltar and Morocco; (5) having Spain define neutral and belligerent rights in such a way as to resist the expected British blockade; (6) supplying weapons to Spain if they were needed against increased French military aid to the Spanish Republicans; (7) using Spanish docks and manufacturers to supply the weak German navy; (8) impressing Spanish military circles with the technical superiority of Germany; (9) obtaining oil for German U-boats and tenders; and (10) obtaining other supplies for U-boats and tenders. Never mind that German naval power was insufficient to put real muscle behind these various schemes and hopes. Hitler, the politician, gave little thought to his navy's problems. He was confident throughout that England would not fight for Czechoslovakia, and he proved to be right.

Among the ways Spain could be useful to Germany and deserving of more attention was the German navy's need for oil and other supplies for submarines and tenders. Over two-thirds of the oil supplies of the Third Reich had to be imported.[201] Guse, in his basic plan for Spain outlined in April 1938, mentioned Spain's ability to supply Germany with oil. Needless to say, Heye also was interested in looking over the ground for satisfying these German needs during his June trip to Spain, Portugal, and Morocco.

One other possibility to consider was that of Germany obtaining a base from Spain. Ever since the French-Soviet publicity of July 1936 about Sanjurjo's earlier visit to Berlin, there had been much western press speculation and fear that the Germans were angling for a base in Spain, Morocco, or the Canary or Balearic Islands. But an open base similar to Britain's in Gibraltar was pretty much out of the question. If Hitler asked for a base, Spanish nationalism, which he counted on to be primarily directed against Anglo-French interests, would be offended. Second, inasmuch as British, French, and even American observers were closely watching areas such as the Canary Islands,[202] an overt base ran the risk of being attacked openly in the event of general European war. Moreover, it was Hitler's policy to lull the passive governments of England and France to sleep by giving them "assurances" in the west so he could have a free hand in the east.

Nonetheless, Canaris and his colleagues did not seek a "base" in the narrow sense of the word; they had greater ambitions. Before the civil war, Canaris had set up the special secret service, Etappendienst, with its primary goal being to arrange for all of Spain and her dependencies to provide secret economic support to the German navy. From 1934 to 1938 the Etappendicnst was mainly concerned that Spain obtain crude oil from Latin America and the United States so that the Germans could purchase refined petroleum products in Spain in the event of a German-French war.[203] Even though Spain had no oil reserves, a government benevolently neutral toward Germany, and Spanish nearness to French shipping lanes, were keys to the German navy's secret strategy.

From the point of view of the Etappendienst, the civil war only served to disrupt these secret long-range plans, because only a peaceful, prosperous Spain could afford to re-export supplies to the German U-boat fleet. Barcelona—the location in 1934-1935 of a branch of the Deutsche Werke, an Etappendienst front[204]—was held by the Republicans, and the civil war had increased suspicions among Germany's Great Power rivals. The outbreak of civil war in 1936, then, had temporarily forced deactivation of Etappendienst plans for Spain. During the civil war the Legion Condor had no oil problem because Royal Dutch Shell Oil Company, Texas (Oil) Company, and the Standard Oil Company of New Jersey delivered the fuel the Legion needed.[205]

With the prospect in 1938 of a united, friendly government, Spain again was to become one of the four worldwide centers of the Etappendienst.[206] In fact, the country was intended to serve as the German navy's main European base of Etappendienst operations outside the Fatherland. During the summer of 1938 steps were taken to reactivate the Etappendienst, and inspecting supply possibilities in Spain was one of Heye's objectives during his June 1938 trip.

As the summer wore on, the Sudetenland crisis worsened. Admiral Erich Raeder, until then an optimist about splitting Britain and France, came to the pessimistic conclusion on September 9, 1938, that the Czechoslovakian crisis would lead to combined war with Britain, France, and the Soviet Union.[207] Raeder predicted that Germany would eventually lose this war, but he nevertheless planned to send the pocket battleship *Deutschland* into the mid-Atlantic where it would be supplied with oil indirectly through Spain. The battleship was to do as much damage as possible to the British merchant marine before its own eventual defeat.[208] Berlin instructed its naval attaché in Spain that, when the code word *Wundergarten* was sounded, supply service from the German auxiliary *August Schulze,* located off the coast of Spain, would begin.[209] Canaris also provided his agents with cash in U.S. dollars for purchases in Spain for the *August Schulze* and U-boats.[210]

How could the Etappendienst get Spanish cooperation, yet simultaneously keep the service secret from the Versailles powers? In July 1938,

Canaris proposed to disperse secret funds of 11.5 million RM ($4.6 million) in gold and foreign exchange that had been earmarked for OKM oil purchases in such neutral cities as Amsterdam, London, and Zurich. Of this money, 1.5 million RM ($600,000) would be sent to Spain and one million RM ($400,000) to the Canary Islands.[211] The Etappendienst took this security precaution to avoid possible seizure or freezing of their funds by British and French banks.

The Germans had another source of Spanish funds. During 1937 the German firm Schroeder & Devrient of Leipzig printed peseta banknotes for the Franco regime, and the Reichsbank kept some for the Abwehr's future war plans. The Allgemeine Electrikische Gesellschaft (AEG), Schering Drug Company, I.G. Farben, Banco Alemán Transatlántico, and Banco Germano América del Sur were to be the conduits.[212] HISMA-ROWAK also accumulated funds inside Spain for intelligence purposes by retaining Spanish damage payments in pesetas to Legion Condor troops, who received payment in reichsmarks in Germany.[213] By the end of World War II, the Etappendienst front of Deutsche Werke, Barcelona branch, held foreign currencies in some twenty-seven countries from Argentina to India, including Spain.[214]

On August 26, 1938, when so many other naval authorities were mobilizing, the OKM discussed with their Foreign Ministry Spain's role in helping to solve Germany's major problem of oil supply. One of the participants was Consul Jakob Ahlers of Santa Cruz de Tenerife, who had been serving in the Canary Islands since World War I.[215] Ahlers, a member of the Etappendienst, had served in the German navy in World War I and still held a reserve commission. Since the 1920s he had run a business, including coal and oil sales, that monopolized German trade in the Canary Islands; in addition, he did intelligence work for the OKM. Franco called upon Ahlers through his commander in the Canary Islands as early as August 1936 for some special machinery to increase ammunition production.[216] In particular, Ahlers's banking services were at the disposal of the OKM to dispense secret funds to purchase oil, coal, and information.[217]

Besides Ahlers, others who discussed the German navy's oil problem were Ministerialrat Dr. Fritz Fetzer of the OKM, Legationsrat Winzer of the Economics Ministry, and Karl Schwendemann, the foreign ministry chief of the political division for Spain and Portugal.[218] The navy placed on the table on August 26 for discussion the question of the only major oil refinery in Spain, at Santa Cruz de Tenerife in the Canary Islands.

This refinery, with a productive capacity of 5,000 barrels per day, was owned by CEPSA (Compañía Española de Petróleos, Sociedad Anónima) and had been constructed from April to November 1930.[219] Its original capital was 75 million pesetas[220] (worth about $8 million in 1930); 60

percent of its stock was owned by Juan March, [221] the Spanish financier and shipping magnate from Mallorca.

The company traced its origins to the politics of the monarchy and the dictatorship of the late Miguel Primo de Rivera. In 1927 the Spanish petroleum market had been mostly controlled by Royal Dutch Shell and Standard Oil of New Jersey.[222] In June of that year, the Spanish minister of Finance, José Calvo Sotelo, had decreed the confiscation of the retail sales facilities of Shell, Standard, and other private firms, and the creation of the state monopoly known as CAMPSA (Compañía Arrendataria del Monopolio de Petróleos, S.A.).[223] To assure supplies for CAMPSA, the Spaniards wanted independent oil fields and refineries.

By creating CEPSA a few years later, they attempted to establish their own refinery, utilizing crude from independent fields in Venezuela for the monopoly,[224] in which March also held shares.[225] CEPSA, however, was not very successful in gaining a truly independent source of crude oil because of the hostility of the Standard-Shell interests on the supply end of the business. Despite some links with British banks, March, an early Nationalist supporter, was during the fall of 1938 in a position to further German naval ambitions if it could be shown that he could make money by doing so.

The German navy held a discussion in late August 1938 on the question of how to utilize the oil refinery at Santa Cruz de Tenerife in the Canary Islands. Four Germans—Ahlers, Fetzer, Winzer, and Schwendemann—talked of buying oil from Mexico and having it refined in Santa Cruz de Tenerife. They hoped to thwart the plans of British Shell to obtain control of the Spanish refinery and to boycott Mexican oil because of Mexico's March 1938 expropriation of Shell and Standard oil fields. The Germans planned to arrange a three-way barter deal: Mexican crude oil in exchange for German-made tankers and transportation to the refinery in the Canaries. The finished petroleum products would then be used in Spain, with the surplus sold to German submarines. Consequently, Reich officials agreed that the OKM would buy up 50 percent of CEPSA's capital, if necessary, to keep the Shell interests out.[226]

Although the worried talks of August 1938 proved to be a false alarm for the Etappendienst, by the opening of World War II thirteen months later, the OKM and its supply service were able to utilize some of the products of this independent Canary Islands refinery.[227] So as a result of its 1938 war game, the Etappendienst acquired experience that proved useful in 1939 when war actually did break out.

A second function of the Etappendienst network of German agents, who were to purchase and arrange for Spanish supplies with hard currency, was to observe British and French activities. During much of the civil war the Etappendienst did not need to carry out an intelligence mission. Gruppe Nordsee already gathered the necessary intelligence from Spain. In case a general war had broken out in 1938, the intelligence network of the Legion Condor could have been expanded to gather information on a broader basis.

As Franco's Catalan campaign reached its decisive stage in December 1938 and January 1939, Canaris foresaw that the Legion Condor soon would be withdrawn and that new arrangements would have to be made for coordinating German naval intelligence in Spain. On January 12, 1939, Lieutenant Rolf Rüggeberg arrived in Burgos by air to satisfy a Spanish request for a naval instructor at the San Fernando Naval School at Cádiz.[228] Rüggeberg, born in Barcelona of German parents in 1907, had been known to Canaris in 1926,[229] his father having served the kaiser as an agent in World War I.[230] In 1934, the young Rüggeberg was working for naval intelligence in Germany as a radio expert.

When it came time to organize the withdrawal of the Legion Condor, a dispute over Rüggeberg's status arose between naval attaché Meyer-Döhner (who was nominally part of the Legion Condor) and his superior, General Richthofen of the Luftwaffe. Richthofen wanted Rüggeberg, who was officially listed as a member of the Gruppe Nordsee, to return to Germany with everyone else in the Legion Condor. To ensure successful operation of the Etappendienst, however, the navy and Canaris wanted Rüggeberg to remain in Spain.

When Canaris visited Franco in April 1939 to witness the triumph of Nationalist arms, Meyer-Döhner took his quarrel with Richthofen to the Abwehr chief.[231] The upshot was the retention in Spain of Rüggeberg, whose subsequent activities with the Etappendienst were to reveal him as considerably more than a mere instructor.[232] Moreover, not only did Rüggeberg stay, but on April 19, 1939, three naval reserve officers (one of whom was Commander Eberhard Messerschmidt) arrived under civilian cover.[233] Canaris needed these men—along with certain foreign office personnel, including Consul Ahlers in the Canary Islands and Consul Gustavo Drager in Seville—to operate the reorganized intelligence and supply system.[234] Lieutenant Alfred Menzell, the naval attaché aide who was also a member of the Abwehr,[235] assisted the other Etappendienst agents. Stohrer, whose contacts with Canaris had begun in World War I,[236] had knowledge of these plans and activities; some "private" businessmen such as Ernst Klingenberg, an associate of Bernhardt, also were involved.

One would be hasty to conclude from the Rüggeberg incident that Richthofen, Göring's aviation representative in Spain, was seeking to thwart German espionage activity. Rather, Richthofen's objection appears to have stemmed from a lack of communication among German officials, or possibly from interservice rivalry. The Nazi regime was plagued with a good deal of this waste, which often rose from the jealousies of Hitler's lieutenants, and it was exacerbated because the Führer fostered dissension for his own ends. Not wholly content with the agencies officially charged with spying, such as the Abwehr (overseas) and the Gestapo (at home), Göring had his own large-scale intelligence-gathering outfit. Although Göring's Forschungsamt had begun in 1933 with just 120 men, it had developed a staff of 3,500 employees by 1937-1938.[237] Paul Körner, better known as state secretary for the Four-Year Plan under Göring, headed this intelligence agency.

The versatile Göring was the highest-ranking party and military man with direct control over military and economic dealings in Spain during the civil war.[238] As such, the field marshal and his men had contact with Canaris and his agents. The Rüggeberg incident aside, Canaris and Göring generally enjoyed a harmonious relationship. In the first place, the Abwehr and the Forschungsamt made an agreement to exchange intelligence information.[239] As nominal economic dictator, Göring also diverted funds for use by Canaris's agents.[240] Secondly, Göring paid for the entire intelligence and Etappendienst operations; on April 17, 1939, Canaris and Göring agreed to spend $96,000 in foreign exchange in Spain for military intelligence.[241] In addition, Göring dispensed an annual fund of $600,000 for acquiring naval supplies, mostly oil. Beyond the oil fund, the annual expenditure for the Etappendienst worldwide amounted to $1,480,000 as of May 23, 1939.[242]

Nevertheless, the field marshal had his own independent plans for the postwar development of Spain in Germany's larger "New Order." As commissioner for the Four-Year Plan, Göring had jurisdiction over German economic activity in Spain. Also, Göring's Luftwaffe from the end of December 1938 through April 1939 sent at least seven members of the Sonderstab W to Spain.[243] Although their activities are not known, their presence in Spain, and the fact that special transfers of money were secretly made to them, were reasons enough for the documentation of their trip to be kept in Abwehr hands.

More is known about Göring's responsibility for sending a "fishing expedition" to the Canary Islands between July 14 and August 14, 1938. Actually, the fishermen were looking for a site for a military base.[244] Participants in the operation took photos and made many maps of the Canary Islands from a fishing vessel of 456 H.P., the *Richard Ohlrogge*.[245] The main figure in the islands behind this venture was Gustav Winter, who supposedly was seeking a site on which to construct a fish cannery. After his training in Germany as an electrical engineer, Winter had lived in Spain during the 1920s and 1930s. In 1927 he had worked for a Spanish company that brought electricity to Las Palmas, and there he had conceived the idea of developing an uninhabited peninsula on the island of Fuerteventura. Some-

Map 4. The Canary Islands

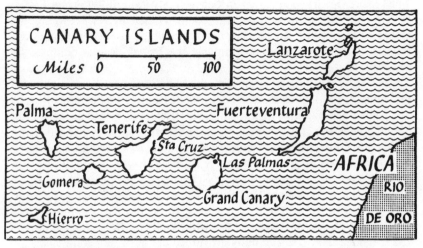

Source: Hugh Thomas, *The Spanish Civil War* (New York, 1961), 130.

time in 1937, he had begun promoting his idea of a German fishing port in the Spanish islands in the Atlantic with Göring's officials (see map 4).[246] Winter's efforts met with some success, and profits from Bernhardt's trading company financed the venture, in whole or in part.[247]

Possibly the Munich settlement caused Göring and his associates to drop their interest in the Canaries. Nothing more was heard of this project for some months, until Ambassador Stohrer and the Foreign Ministry learned of the summer 1938 voyage.[248] In January 1939 Stohrer objected to Göring and Bernhardt about having been left in the dark concerning the project, but by then Göring had lost interest. He sent no further "fishing expeditions" to the Canaries until June 1939.[249]

Such expeditions aside, Göring as the number-two man in the Nazi bureaucracy was the focal point of various people interested in expanding their ties with the new Nationalist Spain. Many Germans brought reports to the field marshal about developments in the Spanish Civil War and about the growing Anglo-German tension in Europe as a whole, as well as occasional reports on activities in Spanish ports and islands. Göring was badly overextended, however, and he did not develop a clear Spanish policy of his own. He merely responded to the events in Spain and to Hitler's overall expansionist ideas in Europe.

In the wake of the Munich crisis, Hitler sought recommendations from Guse, Fricke of Naval Operations, Stohrer, and Ribbentrop about the strategic use of Spain in any future war with Britain. In November 1938, the

Führer told Keitel, the OKW chief, that if Italy and Germany fought Britain and France, Spain should remain benevolently neutral.[250] According to Hitler, Italy was supposed to press Spain to increase its economic and strategic contribution in such a war, to continue its occupation of the Balearic Islands, and even to eliminate the British base at Gibraltar by attacking it.

Hitler further defined Germany's post-civil-war role in Spain to Keitel on March 3, 1939. On the eve of his Czech take-over, the Führer reaffirmed Spain's need to maintain benevolent neutrality in the event of a world war, but he hoped that Franco would build up his army and agree to a bilateral exchange of officers. In consideration of Spanish *Volkscharakter*, however, he said Germany would have to await Franco's decision. Any future economic assistance for rebuilding the Spanish military potential would be under Göring's Four-Year Plan offices, after the Legion Condor was withdrawn.[251]

Hitler's seizure of Prague, and new demands for Danzig in late March 1939, fanned the flames of anti-German feeling in Britain and France and spurred Chamberlain's famous speech to the House of Commons on March 31, guaranteeing the territorial integrity of Poland from German attack. In the midst of these developments, Stohrer and Ribbentrop finally concluded with Spain the long-delayed friendship treaty. It will be recalled that Hitler once had questioned this idea, but in the spring of 1939, when the British Foreign Office was declaiming that there would be no more Munich-type concessions to Germany, the "fostering of comradely military relations" between Spain and Germany took on new meaning.

Franco finally signed the treaty on March 31, 1939, the last day of the civil war. It provided for a military clause, and it pledged collaboration with Italy. If, however, Italy refused to supply Spain's military needs, the way was open for an expanded bilateral German-Spanish military agreement. The time had come for Hitler to tie Franco to the Axis and to ensure that Spain would serve his cause in any future war with the western entente.

Military Plans Grow from Franco's Victory to the Pact of Steel

Just before the German march on Prague in March 1939, General Gastone Gambara, commander of the Italian units in Spain, returned to that country from a brief sojourn in Rome. He carried the Duce's message for Franco, stating that the Italian troops would remain only as long as Franco needed them.[252] Richthofen, then commanding the Legion Condor, agreed that German troops would be withdrawn at the same time. Hitler was prepared to withdraw the Legion Condor as soon as Italy indicated its readiness.[253]

For Hitler, the end of the Spanish Civil War came into sight after the success of Franco's Catalan campaign in January.[254] In a speech before the Reichstag on January 30, 1939, Hitler revealed to the German public for the first time the existence of the Legion Condor.[255] On February 24, as the military situation in Spain looked even more favorable to Franco, the Führer notified the OKW of his decision to give the Legion Condor great publicity upon its victorious return to Germany.[256] Hitler dispatched OKM Commander Pistorius on March 7 to organize the withdrawal of the legion,[257] on whatever final date Franco would set for the departure of German and Italian forces.

The question thereby arose of future military cooperation among Germans, Spaniards, and Italians. In mid-March General Gambara informed Colonel Baron Hans von Funck, German military attaché in Spain, that Franco wanted a preliminary Italian-German military agreement deciding the distribution of the military aid each power would grant Spain after the war.[258] Following the long-established policy of refusing beforehand to divulge German military plans for Spain, Funck did not commit Germany. In a second conversation a few days later, Gambara outlined Spanish military needs and tried to draw out the Germans about what they intended to do. Funck again avoided saying anything specific to Gambara.[259]

Despite Funck's evasiveness, his superiors in Berlin did have in mind several ways in which the Spaniards could be useful in a German war with the West. For instance, by digging trenches in the Pyrenees and thus appearing a menace to France, the Spanish army was expected to divert a French army corps from the Rhine frontier.[260] Yet Italy and Spain would have to carry the burden of Spanish naval rearmament on their own because the Germans offered no specific aid.

In mid-March 1939, Admiral Bastarreche, the commander at Cádiz who had been keeping Meyer-Döhner informed about Spanish fleet construction, represented Franco at the coronation ceremonies of Pope Pius XII. Bastarreche spent part of his fourteen-day stay in Italy conferring with Italian naval leaders, including Rear Admiral Giovanni Remedio Ferretti, who in 1936 had been liaison at Franco's headquarters. He had helped build a blockade headquarters on Mallorca for the Nationalist naval effort.[261] Bastarreche and Ferretti talked about building up the Spanish fleet,[262] and upon his return to Spain, Bastarreche reaffirmed to Meyer-Döhner that the Spaniards would buy the eight Italian destroyers already under contract. The Spanish admiral had no interest in German destroyers, which he claimed had too high a silhouette, but he did want German U-boats. Meyer-Döhner advised the OKM to reject the Spanish bid for German submarines because Germany needed all these vessels it could build for itself.

Despite the caution of Funck and Meyer-Döhner, Göring was ready to implement the military clause of the friendship treaty, concerning German-

Spanish officer consultations.[263] Through Richthofen, Göring invited many Spanish officers in the air and ground forces to come to Germany. Franco answered the invitations by cautioning that before the military talks could be implemented, the Legion Condor must be withdrawn from Spain. He then promised that a Spanish military delegation would go to Germany in connection with the homecoming ceremonies for the legion.[264]

On April 17, the OKW sent to Spanish waters a German training flotilla[265] consisting of practically all the warships Germany had: the pocket battleships (*Deutschland, Graf Spee, Admiral Scheer*), two cruisers, eight destroyers, and eight submarines, accompanied by four supply ships. They planned to stop at Tangier, Ceuta, El Ferrol, and Lisbon from April 18 to May 10.[266] Supplementing the main flotilla, a sailing vessel would put into ports in the Canaries on April 27 and continue on to Brazil.[267]

The visiting German naval officers met with Etappendienst agents in Ceuta and Cádiz; with the Spanish high commissioner for Morocco; with the Moroccan caliph; with Nazi Ortsgruppenleiter (town leader) Langenheim and his son (an Abwehr agent); with Suanzes, the Spanish minister of industry and commerce; and with Bastarreche of the Cádiz naval base. One member of the party, Commodore Karl Dönitz, later famous as World War II commander of the Third Reich's submarine force, took a side trip by auto to Tetuán and concentrated his attention on anti-French, anti-Jewish Moroccans. He wanted to sample Moroccan opinion toward the French, the British, and particularly toward the Arabic translation of *Mein Kampf* and Hitler's speech of April 28, 1939,[268] which reviewed German foreign policy since the Versailles treaty.

Timed to coincide with his fleet's tour of Iberian waters and Spanish bases in North Africa, this was one of Hitler's most significant and well-planned addresses. In his introduction he pretended that he had been a prince of peace; he then denounced British encirclement in general, and specifically the Anglo-German naval arms limitation treaty of 1935. He also reiterated his claim to Danzig, repudiated the German Non-Aggression Pact of 1934 with Poland, and boasted of Axis military strength. Hitler responded publicly with laughter and sarcasm to President Franklin D. Roosevelt's April 15 appeal to him for a pledge of peace to last ten years.[269]

This speech and the German fleet's "training exercise" clearly were directed against Britain, France, and even the United States. For their part, the French saw the German fleet's visit to Spanish waters as part of an all-Europe war scare and a maneuver to avoid a general blockade.[270] When the pocket battleship *Admiral Scheer* stopped in Bilbao, Meyer-Döhner took the opportunity to talk to Suanzes once again about Spain's revised fleet construction plans.[271] The minister intended to build four battleships, fifteen to eighteen cruisers, and twenty-five to forty U-boats, all within eight years. At this time, Suanzes said it was still an open question whether he would accept Italian or German aid—the Bastarreche-Ferretti negotiations in Rome had broken down over financial issues. Although Italy had two contracts on paper to build destroyers and battleships, so far very little had been done about them. The Spanish hint for German hardware brought forth a renewed offer to sell destroyers, which the Spanish navy had already rejected.

Discussion of the battleship project on the Italian end continued when a group of Spanish naval officers arrived in Rome on May 5, at Mussolini's invitation.[272] Later in the month the Italians sent twenty naval officers to Spain, including three rear admirals.[273] Yet they took only another small step on the plans to construct the four battleships. Fundamentally, Italy's military interest in Spain had declined ever since Hitler's seizure of Prague and the end of the civil war. By July the Italian naval construction work at El Ferrol, which had not gone very far in any case, came to an end.

Despite the symbolic value of such visits, the old principle of the original Axis protocols—an Italian sphere of influence in the western Mediterranean in exchange for a German sphere in the east—had become moribund. For Mussolini, the Italian victory at Barcelona had avenged the defeat of Guadalajara. From April to July, he increasingly talked about his ambitions in Yugoslavia and Egypt but ignored Spain.

During April and May, the Germans had been content to leave the March 31 Treaty of Friendship with Spain largely unimplemented. While German-Spanish military relations were confined to exploratory talks, the more important German-Italian military negotiations at this point began and progressed quite rapidly. The OKW, which had parried Italian requests for a military alliance for more than a year, for the first time was eager to proceed. In the initial series of talks, Keitel, the OKW chief, met with the Italian under state secretary for war at Innsbruck on April 4, 1939.[274] Göring followed this with a visit to Libya in early April, and to Rome April 14-17, in order to confer with the Duce, Ciano, King Victor Emmanuel, and others.[275]

The Göring-Mussolini discussions ranged over the whole map of Europe. As far as Spain was concerned,Göring and the Duce agreed that Germany and Italy would jointly grant economic aid to Spain after the civil war. Göring encouraged the Italians to remain in the Balearic Islands and take Tunis from the French.

But Ciano, the Italian foreign minister, pointed out to the Reichsmarshal that Italian deliveries to Spain had already been large and that little payment had been received. Amplifying upon this assertion, the Duce added that Italy, having swallowed Albania, planned no action against France or Tunis for two or three years. With the French, however, Göring took a conciliatory line. Mentioning the German fleet's visit to Spanish waters to the French ambassador in Rome, the Reichsmarshal said the French press exaggerated the threat of war. Göring maintained that the German fleet was engaged only in routine maneuvers and blamed Britain for trying to dominate the Mediterranean.[276]

Göring's talks in Rome brought complaints from Germany's foreign minister, Ribbentrop, for they had not been authorized by the German Foreign Ministry. In turn, Ribbentrop granted permission for the commander in chief of the army (OKH), General Walther von Brauchitsch, to make an official visit.[277] The German army head visited Italy from April 28, the day Hitler publicly denounced the Western democracies, to May 11. Brauchitsch met with Mussolini, the king, Ciano, a war department representative, and the chiefs of staff of the army, air force, navy, and fascist militia.[278] To demonstrate German-Italian alignment, he also inspected Italian troops and military installations in Libya and La Spezia. Finally, on May 9, the anniversary of the founding of the Italian empire, Brauchitsch participated in the bestowal of 138 medals upon Italian soldiers returned from Spain.[279] Afterward, Italian generals were invited to Germany for military maneuvers.[280]

A still more important event for German-Italian military solidarity occurred in Milan. There Ribbentrop made preliminary arrangements for the long-awaited political and military alliance with Italy, triumphantly announced later, during Hitler's visit to Mussolini on May 21-22 in Rome. Ribbentrop told Ciano during their Pact of Steel conversations, May 6-7, that the Germans were satisfied with the attitude of Franco.[281] A reluctant Ciano accepted Ribbentrop's draft on the assumption that it was a defensive treaty to deter England and France and that war was not yet on the horizon. Ribbentrop added that the Axis should strengthen their bonds with Spain in order to pin down French armed forces. In practice, the Axis link with Spain, as far as Hitler and Ribbentrop were concerned, still meant mainly an Italian bond with Spain. The Italians, however, had grown less interested in the western Mediterranean. For one thing, the "war scare," invented by the Fascist party in late 1938 between Italy and France over Corsica and other French western Mediterranean possessions, had disappeared. Again the Duce reiterated what he had told Göring, namely, that he was satisfied that the Spanish Popular Front had been destroyed and that the triumphant new dictator in Spain was emulating Italian Fascism.

The decision of the Duce and Ciano at Milan to postpone war talk[282] was followed by the return of the Corpo Truppe Voluntarie to Italy and the Legion Condor to Germany, after the huge May 19 victory parade in Madrid. The date for the German embarkation was fixed for May 26.[283] Franco gave himself maximum flexibility at a time when he feared the growing Anglo-German tension over Poland.

This chapter has examined German military ideas on the strategic position of Spain. The navy had engaged in certain construction projects in Spain during pre-Nazi times. Since 1933 they had planned to use Spain as a supply point for their submarine operations against the French navy and its merchant shipping. The German intervention in Spain's civil war in July 1936 was not a preconceived military plot to start a general war; in fact, the destructive social conflict of the Spaniards disrupted and weakened the plans of the secret Etappendienst to utilize a healthy Spanish economy.

Hitler's military operations in the Spanish Civil War escalated in three stages: Operation Feuerzauber, July 1936; Operation Otto, September 1936; and operations Luftübung Rügen and Winterübung Hansa in October, dispatching the Legion Condor. Over the course of the civil war, the Legion Condor's five thousand highly trained men were probably essential for Franco's victory. Subsequently they provided Hitler's air force, panzers and signal corps with experienced personnel for the Polish and later campaigns. For Franco the Legion Condor provided a valuable balance to Italy's corps; but in 1937 and 1938 Mussolini, pursuing his own European aims, pushed, with Hitler's encouragement, for even greater glory for the CTV and Italy's Mediterranean navy.

As the civil war developed, the German navy realized belatedly in June 1937 that Spain might be useful in a future war with Britain. The OKM hoped this contingency would never come to pass, but Hitler's April 1938 extended plans for Czechoslovakia encouraged the OKM to expand its plans to use Spain against Britain. At the same time, Franco's victory in the Levante seemed to give Stohrer and Ribbentrop an excuse to sign up Spain with the Axis before the Legion Condor was withdrawn. When Republican resistance revived, however, Hitler did not press for his navy's needs or Ribbentrop's scheme to expand the Anti-Comintern Pact to Spain. Instead, he pinned his immediate hopes on Britain pressuring a weakened France to write off eastern Europe. Hitler won his bluff at Munich, and the decision to tie Spain to the Axis was delayed until Franco occupied Madrid at the end of March 1939.

With relaxation of the September 1938 "period of tension" (as the Germans called the Sudetenland crisis), the German navy did little more about Spain until after the Spanish Civil War was over in 1939. By then, the eyes of Hitler and Chamberlain were turning toward Poland. Hitler would again try previously successful diplomatic bluffs, combining propaganda about communism and national self-determination with military threats. The Treaty of Friendship, signed at Burgos along with the Anti-Comintern Pact, was supposed to ensure that Spain would be a neutral friend in the event of general war. The pattern might be like the pacts with Italy—from the Axis Protocol to the Anti-Comintern Pact and ultimately to the Pact of Steel.

Under the right circumstances, the Spanish pacts could also conceivably be converted into a full-fledged alliance. Indeed, many western leftists and journalists already regarded Franco as fully committed to the Axis at the end of the civil war.

When the German-Spanish Treaty of Friendship was signed, Göring sent out invitations to leaders of the Spanish armed forces to get military discussions under way; Franco ruled that these depended on the return of the Legion Condor to Germany, and talks were delayed two months. During the time between April and June 1939, the German military concentrated on strengthening its ties with Italy, because Germany hoped that the Duce would take the diplomatic offensive against Britain and France in the West.

Most German naval strategists and the Abwehr realized that Franco's aid to the German supply service (Etappendienst) would basically be a small-scale operation. If Germany and Britain were to go to war, the Etappendienst would be pitted against the world's greatest sea power and its potential ally across the Atlantic, in a replay of World War I submarine tactics. Hitler's experimental military and economic relations with Franco seemed to be paying off, but beneath the surface of ideological unity, economic and military differences simmered between the Third Reich and Nationalist Spain.

6

Conclusions

This book has examined three basic questions. First, what role did Adolf Hitler play in bringing Francisco Franco to power in Spain? Second and third, during the years of the Spanish upheaval, what gains did the Führer make in the European balance of power generally and in Franco's Spain specifically? In the decisive years of 1936-1939, Hitler made his Spanish decisions in four interrelated areas: political, military, ideological, and economic. This book has traced the paths of development in those areas.

The failed coup d'etat of July 1936 turned into a long campaign to reconquer Spain, the consequences of which were to eliminate most of the social reforms made by the Second Spanish Republic from 1931 to 1933. When the civil war broke out, Benito Mussolini and Adolph Hitler began pursuing parallel policies toward Spain—their goals being to weaken the influence of the French and, secondarily, the British in that troubled country. The two Axis powers sent Franco organized and effective military aid that outweighed the intervention of other Great Powers. In fact, European liberals were reluctant to act at all, so the Spanish Republicans sought the aid of Soviet military advisors and weapons. Internationally, during 1937, Mussolini took the lead over Hitler, both on the Spanish front and throughout the Mediterranean, in opposing the Soviet Union and France. Hitler welcomed the Duce's imperialist concentration on the southwest, because that meant Austria by 1938 was free for the Führer's taking. The Spanish crisis also helped divert France, Britain, and the USSR in the fall of 1938 from uniting to defend Czechoslovakia against German territorial demands.

The Spanish front seemed to some European military observers to have been bogged down in stalemate during the two years from November 1936 to November 1938. In fact, Franco's troops, city by city, village by village—from Málaga to Bilbao to Vinaroz on the Mediterranean—gradually reconquered Spain from the Left. From the international perspective, Franco won his war in eight decisive stages: (1) the bringing in of Italian and German air transport in July 1936 to help Franco's forces cross the Straits of Gibraltar; (2) the capture of Badajoz on August 14, linking up Franco's troops with those of General Emilio Mola from the north and thereby securing a friendly border with Portugal; (3) Mola's victory at Irún on September 4, sealing off one unfriendly frontier with France; (4) the Nationalist navy's coming to dominate the Straits of Gibraltar in late September and, with the aid of Italian forces, capturing Mallorca in the Balearic Islands; (5) the conquest of the Basque capital of Bilbao in June 1937, which provided El Caudillo with a major industrial base; (6) the decision of Georges Bonnet, the French foreign minister, in June 1938 to seal off the Pyrenees against further substantial clandestine aid by French leftists to the Spanish Republicans; (7) the joint decision in September 1938, on the eve of the Munich Conference, by Juan Negrín, the Republican prime minister, and Stalin to withdraw the International Brigades; and (8) the international inattention to Spain succeeding Munich, while Franco undertook the final assault on the Republican redoubt.

Until Franco's offensive began against Catalonia on December 23, 1938, the front was relatively static. Hitler, Mussolini for the most part, and Stalin continued to provide only enough arms to maintain their respective Spanish friends. Both British and French policymakers, Neville Chamberlain and Georges Bonnet, privately hoped that Franco would win, but they refused to say so publicly. Franco's decisive campaign in Catalonia in January 1939 finally closed the frontier with France, and hundreds of thousands of Loyalists fled into exile.

Although Franco and the Nationalists battled their way to power through their bloody military conquest of Spain, Axis aid was essential. Without the arms and military expertise (total value $569 million) extended on credit from the two Axis dictators, Franco would not have won the civil war. German manpower, while less than Italian, was more effective, concentrating the air, tank, artillery, and communications technical services of the 5,000-man Legion Condor.

In terms of the international balance of power in 1936, the Führer and the Duce transformed a local Spanish struggle into a European diplomatic contest in which developments in Spain served to weaken the ties of France with the Soviet Union and Britain. During the course of the civil war, the Führer concluded anti-Comintern pacts with Japan and Italy, in addition to the Axis agreement with Mussolini. Although stalemated around Madrid, Franco's forces made significant advances in the north and south of Spain in 1937, and Mussolini became heavily involved both on land and in the Mediterranean.

In March 1938, Hitler took Austria; in October, the Sudetenland; and in

March 1939, he seized the remainder of Czechoslovakia. The Austrian and Prague occupations occurred at times when Hitler thought the Spanish crisis was about to end. Then, at the end of the civil war, Hitler capped these diplomatic coups with a bilateral Treaty of Friendship with Spain, Spanish adhesion to the Anti-Comintern Pact, and the solidification of the Rome-Berlin Axis by the Pact of Steel.

In 1935, before the eruption of the Spanish crisis, the British foreign minister, Anthony Eden, had visited the Soviet Union and had speculated about the possibility of an Anglo-French-Soviet coalition against Hitler. In May 1938, Winston Churchill christened the would-be coalition the "Grand Alliance." The war in Spain had made any such deal impossible, however. With the potential "Grand Allies" so badly divided after 1936 that they could not become allied until 1941, the Axis helped to perpetuate the Spanish struggle for nearly three crucial years. If the Axis had left Spain alone, the social crisis of 1936 might well have resolved itself much sooner. As it happened, however, the Axis dictators were influenced to cooperate in Spain in joint opposition to decisions made by the Soviet and French left-wing organizations.

In July 1936, Hitler's military participation was in advance of Mussolini's and Stalin's. By early October, Stalin's involvement had caught up; then Hitler moved ahead again, in late October and in early November, with the dispatch of the Legion Condor. From December 1936 to the end of the war, the Führer refused to increase German support; instead, Italian aid forged ahead. Franco's eventual victory resulted, in part, from the complicated diplomatic maneuvering of the five Great Powers, from which Hitler emerged as the principal winner.

Hitler's motives and tactics in Spain were complex. Neither Mussolini nor Hitler designed his initial technological aid in accordance with a preconceived plan for a new fascist Spain; both lent their money piecemeal, in a half-dozen or so major installments. As the war progressed, the slowness of Franco's armies in the field determined, to some degree, Berlin's and Rome's ad hoc decisions to provide additional military aid for the Nationalist cause.

On the other hand, Hitler's desire to deceive the diplomats of the other Great Powers determined at least two of the three military steps he made in 1936 (Operations Feuerzauber and Luftübung Rügen/Winterübung Hansa). After the major escalation represented by the Legion Condor, Hitler set his subsequent policy of sustaining aid at that level during the rest of the war. His deceit was proven when he secretly sent weapons, ammunition, and supplies to Spain on 134 vessels while continuing discussions in London's ineffective Non-Intervention Committee.[1] Of course, the Italians, Soviets and French were also talking and double-dealing.

Hitler's European strategy was revealed by his encouraging Mussolini to be the prime foreign interventionist in Spain. While he harangued Nürnberg party rallies with preaching against the devil, "communism," he left Franco with the main burden of killing "the reds." For Hitler, the Spanish labyrinth provided a convenient place for experiments—diplomatic, economic, propagandistic, and military. From July 1936 to March 1939, Mussolini cooperated in the main with Hitler's ambitions for Europe, and in general he trumpeted Hitler's Spanish policy as well as his own. During periods in 1937 and 1938, Mussolini adopted Hitler's tactic of merely maintaining Franco's military machine; at other times, the Duce, proud of reviving Italian military might, continued to escalate the war beyond any other nation's intervention. In the summer of 1937 he carried out a "pirate" campaign in the Mediterranean. In the spring of 1938 he joined Franco and the Legion Condor to bomb systematically the port cities of the Spanish Mediterranean coast. Among all the foreign participants in the Spanish upheaval, only the dogged Mussolini showed himself committed to the end to Franco's total victory.

Hitler's reputation as a quintessential propagandist rests, in part, on his successful exploitation of the thirty-two-month-long Spanish war as a crusade against communism. The war's events intensified the negative emotional reaction to communism by many people in Britain, its empire and commonwealth, France, Italy, Japan, the Americas, and much of Europe—except for the Soviet Union and groups among the liberal-socialist Left. In August 1936, Hitler justified to his own people the introduction of the Four-Year Plan in the name of anticommunism. From July to November 1936 he pressed the Japanese military, who ultimately agreed to the Anti-Comintern Pact. During the visit by the Italian foreign minister, Ciano, to Berlin in October to sign the Axis Protocols, Hitler took the opportunity to link the "communist threat" and the Spanish crisis. Göring (Luftwaffe), Himmler (SS), Canaris (military intelligence), Goebbels (general propaganda), Rosenberg (party propaganda), and Ribbentrop (foreign affairs) worked "against communism" with their Italian counterparts in 1936 and 1937. Through the power of German persuasion, Mussolini adhered to the Anti-Comintern Pact in 1937, and Franco finally agreed to join at the end of the civil war in 1939.

Hitler also got much mileage from exploiting the fear of revolution in Spain in his communications with British and French leaders. Notable impacts were made, for instance, on their ambassadors in Berlin, on Lord Halifax during his Berlin visit of November 1937, and on Chamberlain at the Munich Conference. Conservatives everywhere suspected the Soviet Union of a revolutionary role in Spain. Actually the USSR had a dual stance in Spain—preaching democracy and popular front to the Left around the world, while repressing anarchism and Leninist revolution in the Republic itself. Chamberlain, favoring the social status quo in Spain and the "bulwark against communism" claimed by Germany and Italy, supported the repressive Spanish Nationalist movement, appeased the Axis, and undermined the popular fronts that opposed them in Spain and France.

The Germans' delaying role in the Non-Intervention Committee in 1936 and 1937 was tolerated because the British government thought the NIC had importance. The Germans used those discussions mostly to play for time.[2] After February 1938, German bureaucratic paper shuffling at the NIC was less necessary. The focus on intervention then shifted to Anglo-Italian negotiations for mutual withdrawal of foreign troops. The Germans merely backed Mussolini and Franco, who took the burden of stalling in direct negotiations with Britain.[3]

Events during the civil war misled not only European conservatives but also liberals and social democrats. They saw Franco become the chief of state in October 1936 and then make himself the Caudillo of a totalitarian party when he united the Falange with the Carlists in April 1937. In March 1938, Franco publicized his fascist Labor Charter, modeled after Italy's laws, and he adhered to the Anti-Comintern Pact in March of 1939. Thus leftists in the democracies assumed, with Hitler, that by 1939 Franco had become like Mussolini, or Austria's Arthur Seyss-Inquart, Hungary's Admiral Nicholas Horthy, or Czechoslovakia's Father Josef Tiso, all of whom Hitler could manipulate. Leftist propaganda generally portrayed Franco as one more dictator of a monolithic fascism.

Hitler may have hoped that the Nationalist ideological hate for revolution would obligate Franco to join his "New Order." Yet even to Hitler, the New Order was little more than a loose propaganda slogan derived from a racist group called by that name in 1900. The term was first used publicly by the Führer on March 22, 1936, to characterize a peace proposal, but Hitler's famous confidant and first-hand biographer Hermann Rauschning has affirmed that Hitler really meant a new racial order. In 1937, as interpreted by Alfred Rosenberg, the New Order came to mean a general suppression of communism.[4] The slogan also was used outside Germany. In November 1938 the Japanese defined the New Order as Japanese economic and political predominance in China, as opposed to the preceding British and American "capitalistic" order.[5] Thus New Order, like "fascism" and "Axis" and "communism", was used by the anti-Comintern powers to justify their own imperial claims in euphemistic language.

In Spain it is the word fascism that has been subjected to greatest abuse. In 1936 the term was broadly defined by the Left to be equivalent to all forms of reaction.[6] Many conservatives use the word strictly for the Falangist party. Spanish fascism should be compared with Italian fascism and German

National Socialism,[7] for there are similarities among the three. World War I, the Moroccan Wars, the civil war itself, the imperial ambitions of the three "have-not nations," and a hatred of internationalism—these were factors creating pro-fascist sentiment in Germany, Italy, and Spain, and eventually creating fascist regimes. Franco's fascism became overt in April 1937 when he assumed the title of El Caudillo and formed the single legal party in Nationalist Spain.

Debates about the extent to which Hitler, Franco, and Mussolini were or were not fascist, totalitarian or authoritarian[8] generally are not helpful. All three dictators had totalitarian ambitions; they all wanted power to flow to and from themselves. Yet in all three nations, some opposition groups managed to survive, so that totalitarianism was never fully achieved anywhere. All three were fascist in the sense that they repudiated such liberal institutions as parliaments, elections, independent judiciaries, the free press, multiple parties, free religious conscience, and a bill of rights. All three glorified war. All three were anticommunist. From the Marxist point of view, they represented degenerate capitalism trying to preserve itself by resorting to dictatorial militarism.

Still, Hitler's pragmatic economic actions in Spain from 1936 to 1939 proved that he was not a starry-eyed crusader for the anticommunist ideal. Throughout the war the economic role of the Third Reich in Spain continued to grow. Franco's war debts accumulated during the conflict, while Johannes Bernhardt's trading companies made war profits and multiplied investments. The stronger economic influence of Germany in Spain, coupled with Spanish weakness, gave Hitler some additional leverage in the European balance of power.

At the end of the civil war, Hitler, Franco, and Mussolini seemed to be riding the wave of the future. The Führer's experiment in Spain appeared triumphant in all dimensions. Yet, despite the apparent solidarity of the "fascist Axis," Hitler was already encountering difficulties with both Mussolini and Franco. The Spanish experiment as a limited military operation coupled with propaganda was one thing; but in the second half of 1939 it proved to be no firm foundation for a long-range military strategy for Hitler's southern flank.

In the spring of 1939, Franco on the eve of victory joined Hitler's Anti-Comintern Pact. After the diplomatic bombshell of the Nazi-Soviet Non-Aggression Pact of August 23, 1939, however, the Caudillo sent warm congratulations to Germany for the coup.[9] Actually Franco was relieved by the pact, since its effect was to excuse war-ravaged Spain from taking a hostile stand against France. If there had to be a European war, Franco preferred having it fought in the East rather than in western Mediterranean waters. In practice, the Spanish generalissimo gave less weight to sympathy for "Catholic" Poland and antipathy for communism (meaning the Soviet government) than one might suppose from his regime's anticommunist preaching.

Economic destruction wrought by the civil war dictated Spanish neutrality in 1939-1940, although the Caudillo risked occupying Tangier in June 1940 after the fall of the French Third Republic, when Britain was standing alone against the fascists. At that time the Führer took steps to take Gibraltar from Britain through Spain.[10] But Franco's caution kept Spain from throwing in its lot openly with the Axis, as a chilly meeting with Hitler at Hendaye in October 1940 showed.

After Hitler invaded the USSR in June 1941, Franco sent the Blue Division to the eastern front to fight the Soviets. Ramón Serrano Suñer, then foreign minister, publicized this as a great anticommunist crusade. Franco, like Hitler, originally thought that Russia would prove a short campaign, after which he would be in a better bargaining position for Mediterranean concessions. That he was motivated by revenge against Stalin for the Soviet dictator's aid to the Republicans in the Spanish Civil War has been assumed by many; certainly Serrano Suñer's profascist press thirsted for revenge. In any case, 47,000 Spaniards fought in the USSR, and some 4,500 died there.[11]

On the other side, many of the able-bodied Republican refugees in France fought the German invasion in 1940 and joined the Maquis during 1942-1945. Of the 500,000 Spanish Popular Front refugees who fled Franco in 1939, 72,000 were arrested by Vichy France and sent to German concentration camps, where 10,000 to 12,000 of them perished.[12] Thus did the Spanish Civil War merge into World War II on both the eastern and the western fronts.

In September 1942, on the eve of the American landing in French Morocco, uncomfortably close to Spanish territory, Franco fired his brother-in-law, Serrano Suñer, as foreign minister. The American move on the Azores in preparation for the North African landing may have triggered this decisive move toward a more cautious neutrality.[13]

The Anglo-American invasion of Italy in July 1943 brought the downfall of the Duce, Franco's erstwhile ally, and sounded the death knell of the Axis alliance. By October 1943, after Russian troops had made gains during the summer against Hitler's army, the Spanish generalissimo and chief of state hinted to Hitler that the Blue Division should return home. A withdrawal gradually took place during the rest of the European war—although some units of the Blue Division fought to defend Berlin the the last days in April 1945.

While Franco never gave up denouncing communism, he clearly was abandoning his prior close association with his anti-Comintern allies long before the war's end. Following World War II, Franco stayed on as dictator, long after Mussolini and Hitler were dead and discredited. The Falange was downgraded to merely "the Movement," and in 1945 Franco appealed to his monarchist supporters by allowing a referendum to consider the eventual return of the Bourbons. Indeed, when Franco's dictatorship ended thirty years later with his death, Alfonso XIII's grandson became King Juan Carlos.

After fifty years, what is the judgment of history on the civil war that excited a generation of democrats to proclaim it as "the last great cause"? The idealism of those days is hard to recapture in a post-modern era that has been disillusioned by Machiavelli, Orwell, and the American intervention in Vietnam in the name of anticommunism. The horrors of Guernica have dwindled in the flames of Hiroshima and the shadows of thousands of stockpiled nuclear bombs. Still, the continuity of diplomatic history is apparent when one studies the Spanish Civil War in the light of American military and economic dilemmas posed by Latin America. The intervention of the Great Powers in 1936 in Spain has something to tell us about the current American-Soviet economic, political, ideological, and military rivalry in the Third World.

In diplomatic history the place of the Spanish Civil War is secure. As Basil Liddell Hart, one of the greatest military thinkers of the century, put it, the second Great War of the twentieth century began in Spain in July 1936.[14] The Spanish Civil War was indeed an opening round of the great power struggle now called World War II. Fifty years later, ideological rivalries among communism, anticommunism, liberalism, totalitarianism, and democracy continue to trouble the world.

Appendix A.
Note on Monetary Values

To translate the monetary values of the 1930s into values that have real meaning in terms of contemporary purchasing power, there are two ways of measuring inflation: (1) by noting the rise of the cost-of-living index in the United States; and (2) by noting the fall of the value of the peseta relative to the dollar in the international market. In other words, the amount of gasoline an American could buy in 1935 for 44 cents would cost him $3.30 in 1985. Meanwhile, Spanish inflation has been even greater. The Spaniard could have purchased 12.3 cents' worth of gasoline for his one peseta in 1935 but only 1.4 cents' worth in 1980 and .57 cents' worth in 1985.

Prices for 1913-1967 are based on the index in which the years 1957-1959 = 100. In 1967 the U.S. Department of Commerce made a new base of 100. To convert future statistics to the old base, use the following formula:

$$\frac{1967}{\frac{100}{106}} = \frac{1985}{\frac{310}{X}}$$

(*Statistical Abstract of the United States,* 1940, pp. 291, 328; 1965, p. 356; 1970, p. 339; 1975, p. 417; 1986, pp. 471, 858; Hugh Thomas, *Spanish Civil War* [New York, 1977], pp. 971-72.)

Appendix B. German Intelligence Agents in Spain before July 1936

This list is only a tentative beginning to a complex problem. Many questions remain, particularly about the dates of entry into Spain.

The most comprehensive list of German spies in Spain was made by the U.S. government following World War II. It had 104 names of undesirable, black-listed Germans living in Spain. At least 15 of these were living there before July 1936. See Counselor Paul T. Culbertson, Madrid, to Secretary of State, dis. 378, 1 July 1948, SD, 862.20252/7-148 (hereafter cited as "Culbertson Report").

The numbers assigned here to the 60 agents listed also serve as source notes, below. For abbreviations used in the notes, see pp. 163-66.

Name/(Alias)	Profession	Entry into Spain	Place
1. Kühlenthal, Lt. Gen. Erich	Army; military attaché	1928	Paris: Army Abwehr Office for Spain
2. Kühlenthal, Karl Erich (son of Erich? same?)		1935?	(Wife Spanish)
3. Lietzmann, Cmd. Joachim	Navy	1932	Paris: Naval Abwehr Office for Spain
4. Messerschmidt, Lt. Cmd. Eberhard	Navy, Abwehr	1926; Jan. and Sept. 1936	(Traveling Berlin and Spain)
"Ritt, Otto" (same?)	Abwehr	June 1936	Pamplona
5. Ahlers, Jacob ("Ernst Groth")	Consul, Navy, Abwehr	1914	Tenerife, Canary Islands
6. Becker, Otto	Navy, motor sales	1929	Barcelona
7. Bertram, Otto ("Bremen") (See Rüggeberg)	Lufthansa, Abwehr	1935?	Las Palmas, Canary Islands

Name/(Alias)	Profession	Entry into Spain	Place
8. Burbach, Friedhelm	Consul, AO	1935	Bilbao
9. Classen, Richard	Consul, Abwehr	1920s	Cádiz
10. Dede, Hans	Consul, Abwehr, Navy	1935	Mallorca
11. Draeger, Gustav	Consul, Abwehr, Navy	1935?	Seville
12. Eiking, John ("Jean Alexandre Frutos")	Abwehr agent S-2110	1914	San Sebastián
13. Ehrhardt, Eugenio	Abwehr	1935	Bilbao
14. Eitzen, Meino von	Coal, oil dealer	1929	Vigo
15. Flick, Harald	Consular official	1935	Las Palmas
16. Förschler, Pablo	Metallurgist, Navy	1929	Bilbao
17. Fricke, Henrique	Abwehr	1935?	Cartagena
18. Gäbelt, Erich	Business administrator HISMA	1934 1936	Salamanca
19. Geise, Alfred	Abwehr	1935	Ceuta
20. Goss, Franz von ("Grande")	Journalist, Abwehr	1922	Madrid?
21. Goudschall, Hikko Enno	Telegraph agent	1935	Vigo
22. Heinichen, Otto, Korv. K.	Navy	1928	?
23. Janssen, Christian ("Antonio Silva")	Coal, oil dealer, Abwehr	1935	Madrid
24. Klingenberg, Ernst ("Máximo Soler")	Attorney, Abwehr HISMA	1935 1937?	Málaga Salamanca
25. Klumpp, Felix	Engineer, Abwehr agent F-2321	Sept. 1933	Coruña
26. Knobloch, Conrad	Consul	1925	Alicante
27. Knobloch, Hans (son of Conrad?)	?	1925?	Alicante
28. Koss, Maj. Albrecht von	Army, Abwehr I.G. Farben HISMA, Nova	1916 1935? July 1938?	Barcelona Salamanca
29. Kramer, Eugen Ludwig	?	1924	Melilla
30. Lange, Willy	Machinery	1922 July 1936?	Barcelona Cádiz
"Lange" (same as Lange, Willy?)	Army, Abwehr	Oct. 1936?	Cáceres
31. Langenheim, Adolf P.	Mining, AO, Abwehr	1907	Tetuán

Name/(Alias)	Profession	Entry into Spain	Place
32. Langenheim, Heinrich C. (son of Adolf)	Journalist and Translator I.G. Farben Abwehr	1936 1938 1939	London Spain Tetuán
33. Liesau, Franz		1932	?
34. Lippenheide, Friedrich	I.G. Farben	1921	Bilbao
35. Mayrhofer	Telefunken Navy, Abwehr	1922 Jan. 1936	Madrid?
36. Menzell, Lt. Alfred	Navy, Abwehr	1922	Madrid
37. Messner, Otto	Coal, oil, Abwehr	1911	Bilbao
38. Meyer, Conrad	Army, Abwehr	1928?	Vigo
39. Meyer, Kurt	?	1933	Ceuta
40. Moldenhaus, Richard	Chemist, I.G Farben	Sept. 1932	Barcelona
41. Niemann, Edmond ("Pablo García")	Shipper, Abwehr	1934	Las Palmas, Canary Islands
42. Oberbeil, Wilhelm	Abwehr	1934, 1936	Occasional visits
43. Pasch, Karl		1935?	?
44. Pasch, Wilhelm	MAN airlines, zeppelins	1927	?
Pasch, Hermann (same person? brother?)	? HISMA	1935 1937	Bilbao ?
45. Rahn, Wilhelm	Navy	1935?	Tenerife
46. Ratfisch, Werner	Engineer	1914	?
47. Richter, Heinrich	?	1928-1936 1940	El Ksar Spanish Morocco
48. "Rolland, Ino von"	Business representative Journalist, spy	WWI 1934?	Madrid
49. Rüggeberg, Friedrich "Bremen" (Rüggeberg? Bertram?)	Navy, Abwehr, Consul	1907	Barcelona
50. Rüggeberg, Rolf (son of Friedrich)	Navy, Abwehr, I.G. Farben	1934?	Born Barcelona, 1907
51. Schlüssler, Adalbert or Dr. Erich	Navy Schering Drug Co.	1926? ?	Cádiz ?
52. Schneider, J.F.	Abwehr, fishery	1916	Bilbao
53. Schultz, Alfred	Abwehr	?	Bilbao
54. Schultze, Ernst Alexander Karl ("Tinto")	Lufthansa Joined Abwehr	1932 1941	Seville?
55. Schweiger, José	Lufthansa	1926	Lujo?

Name/(Alias)	Profession	Entry into Spain	Place
56. Schwenzner, Dr. Julius	Foreign trade	1927? 1941?	Bilbao
57. Sturm, Juan	Arms sales	1928	Madrid
58. "Wagner, Walter"	DAF	1935	Madrid
59. Winter, Gustav	Engineer	1927?	Canary Islands
60. Winzer, Paul	SS, Gestapo	May 1936	Barcelona

Notes

1. See ch. 5 n 33, below; Angel Viñas, *La Alemania nazi y el 18 de Julio* (Madrid, 1974, 1977), 1st ed., 83. For 1934 and fall 1935 trips, see ibid., 2nd ed., 265-67.
2. "Culbertson Report."
3. See ch. 5, nn 35-38, below.
4. Among the German military, Messerschmidt was probably second only to Canaris in Spanish experience. He went to Spain many times beginning in 1925. He was in Spain on 10 Jan. 1936: FO 371, vol. 120560 W 376/376/41. He was in Berlin 2-7 Aug. 1936: José Ignacio Escobar, *Así empezó* (Madrid, 1974), 103. Between 27 Aug. and 8 Sept. he made a tour of Nationalist Spain for Canaris and the AGK: Minister Huene, Lisbon, to Foreign Ministry, 11 Sept. 1936, *DGFP* ser. D, vol. 3, doc. 80. Also see "Culbertson Report."
5. See ch. 5, pp. 123-24. "Allgemeine Liste der Berichterstatter und Vertrauensmänner," list B, 2 Mar. 1914, OKM Docs., PG 49094.
6. See ch. 5, n 204, below.
7. Viñas, *Alemania*, 1st ed., 353.
8. "Culbertson Report."
9. Viñas, *Alemania*, 1st ed., 353-54. Canaris apparently recruited him.
10. Cmd. Veorger, "Etappenorganisation der Kriegsmarine," 21 Mar. 1947, rep. 107 for U.S. ONI, ONI Doc. 111 S-A 7, U.S. Navy Yard. Also see "Culbertson Report."
11. "Culbertson Report."
12. He was a Spanish national serving the Abwehr in Spain in World War I. In Feb. 1936 he was living in Cherbourg, France, and decided to reactivate his Abwehr status. He returned to Spain in 1940 and served in the Nationalist army. In 1936 his duty was to observe shipping in Cherbourg—apparently that bound for Spain. N.s. R-1 Ga. Abwehr office, Bremen, to Reichskriegsminister, Berlin, rep. Kdos. 35/35, 14 Mar. 1936, Abwehr Docs., ML 37, roll 9; R-1 Ga., Bremen, to RKM, rep. Kdos. 35/36, 25 May 1936; ibid.; questionnaire of "Frutos," n.d. [1941], ibid.
13. Veorger, ONI, 1947.
14. Ibid.
15. Consul Sauermann [Station Las Palmas, on vacation], Saalberg i/Regb., to GFM, 30 July 1936, OKM Docs., PG 80785.
16. Abw. Abt. X [signature illegible], Hamburg, to OKW, Abw. I [Canaris], memo 129/39, 8 Mar. 1939, OKM Docs., PG 48838; Meyer-Döhner to Naval

Attaché Group, rep. 488, 5 July 1939, ibid; declaration, Dr. Julius Schwenzer to OMGUS, Ludwigsburg, 2 Oct. 1946, OMGUS Docs., box 79, part 3/3, file "Repatriation-Schwenzner." He spoke about his own work and that of Förschler. He claimed Förschler did not join the Abwehr until 1941, but it is possible he reported informally before.

17. Veorger, ONI, 1947.
18. "Culbertson Report"; see also ch. 4, n 50, below.
19. Veorger, ONI, 1947.
20. Viñas, *Alemania,* 1st ed., 162; Sabath to Stohrer, memo W 701 g. Rs., 15 May 1939, GFM, 4365/E082242-43.
21. Black List, Counselor F.M. Guerra, Madrid, to Secretary of State, dis. 1843, 20 Mar. 1946, SD, 862.20252/3-2046.
22. "Culbertson Report."
23. Veorger, ONI, 1947.
24. For 1935, ibid.; for 1937, see ch. 4, n 93, below.
25. N.s., Abwehr, Bremen, to Abwehr, Berlin, 15 Sept. 1936, Abwehr Docs., ML 37/9.
26. "Culbertson Report."
27. Ibid.
28. In July and early August 1936, Koss was in Madrid: Viñas, *Alemania,* 1st ed., 427-28. For 1938, "I.G. Farbenindustrie, A.G. Interests in Spain," 116-page report, U.S. Seventh Army, Heidelberg Safehaven Team, 22 July 1945, p. 16, OMGUS Docs., box 76, part 2/3, file "I.G. Farben, Interests in Spain." On 1 July 1938, Koss joined HISMA, branch Nova, S.A., ibid., p. 70.
29. U.S. embassy, Madrid, to OMGUS, dis. 2483, 20 Aug. 1946, OMGUS Docs., box 79, part 2/3, file "Repatriates, Spain."
30. See ch. 3, n 51, below.
31. See ch. 5, nn 16, 17, ch. 4, n 14, below.
32. Heinrich Cromwell Langenheim, son of Adolf, was one-fourth English. He joined the NSDAP in 1933. From 1936 to 1937 he worked in the propaganda section of the British embassy in London for Ribbentrop. He worked for I.G. Farben, 1938-1941, and he told his U.S. interrogators he officially worked for the Abwehr in Spanish Morocco in 1941. Interrogation, Hohenasperg, 2 July 1946, OMGUS Docs., box 79, part 2/3, file "Repatriates." When in 1936 he left Spain is unclear. Ch. 5, n 20, below, shows he was working for the Abwehr at least in 1939; also see n 13 above.
33. "Culbertson Report."
34. Ibid.; Seventh Army, I.G. Farben rep., July 1945, p. 62, cited in n 28 above.
35. Viñas, *Alemania,* 1st ed., 32-33, 77, 91.
36. "Culbertson Report."
37. Interrogation of Otto Messner by Ulrich G. Vodin, Neuengamme- Hamburg, 29 May 1946, OMGUS Docs., box 79, part 2/3, file "Repatriation- Spain."
38. Viñas, *Alemania,* 1st ed., 41; 2nd ed., 246.
39. British Consul General Gascoigne, Tangier, to Sir Roger Makins, FO, 1 July 1940. FO 371, vol. 24447, C 7910/16/41.
40. Interrogation of Richard Moldenhaus by W. Wendell Blanke, Hohenasperg, 9 and 12 September 1946, OMGUS Docs., box 71, part 3/3, file "Spain, Interrogations."

41. See ch. 5, n 16, below.

42. Angel Alcázar de Velasco, *Memorias de un agente secreto* (Barcelona, 1979), 18, 20-21.

43. "Culbertson Report."

44. Ibid. Viñas, *Alemania,* 1st ed., 82, 124-25.

45. OKM, "Organisation und Aufgabe der Etappen," Berlin, Jan. 1939, OKM Docs., PG 49092.

46. "Culbertson Report."

47. Gascoigne, Tangier, to Makins, 1 July 1940, FO 371, vol. 24447, C 7910/16/41.

48. Viñas, *Alemania,* 1st ed., 34, 252, 337. He made several trips to Spain in the 1930s.

49. Friedrich Rüggeberg, Sr., consul in Barcelona, was a German intelligence agent in World War I. British Ambassador Arthur Hardinge, Madrid, to Minister of State Juan Alvarado, 11 May 1917, MAE, "b 3146," file 31. Canaris met him again in Spain in the 1920s. On 16 Jan. 1939, Rüggeberg's son Rolf returned to Barcelona for the Abwehr, but when he or his father left the city is not clear. Lt. Menzell, aide to naval attaché, San Sebastián, to Naval Attaché Group, Berlin, R. 35 g, 16 Jan. 1939, OKM Docs., PG 48838. Rüggeberg Sr. or Jr. may be the same agent as "Bremen," who left Barcelona 29 July 1936 on an Italian vessel bound for Germany. See ch. 5, n 8, below.

50. Ibid.; on Rolf, see Seventh Army, I.G. Farben rep., July 1945, 34, 95, cited in ch. 5, n. 228 below.

51. Meyer-Döhner to Naval Attaché Group, rep. 575, 23 June 1939, OKM Docs., PG 48838; memo of conversation with Adm. Boehm at Ceuta, 27 Apr.-2 May, rep. G 3199 A; at Lisbon, 7 May 1939, OKM Docs., PG 45181.

52. J.F. Schneider, Bilbao, to consulate, San Sebastián, 2 June 1939, GFM, 1308/348298-99. The Nova man was Robert Doelling.

53. Signature 111. [Mayrhofer?], Family Service, Leipzig, to Abwehr Nest (branch office), Bremen, rep. 9 Sch 9549, 30 Nov. 1942, Abwehr Docs., M.L. 37/10.

54. W.W. Blancke, Berlin, to OMGUS and State Dept. dis. 7901, 29 Nov. 1946, OMGUS Docs., box 79, part 3/3, file "Repatriation from Spain, Flight X, General 820.02 a."

55. F.M. Guerra, Madrid, to State Dept., 27 Aug. 1946, SD, 862.20252/8-2746.

56. Schwenzer declaration cited in n 16 above.

57. Viñas, *Oro de Moscú,* 43-44.

58. Viñas, *Alemania,* 1st ed., 311; ch. 4, 58-59, below.

59. "Culbertson Report."

60. Ch. 2, p. 33; Viñas, *Alemania,* 2nd ed., 250-52.

Appendix C.
Chronology

1931

14 Apr.   Second Spanish Republic proclaimed; King Alfonso XIII leaves.
16 June   First series of Premier Manuel Azaña's army reform decrees.
14 Nov.   First issue of *Mundo Obrero* (Communist party organ).

1932

Jan.   Dissolution of the Jesuits; divorce law enacted; cemeteries secularized.
10 Aug.   *Pronunciamiento* of General José Sanjurjo. Upon reaching Seville, Sanjurjo declares martial law. Rising fails.

1933

30 Jan.   Adolf Hitler comes to power in Germany.
20 July   Conclusion of the Concordat between the Reich and Vatican as a means of winning Catholic support.
29 Oct.   Fascist-inspired Falange Española founded in Madrid by José Antonio Primo de Rivera.
19 Nov.   Strong conservative trend evidenced in elections for new Cortes. Francisco Franco's brother-in-law, Ramón Serrano Suñer, elected as Catholic-monarchist.

1934

Jan.   Franco appointed military commander in chief in Morocco.
31 Mar.   Arms agreement between Benito Mussolini and Spanish monarchists.
10 Apr.   German navy draws up plans to obtain secret supplies, particularly oil, from Latin America, Spain, and U.S.; to be delivered in neutral Spain in the event of a German-French war.
Apr.   José Antonio, head of Falange, visits Berlin; meets Hitler and discusses Nazi-Catholic relations with Nazi party ideologist Alfred Rosenberg.
14-15 June Hitler's first meeting with Mussolini in Venice.
4 Oct.   Nationwide general strike in Madrid, Barcelona, the Asturias mining region.

6 Oct.	Leftist revolt in Asturias and Catalonia suppressed by army using Franco's plans.

1935

Apr.	Carlist monarchist group again visits Mussolini.
May	Franco appointed chief of general staff. Catholic José Gil Robles made war minister.
June	Italians give Falange chief José Antonio more than $4,000 monthly (continues through Feb. 1936).
15 Sept.	At Nürnberg Party Day, Joachim von Ribbentrop and an Italian journalist representing Mussolini's newspaper, *Popolo d'Italia*, proclaim a united front against bolshevism.
16-17 Sept.	Admiral Wilhelm Canaris, Hitler's chief of military intelligence, meets with Italian chief of military intelligence Col. Mario Roatta, in Verona. Two powers to work together in military intelligence "against bolshevism."

1936

15 Jan.	Popular Front electoral pact and platform.
16 Feb.	Electoral victory of Popular Front. Azaña government (leftist Republicans without Socialists).
7 Mar.	Hitler's troops reenter Rhineland. Franco posted to Canary Islands.
15 Mar.	Falange outlawed; José Antonio arrested; President Niceto Acalá Zamora impeached.
29 Mar.- 2 Apr.	Italian Chief of Police Arturo Bocchini visits Dachau; confers with Heinrich Himmler, Reinhard Heydrich, head of Gestapo, and Hermann Göring, Reich air minister.
Apr.	German SS reach agreement with Italian police for intelligence cooperation throughout Europe.
29 Apr.	Göring appointed commissioner for foreign exchange and raw materials.
10 May	Azaña becomes president.
13 May	Election of Popular Front in France. León Blum becomes premier in France.
June	Widening of breach between Socialists Indolecio Prieto and Francisco Largo Caballero; increasing violence in streets; clashes of Falange and Socialists.
17 June and 6 July	Colonel Josef Veltjens, reserve air force officer and private arms dealer living in Berlin, contacts right-wing conspirators in Spain.
23 June	Franco gives liberal minister of war a last warning to heed dissatisfaction among officer corps.
	Monarchist Antonio Goicoechea contacts Italian army; Foreign Minister Count Galeazzo Ciano informed of Spanish rightist plans for counterrevolution.
9 July- ca. 14 Aug.	1 German SS *Girgenti* chartered by Veltjens for arms delivery to Spain.
13 July	Assassination of Nationalist bloc leader José Calvo Sotelo.

17 July	Army rising in Morocco.
18 July	Revolt in Spain.
	Serrano-Suñer imprisoned by Republicans in Madrid.
19 July	Franco lands at Tetuán, Morocco, after flight from Canary Islands.
20 July	José Giral's cabinet formed.
	Death of conspirator General Sanjurjo.
21 July	Franco asks Johannes Bernhardt to secure aid from the Reich and sends Luis Bolín to Italy.
	Republican government asks France for aid.
	André Malraux, of French Committee against War and Fascism, flies to Madrid to serve as private volunteer.
ca. July	Franco's brother Nicolás purchases foreign arms in Lisbon.
22-24 July	Premier Blum and foreign minister confer in London with Prime Minister Stanley Baldwin, Foreign Minister Anthony Eden, and Chancellor of the Exchequer Neville Chamberlain.
22 July	Hitler and Ribbentrop meet in Bayreuth with Japanese military attaché, General Hiroshi Oshima, to discuss Anti-Comintern Pact.
24 July	Eden suggests to Portugal a noninterventionist policy in Spanish strife.
	German embassy in London takes up with British Foreign Office reports about deliveries of French planes to Spanish government.
25 July	German Ambassador Ulrich von Hassell calls on Italian Foreign Minister Count Ciano to discuss Spain.
	Hitler decides at Bayreuth to launch Operation Feuerzauber, aid to Franco.
	Mussolini decides to send Savoia bomber-transport planes to Spanish Morocco.
	Split in Blum cabinet develops over aid to Spain.
25-28 July	Count José Quiñones de León, self-appointed rebel "ambassador" in Paris, sends agent to Berlin to appeal for arms for Gen. Emilio Mola.
	Mola's agents meet with Canaris.
26 July	General Miguel Cabanellas establishes Nationalist Junta in Burgos.
	Comintern meeting in Prague discusses Spain.
	Göring creates Sonderstab W[ilberg] in Berlin to direct German intervention.
27 July	Seville under insurgent control of General Gonzalo Queipo de Llano; reinforcement by air from Morocco.
29 July	Bernhardt returns by air from Berlin and Bayreuth to Seville.
	German Ju 52s begin airlift from Morocco to Seville.
30 July	First flight of Savoias arrives in Morocco from Rome.
31 July	Bernhardt and Fernando Carranza organize in Tetuán the Sociedad Hispano-Marroquí de Transportes (HISMA), Ltd., legally controlled on a 50-50 basis.
	Maj. Alexander von Scheele and 85 German "volunteers" depart from Hamburg for Cádiz aboard SS *Usaramo*.
Aug.	German navy temporarily forced to deactivate secret supply service plans for Spain.

Aug.	Hitler issues memo on autarky and communism as prelude to Four-Year Plan.
2 Aug.	Admiral Rolf Carls arrives in Spanish Morocco aboard battleship *Deutschland*. Accompanied by Bernhardt, he visits Franco.
	France announces policy of nonintervention and proposes its Europeanwide adoption.
3 Aug.	Comintern initiates a worldwide call for communists to join volunteers for Republican Spain.
3-7 Aug.	Italian propaganda chief Dino Alfieri travels to Germany. He discusses with his German counterpart, Joseph Paul Goebbels, joint German-Italian press policy against "bolshevik danger" in Spain.
4 Aug.	Canaris confers with Roatta in Rome on Spanish War.
6 Aug.	SS *Usaramo* lands in Spain with German weapons.
	Franco arrives in Seville and establishes headquarters.
12 Aug.	Hitler appoints Ribbentrop ambassador to Britain, but he stays in Germany until 26 October.
	First International Brigade volunteers arrive in Barcelona.
	Germans bomb Republican battleship *Jaime I*.
14 Aug.	Veltjens delivers half-dozen He 51 fighters to Mola at La Coruña.
	Insurgents take Badajoz, securing frontier with Portugal.
15 Aug.	Mussolini sends three Savoia seaplanes to Majorca.
	Franco-British statement on nonintervention issued.
16 Aug.	Japanese agree upon a text with Germany for Anti-Comintern Pact.
22 Aug.	Hitler sends Prince Phillip of Hesse to Italy on special mission to Mussolini.
24 Aug.	Hitler sends Col. Walter Warlimont (Code name "Guido") of Army Economic Welfare Staff, to Spain.
	Italy, Germany, Portugal accept nonintervention "in principle."
	Consul General Antonov-Ovseenko arrives in Barcelona; Soviet Ambassador Rosenberg goes to Madrid.
	Introduction of two-year compulsory military service in Germany.
26 Aug.	Rebel armies occupy Río Tinto mines (British-owned pyrites).
	Italian troops dispatched to Balearic Islands.
26-28 Aug.	Canaris discusses Spain with top Italians.
Aug.	Canaris meets Spanish rebels in Lisbon, visits Seville.
28 Aug.	Italy, the last holdout, finally agrees to French proposal on international Non-Intervention Agreement, which goes into effect.
	Madrid suffers first aerial bombardment.
Sept.	Siege of Madrid, German participation.
	Battles of Vitoria and Zaragoza, German participation.
	German air war against Republican navy in Mediterranean.
1 Sept.	Pope Pius XI receives Spanish religious refugees.
3 Sept.	Franco takes Talavera de la Reina, German participation.
4 Sept.	Largo Caballero brings Socialists into government. Cabinet of leftist Republicans, Socialists, and Communists.
5 Sept.	Rebels take Irún.
	Richard Walther Darré, German minister of food and agriculture,

presses for expansion of Göring's economic jurisdiction with a Four-Year Plan.

6 Sept. Warlimont, Canaris, and Roatta confer with Franco at his headquarters in Cáceres.

9 Sept. First meeting of Non-Intervention Committee (NIC), London. Alexander Orlov of NKVD arrives in Spain. Hitler publicly announces Four-Year Plan, with Göring as commissioner, at Nürnberg Party Day.

13 Sept. Finance Minister Dr. Juan Negrín authorized to hide gold reserves belonging to Bank of Spain.

14 Sept. Pope Pius XI, speaking to Spanish refugees, deplores "truly Satanic hatred of God" displayed in the Spanish Republic.

19 Sept. Hitler expands military intervention with Operation Otto.

22 Sept. Roatta returns to Italy.

23 Sept. Italian reinforcements steam toward Spain. Hans Frank, agent of Hitler, assures Mussolini in Rome that Mediterranean is "a purely Italian sea," and that Baltic is Germany's Mediterranean.

25 Sept. Soviet SS *Neva* arrives at Alicante with food, secret arms, and munitions.

27 Sept. Republican government reorganizes petroleum company CAMPSA to form a general monopoly trading company for Soviet trade, CAMPSA-Gentibus.

28 Sept. Rebels take Toledo with German participation. NIC refuses to hear charges against Portugal. Bernhardt and Warlimont on special mission to Göring to establish new German trading company, ROWAK.

29 Sept. Junta de Defensa Nacional ratifies decision taken at rebel generals' Sept. 21 meeting and designates Franco *Jefe del Estado y Generalísimo de los Ejércitos*. Nationalist naval victory at Cape Espartel achieves naval supremacy.

Late Sept. Franco moves military headquarters to Salamanca, but political center of Nationalist junta remains in Burgos.

30 Sept. Franco goes to Burgos to assume executive authority over Nationalist government.

Oct. Battle at gates of Madrid, German participation.

1 Oct. Franco publicly named generalissimo and chief of state.

3 Oct. Franco creates cabinet (Junta Técnica del Estado) composed of three generals and one diplomat, with his brother Nicolás as general secretary.

6 Oct. Soviets state they will not be bound by Non-Intervention agreement any more than Portugal, Italy, and Germany are.

10 Oct. Göring discusses Frank's sphere-of-influence offer with Ciano in Budapest.

11 Oct. Operation Feuerzauber completed.

15-18 Oct. Göring and his state secretary for the Luftwaffe, General Erhard Milch, fly to Rome, confer with Duce and Italian aviation leaders.

15-22 Oct. Himmler and Heydrich visit Rome.

16 Oct.	SS *Komsomol* unloads 50 Soviet medium tanks at Cartagena.
17 Oct.	Republic establishes training base at Albacete for international volunteers.
21 Oct.	Italy sends two submarines to Spanish waters.
23 Oct.	Loyalist government approves formation of International Brigades.
	Anti-Comintern Pact signed between Japan and Germany.
	Hitler concludes political protocol with Ciano in Berlin, recognizing Mediterranean as "an Italian sea."
24 Oct.	First Russian tanks in action around Aranjuez; Russian officers arrive in Madrid; German-Italian bombers over capital.
	Hitler sends two submarines to Spanish waters, Operation Ursula, to attack Republican vessels.
25 Oct.	510 tons of gold from Bank of Spain leave Cartagena for Odessa.
31 Oct.	Hitler decides to provide Franco with air force of 100 German planes.
	Luftübung Rügen (air) and Winterübung Hansa (naval) operations establish new German unit.
	Canaris goes to Spain to inform Franco of Hitler's decision to send Legion Condor.
	General Hugo Sperrle, first commander of Legion Condor, leaves Germany for Spain via Rome; Wolfram von Richtofen named chief of staff.
	HISMA signs contract with Rif iron mines, agreeing to take 840,000 tons of ore through 31 Dec. 1937.
1 Nov.	Berlin Protocol christened "the Axis" by Mussolini's Milan speech.
4 Nov.	Legion Condor begins landing in Spain.
Nov.	Veltjens joins with Henry Aschpuvis of Hamburg to form shipping company, Hansagesellschaft Aschpuvis & Veltjens. Company's steamship *Urundi* transports brigade of 600 Irish Catholic Fascist Blueshirts, headed by Gen. Eoin O'Duffy, to Franco Spain. Company continues to make arms deliveries through 1938.
6 Nov.	Republican government moves to Valencia.
8 Nov.	Franco fails to take Madrid.
	International Brigades arrive in Madrid.
18 Nov.	Madrid assault suspended. Germany and Italy recognize Nationalist regime at Burgos.
20 Nov.	José Antonio executed in Alicante.
25 Nov.	Germany and Japan publish Anti-Comintern Pact.
28 Nov.	Franco signs with Italy an "anticommunist" and "neutrality" treaty, excluding foreign bases from Spain in any future war.
30 Nov.	Gen. Severiano Martínez Anido, Franco's chief of police, requests that SS send German delegation to Spain to build up Spanish police force.
	German Chargé Wilhelm Faupel meets Franco.
Dec. mid-Jan. 1937	La Rozas-Manzanares Offensive, German participation.
6 Dec.	Joint Italian-German military conference in Rome on expansion of war in Spain.

Mid-Dec.	Attack on Bujalanca, German participation.
	Germans modify Operation Ursula to observation status; Duce increases his patrols to seven submarines.
18 Dec.	First major contingent of Italian volunteers departs from Naples for Cádiz.
Dec.	Warlimont returns from Spain to Germany.
22 Dec.	In Reich Chancellery, Hitler meets with Göring, Blomberg, Wehrmacht Gen. Werner von Fritsch, Faupel, Warlimont and Col. Friedrich Hossbach to limit future German expansion in Spanish war.
Late Dec.	George Orwell arrives in Barcelona, joins POUM militia.

1937

2 Jan.	Italian-British gentleman's agreement.
5-9 Jan.	Canaris in Spain.
15 Jan.	Göring and Mussolini discuss Spain in Rome. Germany would only maintain current strength of Legion Condor.
30 Jan.	Hitler in Reichstag speech denounces Jews, democracy, marxism, and Spanish Left.
1 Feb.	General Wilhelm Keitel proposes that Reich War Ministry set up a propaganda section as a result of Spanish war.
6 Feb.-Mar.	Jarama Offensive, German participation. Nationalist offensive held.
8 Feb.	Nationalists take Málaga, German and Italian participation. Pope Pius XI rejoices.
	Serrano Suñer escapes from Madrid to Burgos.
18 Feb.	Göring and Bernhardt emphasize increased German investment in Spain, particularly in mining; establish Montaña, S.A., for mining investments.
28 Feb.	Abraham Lincoln Brigade first sees action.
5 Mar.	Communist party congress demands that its rival, POUM, be eliminated because of "Trotskyism."
8 Mar.	Italian attack on Guadalajara front, German participation.
15 Mar.	Successful Republican counteroffensive, heavy Italian losses.
19 Mar.	Pope Pius XI issues encyclical condemning atheistic communism.
20 Mar.	Franco pledges neutrality during any future war in a secret protocol signed by Faupel.
Apr.-mid-June	Franco's northern offensive, German participation.
Apr.	Canaris in Spain.
19 Apr.	Franco and Serrano amalgamate Falange and Carlists "from above" into Spain's only totalitarian party, with Franco as El Caudillo.
26 Apr.	Guernica bombed by Legion Condor and Italians.
3-8 May	POUM, Anarchists, and Communists fight each other in Barcelona; "May Days."
May	Mussolini's troops reach maximum of 44,648 in Spain.
17 May	Fall of Largo Caballero, succeeded by government of Juan Negrín.
25 May	Chamberlain succeeds Baldwin as British prime minister.
29 May	Bombing of *Deutschland* by loyalist planes.

31 May	*Deutschland* shells Almería.
1 June	Death of Gen. Mola in airplane accident near Burgos.
12 June	Blomberg visits Rome for military consultation with Italians.
15 June	*Leipzig* alleges attack by unknown submarine off Oran.
16 June	POUM leaders arrested, party suppressed at CP instigation.
18-24 June	Adm. Wilhelm Marschall, German naval operations chief, draws up proposal for Commander-in-Chief Adm. Erich Raeder that assumes, for first time since Versailles treaty, that Great Britain might back a Soviet-French war against Germany. Blomberg draws up series of war possibilities involving France and Britain: Case Green (two-front war with German concentration on Czechoslovakia); Case Red (two-front war with France); Extension Green/Red (war in which Britain would intervene); Case Richard (extension of Spanish Civil War into world war by a "provoked incident").
19 June	Bilbao falls to Nationalists.
19 June-2 July	Pilar Primo de Rivera, of Falange and sister of martyred José Antonio, visits Germany.
June	Dionisio Ridruejo, propagandist for Falange, in Germany to observe international congress of *Kraft durch Freude*, meets Hitler.
23 June	Germany and Italy withdraw from naval patrol of NIC.
Late June	Orwell leaves Spain.
30 June	Portugal ends nonintervention frontier patrol.
1-3 July	Canaris visits Franco's operations to boost morale, promises more aid. Requests intelligence information on Russians and on French Morocco.
1 July	Collective letter of Spanish bishops backs Nationalists.
7-26 July	Brunete Offensive, German participation.
12-16 July	Spain and Germany sign public economic treaty and three secret protocols in Burgos. They postpone comprehensive economic negotiations until end of war and agree to maximize current trade. Spain gives Germany first option on contracts—as opposed to Britain, France, and U.S.—to reconstruct New Spain's economy.
July	Sonderstab W redeploys German reconnaissance squadron, a unit of Legion Condor, from Cádiz to Mallorca.
Aug.	Franco moves military headquarters from Salamanca to Burgos.
5 Aug.	Nicolás Franco goes to Rome to appeal for more naval force to aid Nationalists.
5 Aug. 12 Sept.	Mussolini deploys Mediterranean naval force against European (mainly British) merchant marine; about a dozen ships are sunk.
11 Aug.	Nicolás Franco in Rome agrees to Italian payments agreement.
15-25 Aug.	Santander Offensive, German participation.
21 Aug.	Faupel departs from Spain.
25 Aug.	Conquest of Asturias, German participation.
26 Aug.	Fall of Santander to Nationalists.
6-14 Sept.	Serrano Suñer goes to Nazi party rally at Nürnberg along with Nicolás Franco and Adjutant General José Varela.
10-13 Sept.	Anglo-French Nyon agreements to oppose "piracy," i.e., Italian naval attacks on ships going to Republican Spain.

Mid-Sept.	General secretary of German arms-exports cartel visits Spain looking for postwar contracts.
17 Sept.- 5 Feb. 1938	Nationalist Spaniards step up blockade warfare operations from Balearic Islands region.
23 Sept.	New German Ambassador Eberhard von Stohrer arrives in Spain.
25-29 Sept.	Duce visits Berlin for first time. Axis agreements are reaffirmed. Spheres of influence—Germany would get the East, Italy would control the Mediterranean—are agreed upon.
30 Sept.	British-French-Italian naval understanding reached at Paris.
7 Oct.	Papal nuncio arrives in Salamanca.
12 Oct.	Nicolás Franco contests mining claims of German Montaña S.A.
19 Oct.	Nationalists take Gijón. End of northern campaign.
20 Oct.	German cruiser *Schleswig-Holstein* visits Canary Islands.
22 Oct.	Great Britain sends Robert Hodgson to Salamanca as its "agent."
24 Oct.	Franco declares to Stohrer his willingness to accept responsibility for civil war damages and suggests establishment of a mixed claims commission.
29 Oct.	Negrín government moves to Barcelona.
31 Oct.	Sperrle replaced by Gen. Hellmuth Volkmann as commander of Legion Condor.
5 Nov.	Hitler enunciates Mediterranean policy in Reich Chancellery speech before Blomberg, Göring, and Hossbach. Germany would strengthen Italy's rear; if Italy got into war with Britain and France, Germany would support Italy with raw materials. Germany would let Spanish war drag on and encourage Italy to hang onto Mallorca. Hitler would meanwhile make use of persistence of Spanish war to "settle" Austrian and Czech problems.
6 Nov.	Italy joins Anti-Comintern Pact.
15 Nov.	Franco's brother Ramón shot down in Balearics campaign.
19 Nov.	Lord Halifax visits Hitler.
25 Nov.	Secret German-Spanish police agreement concluded whereby Chief of Police Martínez Anido sends Spaniards to Berlin to learn from Gestapo.
Dec.- Mar. 1938	Spaniards begin work on a naval contract with Italy to build eight destroyers for postwar expansion.
1 Dec.	Japan grants diplomatic recognition to Franco government.
8 Dec.	Nationalist aircraft bombard Barcelona.
15 Dec.	Capture of Teruel by Republicans; Gen. Franco drawn from Madrid siege.
16 Dec.- 6 Jan. 1938	First Battle of Teruel, German participation.

1938

3 Jan.	Franco reorganizes junta to include civilians.
7-22 Jan.	Second Battle of Teruel, German participation.
30 Jan.	Nationalist government completely restructured with abolition of Junta Técnica and introduction of a complete cabinet of ministers, mostly civilians. Serrano Suñer becomes minister of interior.

4 Feb.	Ribbentrop becomes foreign minister.
4-7 Feb.	Alfambra Offensive, German participation.
12 Feb.	Sperrle, former commander of Legion Condor, present at Berchtesgaden when Hitler terrorizes Austrian Chancellor Kurt von Schuschnigg.
14 Feb.	Ciano advises Gen. Alberto Pariani, under secretary for war, that military staff talks with OKW should soon begin.
17-23 Feb.	Third Battle of Teruel, German participation.
20 Feb.	Lord Halifax replaces Eden at British Foreign Office.
23 Feb.	Reconquest of Teruel by Nationalists; Nationalist offensive on Aragón front.
26 Feb.	HISMA-ROWAK asks for repayment of loans. Franco creates bureau of military acquisitions in office of vice-presidency, then under Gen. Count Francisco Gómez-Jordana, to deal with Germans and ration money for arms purchases with all powers.
Mar.	Nicolás Franco goes to Rome to negotiate payments issue.
6 Mar.	British cruiser *Arethusa* helps ward off attack by Legion Condor planes on port of Barcelona.
9 Mar.	Nationalist offensive launched in Aragón, German participation. Franco decrees Labor Charter modeled after Italy's Fascist system.
11 Mar.	Hitler occupies Austria.
13 Mar.	Second Blum prime ministry begins in France. Blum reopens French-Spanish frontier to arms shipments.
16 Mar.	Italian bombers begin regular night raids on Barcelona. Pope Pius XI protests on 24 March.
21 Mar.	First Nationalist Offensive toward Mediterranean, German participation.
5 Apr.	Negrín government reorganized; Prieto resigns from cabinet as minister of defense. Canaris, in Spain to assess Franco's Mediterranean campaign, reports that Franco is too independent.
22 Apr.	Hitler again steps up war plan against Czechoslovakia.
26 Apr.	Vice Adm. Günther Guse, OKM operations, draws up plan for Spain to be benevolently neutral in favor of Germany in any future war.
2-5 May	Hitler visits Mussolini and Pope Pius XI in Rome.
5 May	Jesuits reestablished in Nationalist Spain.
24 May	Nicolás Franco, in Rome, agrees to regular monthly repayment schedule.
2 June	The Caudillo appoints Nicolás Franco ambassador to Portugal.
Mid-June-27 June	Lt. Com. Hellmuth Heye, on behalf of German navy, inspects supply possibilities in Spain, making secret trip to Iberia and Morocco.
13 June	French close Pyrenean frontier.
19 June	Serrano Suñer attacks Jews in speech in Bilbao.
25 June	Negrín's government orders that religious services be provided for Republican troops desiring them.
Late June	Germans cease delivery of replacements for Legion Condor for about three months.

July	Burgos begins monthly payment in hard currency to both Rome and Berlin.
14 July-14 Aug.	Göring sends top secret intelligence mission on "fishing expedition" to Canary Islands looking for site for military base. Foreign ministry and navy are not informed.
24 July	Second Mediterranean Offensive.
	Republican counterattack on Ebro launched, German participation.
25 July-16 Nov.	Ebro Defensive battle, German participation.
Late Aug.-Sept.	German arms salesman Hans Eltze, director of Rheinmetall-Borsig, goes to Spain to survey Spanish post–civil war naval needs.
21-28 Aug.	Canaris brings Don Juan, son of ex-King Alfonso, to tour military and naval installations in Germany.
26 Aug.	German navy, foreign ministry, and economics ministry plan three-way barter deal: Mexican crude oil in exchange for German-made tankers and transportation to Spain's major oil refinery at Santa Cruz de Tenerife in Canary Islands, to supply German U-boats.
27 Aug.	Canaris opposes risking war with Britain, first unambiguous evidence of his opposition to Hitler's foreign policy.
9 Sept.	Czech crisis prompts Adm. Raeder to plan sending pocket battleship *Deutschland* into mid-Atlantic to be supplied with oil indirectly through Spain. 1935 naval supply service plans reactivated. Canaris provides agents with U.S. dollars for purchases in Spain for oil tender *August Schulze* and U-boats.
21 Sept.	Negrín at League of Nations announces plans for withdrawal of International Brigades.
27 Sept.	Franco annoys Hitler by declaring to French that Spain would be neutral if Germany were involved in war with Britain and France over Czechoslovakia.
29 Sept.	Four capitalist powers conclude Munich Agreement to press Czechoslovakia to hand over Sudetenland to Third Reich.
30 Sept.	At Munich, Chamberlain and Hitler discuss Spain.
Late Oct.	Germans resupply run-down Legion Condor.
31 Oct.	Volkmann replaced as commander of Legion Condor by Gen. Richthofen, former chief of staff.
Nov.	Montaña dispute resolved with compromise.
	Bernhardt reorganizes HISMA and Montaña into a holding company of 14 subsidiaries, SOFINDUS, incorporated in Lisbon.
9 Nov.	*Kristallnacht*: anti-semitic excesses in Germany after murder by a Jew of Ernst von Rath, a member of German embassy in Paris.
16 Nov.	Anglo-Italian agreement: Mussolini withdraws 10,000 troops from Spain.
	Republican retreat from the Ebro; farewell parade for International Brigades.
6 Dec.	Ribbentrop in Paris concludes nonaggression pact with France. Foreign Minister Georges Bonnet condemns communism in Spain. Spanish Ambassador Antonio Magaz signs in Berlin a plywood (*Okume*) protocol with ROWAK, providing for German airplane industry for 1939 and 1940.

14 Dec.	French-German Treaty of Friendship signed in Paris.
23 Dec.- 10 Feb.	Nationalist offensive overruns Catalonia.
End of Dec.- Apr. 1939	Luftwaffe sends seven members of Sonderstab W to Spain to survey postwar needs.

1939

10-12 Jan.	Chamberlain and Halifax visit Mussolini in Rome.
12 Jan.	Lt. Rolf Rüggeberg, Canaris's agent, arrives in Burgos by air to satisfy Spanish request for naval instructor at San Fernando Naval School at Cádiz. Remains into World War II era.
26 Jan.	Franco enters Barcelona; German participation.
30 Jan.	Hitler speech "recognizes" Legion Condor for first time.
1 Feb.	In its last session on Spanish soil, Republican Cortes convenes at Figueras.
5-9 Feb.	Mass Loyalist flight over French frontier; Nationalists complete occupation of Catalonia.
7 Feb.	Republican President Azaña goes into exile in France.
9 Feb.	Minorca transferred to Nationalists.
24 Feb.	Azaña resigns.
27 Feb.	French and British recognize Burgos.
1 Mar.	Russia withdraws from NIC.
5 Mar.	Anti-Communist coup of Col. Segismundo Casado. Appointment of Communist military leaders by Negrín.
Mar.	Juan Suanzes, Nationalist commerce minister, proposes ten-year construction program that would include 4 battleships, 12 cruisers, 60 destroyers, and an unspecified number of submarines.
7-11 Mar.	Communist revolt in Madrid.
15 Mar.	German occupation of Prague by Hitler.
Mid-Mar.-end of month	Admiral Francisco Bastarreche, commander at Cádiz, goes to Italy to confer with Italian naval leaders about buying 8 Italian destroyers already under contract. Talks break down over financial issues.
27 Mar.	Spain joins Anti-Comintern Pact.
27-29 Mar.	Madrid Offensive, German participation.
28 Mar.	Nationalist entry into Madrid.
31 Mar.	Spanish Foreign Minister Gómez Jordana signs, in Burgos, German-Spanish Treaty of Friendship, which binds Spain to benevolent neutrality. Canaris presses Franco to publicize Spain's attachment to Axis and Anti-Comintern Pact. Chamberlain speech in House of Commons guarantees Poland.
1 Apr.	Surrender of Republican armies. Franco proclaims, "The war has ended." Pope Pius XII congratulates Franco.
4 Apr.	Gen. Keitel, head of OKW, meets with Pariani, Italian under state secretary for war, at Innsbruck to discuss military alliance.
7 Apr.	Mussolini invades Albania without giving Germans notice.
11 or 12 Apr.	Mussolini decides to withdraw troops from Spain.
14-17 Apr.	Göring visits Libya and Rome to confer with Duce, Ciano, and the

king. Discussions range over whole map of Europe. Göring and duce agree to joint German-Italian economic aid to Spain to stave off Anglo-French influence.

17 Apr. OKM sends German training flotilla, consisting of practically all of
10 May   Germany's warships, to Spanish waters.

28 Apr. Hitler speech reviews German foreign policy since Versailles treaty; makes verbal attacks on Britain, France, and U.S.; denounces Anglo-German naval arms limitation treaty of 1935; reiterates his claim to Danzig; and repudiates German-Polish, Non-Aggression Pact of 1934.

5 May   Spanish naval officers arrive in Rome to discuss battleship construction project.

6-7 May German-Italian military alliance, Pact of Steel, signed in Rome. Ribbentrop tells Ciano that Germans are satisfied with attitude of Franco.

13 May- Italy sends twenty naval officers to Spain to study joint construction.
1 June

19 May   Victory parade in Madrid; Legion Condor and CTV participate.

22 May   Pact of Steel affirmed as Hitler visits Rome.

26 May   Legion Condor departs from Vigo, accompanied by Spanish officer delegation.
         CTV leaves Cádiz, accompanied by Spanish delegation headed by Serrano Suñer and Gen. Alfredo Kindelàn.

5-13 June Victory celebrations in Italy.

6 June   Victory parade of Legion Condor in Berlin.

9 June- Göring sends another exploratory fishing vessel to Canary Islands.
3 July   German Foreign Ministry objects.

July   Canaris goes to Spain to prepare for intelligence and supply activities needed for wider war with West.

10 Aug. Spanish cabinet reshuffled.

23 Aug. Hitler-Stalin Pact; Ribbentrop and Molotov sign Non-Aggression Pact in Moscow.

1 Sept. Germany invades Poland.

3 Sept. Outbreak of World War II. Britain and France declare war on Germany.
         Spain proclaims neutrality.
         Seat of government returns to Madrid.

1940

18 Oct. Serrano Suñer appointed foreign minister (lasts until 3 Sept. 1942).

23 Oct. Hitler and Franco meet at Hendaye.

1941

22 June Spanish Blue Division recruited for USSR.

Notes

Abbreviations

WORKS CITED

ACP	American Committee Project [American Historical Association Committee for the Study of War Documents], German Foreign Ministry Records, 1867-1920. Microcopy T-149, National Archives, Washington, D.C.
Berlin Doc. Cent. Rec.	Nazi Party Records. Microcopy T-580, Berlin Document Center, West Berlin, and Washington, D.C.
CGG	Cuartel General del Generalísimo [Franco Headquarters documents from Spanish Civil War]. Military Archives, Madrid.
Comm. Dept.	U.S. Department of Commerce, Business and Economic Branch [files from 1930s]. National Archives, Washington, D.C.
Cult.	German Records of Nazi Cultural and Research Institutions. Microcopy T-82, National Archives, Washington, D.C.
DAI	Deutsches Ausland-Institut, Stuttgart [German Foreign Institute concerned with Germans who had emigrated abroad]. Microcopy T-81, National Archives, Washington, D.C.
DBFP	*Documents on British Foreign Policy* [publication of the British Foreign Office]. H. M. Stationery Office, London, 1949 seq.
DDF	*Documents diplomatiques français, 1932-1939* [publication of the French Ministry of Foreign Affairs]. Paris: Imprimerie Nationale, 1966 sq.
DDI	*I documenti diplomatici italiani* [publication of the Italian Ministry of Foreign Affairs]. Rome: Libreria dello stato, 1952-1957.
DGFP	*Documents on German Foreign Policy* [publication of the Department of State/ Foreign Office/ French Ministry of

Foreign Affairs; series C and D chosen by a team of scholars to shed light on the origins of World War II]. Washington, D.C.: Government Printing Office, 1949 seq.

DIA   *Documents on International Affairs, 1937* [published in London by the Royal Institute of International Affairs, a nongovernmental organization]. Ed. Stephen Heald. London: Oxford Univ. Press, 1939.

DS   U.S. Department of State files. National Archives, Washington, D.C.

Duce Files   Personal Papers of Benito Mussolini [files captured by U.S. government at the end of World War II]. Microcopy T-586, National Archives, Washington, D.C.

Eco. (Germ)   Reichswirtschaftsministerium [records of Reich Ministry of Economics]. Microcopy T-71, National Archives, Washington, D.C.

FO   British Foreign Office [records for 1930s]. Public Record Office, London and Kew.

FRUS   *Papers Relating to the Foreign Relations of the United States* [Department of State], 1936-39. Washington, D.C.: Government Printing Office, 1954-1956.

GFM   German Foreign Ministry, Berlin [records for the Nazi era on microfilm]. Microcopy T-120, National Archives, Washington, D.C.

IMT   *Trial of the Major War Criminals before the International Military Tribunal* [published version of proceedings of International Military Tribunal (Four-Power Tribunal set up at Nürnberg to try 22 major German war criminals)]. Nürnberg: International Military Tribunal, 1946.

"IMT Nürnberg Trial"   Unpublished documents of IMT. National Archives, Washington, D.C.

JNA Docs.   Documents of the Jefatura Nacional de Adquisiciones [Spanish Nationalist military procurement office]. Archivo Histórico Nacional, Madrid.

MAE   Ministerio Asúntos Exteriores [Spanish Foreign Ministry]. Records at the ministry, Madrid; some files, including CAMPSA-Gentibus, at Spanish government archives. Alcalá de Henares.

MFA   Militärgeschichtliches Forschungs Amt. Military History Research Office, Freiburg im Breisgau.

Min. Cult.   Records of the Italian Ministry of Popular Culture and Italian Foreign Office, 1922-1944 [captured by U.S. government at the end of World War II]. Microcopy T-586, National Archives, Washington, D.C.

Misc. Germ. Rec.   Miscellaneous German Records Collection [filmed at Alexandria, Va.; part of World War II Collection]. Microcopy T-84, National Archives, Washington, D.C.

ML   Marineleitung [German Abwehr Documents, Nest Bremen]. National Archives, Washington, D.C.

NCA	*Nazi Conspracy and Aggression*, ed. Department of Defense, Office of Chief of Counsel for the Prosecution of Axis Criminality [highlights from IMT, an incomplete but handy guide to a larger body of records]. 8 vols. and 2 supplements; Washington, D.C.: Government Printing Office, 1946-1948.
NSDAP	National Sozialistische Deutsche Arbeiter Partei [filmed at the Berlin Document Center by the AHA]. Microcopy T-580, National Archives, Washington, D.C.
OKH Docs.	Documents of Oberkommando des Heeres [records of Headquarters, German Army High Command]. Microcopy T-78, National Archives, Washington, D.C.
OKM Docs.	Documents of Oberkommando der Kriegsmarine [High Command of the German Navy]. Microcopy T-1022, National Archives, Washington, D.C.
OKW Docs.	Oberkommando der Wehrmacht [High Command of the German Armed Forces, Hitler's military staff as Supreme Commander of the Armed Forces], Microcopy T-77. OKW, Wehrkreise [Records of German Army Areas], Microcopy T-79. Unfilmed records listed by item number. National Archives, Washington, D.C.
OMGUS	Office of Military Government of the United States [in charge of administering Germany after World War II]. Records at National Archives, Suitland, Md.
ONI	United States Office of Naval Intelligence. Records at National Archives, Washington, D.C.
PM	British Prime Minister. Records at Public Record Office, London and Kew.
Prop.	Reichsministerium für Volksaufklärung und Propaganda. Microcopy T-580, National Archives, Washington, D.C. [Originals at Berlin Document Center.]
SS Rec.	Reichsführer SS und Chef der Deutschen Polizei [records of the Schutz Staffeln (Black Shirt elite guards)]. Microcopy T-175, National Archives, Washington, D.C.
TWC	*Trials of War Criminals before the Nuernberg Military Tribunals under Control Council Law No. 10, October 1946-April 1949* [publication of the twelve subsequent proceedings at Nürnberg against lesser war criminals, conducted by Office of Chief Counsel for War Crimes, U.S. Army]. 15 vols. Nürnberg, 1946-1949.
"U.S. Army, Nurnberg Trials"	Unpublished documents of the twelve subsequent U.S. trials. National Archives, Washington, D.C.

OTHER ABBREVIATIONS USED

CAMPSA	Compañía Arrendataria del Monopolio de Petróleos Sociedad Anónima [Spanish government oil company]
CHADE	Compañía Hispano Americana de Electricidad

dis.   dispatch
doc.   document
g. Kdos.   Geheime Kommandosache [top secret military]
NIC   Non-Intervention Committee
n.s.   No signature on document
OKM B.Z.   Oberkommando der Kriegsmarine, Office B [General Marine Office], Zentralgruppe, Planning Section
OKW W.Z.   Oberkommando der Werhmacht, Zentralgruppe, Planning Section
PRO   British Public Record Office, London and Kew
Ref D   Referat Deutschland [Domestic Section of the German Foreign Ministry]
rep.   report
tel.   telegram
W.A.   Wehrmacht, Office in Reich War Ministery [functions absorbed by OKW after February 1938]

Chapter 1. Hitler's Diplomatic Policy toward Spain

1. The above story is now well known. Hugh Thomas, *The Spanish Civil War* (New York, 1961; 2nd ed., 1965; 3rd ed., 1977; 4th ed., 1986) is the most comprehensive account in English of the civil war as a whole.

2. Robert H. Whealey, "Economic Influence of the Great Powers in the Spanish Civil War," *International History Review* 5 (May 1983): 230-33.

3. Angel Viñas, *La Alemania nazi y el 18 de Julio: Antecedentes de la intervención alemana en la guerra española*, 2nd ed. (Madrid: Alianza Editorial, 1977), Chs. 1-3.

4. Memo, conversation of Secretary of State Cordell Hull with Spanish Ambassador, Washington, 11 May 1936, *FRUS*, 1936, 2:294.

5. "Die Industrie Spanien," Institut für Weltwirtschaft, August 1940, Misc. Germ. Rec., microcopy T-84, serial 152, frames 1437265-377, 314.

6. See Virgilio Sevillano Carbajal, *¿La España de quien? Ingleses, franceses y alemanes en este país* (Madrid, Feb. 1936), 49, 130, 164, 184.

7. Consul Otto Köcher, Barcelona, to GFM, Dis. 409, 27 June 1935, GFM, microcopy T-120, serial 8425, frame E593094.

8. The Auslandsorganisation (AO), the party agency responsible for the Germans living in Spain, reported 12,000-15,000. Erwin Burbach, Berlin, to ambassador in Spain, 12 Aug. 1937, GFM, 4365/E082875-81. The new German ambassador, Eberhard von Stohrer, quoted these figures to the Foreign Ministry: monthly report, Stohrer to GFM, 25 Oct. 1937, in *DGFP*, Ser. D, 3, doc. 455.

9. Head of the German School in Barcelona, Kurt Harrass, to DAI, Stuttgart, 9 Mar. 1940, DAI Records, microcopy T-81, serial 829, frames 5403163-64.

10. See first document in file, trip of Capt. Canaris, OKM Docs. (microfilmed), Brit. accession no. PG 48903, microcopy T-1022; memo, State Secretary Carl von Schubert, 13 Jan 1925, GFM, 4596/E187722.

11. Canaris, Madrid, to GFM, Dis. A 32173, n.d. (received 27 Nov. 1916),

ACP, microcopy T-149, reel 357, frames 00299-302; published in Viñas, *Alemania*, 1st ed., appendix doc. 1. The first edition of *Alemania* (1974) gives a fuller account about Canaris than the second edition (1977).

12. Viñas, *Alemania*, 1st ed., documents trips by Canaris to Spain: first and second trips, pp. 29-30; third (1922), 32; fourth and fifth (1925), 40, 42; sixth (1926), 47-49; seventh, eighth, and ninth (1927), 62, 65, 66; tenth (1928), 70; and eleventh (1930), 74.

13. Memo, Capt. Walther Lohmann, chief of Naval Transport Department, Naval Staff in Reichswehrministerium, to State Secretary Wilhelm Kempner, Reich Chancellery, 29 Mar. 1926, GFM, 4530/141228-38.

14. For more information, see Vice Adm. Kurt Assmann and Vice Adm. Walter Gladisch, "The Operational and Tactical Considerations of the German Navy and the Consequent Measures Taken for Its Expansion between 1919-1939," *Nazi Conspiracy and Aggression*, vols. 1-8, supplements A and B (Washington, D.C., 1946-48), supp. A, doc. D 854; Capt. Adalbert Schuessler, *The Fight of the Navy against Versailles, 1919-1935* (Berlin: OKM, Navy Manual 352, 1937); extract in "Leeb Case," *TWC*, vol. 10, doc. C-156; Chargé Völckers, Madrid, to GFM, dis. 3186, 20 Sept. 1934, GFM, 8410/E592449-56.

15. Memo, Ambassador Welczeck, Madrid, 26 Jan. 1933, GFM, 6140/E459445-48; Welczeck to GFM, dis. 250, 27 Jan. 1933, GFM, 6140/E459142-44; memo [Adm. Heusinger von Waldegg?] to GFM. B.Z./5181/33g. Kdos,. 22 Feb. 1933, GFM, 6140/E4591616-62.

16. On early war plans, see D.C. Watt, "Appeasement: The Rise of a Revisionist School?" *Political Quarterly* 36 (Apr.-June 1965): 191-213, 204. For more on German war plans, see OKM Docs., files PG 31058, PG 34017, PG 34056, PG 34061, PG 34334, PG 34562; MFA/II M 57/66, and MFA/II M 58/3; Carl-Axel Gemzell, *Raeder, Hitler und Skandinavien: Der Kampf für einen maritimen Operationsplan* (Lund, Sweden, 1965), 31, 42-46.

17. Canaris, Fleet Command Kiel, to Chief of Navy Raeder, rep. 708/33 A G. Kdos., 6 Sept. 1933, OKM Docs., PG 33418.

18. Adolf Hitler, *Hitler's Secret Book* (New York, 1961), 209.

19. Ambassador Welczeck, Madrid, to Head of Western European Desk, Gerhard Köpke, tel. 32, 26 Apr. 1934, GFM, 8411/E592499; Welczeck to GFM, tel. 36, 2 May 1935, GFM, 8411/E592500.

20. Rosenberg conversation with Hitler, 16 Sept. 1940, *Das politische Tagebuch Alfred Rosenbergs, 1934/35 und 1939/40* (Göttingen, 1956), 123.

21. Interrogation of José Antonio by Republican police, Alicante, Nov. 1936, ed. and introd. by Ricardo de la Cierva, "El interrogatorio de José Antonio," *Historia y Vida* 88 (July 1975): 50-63, 56.

22. Jorge Vigón, *General Mola: El conspirador* (Barcelona, 1957), 174-75.

23. Viñas, *Alemania*, 2nd. ed., 322-24; Luis Bolín, *Spain: The Vital Years* (London, 1967), 52; Robert A. Friedlander, "Great Power Politics and Spain's Civil War," *Historian* 28 (Nov. 1965): 77-79.

24. Christopher Fiessler, Seville, to GFM, 27 July 1936, GFM, 3371/E010615; Vice Consul Wegener, Tetuán, to GFM, 24 July 1936, *DGFP*, ser. D, 3, doc. 6; Viñas, *Alemania*, 2nd ed., 337-43; Hans-Henning Abendroth, "Die deutsche Intervention im spanischen Bürgerkrieg," *Vierteljahreshefte für Zeitgeschichte* 30 (Jan. 1982): 117-29; and Abendroth, *Mittelsmann zwischen Franco und Hitler:*

Johannes Bernhardt erinnert 1936 (Markthedenfeld, 1978), 36 (hereafter cited as *Bernhardt*).

25. Ernst Bohle, chief of the Auslandsorganisation, to Foreign Ministry's Protocol Department, 7 July 1939, with enclosure, 5 July 1939, editor's note, *DGFP*, ser. D, 3: 1-2. For complete text, see GFM, 5448/E356185-90, See also memo, Hans Dieckhoff, director of Political Department, GFM, Berlin, 25 July 1936, *DGFP*, ser. D, 3, doc. 10; [Cmd. Pistorius], Berlin, rep. OKM A VI S 4385/39, "Tätigkeitsbericht der Schiffahrts Abteilung (OKM A VI) im Dienste des Sonderstabes W während des Spanienkrieges 26-7-1936 bis 1-6-1939," OKM Docs., PG 80769, microcopy T 1022 (hereafter cited as "Pistorius Report"). The Ju. 52 D-APOK left Tetuán at 5:50 A.M. and arrived in Seville at 6:36 A.M. on 23 July. Flight rep. commanders of African Air Force, Cmd. Julio García de Cacéros, Tetuán, to General of African Army [Franco], 23 July 1936, Cuartel General de Generalísimo, CGG, shelf 6, bundle 316, file 1. For Bernhardt's account, see Viñas, *Alemania*, 1st. ed., 411-19; also, Hans-Henning Abendroth, *Hitler in der spanischen Arena: Die deutschspanischen Beziehungen im Spannungsfeld der europäischen Interessen-Politik von Ausbruch des Bürgerkrieges bis zum Ausbruch des Weltkrieges 1936-1939* (Paderborn, 1973), 33 n 95.

26. Author's interview with former State Secretary for Air Erhard Milch, Düsseldorf, 6 July 1971; Viñas, *Alemania*, 1st ed., 409-11, 418, 427.

27. Viñas, 2nd ed., 338, 343; Abendroth, *Bernhardt*, 36.

28. Interview of Bernhardt by Leonard Horwin, 27 March 1946, enclosed in rep., Commercial Attaché Harold Randall, Madrid, to Secretary of State, dis. 1876, 30 March 1946, DS, Decimal File 800.515/3-3046.

29. Hellmuth Wilberg, "Auf geheimen Befehl," *Der Adler*, 8 (Sonderheft Legion Condor an die Front, 1 June 1939): 8; testimony of Col. Erwin Jaenecke to Soviet government, 24 May 1946, in "Dokumente über Franco und sein Regime," *Beilage zur Neuen Zeit*, no. 13 (1 July 1946), 10; Counselor Alexander Kirk, Berlin, to U.S. Secretary of State Hull, dis. 1005, 16 June 1939, DS, 852.00/9262; British Air Attaché Captain J.L. Vachell, Berlin, to FO, memo 549/39, 13 June 1939, FO, Record Group 371, vol. 24120, W 9431/5/41, London. The U.S. naval asst. attaché, Lt. Cmd. P.E. Pihl, Berlin, also sent a detailed report, 13 June 1939, to ONI, Registration File 15373E-c-10-j. Bernhardt told Abendroth in 1976 that Franco asked for only ten Ju 52s and received only ten (Abendroth, *Bernhardt*, 56).

30. "Pistorius Report," June 1939, OKM Docs., PG 80769. Bernhardt told Abendroth that Hitler conferred with Göring and Blomberg at 1:30 A.M. on 26 July (Abendroth, *Bernhardt*, 36).

31. There is no collection of Sonderstab W records, but scattered copies of reports exist. For example, in 1938 its personnel included Air Force Gen. Karl Schweikard, who replaced Wilberg, Majors Scheer and Karmainski of the army, and Lt. Cmdr. Müller of the navy. Officer list, OKW (WZ) to Economic Staff, 600/38 g., 1 Dec. 1938, OKW, microcopy T-77, serial 28, frames 738536-49,49.

32. Interview of Milch by Whealey, 6 July 1971, Düsseldorf.

33. Chief of Sonderstab W. Gen. Schweikard to GFM, dis. 6415/39 g., 27 April 1939, GFM, 4366/E082304-08.

34. "Pistorius Report," June 1939, OKM Docs., PG 80769.

35. Wilberg, *Der Adler*, 1; Milch "Merkbuch," 27 July 1936, MS found in military archives at Freiburg, Germany, Militärgeschichtliches Forschungsamt (hereafter cited as MFA); Viñas, *Alemania*, 2nd ed., 337-45.

36. [Commander of African Air Force, Cmd. Julio] García de Caceros, Tetuán, to [General of African Army, Franco], reports, 28 and 29 July 1936, CGG, shelf 6, bundle 316, file 1. R. Dan Richardson, "The First Military Aircraft: Wings over the Straits of Gibraltar," *Aerospace Historian* 34 (June 1987): 19-23, emphasizes Franco's originality in starting the airlift on 20 July with two or three of his own planes before the arrival of foreign aircraft.

37. "Legion Condor," *Die Wehrmacht* (7 June 1939), 4-8.

38. Gen. Karl Schweikard, "Zu dem Stand der Bearbeitung der Geschichte der Legion Condor," *MS.* (Berlin, Luftwaffe, 8 Mar. 1940), MFA/II L 234/75, vol. 1, 1-26.

39. Raymond Proctor, *Hitler's Luftwaffe in the Spanish Civil War* (Westport, Conn., 1983), 36.

40. Schweikard, "Zu dem Stand," 66-68.

41. Testimony, Warlimont at Nürnberg, 21 June 1948, "U.S. Army, Nurnberg Trials," "Leeb Case," microcopy edition M 898, reel 8, transcript of trial.

42. "Pistorius Report," June 1939, OKM Docs.; testimony, Jaenecke, *Neue Zeit*, 1 July 1946, 9-14. The name *"Legion Condor"* originated with the Spaniards and is not, therefore, "Legion Kondor" or "Condor Legion." Milch used the term in his calendar diary on 7 Nov. 1936. Milch, "Merkbuch," MS in MFA.

43. Report A, 1392, OKM Operations, Adm. Günther Guse to Commander of Spanish squadron, 19 Sept. 1936, OKM Docs., PG 33308, p. 16.

44. Manfred Merkes, *Die deutsche Politik gegenüber dem spanischen Bürgerkrieg 1936-1939*, 2nd ed. (Bonn, 1969), annex 7, lists all the code names, but he is vague about the sources and some of the dates. In the air force records, "Luftübung Rügen" referred to the entire German operation in Spain, including support for Franco's army.

45. Henry Buckley, *Life and Death of the Spanish Republic* (London, 1940), 203; Geneviève Tabouis, *They Called Me Cassandra* (New York, 1942), 297; Julio Alvarez del Vayo, *Freedom's Battle* (London, 1940), 17; *La Voz*, Madrid, 1 Feb. 1936, p. 5, col. 3, reported from Lisbon that Sanjurjo was leaving Portugal for Germany on that date; Ramón Garriga, *Las relaciones secretas entre Franco y Hitler* (Buenos Aires, 1965), 77-78.

46. *Pravda*, 12 Mar. 1936, p. 5, col. 5, cited by Marion Einhorn, *Die ökonomischen Hintergründe der faschistischen deutschen Intervention in Spanien 1936-1939* (East Berlin, 1962), 84.

47. Copy of text (address by General Reichenau to National Socialist party, Leipzig, June 1938, in English), sent to Lord Halifax by MP Ellen Wilkinson, British Cabinet Papers, Cabinet 64/19.

48. *New Republic*, 25 Nov. 1936, pp. 95-96, citing *The Week*. Later in 1936, the FO and U.S. State Department picked up the testing and training story from the German military. British Military Attaché Col. F. Elliot Hotblack to FO, Berlin, 16 Dec. 1936, FO/371, vol. 20590, W 18862/9549/41; Ambassador William E. Dodd, Berlin, to Hull, 14 Dec. 1936, *FRUS*, 1936, 2:612. See also Abendroth, "Deutsche intervention," 126; testimony, Jaenecke, *Neue Zeit* 1 July 1946, 10. The Legion Condor in 1936 was seriously interested in technical lessons; the best account of these is Edward L. Homze, *Arming the Luftwaffe* (Lincoln, Neb., 1976), 172-73.

49. Adolf Hitler, *Mein Kampf* ([1925] New York, 1939), 809, 986.

50. Neurath conversation with Italian Ambassador, 2 May 1935, *DGFP*, ser. C, vol. 4, doc. 63.

51. Robert H. Whealey, "Mussolini's Ideological Diplomacy: An Unpublished Document," *Journal of Modern History* 39 (Dec. 1967): 432-37; Jens Peterson, *Hitler-Mussolini: Die Entstehung der Achse Berlin-Rom* (Tübingen, 1973); Wolfgang Schieder and Christof Dipper, eds., *Der spanische Bürgerkrieg in der internationalen Politik 1936-1939* (Munich, 1976), 91-94; Donald M. McKale, *The Swastika outside Germany* (Kent, Ohio, 1977), 27.

52. *DGFP*, ser. C, vol. 4, docs. 63, 487, 497, 506.

53. Ambassador Ulrich von Hassell, Rome, to GFM, 6 Jan. 1936, ibid, doc. 485; memo, Hassell conversation with Führer, 20 Jan. 1936, ibid, doc. 506.

54. Text of speech by Hitler, 25 May 1935, *DGFP*, ser. C, vol. 4, p. 171.

55. There is no record of the text, but the agreement was made between 24 May and 1 June 1935, ibid, p. 328 n 2.

56. Memo by Hassell of conversation, Italian Ambassador Attolico, Foreign Minister Neurath, and Hitler, 20 Feb. 1936, ibid., doc. 575; Hassell to GFM, 22 Feb. 1936, ibid., doc. 579.

57. Ambassador Bernardo Attolico in talks with GFM in May 1936, Elizabeth Wiskemann, *The Rome-Berlin Axis: A History of the Relations between Hitler and Mussolini* (London, 1949), 57.

58. Counselor Kurt Reith, Paris, to GFM, dis. A 3397, 5 Nov. 1926, GFM, L187-L055921-22. Mussolini proclaimed his Mediterranean ambitions as early as May 1919: McGregor Knox, "Conquest, Foreign and Domestic in Fascist Italy and Nazi Germany," *JMH* 56 (Mar. 1984): 17 n 56.

59. Raffaele Guariglia, *Ricordi, 1922-1946* (Naples, 1950), appendix B, conversation of Foreign Minister Fulvio Suvich with Spanish ambassador, Rome, 3 Sept. 1932.

60. Text and comments by William C. Askew, "Italian Intervention in Spain: The Agreements of March 31, 1934, with the Spanish Monarchist Parties," *JHM* 24 (June 1952): 181-83.

61. Massimo Mazzetti, "I Contatti del governo italiano con i conspirator Militari Spagnoli prima del lugio, 1936," *Storia Contemporena* (Dec. 1979), 1186.

62. Testimony of Capt. Mario Petrangnani, 2 Feb. 1945, Italy, *Il processo Roatta, I documenti*, 2nd. ed. (Rome, 1945), 1:35-57.

63. Italian citizen Giuseppi Pontoni, Longerone, to Mussolini, 16 Nov. 1937, Duce Files, microcopy T-586, container 1062, frames 063004-14.

64. Douglas W. Foard, "The Forgotten Falangist: Ernesto Gimenez Caballero," *Journal of Contemporary History* 10 (Jan. 1975): 3-18, 10.

65. For more details, see Stanley G. Payne, *Falange: A History of Spanish Fascism* (Stanford, Calif., 1961), and Herbert R. Southworth, "The Falange: An Analysis of Spain's Fascist Heritage," in Paul Preston, ed., *Spain in Crisis: The Evolution and Decline of the Franco Regime* (New York, 1976), 1-22.

66. Chef de Cabinet in Ministry of Popular Culture, Celso Luciano, Rome, to Italian consul and press attaché, Amedeo Landini, Paris, 3 June 1935, Min. Cult., container 472, frame 042121.

67. Luciano to Landini, monthly payments from 28 July 1935 to 3 Jan. 1936, ibid., frames 472/042122-28; 4 Feb.-1 July 1936, frames 042129-33, 41 (see appendix A for inflation and real values).

68. Mazzetti, "Contatti," 1186-87.

69. Pedro Sáinz-Rodríguez, *Testimonio y recuerdos* (Barcelona, 1978), 232-86.

70. Ibid., 385.
71. Manlio Gabrielli, *Una Guerra Civile per la liberta: La Spagna degli anni '30 alla luce degli anni '60* (Rome, 1966), 11.
72. John F. Coverdale, in *Italian Intervention in the Spanish Civil War* (Princeton, 1975), 57, 60, 62-63, uses unpublished Italian Foreign Ministry and naval archives but reports nothing on Italian intervention plans, even as late as 13 July 1936.
73. They arrived on 21 July and talked to the foreign minister on 22 July. Bolín, *Vital Years*, 167-68.
74. Ibid., 10-11; Whealey, "Economic Influence," 235.
75. Possibly on 20 July, but more probably on 21 July for the first time; second time on 23 July. Col. Emilio Faldella [formerly in Italian military intelligence], Rome, to José Luis Alcofar Nassaes, *La marina italiana en la guerra de España* (Madrid, 1976), 37-38.
76. For the foreign minister's worries, see Sáinz, *Testimonio*, 235. For the War Ministry's opposition, see Alcofar, *Marina*, 37.
77. Sáinz, *Testimonio*, 386. On March's aid, see Whealey, "Economic Influence," 235.
78. Roberto Cantalupo, *Fu la Spagna* (Milan, 1948), 63; Bolín, *Vital Years*, 52-53, 167-90; Robert A. Friedlander, "The July 1936 Military Rebellion in Spain: Background and Beginnings," Ph.D. diss. (Northwestern University, June 1963), 215-25. His later article changes the tone and emphasis; there Hitler followed Mussolini. Friedlander, "Great Power Politics," 77-78. His original work is better in light of Bolín. Coverdale, *Italian Intervention*, 3, follows Bolín, *Vital Years*, 60, 70-71. Bolín was Franco's messenger to the Duce. Coverdale also employs two other weak Italian sources but adds nothing new from the Italian Foreign Ministry archives on this vital issue. The difficulty with all the memoirs is that the date of Mussolini's decision, 25-27 July, is left hazy.
79. Interview of Milch by Whealey, Düsseldorf, 6 July 1971. Also interview of Helmuth Wohlthat by Whealey, New York, 3 Jan. 1970. There is some vague documentation that Hans Frank may have been Hitler's liaison to Rome in July (see below, chap. 3, n. 31).
80. Norman H. Baynes, ed., *The Speeches of Adolf Hitler*, 2 vols. (London, 1942), 2:1674.
81. Memo, conversation of Ciano with Hassell, 26 July 1936, *Ciano's Diplomatic Papers* (London, 1948), 20-21; Whealey, "Mussolini's Diplomacy."
82. The nine Italian planes arrived in Melilla at 9 A.M. on 30 July. Radio report, Melilla, to Army of Africa [Franco], Tetuán, 30 July 1936, CGG, shelf 6, bundle 316, file 52. The first Italian crew ready for operations arrived in Tetuán from Melilla at 7:07 P.M., 31 July. Flight log, chief of African Air Force, Cmd. García, month of July, Tetuán, to Army of Africa [Franco], ibid., file 1.
83. On 29 July, the Ju 52s made two trips across the straits; on 30 July, four; 31 July, two; 1 Aug., two; 2 Aug., two; but on 3 Aug., missing or no flights. On 4 Aug., three Sa 81s made one reconnaissance flight; and as of 12 Aug., twenty-three Sa 81s had made seven reconnaissance flights for the month of August; ibid., file 2. Franco, in his own hand, complained that the Italian planes were paralyzed because of mechanical trouble and could not engage in combat bombing. Moreover, the Italians lacked quality gasoline. Radio, Franco to Mola, 1 Aug. 1936, ibid., bundle 337, file 35.

84. Vice Consul Wegener, Tetuán, to GFM, 3 Aug. 1936, *DGFP*, ser. D, vol. 3, doc. 27.

85. Memo, Duce's private secretary, "Weapons for Spain," Rome, 23 Sept. 1936, Duce Files, 1062/062961-65.

86. "Pistorius Report," June 1939, OKM Docs., file PG 80769.

87. Minister Franticek Chvalkovsky, Rome, to Czech Foreign Minister Kamil Krofta, political report 146, 5 Aug. 1936, GFM, 1809/413290-91 (see Bibliographical Note below, p. 221).

88. Memo, state secretary in Reich Chancellery, Otto von Meissner, to GFM, 3 Aug. 1936, GFM, 3236/D700759; Meissner to GFM, 7 Aug. 1936, GFM, D700760.

89. Memo, conversation of Canaris with Roatta, Bolzano, 4 Aug. 1936, OKM Docs., file PG 80604 (see also above, pp. 95-101).

90. José Ignacio Escobar (Marqués de Valdeiglesias), *Así empezó* (Madrid, 1974), 118.

91. Radio message in Franco's hand (Badajoz?) to Mola (Valladolid?), 3 Aug. 1936, CGG, shelf 6, bundle 337, file 35; Mola to Franco, 3 Aug. 1936, CGG, shelf 1, bundle 40, file 40; Mola, Burgos, to "a Spanish personality" (Agramonte? or Spanish military attaché), Berlin, 3 Aug. 1936, OKM Docs., file PG 80786.

92. Mola told this to his unofficial roving ambassador to France and Germany on 12 Aug. in Burgos. Escobar, *Así empezó*, 119.

93. Fernando de los Ríos, Paris, to Giral, 25 July 1936, with copy to Chargé General Faupel by General Franco, 2 Dec. 1936, GFM, 649/255382-88. Also see Thomas, *Spanish Civil War*, 350; *DDF*, 3:52; William Foss and Cecil Gerahty, *The Spanish Arena* (London, 1938), 322; Director of Political Affairs Robert Coulondre, Paris, to Foreign Minister Yvon Delbos, 23 July 1936, unsigned minute, 24 July 1936, *DDF*, ser. 2, vol. 3, doc. 17, 25; Consul Wegener, Tangier, to GFM, 24 July 1936, *DGFP*, ser. D, vol. 3, doc. 7.

94. Testimony of Léon Blum to French Chamber of Deputies, 23 July 1947, *Rapport fait au nom de la commission chargée d'enquêter sur les événements survenus en France de 1933 à 1945*, 1947 session, Annexes, 1:215-20 (hereafter cited as *Evénéments*).

95. Louis Levy, *The Truth about France* (London, 1941), 113; dateline London, *New York Times*, 25 July 1936, p. 3, col. 7.

96. *The Memoirs of Anthony Eden, Earl of Avon: Facing the Dictators* (Boston, 1962), 456.

97. M.D. Gallagher, "Léon Blum and the Spanish Civil War," *JCH* 6 (July 1971); Thomas, *Spanish Civil War*, 334; Eugen Weber, *Action Française* (Stanford, Calif., 1962), 382; Joel Colton, *Léon Blum: Humanist in Politics* (New York, 1966), 237-42; Jean Lacouture, *Léon Blum* (New York, 1982), 307-26.

98. Naval Attaché Capt. T.E. Chandler, Paris, to ONI, 28 July 1936, ONI Docs., 15373 D—C-10-j.

99. Memo of Sir George Mounsey, Western Department, 23 July 1936, with minute of legal officer, seen by Under State Secretary Sir Robert Vansittart and Eden on 24 July, FO/371, vol. 20524, W 6996/62/41.

100. "In July," Bismarck, London, to State Secretary Dieckhoff, 3 Nov. 1936, GFM, 387/211435-39.

101. Thomas Jones, *A Diary with Letters, 1931-1950* (Oxford, 1954), 231.

102. Ambassador Welczeck to GFM, 23 July 1936, 9:35 A.M., *DGFP*, ser. D, vol. 3, doc. 3; copy to Reich War Ministry Auslands Abteilung 1 [Canaris], OKM Docs., PG 80785; Welczeck to GFM, dis. A 3158, 23 July 1936, GFM, 1819/415889-91; dateline Paris, 25 July, *New York Times*, 26 July 1936, p. 24, col. 1.

103. Chargé Bismarck to GFM, telegram 150, 25 July 1936, GFM, 649/255309.

104. Secretary E. Harold Bielfeld, London, to GFM, enclosure to report A 3036, 29 July 1936, GFM, 3610/E026937-45.

105. Weber, *Action Française*, 382; George Windell, "Léon Blum and the Crisis over Spain, 1936," *Historian* 24 (August 1962): 423-49; Gallagher, "Leon Blum," 56-64; David Carlton, "Eden, Blum and the Origin of Non-Intervention," *JCH* 6 (July 1971): 40-55; also Carlton, *Anthony Eden: A Biography* (London, 1981), 86-92; Jill Edwards, *The British Government and the Spanish Civil War, 1936-1939* (London, 1979), 15-30; Lacouture, *Blum*, 307-26.

106. Pertinax [A. Geraud], *The Gravediggers of France* (Garden City, N.Y., 1944), 433; Nathanael Greene, *Crisis and Decline: The French Socialist Party in the Popular Front Era* (Ithaca, N.Y., 1969), 78-89; Carlton, "Eden, Blum," 49; Gallagher, "Léon Blum," 62; Glyn Stone, "Britain, Non-Intervention and the Spanish Civil War," *European Studies Review* (Jan. 1979), 129-49.

107. Delbos to Auriol, 26 July 1936; Delbos to Ambassador in Spain, Jean Herbette, 27 July 1936, *DDF*, vol. 3, docs. 33, 34; David W. Pike, *Conjecture, Propaganda, and Deceit and the Spanish Civil War: The International Crisis over Spain, 1936-1939, as Seen in the French Press* (Stanford, Calif., 1968).

108. *The Diplomatic Diaries of Oliver Harvey, 1937-1940*, ed. John Harvey (London, 1970), 249 (hereafter cited as *Harvey Diaries*); Robert Manne, "British Decision for Alliance with Russia, May 1939," *JCH* 9 (July 1974): 3-26.

109. Report of conversation by Rear Adm. Jean Decoux, London, 5 Aug. 1936, *DDF*, vol. 3, doc. 87; Lacouture, *Blum*, 324. The British Foreign Office does not have a Chatfield report but does have a memo of a conversation between Darlan and Vice Adm. Andrew Cunningham, chief of the Mediterranean Fleet, and a memo of First Lord of the Admiralty Sir Samuel Hoare, both on 5 Aug. 1936, FO/371, vol. 20527, W 7781/62/41.

110. Minute by Hoare, ibid.

111. Pierre Cot, *Triumph of Treason* (New York, 1944), 340-46; Léon Blum, testimony, 23 July 1947, *Evénéments*, 218; Cot, "Ce que fut la 'NonIntervention' relachée," *Le Monde*, 21 Nov. 1975.

112. Aide memoire by Portuguese embassy to Seymour, 27 July 1936, minuted by Seymour, Mounsey, Sir Robert Vansittart, and Eden, 29 July, FO/371, vol. 20513, W 7070/933/36.

113. The French text to Britain, Delbos, 2 Aug. 1936, *DDF*, vol. 3, doc. 59; to Germany, 4 Aug. 1936, *DGFP*, ser. D, vol. 3, Doc. 29. The note was drafted and dictated by Foreign Minister Yvon Delbos and Under State Secretary Alexis Léger on 31 July and 1 Aug. John Dreifort, *Yvon Delbos at the Quai d'Orsay* (Manhattan, Kans., 1973), 43; Mounsey received the note on 2 Aug. from the French ambassador and sent it to Deputy Foreign Secretary Lord Halifax, FO/371, vol. 20526 W 7504/62/41. Winston Churchill to Corbin, 31 July 1936, and Churchill to Eden, 7 Aug. 1936, in Martin Gilbert, ed., *Winston S. Churchill*, vol. 5 (Boston, 1977): 307;

private secretary of Eden, Oliver Harvey, *Harvey Diaries* (Mar. 18, 1937), 29. Eden conversation with British Labour party, 19 Aug. 1936, memo, FO/371, vol. 20534, W 9331/62/41; copy to prime minister, PM 1/360.

114. Delbos to Ambassador Charles Corbin, London, 2 Aug. 1936, Delbos to Auriol, 3 Aug. 1936, *DDF*, vol. 3, docs. 59, 66.

115. Corbin to Delbos, 10 Jan. 1937, *DDF*, vol. 4, doc. 271; Spanish Ambassador Luis Araquistain, Paris, to Blum, 13 Feb. 1937, ibid., doc. 441.

116. Pablo D. Azcárate, *Mi embajada en Londres durante la guerra civil española* (Barcelona, 1976), 265.

117. Fritz Hesse, who was a DNB reporter and was privy to Ribbentrop's thinking, believed Hitler's major motive was to weaken France on its southern frontier: *Hitler and the English* (London, 1954), 28. According to Erich Kordt, a member of Ribbentrop's staff and in the London embassy, Hitler preferred the Popular Front government in France as a strain on Anglo-French relations. Hesse, *Nicht aus den Akten* (Stuttgart, 1950), 151.

118. David T. Cattell, *Communism and the Spanish Civil War*, vol. 1 (Berkeley, Calif. 1956), and vol. 2, *Soviet Diplomacy and the Spanish Civil War* (1957); Burnett Bolloten, *The Grand Camouflage: The Communist Conspiracy in the Spanish Civil War* (New York, 1961); 2nd ed. titled *The Spanish Revolution: The Left and the Struggle for Power during the Civil War* (Chapel Hill, N.C. 1979). In 1986 he came out with a third edition, too late for me to use. Neither of these accounts puts any stock in the official justification of Franco and the generals that starting the civil war was necessary to prevent Spain from going communist. Cattell, *Communism*, 1:39-40, 42; Bolloten, *Spanish Revolution*, 11-13, 104-05 n. 6. Stanley G. Payne, *The Spanish Revolution* (New York, 1970), is both the most anti-Russian and the most anti-revolutionary account of the three. E.H. Carr, *The Comintern and the Spanish Civil War*, ed. Tamera Deutscher (New York, 1984), and Jonathan Haslam, *The Soviet Union and the Struggle for Collective Security in Europe, 1933-1939* (New York, 1984), add further Soviet sources.

The basic Soviet account is edited by Academia Nauk CCCP, *Solidarnost Narodov s ispanskoi Respublucoi* (Moscow, 1972) (hereafter cited as *Solidarnost*). It has chapters on twenty-two countries that participated in the International Brigades. The chapter "USSR" (pp. 225-58) is most revealing and includes fifty-five footnotes, seven of which refer to Soviet archives. There is also an English translation, *International Solidarity with the Spanish Republic, 1936-1939* (Moscow, 1975). See also Janet M. Hartley, "Recent Soviet Publications on the Spanish Civil War," *European History Quarterly* 18 (Apr. 1988): 243-48.

Angel Viñas made a major contribution to understanding the Soviet intervention in his *El oro español en la guerra civil* (Madrid, 1976). He was the first, and thus far only, person to use the archives of the Banco de España. Angel Viñas, *El oro de Moscú: Alfa y omega de un mito franquista* (Barcelona, 1979), adds to and subtracts from *Oro español* in a somewhat revised edition. Scholars need both works.

119. Salvador de Madariaga, *Spain: A Modern History* (New York, 1958), 145; Gerald Brenan, *The Spanish Labyrinth*, 2nd ed. (Cambridge, 1950), 224-26.

120. James Joll, "The Making of the Popular Front," in *Decline of the Third Republic* (London, 1959), 36-66; Ronald Tiersky, *French Communism, 1920-1972* (New York, 1974), ch. 3; Jonathan Haslam, "The Comintern and the Origins of the Popular Front, 1934-1935," *Historical Journal* 22 (Sept. 1979): 673-94; Helen Graham and Paul Preston, eds. *The Popular Front in Europe* (New York, 1987), chs.

4 and 5. Despite a promising and good bibliography, Larry Ceplair, *Under the Shadow of War: Fascism, Anti-Fascism and Marxists, 1918-1939* (New York, 1987), adds little to the Spanish story but has a chapter on the French Popular Front. For the text of the Spanish Popular Front program, see *El Socialista*, 16 Jan. 1936, reprinted in *La preguerra española en sus documentos* [1923-1936] (Barcelona, 1970), 404-11.

121. On communist fronts, see Robert Carew-Hunt, "Willi Münzenberg," in *International Communism*, St. Antony Papers, no. 9 (Carbondale, Ill., 1960), 72-87; Jorgen Schleimann, "The Organizational Man: The Life and Work of Willi Münzenberg," *Survey*, no. 55 (Apr. 1965), 64-91; Helmut Gruber, "Willi Münzenberg: Propagandist for and against the Comintern," *International Review of Social History* 10, pt. 2 (1965): 188-210; Babette Gross, *Willi Münzenberg: A Political Biography* (East Lansing, Mich., 1974). For fronts in Spain, see dis. 2660, Ambassador Welczeck, Madrid, to GFM, 22 July 1933, GFM, L 187/L05679-82; *Times* (London), 12 July 1933, p. 13; Bolloten, *Spain and Left*, 131-32. For the attitude toward communism of Manuel Azáña, president of Spain, see Bolloten, *Spanish Revolution*, 443, 452, 466.

122. Often alleged but mostly undocumented. For allegations, see an unsigned research paper written in the spring of 1939 by the Press Department of the German Foreign Ministry, claiming the Spanish Communist party received $65,000 per year in 1935 and 1936 from Moscow: "Beitritt Spaniens zum Anti-Kominternpakt," copy to Ambassador Stohrer, received 23 Apr. 1939, GFM, 462/225750-82, frame 225773. The Italian press attaché in Paris reported to Rome that an employee in the Soviet embassy in Paris had told him that Moscow had sent 80 million francs ($13 million) to the Spanish Communists: report, 17-18 Aug. 1936, Min. Cult., 418/008755-60. Angel Herrera, vocal Catholic editor of *El Debate*, told the British ambassador at the beginning of 1936 that Russians had sent 2 million pesetas ($260,000) for the upcoming elections: Sir Henry Chilton, Madrid, to FO, 7 Jan. 1936, FO/371, vol. 20519, W 342/62/41. The figures do not add up, and none of these observers was in a position to know definitely.

123. Javier Tusell, *Las elecciones de Frente Popular* (Madrid, 1971), 2:83.

124. Cattell, *Communism*, 39-40, 42; Bolloten, *Spanish Revolution*, 104-05. Even conservative Spanish historians who defended the Franco regime eventually repudiated the charge of a leftist revolutionary plot. Ricardo de la Cierva, *Historia ilustrada de la guerra civil española* (Madrid, 1970), 12. See Arthur F. Loveday, *World War in Spain* (London, 1939), appendix 2, for the original Nationalist charge. For a comprehensive study of the phony Soviet plot, see Herbert R. Southworth, "Conspiración contra la República," *Historia 16*, 3, no. 26 (June 1978): 41-57.

125. There are few historians who directly contradict each other as much as Richard A.H. Robinson and Paul Preston. Both claim to tell what exactly went on in Spain from February 1936 to 18 July 1936 but the stories differ greatly. Compare Robinson's more conservative account with Preston's: Robinson, *The Origins of Franco's Spain: The Right, the Republic and Revolution, 1931-1936* (Pittsburgh, Pa., 1970), ch. 6; Preston, *The Coming of the Spanish Civil War: Reform, Reaction and Revolution in the Second Republic, 1931-1936* (New York, 1978), ch. 7. Aviva and Isaac Aviv, "The Madrid Working Class, the Spanish Socialist Party and the Collapse of the Second Republic (1934-1936)," *JCH* 16 (April 1981): 229-50, is closer to Preston than to Robinson. What is clear is the growing polarization between the Catholics and the rich on one side and the Socialists and the poor on the other.

126. In addition to Robinson and Preston, see Brenan, *Labyrinth*, ch. 13; Madariaga, *Spain*, bk. 2, ch. 6; Thomas, *Spanish Civil War*, chs. 11, 12, and 13; Gabriel Jackson, *The Spanish Republic and the Civil War, 1931-1939* (Princeton, N.J., 1965), ch. 11; Bolloten, *Spanish Revoluion*, ch. 1; Martin Blinkhorn, *Carlism and the Crisis in Spain, 1931-1939* (Cambridge, England, 1975), ch. 10; Payne, *Falange*, ch. 9; Payne, *Spanish Revolution*, ch. 9; Raymond Carr, *The Spanish Tragedy: The Civil War in Perspective* (London, 1977), ch. 6; Ronald Fraser, *Blood of Spain: An Oral History of the Spanish Civil War* (New York, 1979), ch. 2; Juan Linz, "The Breakdown of Democratic Regimes: Crisis, Breakdown and Re-equiliberation," in *Fascism: A Readers Guide: Analysis, Interpretation, Bibliography* (Berkeley, Calif., 1976), pt. 1, 1-124, pt. 2, 142-215. All discuss the developing Spanish crisis in the sprng of 1936.

127. Most of the above authors cite the statistics of Gil Robles, a right-wing partisan who gave a speech in the Cortes on 16 June 1936, alleging that 269 people had been victims of political murder and 251 churches had been burned since the February elections. Payne cites leading Francoist historian Eduardo Comin Colomer, who claims to have seen police statistics to the effect that 215 people were killed between 17 Feb. and 17 July. Stanley G. Payne, *Politics and Society in Twentieth Century Spain*, (New York, 1976), 138. Now that the Spanish archives are opening up, an analysis should be made, province by province, of civil guard records and the provincial press to discover exactly who was responsible for what.

128. First proclaimed by George Orwell, *Homage to Catalonia* (London, 1938), and well documented by Bolloten, *Spanish Revolution*. Bolloten's first version, *Grand Camouflage*, is even more revolutionary in tone.

129. Gruber, "Willi Münzenberg," 193, 198-99; Walter Kritvitsky, *In Stalin's Secret Service* (New York, 1939), 78. For a revealing comment by Karl Radek about Stalin's conservative attitude toward revolution in Spain, see Chargé Jean Payart, Moscow, to Delbos, 2 Oct. 1936, *DDF*, vol. 3, doc. 310.

130. For France, counselor [Dirk Forster?], Paris, to GFM, rep. A 3209, 1 Aug. 1936, GFM, 655/257371; for Belgium, Counselor Brauer, Brussels, to GFM, tel. 40, 2 Aug. 1936, GFM, 655/257372-73.

131. Joaquín Arrarás, ed., *Historia de la Cruzada española* (Madrid, 1940), 38:99; Thomas, *Spanish Civil War*, 214, 232; Jean Creach, *Le Monde*, 20-21 Dec. 1950; *Le Matin*, 6 Aug. 1936; (dateline Paris), *New York Times*, 7 Aug. 1936, p. 3, col. 3; ibid., 11 Aug., p. 2, col. 4. The Comintern did publish a report on July 21 that the World Committee against War and Fascism called for solidarity with Spain. Haslam, *Collective Security*, 10.

132. U.S. naval attache report, Cmd. T.E. Chandler, Paris, to ONI, 4 Aug. 1936, ONI Docs., 15373D—C-10-j, quoting the French right-wing *Le Matin*.

133. Janet Flanner, *Men and Monuments* (New York, 1957), 38-39, says Malraux left on 20 July. Jean Lacouture, *André Malraux* (New York, 1975), 237, says he left on 21 July.

134. André Malraux, *Man's Hope* (New York, 1938), 96; tel., U.S. navy U.S.S. *Quincy*, Spanish waters, to U.S. State Department, received 14 Aug. 1936, DS, 852.00/2589; uncensored report, Madrid via Hendaye, 17 Aug., *New York Times*, 18 Aug. 1936, p.2, col. 2, 26 Aug. 1936, p.3, col. 3.

135. Margaret Slaughter, "Italian Antifascism: The Italian Volunteers in the Spanish Civil War" (Ph.D. diss., University of New Mexico, 1973), 48.

136. Paris report, A 3209, 1 Aug., 1936, GFM, 655/257371.

137. Walter Ulbricht, *Zur Geschichte der deutschen Arbeiterbewegung: Aus Reden und Aufsätzen*, 2 (Berlin, 1954): 223-24.

138. Village of Cérèbère, France, 10 Aug., *New York Times*, 11 Aug. 1936, p.2, col. 3; ibid., 19 Aug. 1936, p. 2, col. 5; Casanova [pseud.], "Ce que fut le role des volontaires," *La Lutte Ouvrière*, no. 114, 24 Mar. 1939; Mary Low and Juan Brea, *Red Spanish Notebook: The First Six Months of the Revolution and the Civil War* (London, 1937), 7, 69, 148; *John Cornford: A Memoir* (London, 1938), 199; Carlo Rosselli, "The Diary of a Militiaman," in Francis Keene, ed., *Neither Liberty Nor Bread: The Meaning and Tragedy of Fascism* (New York, 1940), 253.

139. Cattell, *Communism*, 70.

140. The British tapped the telephone of Auriol, the French minister of finance, and learned that he gave direct orders for arms delivery to the last Republicans defending Irún. Ambassador Sir Henry Chilton, Hendaye, to FO, 8 Sept. 1936, FO/371, vol. 20576, W 10993/9549/41. For testimony of a French customs official, see Greene, *Crisis and Decline*, 89. Pike, *Conjecture*, 48, cites a French War Ministry document of 4 Sept. 1936 from Paris to the Haute Garonne region to make sure that the border patrols "were not too efficient"; also see Lacouture, *Blum*, 345.

141. On 12 Sept., according to Haslam, *Collective Security*, 115; on 14 Sept., according to Whealey, "Economic Influence," 241. Viñas, *Oro de Moscú*, 152-55, concluded that the USSR sent its first military aid in September. The Comintern met 18 Sept. in Moscow and heard reports from André Marty and Jules Duclos from Spain. E.H. Carr, *Comintern*, 20.

142. Viñas, *Oro español*, 152-55; Willard C. Frank, "The Soviet Navy and the Spanish Civil War," in David H. White, ed., *Proceedings of the Conference on War and Diplomacy, 1976* (Charleston, S.C. 1976), 68; Gabrielli, *Guerra*, 44-47.

143. Gabrielli, *Guerra*, 47.

144. See Whealey, "Economic Influence," 242.

145. The $755 million is a maximum: Viñas, *Oro español*, 499. Viñas, in *Oro de Moscú*, 437, says perhaps $744 million. The problem is that figures for Republican exports that supplemented the gold are in doubt. Gold bullion worth $207 million was sent directly to Paris: Viñas, *Oro español*, 66. To this, add $20 million in silver coins transported to the U.S. and France, plus $3 million in precious metals and jewels collected from private sources (ibid., 447), and possibly another $7 million generated by exports (ibid., 448, based on very shaky statistics) for the total of $237 million.

146. For the amount sent to the USSR by Spain, see Viñas, *Oro español*, 210 n 66; as 510 tons, ibid., 201-03. For the amount sent by Moscow to Paris, see ibid., 236-37, 242 n 83, 244 n 84, 249. The $340 million was used until April 1938.

147. The original CAMPSA, the Spanish oil monopoly, had contracts in the Soviet Union through petroleum purchases. Some twelve file boxes of CAMPSA Gentibus's documents, mostly for 1938, are located at the Foreign Ministry archive, MAE, Archivo General de Alcalá (MAE/AGA), boxes 5192-5204.

148. The $131.5 million used in 1937 in Moscow is cited in Viñas, *Oro español*, 236-37. The $85 million credit is claimed by the Soviet Foreign Ministry, cited in *Solidarnost*, 240 n 31. A British Communist also cites this: Andrew Rothstein, *The Munich Conspiracy* (London, 1958), 33. All the $131.5 million was used by the end of 1937. In March 1938, the USSR began utilizing another $36.2

million in gold, part of which was spent in Moscow: Viñas, *Oro de Moscú*, 403. Apparently the $85 million in supplies were gradually extended on credit by the Soviets from about June 1938 to about November 1938, after they exhausted Spain's gold reserves: ibid., 410. Also, only part of this was spent in Moscow.

149. Details are developed by R. Dan Richardson, *Comintern Army: The International Brigades in the Spanish Civil War* (Lexington, Ky., 1982).

150. Whealey, "Economic Influence," 229-35.

151. Whealey, "How Franco Financed His War, Reconsidered."

152. *Solidarnost*, 255. Republican War Minister Indalecio Prieto told a British air force officer there were fewer than 300 Russians in Spain. Cmd. R.V. Goddard to Walter Roberts, 15 Mar. 1938, FO/371, W3987/1245/41. Negrín told one of Britain's League of Nations Withdrawal Commission delegates, R.C. Skirine Stevenson, that the maximum number of Russians ever in Spain was 850 and that there were none on 25 Nov. 1938: ibid., W 16041/29/41.

153. Report on the first planes by French air attaché to Ambassador Jean Herbette, San Sebastián, 6 Oct. 1936, *DDF*, vol. 3, doc. 316. This was also admitted by Soviet Consul Vladimir Antonov-Ovseenko to German Consul Otto Köcher, Barcelona, to GFM, dis. 730, 12 Oct. 1936, GFM, 6488/E 486036-40); Consul Norman King, Barcelona, to FO, 10 Oct 1936, FO/371, vol. 20580, W 13371/9549/41. For Portuguese, Italian, and Soviet confirmation that Russian airmen were already in Spain in September, see Gabrielli, *Guerra*, 47, and Frank, *Proceedings*, 68.

154. Patrick Laureau, "L'Aviation Sovietique en Espagne en 1936 L'Echelon Precurseur," *Melanges de la case de Velazquez* 21 (Paris, 1985): 318-19, 328.

155. Most of the sources cite 60 percent, which apparently originated with the official Communist International. Ex-brigader William Herrick claims this was part of the official down-playing of communist intervention by Moscow and that, from his observations, the Communist Party membership in U.S. units was over 90 percent (statement to Conference on Spanish Civil War at Siena College, N.Y., June 1986).

156. Thomas, *Spanish Civil War*, 455; Jef Last, *The Spanish Tragedy* (London, 1939), 83; Robert G. Colodny, *The Struggle for Madrid: The Central Epic of the Spanish Conflict* (New York, 1958), 60.

157. Andreu Castelles, *Las Brigadas Internacionales de la guerra de España* (Barcelona, 1974), 380-82

158. The conservative is Andreu Castelles; the liberal is Hugh Thomas, *Spanish Civil War*, 982-83.

159. See ch. 5, p. 103, above.

160. Shannon E. Fleming, "A Firm Bulwark for the Defence of Western Civilization: The Nationalists' Uses of the Moroccan Protectorate during the Spanish Civil War" (paper, AHA Conference, Chicago, Dec. 1986).

161. E.H. Carr, *Comintern*, 58, cites a Soviet source published in 1981.

162. See ch. 5, p. 103.

163. Whealey, "Economic Influence," 243-46.

164. The frontier was closed on 13 June. Robert H. Whealey "Foreign Intervention in the Spanish Civil War," in Raymond Carr, ed., *The Republic and the Civil War in Spain* (New York, 1971), 226 n 28; Anthony Adamthwaite, *France and the Coming of the Second World War* (London, 1977), 188.

165. Aide to U.S. naval attaché, Lt. Cmd. R.H. Hillenkoetter, Paris, to ONI, 1 Aug. 1938, ONI Docs., 176212B C-10-a.

166. Viñas, *Oro de Moscú*, 406-07. Circumstantial evidence leads me to believe that Stalin concluded that the Republicans would lose by November 1937. Then his hopes revived briefly from March to April 1938 while Blum ruled France for the second time. Whealey, "Foreign Interventions," 225-26. But some Soviet aid continued to the end of the war.

Chapter 2. The Ideology of Anticommunism

1. Summary of interrogation of Herbert von Dirksen by DeWitt C. Poole, Wiesbaden, 8-13 Sept. 1945, "Reports on Interrogations of German Prisoners of War," made by members of the U.S. Department of State, National Archives (interrogations hereafter cited as "Poole Mission").

2. According to a typed MS by Raumer written in 1955, "Aufzeichnung über die Jahre 1935-38 im Büro Ribbentrop," cited in Theo Sommer, *Deutschland und Japan zwischen den Mächten 1935-1940: Vom Antikominternpakt zum Dreimächte Pakt* (Tübingen, 1962), 27.

3. L. Ohata and F. Fokushiro, "The Anti-Comintern Pact, 1935-1939" in James W. Morley, ed., *Deterrent Diplomacy: Japan, Germany, and the USSR, (1935-40)*, (New York, 1977), 29-32.

4. Ribbentrop, memo for the Führer, Berlin, 16 Aug. 1936, GFM, 3245/ E000071-72. Also see Gerhard Weinberg, "Die Geheimen Abkommen zum Anti-Kominternpakt," *Vierteljahreshefte für Zeitgeschichte* 2 (Apr. 1954): 193-201.

5. Sommer, *Deutschland und Japan*, 33; Frank Iklé, *German-Japanese Relations, 1936-1940* (New York, 1956), 29, 35.

6. Ohata and Fokushiro, "Anti-Comintern Pact," 35.

7. Raumer to Hitler, 19 Nov. 1936, GFM, 3245/E000085; text, *DIA*, 297-300. Matzuoka, Japan's foreign minister, 1940-41, in Nov. 1936 called the Spanish Civil War the best example of "communist subversion." Yosuke Matzuoka, *Die Bedeutung des Deutsch-Japanischen Abkommens gegen die Kommunistische Internationale* (Tokyo, [1939-1940]), 13.

8. Alan Bullock, *Hitler: A Study in Tyranny* (New York, 1962), 317, 492, 513-15; Gerhard L. Weinberg, *The Foreign Policy of Hitler's Germany* (Chicago, 1970), 1: 5 n 13, 75.

9. Both Mussolini and Göring echoed this contempt at their meeting in Rome, Jan. 1937. Paul Schmidt, *Hitler's Interpreter* (London, 1950), 63.

10. Chargé Alexander Kirk, Rome, to Secretary Hull, 8 Aug. 1936, *FRUS*, 1936, 2:435; conversation, U.S. Ambassador William C. Bullitt with Italian Ambassador in Paris, to Hull, 27 Nov. 1936, ibid., 576-77; *New York Times*, 16 Nov. 1936, p. 41, col. 1; 21 Nov. 1936, p. 1, col. 7.

11. Quoted as 30 Jan. 1939 in Einhorn, *Faschistische deutsche Intervention*, 106.

12. Langenheim, Tangier, to Göring, 29 July 1936, *DGFP,* ser. D, vol. 3, doc. 16.

13. Albert Speer, *Spandau* (New York, 1976), 167.

14. Bullock, *Hitler*, 128, 334, 354, 377, 489; Baynes, *Speeches of Hitler*, 1: 665; 2: 993, 1271, 1293.

15. Kurt G.W. Ludecke, *I Knew Hitler* (London, 1938), 492.

16. Bullock, *Hitler*, 234.

17. Ambassador Dodd, Berlin, to Hull, 8 Mar. 1936, *FRUS*, 1936, 1:215-16; Vojtech Mastny, Berlin, to Czech Foreign Ministry, report 55, 1 June 1936, GFM, 1809/473162-84.

18. Memo of conversation by Otto von Meissner, 9 June 1936, *DGFP*, ser. C, vol. 5, doc. 362.

19. British under state secretary in the Foreign Office, Sir Robert Vansittart, in the first week of August 1936, FO/371; French Ambassador François-Poncet, Berlin, to Delbos, 7 Aug. 1936, DDF, vol. 3, doc. 100; Bismarck, London, to Dieckhoff, 7 Oct. 1936, GFM, 387/211432-34; to Adm. Nicholas Horthy, regent of Hungary, 23 Aug. 1936, Emil Vadney (Vienna, 23 Aug. 1936), *in New York Times*, 24 Aug. 1936, p. 3, col. 1; *Ciano's Diplomatic Papers* (7 Sept. 1936), 35-38; Hitler's speech to the public justifying extension of military conscription (24 Aug. 1936), Baynes, *Hitler's Speeches*, 2: 1327; Hitler to François-Poncet, 2 Sept. 1936, and François-Poncet, Berlin, to Delbos, 10 Oct. 1936, *DDF*, vol. 3, doc. 334; Hitler's memo for speech delivered 9 Sept. 1936 as justification for introducing the economic planning of the Four-Year Plan, n.d. (Aug. 1936], *TWC*, vol. 21, doc. NI 4955; Hitler to Michael Cardinal Faulhauber, 4 Nov. 1936, in Guenter Lewy, *The Catholic Church and Nazi Germany* (New York, 1964), 207; Hitler to Austrian State Secretary Guido Schmidt, 19 Nov. 1936, and Reichs Chancellor Otto von Meissner to Foreign Minister Neurath, 20 Nov. 1936, *DGFP*, ser. D, vol. 1, doc. 181; discussion with Lord Lothian, 4 May 1937, text printed as Appendix III b in J.R.M. Butler, *Lord Lothian* (New York, 1960). Also see Lothian memo to Chamberlain, 11 May 1937, PM 1/215, London, PRO.

20. Memo of conversation, Berlin, 19 Nov. 1937, *DGFP*, ser. D, vol. 1, doc. 31; Earl of Birkenhead, *The Life of Lord Halifax* (London, 1965), 231, 368. Halifax informed others of Hitler's convincing anticommunism. *Harvey Diaries* (5 Dec. 1937), 63; *'Chips': The Diaries of Sir Henry Channon*, ed. Robert Rhodes James (London, 1967), 5 Dec. 1937, 108; Lois G. Schwoerer, "Lord Halifax's Visit to Germany: November 1937," *Historian* 32 (May 1970): 353-75.

21. Memo of conversation, Hitler and Chamberlain, signed by interpreter Paul Schmidt, 1 Oct. 1938, *DGFP*, ser. D, vol. 4, doc. 247; Chamberlain, minute, 30 Sept. 1938, *DBFP*, vol. 2, doc. 1228.

22. Chamberlain's talk with Hitler, 30 Sept. 1938, FO/371, vol. 22661, W 13353/86/41; Chamberlain to George VI, 30 Sept. 1938, in John Wheeler-Bennett, *King George VI: His Life and Reign* (New York, 1958), 346-47.

23. Note, Alexis Léger, undersecretary of state, Paris, 7 Dec. 1938, *DDF*, vol. 13, doc. 58.

24. Hitler's two-hour speech, *On National Socialism and World Relations* (Berlin, 1937), 8, 10, 32, 33, 35. Also see Bullock, *Hitler*, 365. A list of complete biographies is in John Hiden and John Farquharson, *Explaining Hitler's Germany: Historians and the Third Reich* (Totowa, N.J., 1983).

25. Charles A. Micaud, *The French Right and Nazi Germany* (Durham, N.C., 1943), 116, 120; Martin Gilbert and Richard Gott, *The Appeasers* (Boston, 1963), 7-8, 26-28, 51-52, 240; Margaret George, *The Warped Vision: British Foreign Policy, 1933-1939* (Pittsburgh, 1965), 146-53.

26. See SS Rec., microcopy T-175, serial 287.

27. On the basis of examination of all promising serials about the SS and the Gestapo available on microfilm (T-175), the German reports expressed a vague anxiety, rather than conveying accurate information, about what Spanish communists were actually doing. The serials scanned included sixty-three German Foreign Ministry files (T-120) dealing with communism, Marxism, and socialism in the USSR, Spain, France, and Czechoslovakia in the decisive months before July 1936. Sixty-seven additional serials, covering the broad period from 1931 to 1935, were also examined. In the SS Records, forty-one serials were examined.

28. Chargé Hans Völckers to GFM, dis. 1300, 24 Apr. 1936, GFM, 8400/ E592318-20.

29. The agents were Vittorio Codovilla and Boris Stepanov. Jesus Hernández, ex-Communist editor of *Mundo Obrero*, the major Spanish Communist daily, says Codovilla was an Italian: *La grande trahison* (Paris, 1953), 12; Bolloten, *Spanish Revolution*, 133 n 77, cites Enrique Castro, another ex-Communist, and says Codovilla was an Argentine.

30. Schwendemann, Madrid, to GFM, copy to OKM, tel. 63, 1 Aug. 1936, OKM Docs., PG 80785.

31. This section's German title was Referat Deutschland (hereafter cited as Ref. D.). Legation Counselor Emil Schumberg, Ref. D., to Vico von Bülow-Schwante, Ref. D., 19 Nov. 1936, GFM, 1949/436413-14.

32. Counselor Dr. Hans Röhreck, Ref. D., to Welczeck, Madrid, tel. 4, 19 Jan. 1934, GFM, 8411/E592569; Röhreck to Liaison NSDAP and SS Untersturmbahnführer Christen Scholtz, 28 Mar. 1934, ibid., 8411/E592483.

33. Dr. Friedrich Mahlo, propaganda ministry, to GFM, memo II 2407, 10 Jan. 1936, GFM, 1949/436409-10; Goebbels to Ribbentrop, memo II 2407/26, 8 Dec. 1936, GFM, 1949/436426-27. Professor Vincente Gay met Goebbels in September 1929 and later published a book in Spanish about the "new Germany," cited in Z.A.B. Zeman, *Nazi Propaganda* (London, 1964), 89.

34. Dr. Adolf Ehrt [editor for the Anti-Komintern], *Der Weltbolschewismus: Ein internationales Gemeinschaftswerk über die bolschewistiche Wühlarbeit und Umsturzversuche der Komintern in allen Ländern* (Leipzig, 1936). It was published early in 1936, before the civil war. Julia Sywottek, *Mobilmachung für den totalen Krieg* (Opladen, 1976), 110, 114-18, has more general discussion of Goebbels's anticommunist propaganda techniques for the 1936-1939 period.

35. Propaganda ministry (n. s.) to German embassy in Madrid, memo II 3/11, 5 June 1936, GFM, 347/201133.

36. Zeman, *Nazi Propaganda*, 85. Noteworthy in the *Goebbels Diary, 1939-1941* (London, 1982) is how utterly indifferent the private Goebbels was toward the concepts of communism, Marxism, or revolution. The few references to bolshevism refer to Russian ignorance or deliberate Russian lying.

37. State Secretary Bernhard von Bülow to Welczeck, Madrid, 20 Mar. 1928, GFM, 6141/E459192-98.

38. This early Abwehr project was described in a later dispatch: Welczeck, Paris, to GFM, dis. A 490, 3 Feb. 1937, GFM, 1104/319170-73.

39. Does the Pentagon or the CIA still hold captured Abwehr records from World War II on Communist agents?

40. Vico von Bülow-Schwante, Ref. D., to State Secretary B. von Bülow, 14 Mar. 1935, GFM, 6141/E459241-42.

41. Ibid.

42. Bülow-Schwante, GFM, to Department I Leg. Rat Ludwig Mayr, 4 May 1936, GFM, 6987/E52262.

43. German embassy, Madrid, to Spanish minister of state, note verbale 121, 13 June 1936, GFM, 4410/E0837838.

44. One great problem with documentation is that there is strong evidence that some of the special files of the Gestapo on Spanish Communists for 1936 were destroyed or not released. Compare SS Rec. 283/277816-34; 289/2784746; 291/2787485-506; 318/28192936-64; 301/2799304,2798327; 490/9351711-2140; 379/2895216.

45. Gestapo Section II/121, n.s., "Monthly Report on the Leftist Movement in June 1936," SS Rec. 291/2787485-506, 500.

46. SS Ob. Sbf. Heinrich Müller to Walther Hindrichs, Ref. D., GFM, rep. II 512, 5 Aug. 1936, GFM, 4853/E2477467; Müller to Bülow-Schwante, GFM, rep. SPP/II J 2033/36 g., 24 Nov. 1936, GFM, 4853/E247748-49.

Viñas interprets these documents differently. He implies that Winzer wanted to observe the tactics of "the Third International," implying the Spanish Communist party. Viñas, *Alemania*, 2nd. ed., 249-53. If so, Winzer apparently discovered little or nothing. In contrast to the German lack of interest in Spain at this time, the Gestapo were closely watching activities of French Communists. See Counselor Forster, Paris, dis. A 552, 19 Sept. 1936, GFM, 303/186785-803. For Gestapo reports on the democratic socialists in Paris, see reports of Ob. G. fü. Werner Best to Comrade Schimpke, Leiter Hauptbüro, GFM, in GFM, 1568/379488-92, 379500, 379516-27, 379542, 379581-83, 379609, 379620-21; also GFM serials 1573 and K 2151; and SS Rec. serials 283 and 490.

47. Schwendemann, Madrid, to GFM, tel. 75, 25 July 1936, GFM, 4853/E247746.

48. SS Ob. Sbf. Müller to Counselor Hindrichs, Ref. D., GFM, rep. II 512, 5 Aug. 1936, GFM, 4853/E247746.

49. As an example, see Phillips, Rome, to Hull, 7 and 12 Jan. 1937, *FRUS*, 1937, 1: 216, 227.

50. Memo by Friedrich Gaus, Legal Dept., Berlin, 7 Jan. 1937, *DGFP*, ser. D, vol. 3, doc. 189; Galeazzo Ciano, *Ciano's Hidden Diary, 1937-1938* (New York, 1953), 23 Aug. 1937, 10 July 1938, 3, 9, 135; *Ciano's Diaries, 1939-1943* (New York, 1946), 5 Jan. 1939, 6.

51. On domestic questions, a Hitler-Mussolini alliance would have been feasible even in the early 1920s. For early Nazi-Fascist contacts, see Alan Cassels, "Mussolini and German Nationalism, 1922-1925," *JMH* 35 (June 1963): 137-57; and Alan Cassels, *Mussolini's Early Diplomacy* (Princeton, N.J., 1970).

52. *Times* (London), 15 Apr. 1933, 9.

53. Ibid., 30 May 1933, 15.

54. Philip V. Cannistraro and Edward D. Wynot, Jr., "On the Dynamics of Anti-Communism as a Foundation of Fascist Foreign Policy, 1933-1943," *Politico* 38 (Dec. 1973): 653. Cannistraro uses Italian archives.

55. Seppo Kuusisto, *Alfred Rosenberg in der nationalsozialistis Aussenpolitik 1933-39* (Helsinki, 1984), 122, 131.

56. Ibid., 375-80.

57. Memo, Rudolf Likus, Nürnberg, 15 Sept. 1935, GFM, 43/28665.

58. *DGFP*, ser. C, vol. 4, docs. 63, 109, 121, 164, 485, 575.

59. Canaris to GFM, Abw. Abt. Chef 22/35 Kdos, 19 Sept. 1935, GFM, 5573/ E399912-17.

60. By courier, Bülow-Schwante to Hassell, ambassador in Rome, 27 Nov. 1935, GFM, 8039/E578219.

61. Minute on program, printed schedule of visit, Berlin Doc. Cent. Rec., roll 71, order 338; memo, Counselor Schumberg, Ref. D., to Pol II, It., 6 Apr. 1936, GFM, 1104/319096-100.

62. Memo, Schumberg, Ref. D., to Reichs Minister Neurath, 26 Oct. 1936, GFM, 1104/319104-110.

63. Text, Hitler-Ciano Protocol, *DGFP*, ser. C, vol. 5, doc. 624.

64. Cannistraro and Wynot, "Anti-Communism," 660.

65. Hitler's anticommunist propaganda has been interpreted differently by Abendroth, *Hitler*, 19, 28-31, 59-61, 68, and Merkes, *Bürgerkrieg*, 34, 36, 59. These two leading West German conservative historians of the Spanish Civil War explain the behavior of the government of the Third Reich as "sincerely" anticommunist. For them, Hitler's anticommunism was more than propaganda. They quote at face value Hitler's many denunciations of bolshevism, almost as if the mere reiteration of the word justified the military intervention of the Legion Condor in the Spanish Civil War. Another interpretation of Hitler's behavior is that he was essentially nihilistic and was a great improvisor, rather than at times having a definite plan. For this view, see Schieder and Dipper (especially the chapter written by Schieder), *Der spanische Bürgerkrieg*, 168.

66. See list of biographies of Francisco Franco y Bahamonde in Robert H. Whealey, "Franco," in *Historical Dictionary of the Spanish Civil War*, ed James Cortada (Westport, Conn., 1982) (hereafter cited as *Historical Dictionary*); and bibliography in Stanley Payne, *The Franco Regime, 1936-1939* (Madison: Univ. of Wisconsin Press, 1987).

67. According to his cousin, Franco voted for Monarchists in April 1931: Francisco Franco Salgado-Áraujo, *Mi vida junto a Franco* (Barcelona, 1977), 93, 122, 124.

68. Bolín, *Vital Years*, 10-11.

69. Juan Vidal, CHADE, Brussels, to U.S. ambassador in San Sebastián, copy to British FO, 27 May 1939, FO/371, vol. 24130, W 9137/8/41.

70. Besides Friedlander, "July Rebellion," and Preston, *Coming of War*, ch. 7, see also Blinkhorn, *Carlism*, 238, 241, 247.

71. Emilio Mola-Vidal, *Memorias*, 2nd ed. (Barcelona, 1977 [originally published 1932]), 42-65.

72. Copy of report on criminal policy (signature illegible), Berlin, to GFM, Political Dept. Spain II, n.d. (cover letter dated 26 Feb. 1931), GFM L 187/ L05257-60.

73. Salgado, *Vida*, 126.

74. To Manuel Portela Valladares. Francisco Franco Salgado, *Mis conversaciones privadas con Franco* (Barcelona, 1976). These are diaries rather than memoirs and are based on conversations with a much older Franco, thirty years after the key events (see entry for 9 Mar. 1968, p. 523).

75. Letter to Santiago Casares Quiroga. Document printed in Joaquín Arrarás, *Francisco Franco*, 9th ed. (London, 1938), 160-63. This was the first official biography of Franco, originally published in Burgos in 1937 and translated into many languages. Franco told journalist Valenti Galarza in August 1937 that the

assassination of Calvo Sotelo on 12-13 July was decisive for his decision. José Gil-Robles, *No fué posible la paz* (Buenos Aires, 1968), 780.

76. Salgado, *Vida*, 108; Salgado, *Conversaciones* (27 Mar. 1967), 499.

77. Sáinz, *Testimonio* (Barcelona, 1978), 340-41.

78. What Franco thought of Catholicism is discussed in George Hills's admiring *Franco* (London, 1967), 229-304. For more critical views see Norman Cooper, "The Church: From Crusade to Christianity," in Paul Preston, ed., *Spain in Crisis* (New York, 1976), 48-81; Frances Lannon, "The Church's Crusade against the Republic," in Paul Preston, ed., *Revolution and War in Spain, 1931-1939* (New York, 1984), 35-58; Stanley Payne, *Spanish Catholicism: An Historical Overview* (Madison, Wis., 1984), chs. 6 and 7. Despite its title, the introduction of Javier Tusell, *Franco y los católicos: La política interior española entre 1945 y 1947* (Madrid, 1984), 17-24, covers the years 1936-1937.

79. Radio, Franco, Tetuán, to Commander of Civil Guard, Almería, 21 July 1936, CGG, shelf 6, bundle 337, file 7.

80. Salgado, *Vida*, 137; Salgado, *Conversaciones* (Apr. 1968), 526.

81. Chief of Staff, n.s., Army of the South [Tetuán], to commander of Santa Cruz de Tenerife, 30 July 1936, CGG, shelf 1, bundle 47, file 91.

82. He told the German consul in Tetuán on 24 July that he was fighting "a Soviet dictatorship": *DGFP*, ser. D, vol. 3, doc. 7; also see Bernhardt's interview with Angel Viñas in 1977 edition of Viñas, *Alemania*, 324.

83. Bolín, *Vital Years*, 171.

84. For Bolín's views on communism, see ibid., 67, 112, 149-51, 154, 214.

85. Pike, *Conjecture*, 39; *New York Times*, 30 July 1936 (dispatched 29 July), p. 2, col. 6.

86. Draft, n.s.; English text enclosed with letter, Portago, Hotel Dorchester, to Bolín [Seville?] 18 Aug. 1936. Franco approved this and made a similar declaration to Herbert Knickerbocker of International News Service: Bolín to Portago, n.d. (27 Aug.?) 1936, CGG, shelf 1, bundle 54, file 27.

87. Memoirs of chief of military intelligence abroad, José Bertrán y Musitu, *Experiencias de los Servicios de Información del Nordeste de España* (Madrid, 1940), 151.

88. The letter is handwritten in bad French, probably by a radio clerk, and was dispatched through Franco's High Commissioner for Morocco, Gen. José Millán Astray, n.s. [Franco] to Pétain, n.d. [Aug. 1936], CGG, shelf 1, bundle 40, file 33.

89. Speech, Franco, Tenerife, 18 July 1936, in *Partes oficiales de guerra 1936-1939*, ed. Col. José María Gárate Córdoba, SHM, 1 (Madrid, 1977): 2-3; *La guerra de España en sus documentos*, ed. Fernando Díaz-Plaja, 1 (Barcelona, 1970): 11-13. This is dated 17 July and reported in *ABC* (Seville) on 23 July. See also Salgado, *Conversaciones*, 499, 524, 526.

90. Col. Faldella, Rome, n.d. [1972-1975], to Alcofar: Alcofar, *Marina*, 101.

91. After Bernhardt had this interview at Cáceres, Nicolás Franco on Sept. 27 announced to Bernhardt Franco's favorable decision. Bernhardt and Warlimont immediately flew to Berlin. On 28 Sept. Bernhardt told Göring, who then told the delighted Führer. Abendroth, *Bernhardt*, 49-53.

92. Lt. Col. [Villanueva?], Sect. II, Hq Generalissimo (Intelligence), Salamanca, to Sect IV (supply), 7 May 1937, CGG, shelf 11, bundle 563, file 109.

93. Whealey, "Franco."

94. See Serrano's memoirs on Spanish fascism, mentioned in Conclusion, above. For a liberal critic of Serrano, see memo, n.s., "The Legal Position of the Spanish Falange," n.d. [1944?], U.S. Department of Justice, Record Group 60, Latin America Section, National Archives, Washington D.C., box 9, file "South American Falange," 26, 27, 33, 35.

Chapter 3. The Diplomacy of the Anti-Comintern Bloc

1. Memo by Canaris, 5 Aug. 1936, OKM Docs. PG 80604.
2. Hesse arrived in Rome on 22 or 23 Aug. Col. Faldella to Alcofar [1972-1975?], Alcofar, *Marina*, 67.
3. Michaelis Meir, "La prima missione del principe de Assia presso Mussolini Agosto '36," *Nuova rivista storica* 55 (May-Aug. 1971), docs. on pp. 369-70.
4. Memo of conversation with Raeder, Dieckhoff, Berlin, 22 Aug. 1936, with annex, memo for Hitler on Spain, *DGFP*, ser. D, vol. 3, doc. 50.
5. Gen. Schweikard, Sonderstab W, 8 Mar. 1940, MFA/II L234/75, vol. 1, p. 66; Adm. Guse, OKM, to Spanish squadron, rep. A/392, 19 Sept 1936, OKM Docs., PG 33308, p. 16; Proctor, *Luftwaffe*, 46.
6. Warlimont interrogation, Oberursel, 17 Sept. 1945, "Poole Mission"; Einhorn, *Faschistische deutsche Intervention*, 119.
7. Testimony, Col. Faldella, who went on the Warlimont-Roatta mission, in Alcofar, *Marina*, 67.
8. Memo, Duce's private secretary, n.s., "Spanish Question: Activities of the SIM," Rome, n.d. [23? Sept. 1936], Duce Files, 1062/062956-60.
9. Interrogation of Warlimont, 17 Sept. 1945, "Poole Mission."
10. Ibid.; memo, Sept. 1936, Duce Files, 1062/062956-60; tel., Col. [Francisco Martín Moreno], chief of staff, Cáceres, to Mola, 8 Sept. 1936, CGG, shelf 1, bundle 41, file 94.
11. Col. Alfred Jodl to commander of the army, memo, W.A. 1686/36 geh. L I a, 8 Sept. 1936, OKH Docs., 328/6321191.
12. According to Col. Faldella: Alcofar, *Marina*, 68.
13. Rep. no. 4, "Guido" [Warlimont], [Salamanca], to Gen. Wilberg, 10 Oct. 1936, OKM Docs., PG 80777; also enclosure 3 dated 13 Oct., chart of organization. Warlimont's point of view is expounded in Proctor, *Luftwaffe*, 71-78, 259-60.
14. Testimony, Warlimont at Nürnberg, 21 June 1948, "U.S. Army, Nurnberg Trials," "Leeb Case" microcopy edition M 898, reel 8.
15. Sáinz, *Testimonio*, 385.
16. Coverdale, *Italian Intervention*, 133; Vice Consul Alan Hillgarth, Palma de Mallorca, to Consul King, Barcelona, and Eden, memo 3, 26 Aug. 1936, FO/371, vol. 20537, W 10418/62/41.
17. Rear Adm. [D.F. Sommerville?], British observation squadron [Crus. H.M.S. *Galatea*?] [Tangier], to Admiralty and FO, received 15 Aug. 1936, FO/371, vol. 20531, W 8759/62/41.
18. Consul Hans Dede, Palma de Mallorca, to GFM, dis. 421, 26 Sept. 1936, GFM, 1547/376029.
19. According to testimony of a Spanish Republican refugee to the Spanish

consul in Oran, published in *La Claridad*, 3 Oct. 1936, translated by GFM, in GFM, 1547/376023-28.

20. Memo, Duce's private secretary, n.s., "Weapons for Spain," Rome, [23? Sept. 1936] Duce files, 1062/062961-65. The British calculated 24 planes and 100 Italians by the end of October. H.M.S. *Shropshire*, Palma de Mallorca, to Admiralty and FO, received 9 Nov. 1936, FO/371, vol. 20551, W 16999/62/41.

21. Memo, "Spanish Question: Activities of the SIM," [23 Sept. 1936], Duce Files, 1062/062956-60. The German naval attaché in Spain later discusses Ferretti in connection with the Balearic Island operations. Naval Attaché Cmdr. Meyer-Döhner, San Sebastián, to Cmd. Mirow, chief of Attaché Group, OKM, rep. 307, 27 Mar. 1939; ibid., rep. 607 g., 3 July 1939, OKM Docs., PG 80730. According to Meyer-Döhner, Ferretti had served in the Balearic Islands from September to December 1936. His wife was originally from Mahón, Minorca. In early 1939 he served at Taranto, Italy. Adm. Juan Cervera-Valderrama, *Memorias de guerra: Mi labor en el estado mayor de la armada afecto al cuartel general del generalísimo durante la Guerra de Liberación Nacional 1936-1939* (Madrid, 1968), 28.

22. Hillgarth to King and Eden, memo 5, 29 Aug. 1936, FO/371, vol. 20538, W 10865/62/41; Hassell to Foreign Ministry, 20 Dec. 1936, *DGFP*, ser. D, vol. 3, doc. 158.

23. Coverdale, *Italian Intervention*, 134.

24. Willard C. Frank, in "Naval Operations in the Spanish Civil War, 1936-1939," *Naval War College Review* 37 (Jan.-Feb. 1984): 30, says the first Italian naval commander on Mallorca was Capt. Carlo Margottini.

25. Memo, "Weapons for Spain," Duce Files, 1062/062961-65. Additional figures from Spanish Archives are in Jesús Salas-Larrazábal, *La intervención extranjera en la guerra de España* (Madrid, 1974), 318-21.

26. "Pistorius Report," June 1939, OKM Docs., PG 80769.

27. Pedrazzi to Ciano, 8 Sept. 1936, in Italian Foreign Ministry records, cited by Coverdale, *Italian Intervention*, 120-21.

28. Ambassador Sir Eric Phipps, Berlin, to FO, 7 Jan. 1936, FO/371, vol. 19938, C 145/145/18.

29. Memo, Ciano conversation with Frank, 23 Sept. 1936, *Ciano's Diplomatic Papers*, 43-48; memo by Frank, *DGFP*, ser. C, vol. 5, doc. 553.

30. See note 29, above.

31. Gerhard L. Weinberg says Frank visited Rome in late July: *Foreign Policy of Hitler's Germany*, 1:333; Meir says Frank visited in April: "La prima missione," 369.

32. Minister Hans Georg von Mackensen, Budapest, to Neurath, 14 Oct. 1936, *DGFP*, ser. C, vol. 5, doc. 600; Mackensen, Rome to GFM, 24 Mar. 1939, *DGFP*, ser. D, vol. 6, doc. 86.

33. Milch, "Merkbuch," 15 and 18 Oct. 1936, MFA; also Minister Chaval-kovsky to Krofta, political rep. 169, 17 Oct. 1936, GFM, 1809/413299-300; note by Hassell, n.d. [Nov. 1936], GFM, 3793/E042492.

34. Memo, Ciano conversation with Neurath, Berlin, 21 Oct. 1936, *Ciano's Diplomatic Papers*, 52-55; memo, Ciano conversation with Hitler, Berchtesgaden, 24 Oct. 1936, ibid., 55-60; text, protocol, 23 Oct. 1936, *DGFP*, ser. C, vol. 5, doc. 624.

35. Memo, Ciano, conversation with Hitler, Berchtesgaden, 24 Oct. 1936, *Ciano's Diplomatic Papers*, 56-60.

36. Neurath to all German diplomatic missions in Europe, circular tel., 30 Sept. 1936, *DGFP*, ser. D, vol. 1, doc. 1. Between Ciano's Oct. 1936 visit and Mussolini's Sept. 1937 visit, Göring visited Italy in Jan. 1937: ibid., docs. 204-08; and Neurath visited Rome in May 1937: *DGFP*, ser. C, vol. 6, docs. 347, 350.

37. *Ciano's Hidden Diary* (11 Feb. 1938), 73.

38. Ibid. 24 Feb. 1938, 80.

39. Blomberg to Canaris, 30 Oct. 1936, enclosure, Neurath to Hassell, *DGFP*, ser. D, vol. 3, doc. 113; Abendroth, *Hitler*, 63.

40. Memo, Ciano, conversation with Hitler, 24 Oct. 1936, *Ciano's Diplomatic Papers*, 55-60.

41. Texts of the original plans have been lost. Referred to in Col. Wolff, chief of staff, Luftkreis Kommando V, Munich, to commander of LKKV (Sperrle), 1 Nov. 1936. Reference to RLM LA 8888 g Kdc. A II, 31 Oct. 1936, MFA, file E948, Freiburg. Milch says the large German unit was decided upon 29 Oct. as a result of the Russian activity in Spain. Sperrle departed from Rome on 4 Nov., Milch, "Merkbuch," MFA.

42. Neurath to Hassell, 30 Oct. 1936, *DGFP*, ser. D, vol. 3, doc. 113; portrait of Sperrle, Proctor, *Luftwaffe*, 59.

43. Interrogation of Sperrle at Nürnberg, by Lt. John Martin, 2 Oct. 1945, p. 2, "IMT Nürnberg Trials."

44. General Blomberg to GFM, 21 Jan. 1929, GFM, L758/L224656-57; subsequent documents in serial L758.

45. Richthofen served as chief of staff to both Sperrle and his successor, Gen. Helmuth Volkmann, when they commanded the Legion Condor. In November 1938 Richthofen became the last commander of the legion. Personnel list in *DGFP*, ser. D, vol. 3. The importance of Richthofen's personality was stressed by Milch in an interview with Whealey, 6 July 1971, Düsseldorf.

46. Lt. Col. Julio [Solsalarce?], Legal Dept. Cáceres, to Sect. 1, Salamanca, 3 Jan. 1937, CGG, shelf 1, bundle 63, file 67. This document lists expenses and payments to Germans dating back to Sept. 1936. Accounting Dept., 3rd Div. [Queipo de Llano], signed by Manuel [Guillén Silva?], Seville, to Franco, Aug. 1936. This was an agreement to pay Col. Rugiero Bonomi, an Italian legionnaire, 19,000 pesetas. CGG, shelf 1, bundle 62, file 5.

47. "Four" comes from Schweikard, "Geschichte der Legion Condor," 66-68, in MFA; "five" is from Franco's personnel chart. He used the code name "Negrillos" (black ones) for Germans. Chart, Sect. III (operations), 12 Oct. 1936, CGG, shelf 1, bundle 91, file 3. There were five Germans giving instructions to sixty-five Spaniards in the unit. Also see Rainer Hans-Joachim Feldt, "An Account of the Activities of the Condor Legion during the Spanish Civil War" (M.A. thesis, 1981), 70.

48. The figure twenty-four tanks comes from Schweikard, "Geschichte der Legion Condor," 66-68, in MFA. The naval records also in MFA, MA, RL 2 IV /1 part 2, p. 21, say twenty-four tanks from 28 Aug. to 30 Sept. The figure thirty is from José María Gárate Córdoba, *La guerra de las Españas; Breve historia de la guerra del 36* (Barcelona, 1976), 237.

49. About 17 Sept., see Gárate Córdoba, *La guerra*, 237. The colonel is an official historian at the Servicio Histórico Militar. On 22 Sept., Franco's headquarters called for tank drivers and mechanics who preferably could speak German. Sect. I (administration), Cáceres, to Col. Asesino, Cavalry, Talavera de la Reina, 22 Sept. 1936, CGG, shelf 1, bundle 44, file 49. Franco may have regarded the Germans

under him as only volunteers in his legion; but the Germans, even during Operation Feuerzauber in July through September 1936, were organized in a separate military unit disguised as a transportation company under the command of Sonderstab W (see above, ch. 4, pp. 72-80).

50. Memo, Col. Francisco Martín Moreno, chief of staff, n.d. [13 Oct.-6? Nov. 1936], CGG, shelf 1, bundle 60, file 68.

51. Testimony, Warlimont at Nürnberg, 21 June 1948, "Leeb Case," "U.S. Army, Nurnberg Trials," M 898/R8. An organization table of the Germans in Spain is found in enclosure 3 of rep. 4, "Guido" [Warlimont], [Salamanca], to General Wilberg, 13 Oct. 1936, OKM, Docs., PG 80777.

52. In the table (see note 51, above), Warlimont had as his intelligence officer "Linde," while his administrative officer for general army tasks was "Lange." There is a problem of identifying these men. Differing clues are found in note, n.d., [chief of staff], [Salamanca], to Junta Técnica, Burgos, 12 Oct. 1936, CGG, shelf 1, bundle 41, file 61; handnote, n.d. on memo, Martín Moreno [13 Oct.-6 Nov], CGG, shelf 1, bundle 60, file 68; Viñas, *Alemania*, 1st ed., 326; Adm. Juan Cervera-Valderrama, *Memorias de guerra*, 27; Donald Heath, director of political affairs, Germany, to Col. D.L. Robinson, director of financial division, Office of Political Affairs, 6 Feb. 1946, OMGUS Docs. box 64, part 2/3, file "External Assets Spain"; Legion Condor personnel list, K 88, n.s., n.d. [1939-1940], MFA/LII 1010. Most likely "Lange" was a cover name for one of the first military attachés, Col. Freiherr Hans von Funck or Naval Commander Gerhard Wagner. Note, Operations Col. Antonio Barroso, n.d. [24 Apr.-16 May 1938], CGG/ shelf 1, bundle 42, file 88; testimony of Warlimont at Nürnberg, 21 June 1948, "Leeb Case," "U.S. Army, Nurnberg Trials," M898/R8; and affidavit of Wagner, 5 Feb. 1948, R 50, Warlimont Defense Doc. no 59.

53. Franco still tried unsuccessfully to recruit German volunteers for the Spanish Foreign Legion. Ambassador José Antonio Estrada, Berlin, to Secretary of external relations [Francisco Sangroniz], Salamanca, 4 Jan. 1937; veto, Gen. Martín, chief of staff, 19 Jan. 1937, CGG, shelf 1, bundle 60, file 71. Two hundred Austrians, however, volunteered via Genoa. They joined the Falange, not the legion. Herbert Heide [Austrian volunteer], Burgos, to Carlos Padrós, chef de cabinet, 2d Division, Seville, 15 Aug. 1937, CGG, shelf 1, bundle 61, file 67.

54. Carlito Freiro, Brazil, to Radio Tenerife, 2 Sept. 1936, CGG, shelf 6, bundle 318, file 80.

55. Signed Ahrenhold in *Gaceta Atlántica*, KTB, F/88, Von Rohden Collection of Research Materials on the Role of the German Air Force in World War II, 1911-1947, Washington, D.C., National Archives, microcopy T-971, roll 20, frames 711-15. The translation is my own.

56. "Pistorius Report," June 1939, OKM Docs., PG 80769. An account of the military operations of the war is the great strength of Merkes, *Bürgerkrieg*.

57. Hermann Plöcher, "The German Air Force in the Spanish Civil War," U.S. Defense Department, Air Force, *Ms* AF/150, p. 17, National Archives, RG 338, Washington, D.C.

58. Frank, "Naval Operations," 34.

59. Text, OKM Docs., PG 80773.

60. Cmd. Attaché Werner Lange, Rome, to OKM, tel. 287, 2 Dec. 1936, OKM Docs., PG80773; Cmdr. of German fleet in Spanish waters, Adm. Hermann Boehm [at sea], to OKM, rep. 14 Dec. 1936, ibid., 7.

61. Rep. Adm. Boehm, 14 Dec. 1936, ibid., 1.

62. Hassell to GFM, 17 Dec. 1936, *DGFP*, ser. D, vol. 3, doc. 156.

63. Biography of Faupel by Rudolf Feistmann, "Franco's Nazi Adviser," *Living Age* 352 (June 1937): 327-30.

64. Coverdale, *Italian Intervention*, 157-58.

65. Ohata and Fokushiro, "Anti-Comintern Pact," 43-45; Hassell, Rome, to GFM, 19 Nov. 1936, 5 Aug. 1937, *DGFP*, ser. C, vol. 6, docs. 44, 508.

66. Eden to Cabinet, FP 36/10, 19 Aug. 1936, Cab 27/626; also copy in FO/371, vol. 20574, W 10452 (A)/9549/41.

67. Text, *Times* (London), 2 Nov. 1936, p. 14, col. 4; memo, Orme Sargent, head of Southern Department, 2 Nov. 1936, FO/371, vol. 20412, R 6646/226/22.

68. Text of final Gentleman's Agreement, *DIA, 1937*, 87; also in *DBFP*, 2nd ser., vol. 17, doc. 530.

69. Told to his minister of education, Giuseppi Bottai, on 31 Oct. 1936: Bottai, *Diario, 1935-1944* (Milan, 1982), 113-14.

70. For details of subtle shifts in the balance of power, see Whealey, "Foreign Intervention."

71. Text of Italian draft translated into English. Enclosure, Hassell to GFM, 1 Dec. 1936, *DGFP*, ser. D, vol. 3, doc. 137.

72. Quoted draft, *DGFP*, ser. D, vol. 3, doc. 137.

73. The Italians told the German ambassador 4,000. Hassell to GFM, 27 Nov. 1936, *DGFP*, ser. D, vol. 3, doc. 130. The Italian Foreign Ministry records say only 3,000. Coverdale, *Italian Intervention*, 167 n 37.

74. Sáinz, *Testimonio*, 238, 384; Antonio Margina Barrio, "El Vaticano contra La Cruzada: El Cardinal Gomá; el fracaso diplomatico del Marqués de Magaz," *Historia 16*, Año 3, no. 22 (Feb. 1978): 39-52.

75. Tel., Magaz, Genoa, to Hdq. of Generalissimo, Salamanca, 6 Nov. 1936, CGG, shelf 1, bundle 60, file 68. Franco answered yes on 8 Nov.

76. Tel., Magaz to Recruitment Officer Manuel Villegas, Sect. IV (supply), Salamanca, 20 Nov. 1936, ibid., bundle 60, file 68.

77. "Mancini" (code name of Roatta), Salamanca, to Operations III, Col. Antonio Barroso, 24 Nov. 1936, CGG, shelf 6, bundle 60, file 68; on 30 Nov. Roatta discussed his plans with Franco, ibid., bundle 314, file 47.

78. Coverdale, *Italian Intervention*, 166-67. According to General Gabrielli, who was the main advocate for Italian expansion, he began the campaign on 20 Nov. over the objections of an overly optimistic Roatta. Gabrielli, *Una Guerra Civile*, 64, 67-70.

79. Fritsch supposedly had a violent discussion with Hitler about the Spanish problem in which he threatened to resign if Hitler didn't stop expanding the war. The day of the discussion is not reported. Capt. Cogswell, Paris, 4 Jan. 1937, ONI Docs., 20533 C—c-10-j. Warlimont was also at the conference and claimed that he, Blomberg, and Col. Beck were also opposed, and that the meeting was on 22 Dec., with Faupel also in attendance (see below, n. 88). Testimony of Warlimont at Nürnberg, 21 June 1948, "Leeb Case," "U.S. Army, Nurnberg Trials," Microfilm, M 898, roll 8.

80. Weizsäcker memos, 18 and 22 Nov. 1936, in *Die Weizsäcker-Papiere, 1933-1950*, ed. Leonidas E. Hill (Frankfurt, 1975), 100-104.

81. Neurath to Hassell, 5 Dec. 1936, *DGFP*, ser. D, vol. 3, doc. 142.

82. Hassell to GFM, 1 Dec. 1936, ibid., doc. 136.

83. Memo, Göring's Chef des Stabsamtes Karl Bodenschatz, 2 Dec. 1936, *NCA*, vol. 6, doc. 347-PS, pp. 199-200. On 2 Dec. Hitler was for caution and Göring for expansion, according to the Italian military attaché in Berlin, Col. E. Marras, quoted in Renzo De Felice, *Mussolini il Duce*, vol. 2, *Lo stato totalitario, 1936-1940* (Turin, 1981), 384.

84. Neurath to Hassell, 5 Dec. 1936, *DGFP*, ser. D, vol. 3, doc. 142.

85. Memo, Dieckhoff, 11 Dec. 1936, ibid., doc. 151; Hassell to Neurath, 17 Dec. 1936, ibid., doc. 156. Hitler discussed Italy for two and one-half hours with Milch on 8 Dec.: Milch, "Merkbuch," in MFA.

86. Rudolf Likus, Dienstelle Ribbentrop, to Ribbentrop, n.d. [ca. 24 Nov. 1936], GFM, 314/190567-69. The name of Faupel was first suggested by Willi Köhn, who accompanied Faupel to Spain as propaganda attaché. Defense document, affidavit von Stohrer, Lugano, 26 Jan. 1948, "Leeb Case," "U.S. Army Nurnberg Trials," M 898, roll 49, Defense Document Sperrle, no. 7.

87. Faupel to Hitler, 10 Dec. 1936, *DGFP*, ser. D, vol. 3, doc. 148.

88. Blomberg to Raeder, 24 Dec. 1936, W.A., no. 72, Chef Sache, OKM Docs., PG 33308, p. 266; interrogation of Warlimont, 17 Sept. 1945, "Poole Mission." (On SS, see below, note 135).

89. Interrogation, 17 Sept. 1945, "Poole Mission," Warlimont paraphrasing Hitler. Additional testimony from GFM in Viñas, *Alemania*, 2nd. ed., 363.

90. Hassell to GFM, 18 Dec. 1936, *DGFP*, ser. D, vol. 3, doc. 157.

91. Memo, n.s., Italian Ministry to Mussolini, 31 Dec. 1936, Duce Files, 1062/062973; Chargé Jules Blondel, Rome, to Delbos, 9 Jan. 1936, *DDF*, 2nd. ser., vol. 4, doc. 270.

92. Coverdale, *Italian Intervention*, 166-69; Alcofar, *Marina*, 128.

93. Memo, Rudolf Likus, Ribb. D., Berlin, 15 Jan. 1937, *DGFP*, ser. D, vol. 3, doc. 203; Hassell, Rome, to foreign minister, 15 Jan. 1937, ibid., doc. 204.

94. Col. Faldella archive, 14-15 Jan., cited by Felice, *Mussolini*, 389-90.

95. Ibid., 415. The German records on Göring's visit are briefer; see *DGFP*, ser. D, vol. 1, docs. 204, 205, 207, 208.

96. Memo [Count Luca Pietromarchi], Spanish Office, Ministry of Foreign Affairs, to Mussolini, 18 Jan. 1937, Duce Files, 1062/062976-78. The Spanish Office, created in December, coordinated Mussolini's Spanish policy and was Italy's parallel to Sonderstab W.

97. From two documents of Italy's Foreign Ministry, reprinted in Ismael Saz and Javier Tusell, eds. *Fascistas en España: La intervención en la Guerra Civil a través de los telegramas de le missione militare Italiana en Spagna 15 Diciembre 1936-31 Marzo 1937* (Madrid, 1981), docs. 7, 8.

98. The lower figure comes from a Spanish military document of Aug. 1938 from Archivo Histórico Militar, cited by Salas, *Intervención Extranjera*, 268. The higher figure is from the Italian archives, Saz and Tusell, *Fascistas*, docs. 7, 8.

99. Whealey, "Economic Influence," 245.

100. Resolution to Fascist Grand Council, 1-2 Mar. 1937, *Il corriere della sera*, 3 Mar., trans., *DIA, 1937*, 266-67.

101. Germany had advanced its representative in Spain from chargé d'affaires to ambassador on 11 Feb. 1937. Editor's note, *DGFP*, ser. D, vol. 3, 243.

102. Gauleiter Heinrich Lohse, Nürnberg, to Rudolf Hess, deputy of the Führer, 9 Sept. 1937, NSDAP Records, Berlin Doc. Cent., 83/Ordner 397.

103. "Pistorious Report," June 1939, OKM Docs.

104. The Hossbach Memorandum, *DGFP*, ser. D, vol. 1, doc. 19. For historiography on the memorandum, see T.W. Mason, "Some Origins of the Second World War," *Past & Present*, no. 29 (Dec. 1964): 67-87; Donald S. Detwiler, "The Origins of the Second World War," *Air University Review* 21 (July-Aug. 1969): 94-101; Göran Henrikson, "Das Nürnberger Dokument 386-PS (das 'Hossbach-Protokoll')," in *Probleme Deutscher Zeitgeschichte*, ed. by Göran Rystad and Svan Tägil (Stockholm, 1971), 151-94; Verner R. Carlson, "The Hossbach Memorandum," *Military Review* 63 (Aug. 1983): 14-30.

105. Coverdale, *Italian Intervention*, 171-72; Whealey, "Foreign Intervention," 232.

106. Col. Erwin Jaenecke, "Erinnerungen aus dem spanischen Buergerkrieg," thirteen-page *MS* written for the U.S. Air Force, Karlsruhe, 2 April 1956, MFA/Lw 107/1, pp. 8-9. A copy of this report is reproduced in a larger study by Karl Drum, "Die deutsche Luftwaffe im spanischen Buergerkrieg," Maxwell Air Force Base, Ala., 1957, and in Freiburg, MFA/Lw I.

107. Memo, Rex Leaper, press department, conversation with Vladimir Poliakoff [a White Russian personal liaison between Chamberlain and Mussolini] to Mounsey, 16 June 1937, FO/371, vol. 21337, W 11877/7/21.

108. Plöcher, "German Air Force" AF 150, 215.

109. Ibid., 227.

110. Weizsäcker to embassy in Rome, 4 Aug. 1937, *DGFP*, ser. D, vol. 3, doc. 407.

111. Naval Attaché Lange to Lt. Cmd. Heye, Operations Section, OKM, tel. no. 118 g. Kdos., 12 Aug. 1937, OKM Docs., PG 80597A.

112. Frank, "Naval Operations," 42.

113. Coverdale, *Italian Intervention*, 312.

114. There was never any doubt in the British Admiralty that the pirates were Italians. On the effectiveness of the Anglo-French countermeasures, see Peter Gretton, "The Nyon Conference—the Naval Aspect," *English Historical Review* 40 (Jan. 1975): 103-12; Stephen Roskill, *Naval Policy between the Wars*, vol. 2, *The Period of Reluctant Rearmament, 1930-1939* (London, 1976), 385-86.

115. Frank, "Naval Operations," 43-45.

116. Text, 28 Sept. 1937, *DIA, 1937*, 298-301.

117. Speer, *Spandau*, 125.

118. Hassell to GFM, 20 Oct. 1937, *DGFP*, ser. D, vol. 1, doc. 10; *Ciano's Hidden Diary*, 24-26; text, *DIA, 1937*, 306-07. Ribbentrop's representative, Raumer, began to discuss Italy's adhesion as early as 26 Feb. 1937. (Hassell to Weizsäcker, GFM 919/295109-10). Hassell to GFM, 24 Mar. 1937, *DGFP*, ser. C, vol. 6, doc. 292.

119. *DGFP*, ser. C, vol. 6, docs. 193, 235, 281, 292, 312, 325, 332, 359, 354, 355, 368, 385; Felice, *Mussolini*, 373 n 78.

120. Attaché Lange, Rome, to Adm. Raeder, G. 347, 27 Jan. 1937, OKM Docs., PG 48832; Lange to OKM, G 738, 15 Feb. 1938, PG 48833.

121. Hassell, Rome, to GFM, 25 Mar. 1937, *DGFP*, ser. D, vol. 3, doc. 236.

122. *Ciano's Hidden Diary* 17 Nov. 1937, 34. He used similar language during a speech made at Genoa, 14 May 1938: Ambassador Georg von Mackensen, Rome, to GFM, 20 May 1938, *DGFP*, ser. D, vol. 1, doc. 769; *Ciano's Hidden Diary* 13 and 14 May, 115-16.

123. Jaenecke, MFA/Lw 107/1, pp. 10-13.

124. Thomas, *Spanish Civil War*, 798-99, 803, 818-19.
125. *Ciano's Hidden Diary* (13 Nov. 1937), 32; (6 Oct. 1938), 175.
126. Ibid. (30 Nov. 1938), 201; *Ciano Diaries, 1939-1943* (8 Jan., 21 Feb. 1939), 8, 31.
127. Ambassador Lord Perth, Rome, to FO, 27 Jan. 1939, FO/371, vol. 24115, W 1557/5/41.
128. *Ciano Diaries, 1939-1943* (8 Jan. 1939), 8.
129. Ibid. (14 Mar. 1939), 42.
130. Ibid. (15 Mar. 1939), 43.
131. Weizsäcker, memo, 6 Apr. 1939, *DGFP*, series D, vol. 6, doc. 170.
132. *Ciano's Hidden Diary*, 77, 107, 114, 176, 253; *Ciano Diaries, 1939-1943*, 19, 30, 31, 48-51, 54, 56.
133. Langenheim to Göring, 29 July 1936, *DGFP*, ser. D, vol. 3, doc. 16; minute, Hermann Sabath, counselor, Economic Policy Section for Western Europe, Berlin, 27 Nov. 1936, ibid., doc. 132; chief of Auslandsorganisation [Ernst Bohle] to Gen. Faupel, EFH/HN, 12 Mar. 1937, GFM, 269/174284-85; speech, Hitler at reception of Spanish Ambassador Magaz, 6 Aug. 1937, in Baynes, *Speeches of Hitler*, 2:1355-56; speech, Nürnberg Party Day, Sept. 1937, ibid., 1:703.
134. Riemschneider, Sonderstab W, Berlin, to Gestapo, 30 Nov. 1936, document reprinted in Horst Kühne, *Revolutionäre Militärpolitik, 1936-1939: Militärpolitische Aspekte des national revolutionären Kriegs in Spanien* (East Berlin, 1969), doc. 17. On 16 Oct. 1936, Herr Ulrich von Osten of the Abwehr had arrived in Salamanca to advise Franco's police; Chief of Staff [Martín], Salamanca, to Civil Governor, Salamanca, 16 Oct. 1936, CGG, shelf 1, bundle 41, file 105.
135. Tel., Operations III, Salamanca, to General of South, Seville, 26 Jan. 1937, CGG, shelf 6, bundle 327, file 67; Hans Gisevius, *To the Bitter End* (Boston, 1947), 68, 196, 582.
136. Note, Col. Barroso, Sect. III, Salamanca, 23 Jan. 1937, CGG, shelf 6, bundle 327, file 70. Permission was again denied one year later by Barroso, 30 Jan. 1938, ibid., file 80.
137. Tel., Barroso, to Guardia Civil [Seville?], 22 Jan. 1937; tel., Barroso, to Army of South [Queipo de Llano] [Seville], 28 Jan. 1937, ibid., file 69.
138. Viñas, *Alemania*, 2nd ed., 152-53.
139. Memo, Neurath, 18 Nov. [1936], *DGFP*, ser. D, vol. 3, doc. 125.
140. Viñas, *Alemania*, 2nd. ed., 252.
141. Likus [to Ribbentrop], [24 Nov. 1936?], GFM, 314/190567-68.
142. Faupel to GFM, 14 Apr. 1936, *DGFP*, ser. D, vol. 3, doc. 243.
143. Lt. Col. von Doering, commandant of the *Horst Wessel Squadron*.
144. Faupel to Neurath, 10 Dec. 1936, *DGFP*, ser. D, vol. 3, doc. 148.
145. Faupel to GFM, 27 Jan. 1937, ibid., doc. 214.
146. Text, ibid., doc. 234, signed at Salamanca by Franco and Faupel.
147. Ramón Serrano Suñer, *Entre Hendaya y Gibraltar: Noticia y reflecion, frente a una leyenda, sobre nuestra política en dos guerras*, 2nd ed. (Madrid, 1947), 47-49.
148. Faupel to Bohle, and Bohle to Faupel, exchanges of telegrams, 19 June-2 July 1937, GFM, 269/17492-98.
149. See ch. 4, sect. 2.
150. Lohse to Hess, 9 Sept. 1937, Berlin Doc. Cent., 83/Order 397.
151. Mackensen, memo, 20 July 1937, *DGFP*, ser. D, vol. 3, doc. 399. Gen.

Roatta knew about these differences as early as December: tel. of Roatta to Spanish Office, Rome, 19 Dec. 1936, Saz and Tusell, *Fascistas*, doc. 14.

152. Faupel to GFM, 7 July 1937, *DGFP*, ser. D, vol. 3, doc. 386.

153. Mackensen, memo, ibid., doc. 399.

154. Ambassador Prince von Ratibor, Madrid, to GFM, 26 Dec. 1917, ACP, 357/00630-31.

155. *New York Times*, 25 July 1936, p. 3, col. 7.

156. Serrano Suñer, *Entre Hendaya y Gilbraltar*, 77.

157. Dionisio Ridruejo, *Casi unas memorias* (Barcelona, 1976), 187-92.

158. Serrano Suñer, *Entre Hendaya y Gibraltar*, 52, 176-77.

159. List of eight, Delegate for external service [José del Castro], Salamanca, to Operations III, Burgos, n.d. [Oct. 1937], CGG, shelf 6, bundle 327, file 78; FET and JONS, prov. delegate, Burgos, to Sect. III, [15 Oct.1937], ibid.; Lt. Col. [Barroso], Sect. III, Burgos, to chief of staff, Salamanca, 15 Oct. 1937, ibid., bundle 318, file 106; Castro, Salamanca, to Barroso, Burgos, 22 Oct. 1937, ibid.,; program for HJ, n.s., Sect. III, Salamanca, 24 Oct. 1937, bundle 327, file 78.

160. AM/EG, Ricardo de Cuevas, Sub. Sect., Ministry of Industry and Commerce, Bilbao, to Sub. Sect. Foreign Ministry, Burgos, 14 May 1938, MAE, bundle R 1034, file 51.

161. Dionisio Ridruejo, *Escrito en España*, 2nd ed. (Barcelona, 1976), 140.

162. Weinberg, *Foreign Policy*, 2:117. For further details on Ribbentrop's anti-Bolshevik policy in relation to Britain, see Wolfgang Michalka, *Ribbentrop und die deutsche Weltpolitik 1933-1940* (Munich, 1980), 118.

163. *Ciano's Hidden Diary* (9 Nov. 1937), 30. For the text of the Anti-Comintern Agreement signed by Italy, 25 Nov. 1937, see *DIA 1937*, 306-07.

164. Stohrer, "Status of Our *de facto* and *de jure* Relations with Nationalist Spain," Feb. n.d., 1938, *DGFP*, ser. D, Vol. 3, doc. 529.

165. German Foreign Ministry documents, cited in Abendroth, *Hitler*, 216. Martínez-Anido and Himmler also signed a broader agreement on 31 July 1938, ibid.

166. Stohrer, Feb. 1938, *DGFP*, ser. D, vol. 3, doc. 529.

167. Stohrer to Weizsäcker, 1 Mar. 1938, GFM, 4365/E0822261-62.

168. Minister Otto von Erdmannsdorff, Budapest, to GFM, 12 Jan. 1938, copy to Salamanca, *DGFP*, ser. D, vol. 1, doc. 97.

169. Text, n.d. 1938, enclosure to *DGFP*, ser. D, vol. 3, doc. 558. The date can be established as 6 Apr. 1938, since the document mentions a telegram received "yesterday" (5 Apr.).

170. Memo, Ribbentrop to Hitler [6 Apr. 1938], ibid.

171. Hitler's reply, memo, Adjutant Spitzy, Salzburg, to Ribbentrop, 6 Apr. 1938, ibid., Doc. 559.

172. Stohrer to GFM, 4 May 1938, ibid., doc. 582. Compare the April 1938 draft with the final treaty of March 1939, doc. 773.

173. Ribbentrop to Stohrer, 31 May 1938, ibid., doc. 590.

174. Sáinz, *Testimonio*, 270; memo of Count Casa Rojas to Count Jordana, cited in Angel Viñas et al., *Política comercial exterior en España (1931-1975)*, 2 vols. (Madrid, 1979), 1:284.

175. Donald S. Detwiler, *Hitler, Franco und Gilbraltar* (Wiesbaden, 1962), 11-12.

176. Richthofen Tagebuch, 13 Dec. 1938, MFA/Lw/107/1, pp. 2-3.

177. Ambassador Francisco Conde, Rome, to Spanish MAE [Burgos], tel. 601, 14 Sept. 1938, MAE/R1462/37; tels. 615 and 616, ibid.

178. Memo, Stohrer, 18 Dec. 1938, *DGFP*, ser. D, vol. 3, doc. 702.

179. Memo, Stohrer, 3 Nov. 1938, ibid., doc. 690.

180. Memo, Weizsäcker, 23 Dec. 1938, ibid., doc. 705; Counselor of Legation Walter C. Thurston, Barcelona, to Hull, tel. 1150, 27 Dec. 1938, DS, 852.00/8728. Magaz, who had been a Nationalist envoy in Rome in 1936, was transferred as Franco's third representative in Berlin in April 1937. Franco's first unofficial envoy to Berlin was Francisco Agramonte; the second was José Antonio de Estrada, who arrived in December 1936: Salgado, *Vida*, 355-56.

181. Memo of conference, Woermann, 4 Jan. 1939, *DGFP*, ser. D, vol. 3, doc. 708.

182. Stohrer to GFM, tel. 70, 31 Jan. 1939, *DGFP*, ser. D, vol. 3, doc. 721, from GFM, 462/225465.

183. Weizsäcker to Stohrer, tel. 51, 1 Feb. 1939, GFM, 462/225468.

184. Text, *DGFP*, ser. D, vol. 3, doc. 768.

185. Text, ibid., doc. 773.

186. Minutes of Führer's conference in Reich Chancellery, by Adj. Lt. Col. Rudolf Schmundt, ibid., doc. 433. Some historians doubt its authenticity. See Schreiber, *Revisionismus und Weltmachtstreben* (Stuttgart, 1978), 181 n 387.

187. See below, ch. 5, nn. 131-33.

188. The lengthy discussions went nowhere and virtually ended in May and June 1937. Considerable documentation in *DGFP*, ser. C, vols. 5, 6; and *DDF*, ser. 2, vols. 2, 3, and 4.

Chapter 4. The Development of German Economic Interests

1. Interrogation of Fritz Kolbe, official of German Foreign Ministry, by Harold C. Vederler, Wiesbaden, 23-24 Sept. 1945, "Poole Mission." Bernhardt through Viñas implied no prior acquaintance with Göring. Viñas, *Alemania*, 1st ed., 372. Bernhardt was a World War I veteran.

2. Interrogation of Bernhardt by Leonard Horwin, Madrid, 27 Mar. 1946, dis. 1876, DS, 800. 515/3-3046. Bernhardt said then that the firm of H. & O. Wilmer was an agent for Junkers. Also, OMGUS, Financial Division, Financial Investigation Sect., "Report on Investigation of Reichskredit Gesellschaft," OMGUS, 20 Aug. 1946, 116 (mimeographed) (hereafter cited as "OMGUS Report on RKG"); OMGUS Docs., box 61, part 3/2. Also, part 2 of this same collection, Emil Lang, OMGUS, Financial Division, interrogation of Wolf von Ingel, assistant, Foreign Business Sect. of RKG, by Lang in Germany, 2 May 1946, "Interrogation, Exhibits, and Annexes to Report on Reichskredit Gesellschaft," OMGUS, 20 Aug. 1946. Also on Junker agency see declaration, Friedrich Bethke to OMGUS, 21 Aug. 1945, OMGUS Docs., box 57, part 1/2, file "Ministry of Economics"; Horwin, Madrid, to OMGUS, enclosure 2, dis. 3302, 3 Dec. 1946, box 80, part 2/3, file "German Assets, Miscellaneous, Spain."

3. Bernhardt told Viñas this in 1973: *Alemania*, 2nd ed., 322; Abendroth, *Bernhardt*, 14.

4. Horwin-Bernhardt interview, 1946. Bernhardt may have known Yagüe,

who was then in Ceuta, but it was Col. Eduardo Saénz de Buruaga who introduced Bernhardt to Franco at Tetuán on 21 July 1936. Abendroth, *Bernhardt*, 7, 14. Viñas, *Alemania,* 2nd ed., 293, includes Mola and Beigbeder and ignores Queipo and Aranda.

5. Bernhardt, at sea near Vigo, to OKM, 2 Sept. 1936, OKM Docs., PG 80604; Constitution of HISMA in Viñas, *Alemania*, 1st ed., doc. 11; *Boletín oficial del Marruecos español*, no. 11, 20 Apr. 1938; English summary, Vice Consul A. Monck Mason, Tetuán, to Consul E.A. Keeling, Tangier, and FO, 26 April 1938, with enclosure from the *Boletín*, FO/371, vol. 22681, W 5791/1142/41.

6. Viñas, *Alemania*, 1st ed., 464.

7. Carranza, Tetuán, to Nicolás Franco, Salamanca, 8 Mar. 1937. JNA Docs., bundle 187, file 25.

8. Consul William Coultas, Seville, to FO, dis. 42, 11 Apr. 1938, FO 371, vol. 22624, W 5001/29/41.

9. See Whealey, "Economic Influences," 238 n 46. On the foreign exchange mechanism, see Whealey, "How Franco Financed His War," 133-52.

10. Whealey, "How Franco Financed His War," 135.

11. Receipt, Bernhardt, Seville, to Queipo de Llano, 14 Aug. 1936, Salgado, *Vida*, 148. The bank account is named in contract, Miguel Ponte y Manso de Zúñiga and Hermann Paege, 17 Oct. 1936, CGG, shelf 12, bundle 630, file 111.

12. Ibid. Each plane was priced at 85,000 RM CIF.

13. "Pistorius Report," June 1939, OKM Docs., PG 80769.

14. Langenheim to Consul W. Bohn, Tetúan, 18 June 1927, GFM, L 190/L059047-49; Counselor Wilhelm Friedrich von Vietinghoff, San Sebastián, to GFM, dis. 2873, 28 Sept. 1927, ibid., L 190/L059057-58.

15. Gen. Miguel Cabanellas, Burgos, to [Franco], Cáceres, tels. 311-200, 28 Aug. 1936, CGG, shelf 11, bundle 559, file 169.

16. Contract signed by Joaquín Bau, Commission of Industry and Commerce, Burgos, and approved by Nicolás Franco, Salamanca, 3 Nov. 1936, MAE bundle R 1034, file 48.

17. Capt. Ulick de B. Charles, manager, Rio Tinto, Burgos, to Nationalist Spanish Ministry of Industry and Commerce, 28 Nov. 1936, FO/371, vol. 20571, W 17631(B)/4719/41, says 7,000 workers. There were 8,500 workers on 16 July 1936, and 5,400 on 28 Aug., when Franco's army took over the mines, according to a semiofficial historian, David Avery, *Not on Queen Victoria's Birthday: The Story of Rio Tinto Mines* (London, 1974), 369. Also see Charles E. Harvey, "Politics and Pyrites during the Spanish Civil War," *Economic History Review* 31 (Feb. 1978): 89-104.

18. G.K. Logie, Lazard Bros., London, to Waley, Treasury and FO, 6 Feb. 1937, FO/371, vol. 21381, W 3004/40/41.

19. Faupel, Salamanca, to GFM, 20 Jan. 1937, *DGFP*, ser. D, vol. 3, doc. 208; secretary in the Economic Policy Dept. of GFM, Reiner Kreutzwald, to Faupel, 22 July 1937, doc. 401; memo, Kreutzwald, 13 June 1938, ibid., doc. 608.

20. Commercial Attaché Ralph Ackerman, San Sebastián, through Chargé d'Affaires Edwin Wilson, Paris, and Hull, to Bureau of Foreign and Domestic Commerce, tel. 173, 21 June 1939, file 231, "Drug & Chemical Spain," Department of Commerce, Business and Economic Branch, National Archives (hereafter cited as Comm. Dept.).

21. Two letters of Bernhardt to Francisco Franco, 14 Jan., and Nicolás Franco,

22 Jan. 1937, JNA Doc., bundle 187, file 7. Rio Tinto, basically British, also included Rothschilds (French Jewish) investments.

22. Enclosure, Bernhardt to N. Franco, 24 Apr. 1937, ibid., bundle 192, letter file.

23. J. Davidson, secretary, Rio Tinto, London, to Spanish Finance Ministry, Burgos, 26 July 1938, copy to FO, FO/371, vol. 22673, W 11589/386/41.

24. Bernhardt talked with C.B. Jerram of the British Board of Trade in Salamanca. Jerram to FO, 17 Jan. 1938, FO/371, vol. 22681, W 1142/1142/41.

25. Capt. Charles, Rio Tinto, Burgos, to FO, 28 Nov. 1936, vol. 20571, W 17631 (A)/4719/41.

26. Gen. Schweikard to Sonderstab W to Foreign Ministry, 27 Apr. 1939, GFM, 4366/E082304-08; weekly report, General Georg Thomas's adjutant, Rudolf Hünnermann, Reich War Ministry, to Economic Staff Training Sect. (Le), 11 July, 1938, OKW Docs., 105/830878-80.

27. Testimony, Warlimont, at Nürnberg, 21 June 1948, "Leeb Case," "U.S. Army, Nurnberg Trials," M 898, R 8.

28. Bernhardt met with Göring three times between 28 Sept. and 1 Oct. Abendroth, *Bernhardt*, 52-53.

29. Wilhelm Niemann, Foreign Trade Sect. V So, Reich Economics Ministry, to Min. Dirig. Dr. Michel, 18 Apr. 1940, Germ. Eco. Min., 32/426048-70.

30. Clodius to Ritter, 9 Oct. 1936, GFM, 629/251985-86.

31. Minute of telephone conversation by Col. Georg Thomas at OKW with Ministerial Director Meyer of Reich Finance Ministry, Berlin, 9 Oct. 1936, OKW Docs., 35/748082-84.

32. Georg Thomas, "Basic Facts for a History of the German War and Army Economy," *TWC* 7 ("Farben Case"), doc. 2353-PS, pp. 795-98; Georg Thomas, *Geschichte der deutschen Wehr und Rüstungswirtschaft 1918-1943/45*, ed. Wolfgang Birkenfeld (Boppard am Rhein, 1966). The first document in a Four-Year Plan file is a decree of 29 Apr. 1936 appointing Göring commissioner for foreign exchange and raw materials, NSDAP, Berlin Doc. Cent., 51, order 284. Interrogation of Schacht by Lt. Col. Murray Gurfein, 16 Oct. 1945, MS, "IMT Nürnberg Trials"; interrogation of Göring by Col. John Amen, 10 Oct. 1945, *NCA*, supplement B, p. 1151; minute, G.H.S. Pinsent, commercial attaché, Berlin, to FO, 4 May 1936, FO/371, vol. 19932, C 3431/99/18; GFM, serials 8768, 9238, files of Lammers, state secretary in Reich Chancellery.

33. Treue, "Hitlers Denkschrift zum Vierjahresplan 1936," *VJHfZ* (Apr. 1955): 184-203; Weinberg, in *Foreign Policy*, 1:355, says that Hitler first told party leaders to be ready for war in four years in September 1935.

34. Darré to Hitler, 5 Sept. 1936, GFM, 8768/E61109-98; interrogation of Darré by Col. John Monigan, 12 Sept. 1945, MS, "IMT Nürnberg Trials."

35. Speech to Aero Club, 17 Dec. 1936, reported by Ambassador Sir Eric Phipps, Berlin, to FO, 28 Dec. 1936, FO/371, vol. 19937, C 0184/99/18.

36. Abendroth, *Bernhardt*, 52-53.

37. Ibid.

38. Interrogation of Bohle by Emil Lang, 5 Nov. 1946, OMGUS Docs., box 57 part 1/2, file "Bohle."

39. Declaration of Bethke to OMGUS, 21 Aug. 1945, OMGUS Docs., box 57, part 1/2, file "Min. of Economics."

40. Conversation of Thomas with Meyer, Reich Finance Ministry, 9 Oct. 1936, OKW Docs., 35/748082-84; interrogation of Bethke, Frankfurt, 18 Aug. 1945, OMGUS Docs., box 81, part 2/3, file "Spain (Clearing Bethke)"; Abendroth, *Hitler*, 124.

41. The credit was authorized by the Foreign Exchange Control Office of the Reich Economics Ministry, letter of instruction Dev. B 6/54883/36, 26 Oct. 1936. This letter was not found but is referred to by Geiselhardt, counselor in Economics Ministry, to managers of Examining Offices, letter V Exp. 4/23548/38, 4 July 1938, Misc. Germ. Rec., T-84, 152/1437553-54.

42. Generally "mixed companies" like Rheinmetall-Borsig had a managing board, the *Vorstand*, for everyday decisions, and a governing body, the *Aufsichtsrat*, which met annually or semiannually. A particular individual, such as Olscher, often held seats on both kinds of bodies for several companies.

43. "OMGUS Report on RKG," 4, 48.

44. Ministerial Director Landwehr, Foreign Exchange Control Office of Reich Economics Ministry, to Reich commissioners of Supervisory Offices, letter of instruction Dev. B 6/58601/36, 9 Nov. 1936, Germ. Eco. Min., 117/621190.

45. Clipping, "Was ist beim Export nach Spanien zu Beachten?" *Zentralstelle für Interessanten der Leipziger Messe*, no. 1 (Jan. 1937), in files of Industry and Trade Chamber, Coburg, Misc. Germ. Rec., 152/1437610.

46. Herr Riendwiezer, Bruno Dietz Light Bulb and Radio Tube Co., to Industrial and Trade Chamber, Coburg, 10 Dec. 1936, Misc. Germ. Rec., 152/1437622; Herr Russitzen (sp. ?), Reich Economic Chamber, Berlin, to Industrial and Trade Chamber, Coburg, confidential letter 3330/37, 21 July 1937, ibid., 152/1437581.

47. Counselor of legation, Karl Schwendemann, chief of section III, Spanish desk of Foreign Ministry, to Max Wessig, 28 May 1938, GFM, 1568/379652; Schwendemann to Wessig, 10 June 1938, ibid., 1568/379667.

48. "OMGUS Report on RKG," 70-118.

49. For a more complex chart of VIAG, see figure in Federal Economic Administration (Washington), Economic Industrial Staff, Sept. 1946, OMGUS Docs., box 27, part 3/11, file "Control, Ownership and International Relationship of Leading German Combines," appendix D.

50. Bernhardt to N. Franco, 6 Nov. 1936, JNA Docs., bundle 187, file 2; Erich Gäbelt for HISMA to N. Franco, 14 Nov. 1936, ibid., file 3.

51. See Whealey, "Economic Influence," 247 n 83. Also SAFNI, Madrid, to SAFNI, Rome, 3 Sept. 1941, radio intercept CS23638, Ministry of Economic Warfare, PRO FO/837, file 721; Robert H. Whealey, "German-Spanish Relations, January–August 1939: The Failure of Germany to Conclude Economic and Military Agreements with Spain" (Ph.D. diss., Univ. of Michigan, 1963), 100.

52. See Whealey, "Economic Influence," 247 n 84.

53. Memo, Political Div. I, Alexander von Dörnberg, Berlin, 26 Jan. 1937, *DGFP*, ser. D, vol. 3, doc. 213.

54. Memo of director of Economic Policy Dept., Karl Ritter, Berlin, 17 Mar. 1937, ibid., doc. 231.

55. Memo, Economic Policy Dept., Felix Benzler, 23 Feb. 1937, ibid., doc. 223.

56. Ritter to Faupel, Salamanca, 13 May 1937, *DGFP*, ser. D, vol. 3, doc. 256.

57. Faupel to GFM, 21 May 1937, ibid., doc. 263.

58. Viñas, *Alemania*, 2nd ed., 137, 243; Weinberg, *Foreign Policy*, 1:184, 287.

59. Political Director Adolf von Bülow, Berlin, to Hans Völckers, chargé, Madrid, *DGFP*, ser. C, vol. 5, doc. 433; Félix Maíz, *Alzamiento en España* (Pamplona, 1952), 264, and Maíz, *Mola: Aquel Hombre* (Barcelona, 1976), 317; Viñas, *Alemania*, 2nd ed., 140.

60. Testimony of Eric Gritzbach, personal aide to Göring, to Col. Norbert G. Barr, Nürnberg, 20 Apr. 1948, no. 1206 a, MS, "U.S. Army Nürnberg Trials"; testimony, state secretary for VJP (Four-Year Plan), Paul Körner, 29 July-4 Aug. 1938, *TWC*, case 13, p. 837.

61. Viñas, *Alemania*, 2nd ed., 139; on Veltjens's life before 1929, see Walter Zuerl, *Pour-le-Mérite Flieger: Heldentaten und Erlebnisse unserer Kriegsflieger* (Munich, 1938), 456-60.

62. Manfred Funke, *Sanktionen und Kanonen* (Düsseldorf, 1970), 43-44.

63. Viñas, *Alemania*, 1st ed., 314-16.

64. Note verbale 770-3 e/B, [Völckers], Madrid, 13 Aug. 1936, OKM Docs., PG 80786.

65. "Pistorius Report," June 1939, OKM Docs., PG 80769, p. 5.

66. Nationalist conspirator Maíz (*Alzamiento*, 263-64) does not mention the S.S. *Girgenti* but claims Canaris and Veltjens were in Paris on 12 July discussing aid to the rebels with Juan de la Cierva.

67. Radio, Mola to Franco, 14 Aug. 1936, CGG, shelf 6, bundle 337, file 35; interview of Mola, Burgos, 12 Aug. 1936, Escobar, *Así empezó*, 113, 119. Veltjens was introduced to Mola's agent Escobar on 28 July in Berlin. Canaris's agent Messerschmidt joined the arms talks about 2 Aug. Escobar, *Así empezó*, 81-86, 103. Veltjens informed Escobar, representing Mola, that Franco's party (Bernhardt) had already conferred with him; ibid., 110.

68. These munitions had been ordered in Berlin on 29 July; ibid., 91, 115. Franco wrote in code to Canaris ("Willi"), notifying him of their delivery through Portugal to London. "Duncan"—i.e., Falangist Alonso Olano (not Juan de la Cierva), an agent in London—then sent the message from London to Berlin. Col. [Martin Moreno] chief of staff, Cáceres, to Lt. Medina Ayamonte [liaison to Portugal], 17 Sept. 1936, CGG shelf, 1, bundle 41, file 70.

69. "Pistorius Report," June 1939, OKM Docs., PG 80769.

70. Eoin O'Duffy, *Crusade in Spain* (Dublin, 1938), 16.

71. Consul L.M. Robinson, Hamburg, to FO, 5 Apr. 1938, dis. 32, FO/371, vol. 22642, W 4605/83/41.

72. The OKM was certainly in liaison with and assisting Veltjens's Spanish activities after the war began, as part of the OKM Transport Sect. and Operation Otto. Cmd. Schiller to Attaché Kurt Meyer-Döhner, memo R. 2999/37 G Kdos., 6 Apr. 1937, OKM Docs., PG 80597A/II 2. So was the OKW, including Col. Thomas and Gen. Jodl. Jodl, "Tagebuch," 27 and 30 Mar. 1937, *IMT*, vol. 28, doc. 1780 PS.

73. Bills of lading, 1936-1939, Veltjens through HISMA to JNA, JNA Docs., bundle 2, file A 1054, doc. 2; bundle 2, file A 1080; bundle 3, file A 1389; bundle 6, file A 1725; bundle 20, file A 1935; bundle 22, file A 1299; bundle 191, file A 1, 2. See also Proctor, *Luftwaffe*, 34.

74. Erich Gäbelt and Herr Schleich for HISMA, Salamanca, to chief of JNA Gen. Abilio Barbero Saldaña, Burgos, 3 July 1939, JNA Docs., bundle 20, file A 1935.

75. "Pistorius Report" [June 1939], OKM Docs., PG80769, p. 18; Transport Sect., Cmd. Pistorius, OKM, Berlin, to intelligence officer A I a, 30 Sept. 1936, reference to intelligence rep. tel. 7 Kückler, Thorn, Poland, 26 Sept. 1936, OKM Docs., PG 80789; U.S. Air Force, intelligence rep. 9, interview of Adolf Galland, "The Birth, Life and Death of the German Day Fighter," ADI (K) report no. 373, 15 Aug. 1945, p. 5, National Archives, Washington, D.C., Abendroth, *Hitler*, 181.

76. Weekly rep. Ob. Lt. Hünnermann, OKW, Wi, Stab. III, to Economics Staff Training Sect. (Le), 29 Nov. 1938, OKW Docs. 105/830960. See also Weinberg, *Foreign Policy*, 2:147 n 17.

77. Gen. Schweikard, Sonderstab W, to GFM, memo 6415/39 IV a. g. Kdos, 27 Apr. 1939, GFM, 4366/E982304-08.

78. Counselor, C.G. Howell, Madrid, to U.S. State Dept., 15 Jan. 1947, DS, 800.515/1-1547.

79. Heinrich C. Langenheim claimed Bernhardt siphoned off profits from HISMA and invested them in Spanish farms under Spanish names. Interrogation, H. Langenheim at Hohenasperg, 2 July 1946, OMGUS Docs., box 79, part 2/3, file "Repatriates."

80. Consul Bay, Seville, to Hull, dis. 306, 3 Aug. 1938, DS, 652.6217/6; Serrano Suñer, *Entre Hendaya y Gilbraltar*, 50.

81. Ambassador Magaz, Berlin, to secretary of external relations [Burgos], dis. 186, received 10 Sept. 1937, MAE, bundle R 1034, file 52.

82. Niemann, Special Sect., Reich Economics Ministry, to Dr. Michel, 18 Apr. 1940, Germ. Eco. Min., 32/426048-70.

83. Text, *DGFP*, ser. D, vol. 3, doc. 397.

84. Niemann to Michel, 18 Apr. 1940, Germ. Eco. Min., 32/426048.

85. Ibid.

86. For the details of the Montaña investment dispute, see *DGFP*, ser. D, vol. 3, docs. 463-64, 469-70, 632, 642-43, 655, 682-83, 689, 703; Glenn T. Harper, *German Economic Policy during the Spanish Civil War, 1936-1939* (The Hague, 1967), ch. 6; Juan Velarde Fuertes, "Un aspecto del asunto Montaña," *De Economía* 21 (March 1968): 131-55.

87. List, Jan. 1940, GFM, 4365/E082054. Also see list, n.s. [OMGUS], n.d. [1946?], OMGUS Docs., box 12, part 3/31, file "Rowak, Handelsgesellschaft G.m.b.H." 12 pp.

88. For more detail on HISMA-ROWAK, especially for 1937, see Viñas et al., *Política comercial exterior*, 1:166-70.

89. Niemann to Michel, 18 Apr. 1940, Germ. Eco. Min., 32/426048; 2nd Sect., Herbert P. Fales, London, to OMGUS, D. 24, 279 (SH no. 260), 16 July 1945, OMGUS Docs. box 80, part 1/3, file "Rowak."

90. Ministerial director for special tasks in Four-Year Plan, Helmuth Wohlthat, Berlin, rep. W. XXII/247, 15 (?) July 1939, *DGFP*, ser. D, vol. 3, doc. 809, p. 926. For establishment of the date of this document, see Whealey, "German-Spanish Relations," 223 n 1.

91. Whealey, "Economic Influence," 230.

92. Interrogation of Bernhardt by Horwin, 27 Mar. 1946, DS, 800.515/3-3046.

93. Wohlthat, Berlin, rep. W XXII/695, 20 Jan. 1940, GFM, 4365/E082004-42.

94. Bethke, V So, to Anton Wahle, ROWAK, V So 331/39 g., 22 May 1939,

GFM, 5206/E307921-22; Bohle, chief of AO, order 80, 6 Dec. 1938, Berlin Doc. Cent. 55, ordner 294; Roth, Economics Ministry, foreign trade sect. to Schwendemann, V So 131/39 g., 3 Feb. 1939, GFM, 1573/381167-68. Interrogation Ernst Bohle by Emil Lang, 5 Nov. 1946, OMGUS, rep. of Deutsche Bank, exhibit 404, OMGUS Docs., box 61, part 3/2.

95. Wohlthat, Berlin, rep. W XXII/695, 20 Jan. 1940, GFM, 4365/E082004-42.

96. Ibid.

97. Bernhardt, Salamanca, to Nicolás Franco, Burgos, 22 Jan. 1937, JNA Docs., bundle 187, file 7; Bernhardt to F. Franco, 14 Jan. 1937, ibid., bundle 192, letter file.

98. Viñas, *Alemania,* 2nd ed., 234.

99. Copy of contract between Bernhardt, Seville, and Luis Wenzel, representative of Rohstoffhandel der Vereinigten Stahlwerke, Düsseldorf, 7 Oct. 1936, and second contract between Bernhardt and Bau, Nationalist Spanish Ministry of Industry and Commerce, Burgos, 30 Oct. 1936, JNA Docs., bundle 214, file 2.

100. Viñas et al., *Política Comercial Exterior,* 1:246.

101. Felice Guarnieri, *Battaglie economiche fra le due grandi guerre* (Milan, 1953), 2:131-33. The Italian Foreign Ministry Archives include the long negotiations of Nicolás Franco in Rome in 1937-1938; see Coverdale, *Italian Intervention,* 298-346.

102. Capt. Charles, Rio Tinto, Burgos, to FO, 28 Nov. 1936, FO/371, vol. 20571, W 17631(A)/4719/41.

103. Whealey, "How Franco Financed His War."

104. Viñas et al., *Politica Comercial Exterior,* 1:179-80.

105. Coverdale, *Italian Intervention,* 408-10.

106. See table 5, p. 91.

107. Whealey, "Economic Influence," 230, 238.

108. The theme of German economic imperialism is further developed in Robert H. Whealey, "Nazi Economic Imperialism: Spain, 1936-1939," in *Proceedings of the Citadel Symposium on Hitler and National Socialism,* ed. Michael B. Barrett (Charleston, S.C., 1982); and Robert H. Whealey, "Anglo-American Oil Confronts Spanish Nationalism, 1927-31: A Study of Economic Imperialism," *Diplomatic History* 12 (Spring 1988): 111-26.

109. Text, *League of Nations Treaty Series,* 62 (Geneva, 1926): 339-53.

110. Faupel, Salamanca, to GFM, 12 Jan. 1937, *DGFP,* ser. D, vol. 3, doc. 196.

111. Note of Lammers, 15 Jan. 1937, ibid., p. 219 n 2.

112. Text, GFM. 4365/E081984-87.

113. Faupel to GFM, 9 July 1937, *DGFP,* ser. D, vol. 3, doc. 196.

114. Text of public treaty, *Reichsgesetzblatt,* 1937, 2:521-24.

115. *DGFP,* ser. D, vol. 3, docs. 392, 394.

116. [Counselor] Calderón, Berlin, to Foreign Minister [Francisco Gómez Jordana], [Burgos], tel. 126, 7 May 1938, MAE, bundle R 1034, file 61.

117. On 1 Dec. 1938, ROWAK signed a contract with Jesús Gangoiti Barrera, representing the Delegación del Sindicato Madero de la Guinea Continental Española. The protocol was countersigned by Magaz and Under State Secretary Ernst Woermann, and confirmed on 6 Dec.; ibid.

118. Völckers, Madrid, to GFM, dis. 770, 8 Aug. 1936, GFM, 3176/D682852-57.

119. Deutsche Überseeische Bank, n.n., Berlin, to Industry and Trade Chamber, Coburg, circular letter, 22 Feb. 1938, Misc. Germ. Rec., 152/143766; "Memorandum sobre el desenvolvimiento de las futuras relaciones económicas hispanoalemanas," 17 June 1939, GFM, 4366/E082345-50.

120. Minute of Sabath to Ritter, W II 4201, 17 Nov. 1936, with marginal comment, 27 Nov. GFM, 5646/001868-69.

121. Party Comrade Burbach, AO Berlin, to Stohrer, memo Bu/Bö, 12 Aug., 1937, GFM, 4365/E082075-81.

122. Dr. Olscher, Finance Ministry, to GFM, letter A. 3104 Sp. 15 a 1.c., 10 Mar. 1937, GFM, 269/174287-88; Herr Russitzen (sp.?), Reich Economic Chamber, Berlin, to Industrial and Trade Chamber, Coburg, Tgb. 7467/36, 14 Dec. 1936, Misc. Germ. Rec. 152/1437617-18.

123. Deputy of Gauleiter AO [Alfred Hess], Berlin to Bohle, FO, letter He/R, 16 Apr. 1937, GFM, 269/174289-90.

124. Hellermann to Bohle, letter H/Hgs, 15 June 1937, GFM, 269/174291.

125. Memo, Stohrer, San Sebastián, 1 July 1938, GFM, 1606/3875700-05.

126. Official of AO Legal Office, Robert Fischer, Berlin, to Stohrer, tel. no. 1, 1 Jan. 1938, GFM, 269/174311; representative of Hilfsauschuss für Spanien-Deutsche Burbach, Salamanca, to Fischer, 13 Feb. 1938, ibid., 269/174321-23.

127. Burbach to Fischer, 13 Feb. 1938, GFM 269/174321-23.

128. Burbach to Stohrer, memo Bu/Bö, 12 Aug. 1937, GFM, 4365/E082075-81.

129. Hellermann to Alfred Hess, letter H/Bög, 22 Mar. 1938, GFM, 269/174338-39; Party Comrade Knörk for Fischer to Hess, letter Fi/Ro, 3 May, 1938, 269/174340.

130. Memo, Fischer to Schwendemann, 16 June 1939, GFM, 269/174400.

131. Texts of protocols, *DGFP*, ser. D, vol. 3, 12, 15, and 16 July, 1937, docs. 392, 394, 397.

132. Memo, official in GFM Secretariat, Spitzy, to Ribbentrop, 6 April 1938, *DGFP*, ser. D, vol. 3, doc. 559.

133. Memo, Emil Wiehl, director of Economic Policy Dept., GFM, 10 Jan. 1939, ibid., doc. 710.

134. Harper, *Spanish Economy*, 116-19.

135. For more on Nationalist Spain's autarky, see Viñas, *Política comercial exterior*, 1, ch. 3, sect. 6, 290-319.

136. Whealey, "Economic Influence," 231-32.

137. Ibid., 246.

Chapter 5. The Place of Spain in German War Plans

1. The Soviet Union published in East Berlin, in a special supplement to *Neue Zeit*, no. 13 (1 July 1946), 3-18, interrogations of three German officers who emphasized the role of Canaris in connection with the origin of the civil war. There are nine or ten biographers of Canaris listed in Viñas, *Alemania*, and in David Kahn, *Hitler's Spies: German Military Intelligence in World War II* (London, 1978). All should be used with extreme caution.

2. Helmuth Groscurth, *Tagebücher eines Abwehroffiziers 1938-1940: Mit weiteren Dokumenten zur Militäropposition gegen Hitler*, ed. Helmut Krausnick, Harold C. Deutsch, and Hildegard von Kotze (Stuttgart, 1970), 104.

3. Lais, chief of Information Sect., Italian Naval Ministry, to Chief of Staff Adm. Cavagnari, 22 July 1939, *DDI*, 8th ser. (1935-1939), vols. 12, 13; 9th ser. (1939-1943), vols. 1, 2 (Rome, 1952-1957), vol. 12, doc. 648.

4. According to Polish Foreign Minister, Josef Beck. Jan Szembeck, *Journal* (Paris, 1952) 9 July 1935, 106; Whealey, "Mussolini's Diplomacy."

5. Gert Buchheit, *Der deutsche Geheimdienst: Geschichte der militärischen Abwehr* (Munich, 1966), 58.

6. Canaris to Adm. Raeder, dis. 30/35, 12 Nov. 1935, OKM Docs., PG 48899, p. 302.

7. For the best account see Viñas, *Alemania,* 1st ed., 29, 30, 32, 40, 42, 47-49, 62, 65-66, 69, 70, 74, 79-80, 173. A contemporary document is Canaris, Fleet Command Kiel, to Chief of Navy Raeder, rep. 708/33 A G. Kdos., 6 Sept. 1933, OKM Docs., PG 33418.

8. At least as early as 19 July 1936, Canaris's agent, "Bremen," stationed in Barcelona, was observing the failure of Spanish officers to seize the city. "Bremen" to chief of staff (1a) of Abwehr, rep. 231, 29 July 1936, OKM Docs., PG 80785, This is a detailed eyewitness report of events during 19-22 July. There is no explanation for the delay in composing and sending the report until 29 July. Reference is made to a report 230 of 27 July (not found). "Bremen's" report 231 was published in Spanish by Angel Viñas, "Los espiás nazis entran en la guerra civil," *Historia Internacional*, no. 7 (Oct. 1975): 27-29. See below n 35 and also ch. 4 nn 56-59.

9. Karl Heinz Abshagen, *Canaris* (London, 1956), 107-14; Ian G. Colvin, *Master Spy* (New York, 1951), 30-35; André Brissaud, *Canaris* (London, 1973), 34-35.

10. Frank Jellinek, *The Civil War in Spain* (London, 1938), 280-82.

11. Ambassador Welczeck, Paris, to GFM, dis. A 490, 3 Feb. 1937, GFM, 1104/319170-73. Viñas, *Alemania,* 1st ed., 171-73, 215-16, 338.

12. OKM Docs., files PG 31058, PG 34017, PG 34056, PG 34061, PG 34334, PG 34562. Also OKM Docs., files MFA/II M 57/66, MFA/II M58/3; Gemzell, *Raeder, Hitler, und Skandinavien*, 31, 42-46. For early war plans, see Watt, "Appeasement," 204.

13. For the names of these more than fifty men, see below, appendix B. See pp. 121-25 for the operation of the Etappendienst supply service.

14. Helmut Krausnick, "Canaris," *Neue deutsche Biographie*, 3 (Berlin, 1957): 116.

15. Roger Manvell and Heinrich Fraenkel, *The Canaris Conspiracy* (New York, 1969), 6.

16. This account is based on conversations the military attaché in Tangier (1942-1944) later had with Langenheim and Niemann. Testimony of Hans Remer, 16 May 1946, *Neue Zeit*, 1 July 1946, 6-8. Rudolf Bamler, in "Die Rolle des deutschen Militärischen Geheimdienstes bei der Vorbereitung und Provozierung des Zweiten Weltkrieges," *Arbeitsgemeinschaft ehemaliger Offiziere, Mitteilungsblatt* 2 (East Berlin, 1958): 3-6, says Niemann was always an agent and immediately reported to Canaris before he and his companions left Tetuán. There is also a biographical sketch of Edmond Niemann in W. Wendell Blanke, OMGUS, to Lt.

Lowenstein, Central Intelligence Officer, Camp 76, n.d. [Aug. 1946], OMGUS Docs., box 79, part 3/3, file "Repatriation from Spain—Flight X, General 820.02," p. 15. But it adds nothing to the story of the first week of war in July.

17. Viñas's interview of Bernhardt appears in *Alemania*, 1st ed., 411-16, especially 413 and 416. Although generally highly documented, one weakness of Viñas is that he puts so much faith in Bernhardt's 1973 recollections that he sometimes underplays the contemporary documents. But he is correct in regarding with suspicion the accounts of those who testified to Soviet authorities. In general I have used Viñas's first edition throughout this section because it has more information about Canaris. In the second edition, he cut most of the material, emphasizing more strongly that all the documentation about Canaris is speculative. Also see Abendroth, *Bernhardt*, 33.

18. Viñas may dismiss the idea that Langenheim was a part-time Abwehr agent because he was also Ortsgruppenleiter for the NSDAP for Tetuán. A Spanish document casts doubt on the "too old to spy" theory. Langenheim sent his mail to Berlin by plane from Seville to the German minister in Lisbon because he assumed the British opened his regular mail. Tel., Chief of staff, Army of Africa [Franco], Seville, to 2nd Division Aerodrome, Tablada [Queipo de Llano], 9 Aug. 1936, CGG, shelf 1, bundle 39, file 128.

19. Abendroth, *Bernhardt* [on Langenheim], 14, 15, 25, 33, 42.

20. Adm. Boehm, Lisbon, to OKM, rep. G 3199A, 7 May 1939, OKM Docs., PG 45181; Consul Alvary J. Gascoigne, Tangier, to Roger Makins, Central Dept., 1 July 1940, dis. 316/25, FO 371, vol. 24447, C 7910/16/41. U.S. intelligence regarded both father and son (Heinrich) as dangerous agents. "Diplomatic Agent" Paul Alling, to Dept. of State, dis. 37, Tangier, 30 July 1945, OMGUS Docs., box 108, part 2/15, file "Departure of Axis Agents and Other Persons."

21. Gascoigne, Tangier, to Makins, 1 July 1940, FO 371, vol. 24447, C 7910/16/41.

22. Their source is the editor's note, *DGFP*, ser. D, vol. 3, p. 2. The note is based on a document written in 1939 by the Protocol Dept. of the German Foreign Ministry. According to Bernhardt the three armed services officers conferred with Hitler immediately after Bernhardt left Hitler, at 1:30 A.M., 26 July. Abendroth, *Bernhardt*, 33. Warlimont told Albert C. Horton in August 1961 that Canaris was at Bayreuth. Horton, "Germany and the Spanish Civil War" (Ph.D. diss., Columbia University, August 1966), 30.

23. "Pistorius Report," July 1939, OKM Docs., PG 80769. Abendroth says the naval officer was Captain Coupette. Abendroth, *Bernhardt*, 33. Earlier he mentioned Lindau: Abendroth, *Bürgerkreig*, 334 n 103.

24. Interrogation of Bohle by Emil Lang, 5 Nov. 1946, OMGUS Docs., box 61, part 3/2, rep. "Deutsche Bank," exhibit 404. Not seen by Viñas.

25. Abendroth, *Bernhardt*, 30-31; Viñas, *Alemania*, 2nd ed., 340.

26. Testimony of Bamler, 12 May 1946, in *Neue Zeit*, 1 July 1946, 4.

27. Göring claimed to have been instrumental in getting Hitler to intervene in July 1936. Testimony, 14 Mar. 1946, *ITM*, 9:280-81; interrogation of Göring by U.S. Army, 15 Aug. 1945, "Poole Mission." In view of Göring's penchant for putting himself in the limelight, this cannot be taken as conclusive (see ch. 2, p. 7). He specifically downgraded the role of Canaris. But after 26 July Göring's role became key—especially on 2 Dec. 1936, when he told his top air force personnel that it was Italy's responsibility to take more of a military lead in Spain. Memo, chief

of Göring's Stabsamt, Bodenschatz, 2 Dec. 1936, *NCA*, 6, doc. 3474-PS, pp. 199-200.

28. Statement of Milch to Whealey, Düsseldorf, 6 July 1971. Milch made the same point to Abendroth, *Hitler*, 28.

29. Milch, "Merkbuch," 26 July 1936, in MFA.

30. Félix Maíz was a messenger in Spain for Mola in the vital spring of 1936, and he has written two versions of his memoirs. In the 1952 version, he informed the world that he met with an anonymous Abwehr agent in Pamplona for three hours on 27 June 1936. He also asserted, on the basis of secondhand knowledge, that Admiral Canaris met on 12 July in Paris with a German arms dealer and a Spanish agent for the conspiracy, Juan de la Cierva, an aeronautical inventor who visited from London. Maíz, *Alzamiento en España*, 85, 109, 179, 188, 190, 263-64. In 1976 he published a more detailed account that added the information about the anonymous Abwehr agent, who had a name like "Otto Rit . . ." and was also in contact with Canaris and Cierva in Paris in June. The Maíz story about Canaris in Paris apparently originated from Capt. Barrera, who informed Maíz on 12 July about the meeting with Juan de la Cierva. Maíz, *Mola*, 281, 317-18, 322. Throughout both books, the accounts of what was said and done by Canaris, his agent "Otto," and the arms dealer are left vague. Furthermore, little other information confirms the story, except a vague report that "Veltjens" may have been involved, dated 9 July 1936, *DGFP*, ser. C, vol. 5, doc. 433 (see also above ch. 4 nn 56, 57). For further discussion see Weinberg, *Foreign Policy*, 1:286-88, 2:147 n 17; Viñas, *Alemania*, 1st ed., 280-84, 311-16; Friedlander, "Great Power Politics," n 75.

31. *Neue Zeit*, 1 July 1946, 4.

32. Ibid.; Jellinek, *Civil War*, 280-82.

33. High commissioner for Spanish Morocco, Lt. Col. Juan Beigbeder, to military attaché, Lt. Gen. Erich Kühlenthal, in Paris [also appointed to Madrid and Lisbon], 22 July 1936, *DGFP*, ser. D, vol. 3, doc. 2. Viñas makes too much of the fact that the Foreign Ministry delayed sending this particular telegram to the War Ministry until 24 July: *Alemania*, 2nd ed., 322. Surely the Abwehr had another copy. In fact, a copy of the published doc. 3 in *DGFP*—a report by Welczeck on 23 July, detailing France's plans to send bombers and artillery pieces to Republican Spain— is in the Abwehr files, OKM Docs., PG 80785.

34. Escobar, *Así empezó*, 69-74, 81-87, 103.

35. Viñas differs from this view and assumes Canaris was surprised; *Alemania*, 2nd ed., 272. What happened to Lietzmann's reports from 8 July to 27 Aug.? Canaris had at least fifty possible reporters in the two zones of Spain, besides attachés Kühlenthal and Joachim Lietzmann in Paris (see appendix B). What happened to their complete reports? Viñas overcompensates for the sensationalized biographies of Colvin, Abshagen, and Brissaud as well as testimony given to the Soviets, and plays Canaris's role down to the minimum. He also elaborates on his thesis that Canaris, in July 1936, was surprised and unprepared (Viñas, "Los espías," 18-19). Viñas analyzes the documents available with great care, but he writes as if what now exists in archives is all that ever existed. Certain aspects of the complex events of the seven days in July may have been surprising, but by the evening of 25 July, Canaris should have had quite a folder on events in Spain.

36. *DGFP*, ser. D, vol. 3, docs. 25, 41, 43, 59; Naval Attaché Cmd. Lietzmann, Paris, to Canaris, tel. 418, 2 Aug. 1936, tel. 422, 4 Aug., GFM, 665/257364, 257382.

37. Testimony of Count Du Moulin, German counselor in Lisbon embassy (1936), to Viñas [1973], *Alemania*, 1st ed., 428.

38. Testimony, Warlimont at Nürnberg. 21 June 1948, "Leeb Case," "U.S. Army, Nurnberg Trials," M 898, R-8.

39. Neurath, Berlin, to Hassell, Rome, 30 Oct. 1936, *DGFP*, ser. D, vol. 3, doc. 113; confirmed by Roatta, tel. to Spanish Office, 12 Jan 1937, Saz and Tusell, *Fascistas*, doc. 94.

40. Hassell to GFM, 1 Dec. 1936, *DGFP*, ser. D, vol. 3, doc. 136; Political Director Dieckhoff, Berlin, to Hassell, 2 Dec. 1936, ibid., 139; Hassell to GFM, 29 Dec. 1936, ibid., doc. 170.

41. For the first trip, in Jan. 1937, see Gen. Alfred Jodl, "Tagebuch," 5, 7, and 9 Jan. 1937, *IMT*, 28, doc. 1780-PS pp. 346-47; second trip, in April 1937, Merkes, *Bürgerkrieg*, 115.

42. Mackensen, Berlin, 20 July 1937, *DGFP*, ser. D, vol. 3, doc. 399.

43. Memo, n.s. [Barroso?], Sect. III, n.d. [1-3 July 1937], CGG, shelf 6, bundle 314, file 28. Viñas on Sacro Lirio, *Alemania*, 1st ed., 42, 72.

44. N.s. [British diplomatic agent], Salamanca, to FO, [30] Jan. 1938, FO 371, vol. 22621, W 2128/29/41.

45. Ambassador Stohrer, Salamanca, to Mackensen, *DGFP*, ser. D, vol. 3, doc. 503; Canaris through Stohrer, Salamanca, to GFM and Wehrmacht, 5 Apr. 1938, ibid., doc. 557; Ribbentrop, memo for Hitler [6 Apr. 1938], ibid., docs. 558, 559, 560; "Guillermo" [Canaris] through Stohrer to Wehrmacht and GFM, 27 Oct. 1938, ibid., doc. 687.

46. Stohrer, San Sebastián, to GFM, 31 Mar. 1939, ibid., doc. 772, 3 Apr., doc. 777, 4 Apr., doc. 778.

47. Attaché Meyer-Döhner to OKM, military attaché rep. 80/392 g., 16 Sept. 1939, OKM Docs., PG 48843, pp. 73-83.

48. Manvell and Fraenkel, *Canaris Conspiracy*, 6.

49. Léon Papeleux, *L'amiral Canaris entre Franco et Hitler* (Paris, 1977), 110.

50. Ten-page plan sent as enclosure by Adm. Walther Gladisch, Operations (Marine Leitung), to Adm. Raeder, memo 708/33 A, 6 Sept. 1933, OKM Docs., MFA/II M-57.

51. Military Attaché Maj. Truman Smith, Berlin, to ONI, rep. 14,830, 24 Aug. 1936, ONI Docs., 20536—C-10-j.

52. Interview, Wohlthat by Whealey, New York, 23 Mar. 1970. Wohlthat met Canaris in 1933 and had from fifty to a hundred talks with him. He claimed Canaris began his opposition to Hitler in 1936. Interview, New York, 3 Jan. 1970.

53. Schweikard, rep., 8 Mar. 1940, MFA/II L234/75, 1:45.

54. Ibid., 153.

55. At the time of the Ebro offensive in August 1938, there were 140 machines in the legion, 220 in the CTV, and 140 in the Spanish Nationalist air force. Rep., Schweikard, 8 Mar. 1940, MFA/II L 234/75, 1:10. Merkes, *Bürgerkrieg*, 94, says 150. British military intelligence reported that the Legion had 146 planes in December 1938, compared with 182 for the Italian CTV. Col. F. Beaumont-Nesbett et al. to Committee of Imperial Defense, rep. DCOS 140; rep. JIC 94, 10 June 1939, GB Cab. 54/6, para. 48.

56. The number of German troops sent via marine transport was 16,846, and 16,524 returned. In addition, some 31 were killed on the battleship *Deutschland*, not

included in these figures. Rep. OKM A VI S 4385/39 [Commander Pistorius] [June 1939], enclosure 5, "Pistorius Report," OKM Docs., PG 80769; Thomas, *Spanish Civil War*, 1st ed., appendix; Salas, *Intervención* (in annex 13), lists 271 of the dead by name from a list published in Feb. 1941. Somewhat fewer than 322 deaths are given by Raymond Proctor in "Condor Legion," *Historical Dictionary*. According to Proctor, a total of 19,000 men served. The maximum number of troops at one time was 5,136, which he breaks down into 4,383 men, 281 officers, and 472 civilians. MFA Doc., May 1939. Proctor, *Luftwaffe*, 253. Feldt uses a list of medal winners published in 1943 to show that 17,920 served and 315 were killed. Feldt, "Condor Legion," 139.

57. According to Proctor, *Luftwaffe*, the Germans only lost 72 planes in combat during the entire war. The rest were accidents. Good statistics on the planes that were destroyed are hard to find because the Sonderstab W records were lost. Salas, *Intervención extranjera*, 331, using a complex series of Spanish military archives which he does not cite specifically, claims the maximum loss was fewer than 100 planes.

58. Lt. Gen. Volkmann, Sonderstab W, to OKM, annual rep. no. 2585, Dec. 1938, OKM Docs., PG 80836.

59. There were twenty-four German military units in Spain according to Merkes, *Bürgerkrieg*, appendix 7. But the list is incomplete. There were at least thirty. Ramón Garriga, *La Legión Condor* (Madrid, 1975), has no footnotes and no bibliography. Merkes, *Bürgerkrieg*, has a list of the memoirs of ex-Legionnaires. U.S. Naval Attaché Lt. Cmd. P.E. Pihl, Berlin, to ONI, rep. 362, 13 June, 1939, ONI Docs., 15373E—C-10-j; Homze, *Luftwaffe*, 170-73.

60. Ramón Salas Larrazábal, *Historia del ejército popular de la República*, 4 vols. (Madrid, 1973), vol. 4, doc. 48. Table calculated from documents in CGG but no specific citations. Pihl report, ONI, June 13, 1939.

61. Feldt, "Condor Legion," 130.

62. Note, Lt. Col. Antonio Barroso, Operations [Burgos], n.d. [24 Apr.–16 May 1938], CGG, shelf 1, bundle 42, file 88.

63. Ibid.; note, Operations, Sect. III, 24 Oct. 1936, CGG, shelf 6, bundle 314, file 40, p. 19. Drohne had a special status; it was not an integral part of the Legion Condor. Proctor, *Luftwaffe*, 60-61.

64. Feldt, "Condor Legion," 71.

65. Ambassador Henderson, Berlin, summarized German press reports to Foreign Office, 31 May 1939, FO/371, vol. 24119, W 8593/5/41.

66. Salas, *Intervención extranjera*, 423; Albert Kesselring, *The Memoirs of Field Marshal Kesselring* (London, 1953), 30; British Chief of Staff Gen. D.F. Anderson et al. to CID, rep. COS 622 (JIC), 6 Oct. 1937, Cab 53/33; Proctor, *Luftwaffe*, 256, 259. (The Me 109 was officially called the Bf 109, but later the more well known Me was used.)

67. Salvador Rello, *La Aviación en la guerra de España* (Madrid, 1969), vol. 1, no page numbers, a picture handbook.

68. Proctor, *Luftwaffe*, 253.

69. Ibid., 262.

70. Coverdale's thesis, "Italian Intervention in the Spanish Civil War, July 1936-March 1937" (Ph.D. diss., Univ. of Wisconsin, 1971), 195, says 48,000. In this book he cites Italian Foreign Ministry archives to the effect that as of 18 Feb. 1937, Mussolini had sent a total of 48,823 men to Spain cumulatively. *Italian*

Intervention, 175. Saz and Tusell later published from two Italian Foreign Ministry memoranda a grand total of 44,648 as of May 1937. *Fascistas*, docs. 7, 8.

71. The figure 3,819 is from Italian archives. Coverdale, *Italian Intervention*, appendix D, p. 418. The figure is given as a round 4,000 according to Asst. Air Attaché J.A. Dixon in conversation with Gen. Llanderas, San Sebastián, to Ambas-sador Sir Maurice Peterson, 15 June 1939, FO/371, vol. 24120, W 9387/5/41.

72. Coverdale, *Italian Intervention*, 393, citing Italian archives.

73. According to Salas (*Intervención extranjera*, 439), there were 593 German planes (unfootnoted calculations). This was probably an underestimate. Col. Jae-necke of the Sonderstab W reported to the OKM that delivery up to 1 Nov. 1937 was 135 to the Nationalist Air Force and 384 to the Legion Condor, a total of 519 planes. Jaenecke, no. 16, 750/37, 5 Nov. 1937, OKM Docs., PG 33310, p. 302. The 708 planes figure is given by Willard Frank, "Naval Operations," 54.

74. Based on extrapolation of appendix 8 in Jesús Salas Larrazábal, *Air War over Spain* (London, 1969). His table gives the total of each aircraft type used by the "Nationalists" on 23 Dec. 1938, then totaling 489. But he is unclear about the Balearic Island units and obscures the numbers of CTV and of Condor planes in the total.

75. Col. Beaumont-Nesbett to CID, rep. DCOS 140, JIC 95, 10 June 1939, Cab 54/6.

76. Castelles, *Brigadas*, 383.

77. Stanley Payne, *Politics and Military in Modern Spain* (Stanford, 1967), 385, says January. Proctor, *Luftwaffe*, 118, says March.

78. Merkes, *Bürgerkrieg*, lists all thirty in annex 8; see also my chronology. Proctor, *Luftwaffe*, has maps for seventeen of these battles.

79. Herbert R. Southworth, *Guernica! Guernica! A Study of Journalism, Diplomacy, Propaganda and History* (Berkeley, 1977); Klaus A. Maier, *Guernica 26.4.1937: Die deutsche Intervention in Spanien und der "Fall Guernica"* (Freiburg, 1975); and Gordon Thomas and Max Witts, *Guernica: The Crucible of World War II* (New York, 1975). Proctor, *Luftwaffe*, 128-30, endorses Maier as the best source on the military aspects of the subject. Southworth has developed the political side of the question.

80. The blockade with its major base at Mallorca was declared by the Nationalists on 13 Sept. 1936. Consul William E. Chapman, Bilbao, via Destroyer *USS Kane*, to Hull, 13 Sept. 1936, *FRUS* 1936, 2:715. Cervera, *Memorias*, 422. Willard Frank emphasizes the important battle of Cape Espartel, 29 Sept. 1936, in which the Republican navy lost control of the Straits. "Naval Operations," 31.

81. Committee of British Shipowners to FO, memo no. 2, 12 Jan. 1939, FO/371, vol. 29114, W 850/5/41.

82. Parliamentary question drafted by Counsellor Kenneth Johnson, 2 Feb. 1939, FO/371, vol. 24109, W 1947/4/41.

83. If one analyzes the above British statistics according to date and location of sinking.

84. Roatta to Spanish Office, 19 Jan. 1937, *Saz and Tusell, Fascistas*, doc. 157.

85. Plöcher, German Air Force, rep. 150, 113-16.

86. Ibid., 91, 102, 181.

87. Basil Liddell Hart, *The German Generals Talk* (New York, 1948), 93.

88. Adolf Galland, *The First and Last: The Rise and Fall of the German Fighter Forces, 1938-1945* (London, 1954), 49. Edward L. Homze, *German*

Military Aviation: A Guide to the Literature (New York, 1984), 88-90, lists published German memoirs of the Legion Condor veterans. Also see Williamson Murray, *Luftwaffe* (Baltimore, 1984), 16-18.

89. Clarence Beck, "A Study of German Involvement in Spain, 1936-1939" (Ph.D. diss., Univ. of New Mexico, 1972), 70.

90. Proctor, *Luftwaffe*, 256.

91. Coverdale, *Italian Intervention*, 110.

92. As the title indicates, the problem with Proctor's *Luftwaffe* is his over-emphasis on air power at the expense of ground forces. The book gets diverted to the heroics of World War I type fighter dogfights but is weak on the role of the Drohne unit.

93. Proctor, "Military History," in *Historical Dictionary*, 523-24; affidavit, Nürnberg, 5 Feb. 1948, Warlimont defense doc. 59, "Leeb Case," "U.S. Army, Nurnberg Trials, microfilm, M 898, R 50; Warlimont testimony, 21 June 1948, ibid., R 8.

94. Merkes, *Bürgerkrieg*, 136 n 335.

95. Ferdinand Miksche, *Attack* (New York, 1942), 17, 22, 26.

96. Feldt, "Condor Legion," 103.

97. Miksche, *Attack*, 29, agrees with Liddell Hart, *German Generals*, 92.

98. Plöcher, Air Force rep. 150, pp. 89, 91, 181, 194.

99. Liddell Hart, *German Generals*, 92. Perhaps Thoma exaggerated his own importance. General Heinz Guderian ignores Spain and only mentions having met Thoma on the Russian front in 1941. Guderian, *Panzer Leader* (New York, 1952), 180.

100. Liddell Hart, *German Generals*, 92.

101. Memo, Georg Thomas, Berlin, May 24 1939, *IMT* 36, doc. EC 24, p. 122. S.J. Lewis, *Forgotten Legions* (New York, 1986), 45, goes too far in asserting that neither Guderian nor Thoma invented the Blitzkrieg, because Lewis did not study the Spanish operations. He is wrong in assuming (p. 52) that the word *Blitzkrieg* was invented by an American military writer in August 1939.

102. Coverdale, *Italian Intervention*, 115, 410.

103. Robert J. Young, "French Military Intelligence and Nazi Germany, 1938-1939," in Ernest May, ed., *Knowing One's Enemies: Intelligence Assessments before the Two World Wars* (Princeton, 1985), 303.

104. Liddell Hart, *German Generals*, 92.

105. Viñas, *Guerra, Dinero, Dictadura: Ayuda fascista y autarquía en la España de Franco* (Barcelona, 1984), 102-06, 111-12.

106. The sources vary as to the exact number of dead and wounded as a result of the bombing.

107. Col. Jaenecke, Sonderstab W, to OKM, rep. 6283/37 g, 18 May 1937, OKM Docs., PG 80604.

108. Madeline Astorkia, "L'Aviation et la Guerre d'Espagne: La cinquième arme face aux exigences de la guerre moderne," in *Deutschland und Frankreich 1936-1939*, ed. Klaus Hinderbrand and Karl Ferdinand Warner (Munich, 1981), 339.

109. Proctor, *Luftwaffe*, 258.

110. Williamson Murray, *The Change in the European Balance of Power, 1938-1939: The Path to Ruin* (Princeton, 1984), 42-43.

111. Homze, *Luftwaffe*, 172-73.

112. Proctor, *Luftwaffe*, 260.

113. Plöcher, Air Force rep. 150, pp. 40, 48.

114. German Mission, Burgos, to Headquarters Sect. IV (Supply), 25 Dec. 1937, CGG, shelf 13, bundle 656, file 158.

115. Asher Lee, *The German Air Force* (London, 1946), 25.

116. Proctor, *Luftwaffe*, 262.

117. Plöcher, Air Force rep. 150, p. 167.

118. Keitel to OKM, Operations, rep. WA 15/37 Ch SL la, 1 Feb. 1937, OKM Docs., PG 33309, p. 67. Also with the GFM, Keitel to Weizsäcker, 2 Dec. 1936, *DGFP*, ser. D, vol. 3, doc. 138.

119. Kurt Schuschnigg, *Austrian Requiem* (New York, 1946), 11-19; Speech, Gauleiter Friedrich Rainer, Klagenfurt, Austria to Gau Karinthia, 11 Mar. 1942, *TWC* 12, "Leeb Case", doc. 4005-PS.

120. Ferdinand Miksche, *Paratroops* (New York, 1943), 182-83.

121. Ibid., 240.

122. Ambassador Josephus Daniels, Mexico City, to Secretary of State, 28 July 1939, ONI Docs., Reg. 22512 D—C-10-k., reported on "Luis Vent-Salazar," a veteran of the Legion Condor working against Britain in Mexico and Guatemala. U.S. diplomats also reported on the activities of one Herr "von Holstein." U.S. Naval Attaché Maj. F.H. Lemson-Schribner, USMC, Mexico City, to ONI, 13 Dec. 1939, ONI Docs., 22512 E—C-10-k.

123. On Göring's views, see Kesselring, *Memoirs*, 42. On von Thoma, see Liddell Hart, *German Generals*, 156.

124. Southworth, *Guernica! Guernica!* 203-04 n 129.

125. Jordana quotes Franco. Stohrer, San Sebastián, to GFM, 15 July 1938, *DGFP*, ser. D, vol. 3, doc. 638.

126. Murray, *Balance of Power*, 43.

127. U.S. Naval Attaché Lt. Cmd. P.E. Pihl, Berlin, to ONI, rep. 362, 13 June 1939, ONI Docs., 15373E-C-10-j.

128. Memo, Lt. Cmd. Hans Schottky, transport officer, Salamanca, to Sonderstab W. 17 Mar. 1937, OKM Docs., PG 80695.

129. Abendroth, *Hitler*, 147.

130. Pihl report, ONI, 13 June 1939.

131. Unnumbered rep. n.s., 3 Abt. Skl [Naval Intelligence], to GFM, 10 Apr. 1938, GFM, 1568/379629-33. See also, report on British ships in the Bilbao-Santander area, radio rep. U-35 through "Partner" to [A 1] Naval Command Office, OKM, 16 July 1937, OKM Docs., PG 80597C.

132. Michalka, *Ribbentrop*, 161.

133. Joseph Henke's thorough study of Hitler's views dates Ribbentrop's shift against Britain to 21 May 1937. Military planning against Britain began in June: *England in Hitlers politischem Kalkül 1935-1939*(Boppard am Rhein, 1973), 64-65. Further German literature on the naval aspects of the issue is discussed by Keith W. Bird, *German Naval History: A Guide to the Literature* (New York, 1985), 557-58.

134. Chargé Bielfeld, London, to GFM, 31 July 1936, *DGFP*, ser. D, vol. 3, doc. 19; Eden, *Memoirs*, 484-87.

135. Neurath to Ribbentrop, embassy in London, 30 May 1937, *DGFP*, ser. D, vol. 3, doc. 167; memo, Foreign Minister Neurath, 31 May, ibid., doc. 270.

136. Neurath to Ribbentrop, 30 May 1937, ibid., doc. 268.

137. Ibid., docs. 267-85, 287-95, 298-300, 303-05.

138. Count Massimo Magistrati, *L'Italia a Berlino 1937-1939* (Verona, 1956), 40; Hassell to GFM, 12 June 1937, *DGFP*, ser. D, vol. 3, doc. 306.

139. Mackensen, Berlin, to German embassy in London, 20 June 1937, *DGFP*, ser. D, vol. 3, doc. 346; memo of conversation, Neurath and Göring, signed by Keitel, rep. 106/37 g. Kdos. (L) 1b, to OKM, 21 June 1937, OKM Docs., PG 33309; testimony of Capt. Fritz Wiedemann, adjutant to the Führer, to Howard A. Brundage at Nürnberg, 18 Oct. 1945, 24-page MS "IMT Nürnberg Trials," p. 5; testimony of Neurath to J.J. Monigan, 3 Oct. 1945, *NCA*, Supp. B., 1488.

140. This is what Neurath told the French. François-Poncet to Delbos, 19 June 1937, *DDF*, 2nd series, vol. 6, doc. 29.

141. Commander, Spanish Reconnaisance Fleet, Adm. Rolf Carls, to OKM, 1 and 23 Aug. 1937, cited in Merkes, *Bürgerkrieg*, 275. Merkes also believes that either a "Spanish Red" submarine or a Soviet U-boat was involved, but he offers no evidence despite his heavy documentation (pp. 294-95). Delbos did not believe the story and wanted the Non-Intervention Committee to interrogate the officers and examine the log of the *Leipzig*. Delbos to French Ambassador in London, 20 June 1937, *DDF*, 2nd series, vol. 6, doc. 99. Needless to add, nothing came of this proposal.

142. Kriegstagebuch of *Leipzig*, 15 June 1937, cited by Abendroth, *Hitler*, 170; KTB, Adm. Fischel, *Deutschland*, 28 June 1937, cited by Stephen Tanner, "German Naval Intervention in the Spanish Civil War: As Reflected by the German Records, 1936-1939" (Ph.D. diss., American University, 1976), 245. Weinberg, *Foreign Policy*, 2: 101 n 14, agrees with this judgment on the *Leipzig*. Rear Adm. Alberto Bastarreche told the British navy that "officially" the *Leipzig* was attacked by a sub, but "unofficially" it was a fish. HMS *Galatea*, Gilbraltar, to FO, rep. 534/S 6, 12 July 1937, FO 371, vol. 21298, W14202/1/41, For further details see K. Westmann, "Juni 1937—Die Provokation des leichten Kreuzers 'Leipzig,'" *Marinewesen* 7 (1968): 747-52; Oswald Hauser, "England und Hitler, 1936-1939" in *Geschichte und Gegenwart* (Neumünster, 1980), 368.

143. Testimony, Wiedemann to Brundage, Nürnberg, 9 Oct. 1945, "IMT Nürnberg Trials," 24.

144. C.A.E. Schuckburgh, minute, 14 June, to Eden's tel. to Henderson, 10 June 1937, FO/371, vol. 21336, W 11261/7/41; Henderson to Weizsäcker, 10 June 1937, *DGFP*, ser. D, vol. 3, doc. 290.

145. Mackensen to Ribbentrop, 15 June 1937, *DGFP*, ser. D, vol. 3, doc. 326; Woermann, London, to GFM, 18 June, ibid., doc. 338.

146. Neurath to British ambassador, 23 June 1937, ibid., doc. 334.

147. Marschall for Raeder to Fleet Commands, A I a 33/37 g. Kdos., Chef Sache, 18 June 1937, OKM Docs., PG 34562.

148. Blomberg to Fritsch, Raeder, and Göring, 24 June 1937, *NCA*, vol. 4, Doc. C-175.

149. Guse to Fleet Commander, 3 Nov. 1937, A I a 1162/376, OKM Docs., PG 34480.

150. Text, *DBFP*, 2nd ser., vol. 19, doc. 169.

151. Ibid., doc. 214.

152. Naval Attaché Werner Lange, Rome, to Lt. Cmd. Heye, Operations Sect., OKM, tel. 118 g. Kdos., 12 Aug. 1937, OKM Docs., PG 80597 A.

153. Note verbale, Ciano to Hassell, Rome, 11 Aug. 1937, OKM Docs., PG 80597A.

154. Ciano, *Ciano's Hidden Diary* (24 Oct. 1937), 24.

155. Willard Frank, "The Spanish Civil War and the Coming of the Second World War," *International History Review* 9 (Aug. 1987): 368-409.

156. *Ciano's Hidden Diary* (6 Nov. 1937), 28; Weizsäcker to embassy in Italy, 19 Oct. 1937, *DGFP*, ser. D, vol. 1, doc. 9.

157. Ciano, *Ciano's Hidden Diary* (6 Nov. 1937), 29.

158. Frank, "Naval Operations," 54.

159. Memo, Under State Secretary Georg von Mackensen, conversation with Italian Chargé Massimo Magistrati, Berlin, 29 Dec. 1937, *DGFP*, ser. D, vol. 3, doc. 494; memo, Weizsäcker, 2 Jan. 1938, ibid., doc. 495.

160. Ciano, *Ciano's Hidden Diary* (14 Feb. 1938), 75.

161. Weizsäcker and Gen. Beck privately opposed the Italian military talks. Minute, conversation of Weizsäcker with Beck, 24 Mar. 1938, *Weizsäcker Papiere*, 123-24. Ambassador von Mackensen, Rome, 5 Nov. 1938, *DGFP*, ser. D, vol. 4, doc. 402; Italian Military Attaché Luigi Marras, Innsbruck, to Gen. Pariani, 5 Apr. 1939, *DDI*, 8th ser., 13:423, appendix B. See Mario Toscano, *The Origins of the Pact of Steel* (Baltimore, 1967); and Schreiber, *Revisionismus*, on the complexity of the Italian-German discussions for a military alliance.

162. Hossbach memo, *NCA*, vol. 3, doc. 386-PS.

163. Bullitt, Paris, to Hull, 23 Nov. 1937, *FRUS* 1937, 1:162-77.

164. Memo, Karl Schwendemann, Dept. II, to State Secretary Bernard von Bülow, 12 Aug. 1935, GFM, 5560/E396347-48; Lupin to Sabath, Economic Dept., GFM, 24 Sept. 1935, *DGFP*, ser. C, vol. 4, doc. 303; Lupin to GFM, 19 May 1937, GFM, 4793/E236188-89.

165. Lupin to GFM, rep. 3506/G/37, 4 Sept. 1937, GFM 4896/E254010.

166. Canaris, Salamanca, to OKW through Stohrer, 5 Apr. 1938, *DGFP*, ser. D, vol. 3, doc. 557.

167. Text, ibid., doc. 558.

168. Notes of Führer, signed by Adjutant Col. Schmundt, [April 1938?], *NCA*, vol. 4, doc. 388-PS, item 1.

169. Ambassador Stohrer to GFM, T-114, 8 Mar. 1938; Keitel to Schwendemann, 11 Mar. 1938, GFM 1568/379487, 379509-11.

170. Draft of New Directive Case Green for Hitler by Keitel, 18 June 1938, *NCA*, doc. 388-PS, item 14.

171. Dr. Walther Hoffman to Heye, 8 Apr. 1938, OKM Docs., PG 48901.

172. See ch. 4, above.

173. Meyer-Döhner, Burgos, to OKM, Operations Capt. Lt. Kurt Freiwald, 23 Apr. 1938, OKM Docs., PG 48901.

174. Memo, Capt. Walter Lohmann, chief of Naval Transport Dept., Naval Staff in Reichswehrministerium, to State Secretary Wilhelm Kempner, Reich Chancellery, 29 Mar. 1926, GFM, 4530/141228-38.

175. Guse, OKM, 1 Abt Skl, to OKW (L) [Abteilung Landesverteidigung], minute A I a 16/38 g. Kdos. and A I a 17/38 g Kdos. both 26 Apr. 1938, GFM, 9930/E694848 and E69428-31. The idea was revived in August in a related file, serial M 70. (see below, n 183).

176. Canaris through Stohrer to OKW, 5 Apr. 1938, *DGFP*, ser. D, vol. 3, doc. 557.

177. Whealey, "Foreign Intervention," 226.

178. Col. Jaenecke, "Erinnerungen aus dem Spanischen Buergerkrieg," MFA/ Lw 107/1, pp. 10-13.

179. Memo, Messerschmidt, Berlin, to OKM, 17 May 1938, OKM Docs., PG 48901.

180. Admiral Guse, Operations, to OKM, Construction, rep. A IV 5706 g. Kdos., 7 June 1938; n.s., memo of discussion, by Construction to M Sect., B. 1019/38 g. Kdos., 8 June 1938, OKM Docs., PG 48901.

181. There are two reports on the mission, neither signed by Heye. Cmd. Alfred Eckhardt, OKM Operations, to Gen. Wilberg, Sonderstab W. and Naval Attaché Group, 27 June 1938; Lt. Cmd. Karl Otto Groschupf, OKM Operations, to Naval Attaché Group, 1 Abt Skl Ia 961/38 G, 14 July 1938, OKM Docs., PG 48902.

182. Cervera, *Memorias de guerra*, 208, 213, says December 1937; the memoirs of Felice Guarnieri, *Battaglie economiche*, 2:278, say March 1938.

183. Memo, 1 Abt. Skl. 1c [Seekriegsleitung], drafted by Lt. Com. Karl Heinz Neubauer, signed by Capt. Fricke, to Naval Attaché Group, 18 Aug. 1938, GFM, M70/M002219-21b.

184. Minute, Fricke to OKM Ausland, 1 Abt. SKI, 1c, 31 Aug. 1938, GFM, M70/M002221a-22.

185. Naval Attaché Meyer-Döhner, Burgos, to Minister of Navy Adm. Juan Cervera, 1 Sept. 1938, OKM Docs., PG 80936.

186. Memo, Schwendemann, 30 Aug. 1938, GFM, 1606/385765.

187. Memo, Woermann, with enclosure, aide memoire of Ambassador Magaz, Berlin, 5 Aug. 1938, ibid., 1606/385711-12.

188. Officer in general staff, 5th section, German Air Forces, Hauptmann Hans Wolter, "Extended Case Green" to Air Force Operations staff, memo 28/38 g. Kdos., 25 Aug. 1938, *NCA*, vol. 4, doc. 375-PS.

189. Interrogation of Göring by Col. John Amen, 1 Sept. 1945, MS, "IMT Nürnberg Trials."

190. Attaché Meyer-Döhner, San Sebastián, to Naval Attaché Group, OKM, rep. 211, 27 Feb. 1939, OKM Docs., PG 80730.

191. Attaché Meyer-Döhner to Naval Attaché Group, unnumbered rep. Receiving no. M. Att. 5929, 4 Sept. 1938, OKM Docs., PG 48837.

192. Meyer-Döhner to Naval Attaché Group, rep. 360 g., 13 Apr. 1939, OKM Docs., PG 80730.

193. Adm. Francisco Moreno, *La Guerra en el Mar: Hombres, barcos y honra* (Barcelona, 1959), 55-56.

194. Minute, economic department, Sabath, 4 Dec. 1935, *DGFP*, ser. C, vol. 4, doc. 445; Eltze, Berlin, rep. of Spanish visit, 20 Jan. 1936, GFM, 5561/ E396533-44; Minister Baron Oswald von Hoyningen-Huene, Lisbon, to foreign minister, tel. 215, 1 Dec. 1936, GFM, 4793/E236373.

195. Aide to the Naval Attaché Lt. Menzell, Burgos, to Naval Intelligence, unnumbered rep., receiving no. I Skl 242/38, 18 Aug. 1938, OKM Docs., PG 48837.

196. Known in Spain as Constructora Naval, S.A.

197. Meyer-Döhner to Naval Attaché Group, rep. 1003 g., 5 Nov. 1939, OKM Docs., PG 48837. The number-one base in Spain was El Ferrol, and the number-two base was Cartagena. Vickers controlled the shipyards at both. Willard C. Frank, "Sea

Power, Politics, and the Onset of the Spanish Civil War," (Ph.D. diss., University of Pittsburgh, 1969), 42-43.

198. Meyer-Döhner to Naval Attaché Group, 4 Sept. 1938, OKM Docs., PG 48837.

199. See *DGFP*, ser. D, vol. 3, docs. 658, 659, 661, 664, 666, 669, 670, 673; ibid., vol. 2, docs. 622, 624, 638, 641, 654.

200. Attaché Meyer-Döhner, U-30 in Spanish waters, to OKM, radio rep., 30 Sept. 1938, GFM, M70/M002248. The deputy Spanish chief of naval staff was Rear Adm. Salvador Moreno—brother of Adm. Francisco Moreno, the Operations chief, and brother-in-law of Adm. Bastarreche of the Cádiz command. Three of the most important Spanish naval officers were of the same family; hereditary family traditions die hard in Spain.

201. Wilhelm Meier-Dörnberg, *Die Ölversorgung der Kriegsmarine 1935 bis 1945* (Freiburg, 1973), 29.

202. Report of Darlan-Chatfield conversation by Adm. Decoux, 5 Aug. 1936, *DDF*, 2nd series, vol. 3, doc. 87; HMS *Ramilles* attempted to visit Tenerife, tel., Col. Peral, military commander, Tenerife, to chief of staff, Burgos, 18 Feb. 1938, CGG, shelf 1, bundle 61, file 62; Consul Winfield Scott, Santa Cruz de Tenerife, to Hull, dis. 305, 9 Dec. 1938, SD, 862.3452 a/1; Vice consul S.H.M. Head, Las Palmas, to Consul Eric L. Fox, Tenerife, 27 July 1938, FO/371, vol. 22682, W 11086/1142/41; and Fox to Sir Robert Hodgson, agent in Burgos, 29 Aug. 1938, ibid., paper W 12264.

203. Chief of Abwehr Capt. Konrad Patzig, to Naval Operations, Abwehr rep. 284/34 g. Kdos., 10 Apr. 1934, OKM Docs., PG 33425.

204. Otto Becker, Kiel, to Cmd. H. Zillwood, Audit and Investment Branch, Financial Division, British government in Germany, 21 May 1946, OMGUS Doc., box 74, part 1/3, file "Deutsche Werke Kiel, A.G." Attaché Kurt Meyer-Döhner, San Sebastián, to Attaché Group OKM, dis. 178 g., 19 Dec. 1938, OKM Docs., PG 80730; OKW, Ausl. IV, Werner Dietel, to Meyer-Döhner, unnumbered tel., 27 Aug. 1939, OKM Docs., PG 48843.

205. Whealey, "How Franco Financed," 146; interview of Milch by Whealey, Düsseldorf, 6 July 1971.

206. Roy A. Stratton, "Germany's Secret Supply Service," *United States Naval Institute Proceedings* 79 (Oct. 1953): 1088.

207. Memo, Raeder, Ob. d M. 1 Skl 75/38, 9 Sept. 1938, OKM Docs., PG 30960.

208. OKM, n.s., to naval attaché, Salamanca, memo M 227 g. Kdos., 6 Sept. 1938, OKM Docs., PG 48843. This is the first document in this file and gives general instructions in case of war.

209. OKM 3, Abt., Cmd. Johannes Möller, to naval attaché, Salamanca, 4562/38, 20 Sept. 1939, ibid.

210. Adm. Bürckner, Abwehr, to Naval Attaché Group, rep. 1020/38 g. Kdos. IVa, 31 Dec. 1938, OKM Docs., PG 33613. Since the values of paper reichsmarks and pesetas were artificially fixed, only pounds sterling and dollars had convertible international value.

211. Minute of Reichsbank Conference for OKM, Ob.R.Rat. Wandres, 20 July 1938, copy by OKW IV c to Abwehr, 25 July 1938, OKM Docs., PG 33426.

212. Interrogation, Max Franzbach, Abwehr officer, by 7707 U.S. Military

Intelligence Service Center, Germany, 20 Dec. 1946, OMGUS Docs., box 57, part 1/2, file "Speer & Schacht Interrogation."

213. Weinberg citing ROWAK files in Koblenz. Weinberg, *Foreign Policy* 2:151-52.

214. Declaration, Karl Erk and F. Becker, Kiel, 16 Mar. 1948, OMGUS Docs., box 74, part 1/3, file "Deutsche Werke, Kiel, A.G."

215. Consul Ahlers, Hamburg, to Reich Chancellor Dr. Georg Michaelis, 17 Oct. 1917, ACP 357/99581-83.

216. Chief of staff, Army of Africa, Seville, to chief of ordinance, 25 Aug. 1936, CGG, shelf 6, bundle 314, file 27; Military Cmd. Martínez Fuset, Las Palmas, to General Franco, 29 Aug. 1936, ibid., shelf 1, bundle 63, file 21; Military Cmd., Las Palmas, to Operations Sect. III, Cáceres, 1 Oct. 1936, ibid., shelf 6, bundle 314, file 27.

217. Lt. Cmd. Otto Schniewind, OKM operations, to Kamphoevener, GFM, 1 Skl 122/39, 17 Jan. 1939; Adm. Bürckner, Abwehr, to Naval Attaché Group, 1020/38 g Kdos. IVa, 31 Dec. 1938, OKM Docs., PG 33613.

218. Memo, Schwendemann, 26 Aug. 1938, GFM, 1606/385767-68.

219. *Memoria CEPSA 1930*, 7 (the first annual stockholders' report).

220. Copy of CEPSA charter, six pages, Feb. 1930, MAE, R1781, f29; *Memoria CEPSA 1930*, 5.

221. Memo, Capt. Gottfried Krüger, Abwehr Vb., Intelligence Conference, Berlin, 4 Sept. 1934, OKM Docs., PG 49087.

222. Manager of CAMPSA, n.s., to CAMPSA board, Madrid, 18 Apr. 1938, translated, copy given to State Department, Ambassador Ogden Hammond, Madrid, to Secretary of State Frank B. Kellogg, 6 July 1938, DS, 352.1153/St 2/99. For a general history of the early years of the Spanish oil monopoly, see Whealey, "La diplomacia española del petróleo: De junio de 1927 a abril de 1931," *Cuadernos Económicos de ICE*, no. 10 (Madrid, 1979): 511-31; idem, "Anglo-American Oil Confronts Spanish Nationalism, 1927-31," *Diplomatic History* 12 (Spring 1988): 111-26; and Adrian Shubert, "Oil Companies and Governments: International Reaction to the Nationalisation of the Petroleum Industry in Spain: 1927-1930," *Journal of Contemporary History* 15 (Oct. 1980): 701-20.

223. Dateline Madrid, June 23, *Times* (London), 24 June 1927, p. 15, col. 2; Annual Report of CAMPSA in *Petroleum Times* [Shell Ltd.], 25 (18 April 1931): 594.

224. Mining department, German Economics Ministry, n.s., memo W 4709, 18 Sept. 1944, Germ. Eco. Min., 31/24861-63.

225. Ibid., Whealey, "Diplomacia española del petróleo," 513, 527, 529; enclosure II to letter, Gustavo F. Fliechler, private German oilman, to German Ambassador in Madrid von Stohrer, 25 July 1941, GFM, 1308/348886-91.

226. Memo, Schwendemann, 26 Aug. 1938, GFM, 1606/385767-68.

227. Naval attaché, San Sebastián, through GFM to OKM, tel. 953, 6 Sept. 1939, OKM Docs., PG 48843.

228. Aide Lt. Menzell, San Sebastián, to Naval Attaché Group, rep. 35 g., 16 Jan. 1939, OKM Docs., PG 48838.

229. Minute of Canaris trip, 20 Apr.-8 May 1925, OKM Docs., PG 48903.

230. French ambassador in Madrid to Spanish minister of external affairs, Manuel G. Hontoria, 7 June 1919, MAE [Sect. II?], Política Alemana, 1917-1919,

(bundle 2, no. 2291. This bundle had 110 files. The document was in file no. 52 by my unofficial count. For the problems of these records see Robert H. Whealey, "Opportunities and Disappointments in the Spanish Foreign Ministry Archives," *Archives* 12 (Autumn 1975): 68-73. Rüggeberg Sr. joined the NSDAP on 1 Aug. 1935, Political Director W. Wendell Blancke, Berlin, to Blankinship, Spain, 29 Aug. 1946, OMGUS Docs., box 137, part 1/4, file "Suspicious Johns."

231. Meyer-Döhner, San Sebastián, to Naval Attaché Group, rep. 15/39 g. Kdos., 3 Apr. 1939, OKM Docs., PG 80835.

232. Meyer-Döhner to Naval Attaché Group, rep. 80/39 g. Kdos., 16 Sept. 1939, OKM Docs., PG 48843.

233. Meyer-Döhner to Naval Attaché Group, rep. 24/39, 19 Apr. 1939, OKM Docs., PG 48843.

234. Attaché Meyer-Döhner, San Sebastián, to Attaché Group OKM, dis. 178 g., 19 Dec. 1938, OKM Docs., PG 80730; Party comrade Rudolf Tesmann, AO Berlin, to Robert Fischer, Bohle's legal assistant in Foreign Office, letter Te/Rsz, 5 July 1939, GFM, 269/17401-02; Diebel, OKW, to Meyer-Döhner, unnumbered tel., Ausl. IV, 27 Aug. 1939, OKM Docs., PG 48843.

235. Personnel list, OKW Docs., 28/738541.

236. Viñas, *Alemania*, 2nd ed., 256.

237. Interrogation of Paul Körner by Eric Kaufman, Nürnberg, No. 439 D, 15 Sept. 1947, "U.S. Army, Nürnberg Trials." One of the few surviving Forschungsamt papers is published in David Irving, ed., *Break of Security: The German Secret Intelligence File on Events Leading to the Second World War* (London 1968). See also David Kahn, "Forschungsamt: Nazi Germany's Most Secret Communications Intelligence Agency," *Cryptologia* 2 (Jan. 1978): 12-19, an excerpt from Kahn's *Hitler's Spies*; Michael Geyer, "National Socialist Germany: The Politics of Information," in May, *Knowing One's Enemies* 322-24.

238. See ch. 4, above.

239. Karl Bartz, *The Downfall of the German Secret Service* (London, 1956), 62.

240. Gen. Schweikard, Sonderstab W, to supreme finance president for foreign exchange (Reichsbank), 169/39 III, 29 June 1939, OKW Docs., item 1124. This is part of the T-77 collection and will be microfilmed in the future. "Item" means the originals were seen at Alexandria, Va.; interrogation, Erich Neumann, chief assistant to Paul Körner in the Four-Year Plan, by Mr. Hartmann, Nürnberg, No. 1920 c., 26 Sept. 1947, "U.S. Army, Nurnberg Trials."

241. Canaris and Göring agreement, Chef Ausl. No. 73/39 Kdos. (ZF), 17 Apr. 1939; Canaris to Reich. Eco. Min. Dr. Landwehr, 73/39 g. Kdos. II (ZF II), 5 May 1939, OKW Docs., item 1121a.

242. Canaris to Göring, 59 a 12/13 a, 129/39 g. Kdos. (ZF II), 23 May 1939, ibid.

243. Reg. Rat. Freiherr von Dungen, R.L.M., Industrial Sect. to supreme finance president, Reichsbank Amtsrat Reichelt, LD I Az 66 m 12 no. 1004/39 (Le) g. Kdos., 7 Jan. 1939; Macht, R.L.M., to Reichelt, Az 66 m 12 No. 9187/39 g. Kdos., 30 Mar. 1939; Macht to Reichelt, Az 66 m 12 No. 9215/39 g. Kdos., 13 Apr. 1939; Maj. Gen. Eberhard Fischer, R.L.M., chief of 4th Aviation Bureau, to Reichelt, LD I Az 66 m 12 No. 9295/39 g. Kdos., 29 Apr. 1939, OKW Docs., item 1124. This file was originally part of the Reichsbank's files but was turned over to the

Abwehr. Two other Sonderstab W people are mentioned in similar files, OKW Docs., items 1121a and 1123.

244. Counselor Hermann Sabath, Economic Policy Dept., Berlin, to Stohrer, dis. W 701 g. Rs., 15 May 1939, GFM 4365/E082242-43.

245. Hans Mosolff, Food Business Group of Four-Year Plan, Berlin, rep. Tgb. Gr. 194/38, Aug. [n.d.] 1939, Misc. Germ. Rec., T-84, 152/14737397-424. This and other documents in the file carefully avoid any military or strategic references, except that large docks were to be constructed. The British reported the details of Winter's plan,. Head, Las Palmas, to Fox, Tenerife, 27 July 1938, FO/371, vol. 22682, W11086/1142/41.

246. Draft tel. by Sabath to Madrid embassy, 6 Nov. 1939, GFM, 3868/E054889.

247. Unsigned dispatch, Paris embassy to Foreign Ministry, 1506/42 g., 5 Aug. 1942, GFM, 1308/347060-61; Commercial Attaché Richard Enge, Madrid, to GFM, 21 Oct. 1942, GFM, 1308/347041-42.

248. Stohrer to GFM, dis. 195, 18 Jan. 1939, GFM, 4365/E082246-47.

249. [Signature illegible], Food Division of Four-Year Plan to Supreme Forest Master Menthe, memo G 730 Dr. M/V, 9 June 1939, Misc. Germ. Rec., 152/1437381; [n.s.] captain of M.V. *Eider*, at sea, to Norddeutscher Lloyd, Bremen, 3 July 1939, ibid., 152/1437454-56.

250. Memo, "Notes for Wehrmacht discussions with Italy," 26 Nov. 1938, *DGFP*, ser. D, vol. 4, doc. 411. Keitel sent the memo to Ribbentrop on 30 Nov., stating that it had been drawn up on the Führer's orders in accordance with his detailed intructions.

251. Keitel to Cmd. of Navy Adm. Raeder, W.F.A./L No. 18/39 g. Ia Chef, 3 Mar. 1939, GFM, 8230/E585442-43.

252. Ambassador Eberhard von Stohrer, San Sebastián, to GFM, tel. 223, 10 Mar. 1939, OKM Docs., PG 80676.

253. Memo, Weizsäcker, St. S. 274, 27 Mar. 1939, GFM, 483/23194; memo, Under State Secretary Woermann, 12 Apr. 1939, *DGFP*, ser. D, vol. 3, doc. 785.

254. Carl Goerdler—an anti-Nazi who had contacts with the OKW and Göring, Schacht, Neurath, and Capt. Fritz Wiedemann, Hitler's attaché—claimed that, as late as 15 Jan., Hitler still intended to stay in Spain and to get Franco to close the Straits against France and Britain. Goerdler to British intelligence agent A.P. Young and FO, 15 Jan. 1939. A.P. Young, *The X Documents* (London, 1974), 158-60. The first indirect evidence of Hitler's intention to withdraw the Legion Condor is on 5-6 Jan. when he decided to make a movie of the legion for a Berlin victory spectacle. Minutes by Schwendemann to Culture Sect., 5-6 Jan., GFM, 1573/381000-01.

255. Einhorn, *Die faschistische Intervention*, 106.

256. Propaganda chief of OKW, Maj. Georg von Wedel, to Capt. Hans Gerhard Meyer, 3rd sect., General Staff, Gr. Abt. VII, et al., memo OKW 426/1 II d (W. Pr.), 24 Feb. 1939, OKW Docs., 935/6585567; chief of OKW, Gen. Wilhelm Keitel, to Minister of Propaganda Joseph Goebbels, letters OKW 23/39 g./11 b (W. Pr.), 13 Apr. 1939, OKW Docs., 975/4463888.

257. "Pistorius Report" [June 1939], OKM Docs., PG 80769.

258. Stohrer to GFM, 13 Mar. 1939, *DGFP*, ser. D, vol. 3, doc. 755.

259. Stohrer to GFM, 29 Mar. 1939, with enclosure, military attaché conversation with Gen. Gambara, Logroño, 16 Mar., ibid., doc. 765.

260. Memo, Ciano conversation with Ribbentrop, Milan, 6-7 May, *Ciano's Diplomatic Papers*, 283-86.

261. Cervera, *Memorias de guerra*, 28-30.

262. Meyer-Döhner to Naval Attaché Group, rep. 307 g., 27 Mar. 1939, OKM Docs., PG 80730.

263. Reps., Stohrer from San Sebastián, 31 Mar. 3 and 4 Apr. 1939, *DGFP*, ser. D, vol. 3, docs. 772, 777, 778.

264. Woermann to OKM, OKW, and Oberkommando der Luftwaffe, memo Pol. III 1087 g., 8 May 1939, GFM, M 70/M002269-70b; memo, Stohrer, 14 Apr. 1939, *DGFP*, ser. D, vol. 3, doc. 786. Stohrer brought to Berlin a twenty-five-point outline mentioning military talks, memo Pol. III 1087 g., n.d. [14? Apr.]; annex to above published as doc. 786, GFM 1588/383344-47.

265. Attaché Lange, Rome, to Italian Naval Command [R. Oliva?], G 1215, 17 Apr. 1939, OKM Docs., PG 45181.

266. Supreme Commander of the Navy, n.s., to counselor Kurt von Kamphoevener, GFM, R 910 g., 1 Abt. Skl. c, 4 Apr. 1939, ibid.

267. Supreme Commander of the Navy to naval attaché in Rome, R 900, 1 Abt., Skl., 4 Apr. 1939, ibid.

268. Annex by Dönitz, part of Admiral Boehm's rep., Lisbon, G. 3199 A I, to OKM, 7 May 1939, ibid.

269. Bullock, *Hitler*, 500-504.

270. Chargé Christian Vaux Saint-Cyr, Berlin, to foreign minister, 18 April 1939, *DDF*, 2nd ser. , vol. 15, doc. 436.

271. Meyer-Döhner to Naval Attaché Group, rep. 400 g., 27 Apr. 1939, OKM Docs., PG 48838.

272. Press reports, *DGFP*, ser. D, vol 6, p. 1123 n 5.

273. Meyer-Döhner, San Sebastián, to Legion Condor (S/88 II a), León, rep. 437, 13 May 1939, OKM Docs., PG 48838; Menzell to Naval Attaché Group, rep. 501, 1 June 1939, ibid.

274. Memo of conversation, 12 Apr. 1939, *DGFP*, ser. D, vol. 6, appendix 1, doc. iii, Italian version of talks, Military Attaché Luigi E. Marras to Pariani, Innsbruck, 5 Apr. 1939, *DDI*, 8th ser., vol. 13, appendix 3, doc. 6.

275. Minute, conversation, Göring, Mussolini, and Ciano, 15 Apr. 1939, and conversation, Göring, Mussolini, and Ciano by interpreter Paul Schmidt, 18 Apr. 1939, *DGFP*, ser. D, vol. 6, docs. 205, 211; Mackensen to GFM, Dis. 3367, 26 Apr. 1939, GFM, 8420/E592884-87.

276. Poncet, Rome, to Bonnet, 17 Apr. 1939, *DDF*, 2nd series, vol. 15, doc. 430; memo, Göring-Mussolini conversation, 18 Apr. 1939, *DGFP*, ser. D, vol. 6, doc. 211.

277. Ribbentrop to von Brauchitsch, 18 Apr. 1939, OKH Docs., 252/6232736.

278. According to the schedule set forth in a memo by Lt. Col. Kurt Siewert, staff of von Brauchitsch, Ob. d H. memo 590, 24 Apr. 1939, OKH Docs., 252/6232722-24.

279. Printed program, *Königliches Italienisches Heer: Tag des Heeres* (Rome, 9 May 1939), 2, filmed, OKH Docs., 252/6232762.

280. General Staff Attaché Group [signature illegible] to German military attaché in Rome, Col. Enno von Rintelen, dis. no. Az 3 a/n 39 Att. Gr. III, no. 1116/39, 16 May 1939, OKH Docs., 329/6322914.

281. Ciano, memo of conversation with Ribbentrop, 6-7 May 1939, *Ciano's Diplomatic Papers*, 283-86; Toscano, *Origins of the Pact of Steel*, 289-307.

282. Conversation of Ribbentrop with Ciano, 6-7 May 1939, *DGFP*, series D, vol. 6, doc. 341.

283. Woermann to OKM Naval Attaché Group, 8 May 1939, memo, Pol. III, 1087 g., GFM, M 70/M002269-70.

Chapter 6. Conclusions

1. The list of vessels is in "Pistorius Report," OKM Docs., PG 80769.

2. See a brief description of the NIC documents in the tables of contents of *DGFP*, ser. D, vol. 3, and *DBFP*, series 3.

3. *DGFP*, ser. D, vol. 3, docs. 535, 583, 602, 629, 633, 635-646, 653, 677, 678, 688, 696.

4. For more on the "New Order," see Robert Waite, *The Psychopathic God: Adolf Hitler* (New York, 1977), 92; Hans-Adolf Jacobsen, *National-sozialistische Aussenpolitik 1933-1938* (Frankfurt, A.M., 1968), 54, 333-38; Hermann Rauschning, *Hitler Speaks* (London, 1939), 229-30.

5. James W. Morley, *Deterrent Diplomacy: Japan, Germany, and the USSR (1935-40)* (New York, 1977), 107, 202.

6. Philip Rees has edited a comprehensive bibliography of European fascism: *Fascism and Pre-Fascism in Europe, 1890-1945: A Bibliography of the Extreme Right* (New York, 1984). The general theory, Germany, Italy, and Spain are covered.

7. Macgregor Knox, "Conquest," 1-57.

8. Juan Linz, "Some Notes toward a Comparative Study of Fascism in Sociological Historical Perspective," in *Fascism: A Readers Guide* (1976), 3-121; Linz, "Political Space and Fascism as a Late Comer," in *Who Were the Fascists?* (1981), 153-89.

9. Magaz to Woermann, memo for Ribbentrop, 25 Aug. 1939, GFM, 269/174415.

10. Detwiler, *Hitler, Franco und Gilbraltar*; Charles B. Burdick, *Germany's Military Strategy and Spain in World War II* (Syracuse, N.Y., 1968).

11. See Raymond L. Proctor, *Agony of a Neutral: Spanish-German Wartime Relations and the "Blue Division"* (Moscow, Ida., 1974); Gerald R. Kleinfeld and Lewis A. Tambs, *Hitler's Spanish Legion: The Blue Division in Russia* (Carbondale, Ill., 1979).

12. Sybil Milton, "The Spanish Republican Refugees in France, 1938-41" (paper presented at a conference on "World War II—The 50th Anniversary: 1936, the Spanish Civil War," Siena College, New York, June 1986). The figure of 12,000 is a minimum because it is just for Mauthausen, for which the statistics on Spaniards are available. See also Nancy MacDonald, *Homage to the Spanish Exiles* (New York, 1987); Louis Stein, *Beyond Death and Exile: The Spanish Republicans in France, 1939-1955* (Cambridge, Mass., 1979).

13. David Wingeate Pike, "Franco and the Axis Stigma," *JCH* 17 (July 1982): 369-407.

14. Basil Liddell Hart, *Memoirs* 2 (London, 1965): 142. Also, affirmed by a

first-hand observer at the time, U.S. Ambassador Claude Bowers, *My Mission to Spain: Watching the Rehearsal for World War II* (New York, 1954); Whealey, "Foreign Intervention"; Whealey, "Economic Influence," n 1; Frank elaborated it most systematically in "The Spanish Civil War and the Coming of the Second World War," *IHR* (Aug. 1987).

Bibliographical Note

Unpublished Documentary Sources Used

GERMAN DOCUMENTS

The millions of German documents now available in the United States on microfilm are a great boon to historical scholarship. The guides to these materials are many; see Robert Wolfe, ed., *Captured German and Related Records: A National Archives Conference* (Athens, Ohio: Ohio University Press, 1974). Christopher M. Kimmich has edited a series of five volumes, the first of which was his own *German Foreign Policy, 1981–1945: A Guide to Research and Research Materials* (Wilmington, Del.: Scholarly Resources, 1981). Others in the same series are on France by Robert J. Young, Britain by Sidney Aster, Italy by Alan Cassels, and a fifth, by George Baer, on international organizations.

For new materials, recent articles in the *Vierteljahreshefte für Zeitgeschichte* and the American Historical Association's *Recently Published Articles* are the best way to keep up to date. For general directories of archives and reference works, consult current issues of the American Committee on the History of the Second World War, "Newsletter," ed. Donald S. Detwiler (Carbondale: Southern Illinois Univ.).

GERMAN FOREIGN MINISTRY

For specific information on the use of the ministry's records, *A Catalog of Files and Microfilms of the German Foreign Ministry Archives, 1920-1945*, 4 vols., ed. George Kent (Stanford, Calif.: Stanford Univ. Press, 1961–) is indispensable. This catalogue lists the rolls of microfilm with cross-references to the original German file titles.

One of the more interesting files from the Foreign Ministry for my work was 269. This serial was the file on Spain of Reichsleiter Bohle, containing

435 frames. Bohle, head of the Nazi Party Abroad (AO), was made an under state secretary in the Foreign Ministry, and the file was filmed in its entirety. It covered the period from late 1937 to early 1940. The importance of the file is that it demolishes a myth. Bohle was contacted by Bernhardt in July 1936 when intervention in the Spanish Civil War began. In July 1936 the Spanish Anarchists and Communists captured the files of the AO office in Barcelona, and many excerpts from these documents were distorted and sensationalized by Otto Katz, "Editor of the Brown Book of the Hitler Terror," in *The Nazi Conspiracy in Spain,* trans. Emile Burns (London: Victor Gollancz, 1937).

Bohle was interrogated by the Nürnberg investigators in 1945 and 1946 on the supposition that he was the head of a major international espionage-sabotage network. Serial 269 shows that he was not primarily the sponsor of Fifth Column activities but was mostly interested in private German citizens abroad. His main function was to see that these people were good Nazis, ideologically, and his influence on the determination of foreign policy has been overdrawn. The file contains many papers originating with the party and dealing with such routine matters as seeing that seamen had enough money to get home. The party papers were important for the damages question that bore on Bernhardt's power in Spain. But the significant Nazi was Bernhardt because of his connections with Göring and Franco—not because he was "an agent of Bohle."

More revealing in this file are those papers Bohle received as a Foreign Ministry official. Thus, copies of Stohrer's, Schwendemann's, and Woermann's memoranda are ample. They were given to Bohle for informational purposes. Donald M. McKale, *The Swastika Outside Germany* (Kent, Ohio: Kent State Univ. Press, 1977) is a broad study of the AO and Bohle's activities.

The only other file that, because of its unusual source, needs special comment is serial 1809. This file of Czech Foreign Office materials was captured by the Germans when they took Prague in March 1939 and was translated into German by a team headed by Fritz von Berber. Part of the collection was published as Fritz von Berber, ed., *Veröffentlichungen des Deutschen Instituts für Aussenpolitische Forschung: Europäische Politik 1933-1938 im Spiegel der Prager Akten,* vol. 8 (Essen: Essener Verlagsanstalt, 1941). It was only used marginally in this study.

GERMAN NAVAL RECORDS

Next to the Foreign Ministry Records, the records of the Oberkommando der Kriegsmarine (OKM) were most important. In some respects they were even more important because of their completeness, but substantively they are secondary because this book is not primarily a military history. The OKM documents contain virtually all the reports of Attaché Meyer-Döhner, plus

occasional copies of reports from other German observers in Spain. Therefore, unlike the other German records used, there are no embarrassing gaps
of information.

In 1945, sixty thousand naval files were taken to Tambach Castle. The
British navy then catalogued the records, giving them a number preceded by
the prefix P.G. The U.S. Office of Naval Intelligence obtained microfilmed
versions of 60 percent of the total collection. They are now at the National
Archives in Washington, D.C. Regarding Spain, almost 100 percent were
filmed and are available. The originals remain in Freiburg, West Germany, at
the Militärgeschichtliches Forschungsamt. Some files are still retained in
London. London, Washington, Koblenz, Freiburg, and the University of
Michigan all have catalogues. In addition to Robert Wolfe's guide (p. 219),
there is the important work by Keith W. Bird, *German Naval History: A
Guide to the Literature* (New York: Garland Reference Library of Social
Science, 1985). He has a section on unpublished sources (pp. 57-64) and
one on the Spanish Civil War (pp. 566-70).

OTHER GERMAN AGENCY RECORDS

The AHA Committee for the Study of War Documents began in 1956 to
microfilm tons of records that had been held by the United States Army in
Alexandria, Virginia, since the end of World War II. The project came to a
close in August 1961, but not all of the records held by the army were
declassified. The prefaces to the various guides to this material are indispensable. There are eighty-four mimeographed guides, and additional ones are
expected. Copies of these "Guides to German Records Microfilmed at
Alexandria, Va." can be obtained from the National Archives. The scope of
topics covered in these documents is vast, but their value is mainly for the
study of domestic German developments from 1933 to 1945.

For the study of German-Spanish relations in particular, it is significant
to note the groups of German records *not* available to the Alexandria Project.
Most of the Reich Economics Ministry files were left in what is now East
Germany, so those records filmed at Alexandria (T-71, guide no. 1) are
fragmentary. They do not include the files of ROWAK, or the Mining
Section dealing with Spain, or the Foreign Trade Section, or correspondence
with Helmuth Wohlthat's Four-Year Plan office. Most of these were destroyed, but some ROWAK material is at Koblenz.

The Military Records, OKW Documents T-77(guide no. 5, 7, 17, 18,
19, 80), OKH (Oberkommando des Heeres) Documents T-78 (guide no. 12,
29, 30), and Miscellaneous German Records T-84 (part 2, guide no. 8)
proved to be the major records within the Alexandria group of significance
for this study. We have no Sonderstab W records and only a small fragment
of Legion Condor records concerned with engineering. Very few of the
German military attaché reports (unlike the naval reports) are available. We

know very little about the German army talks with the Spaniards, for virtually no reports from Attaché Funck, San Sebastián, are in the filmed OKW and OKH documents. Some copies of military attaché reports are found in the OKH records, particularly those sent to and from Rome.

The German air force records filmed at Alexandria concern production, testing, and other matters not pertinent to this study. Most of the air force records were destroyed in 1944 by bombing. Some of the General Staff records are in East Germany; others are in Freiburg. The status of the German air force records is described in Horst Boog, "Germanic Air Forces and the Historiography of the Air War," *Aerospace Historian* 31 (March 1984): 38-42. David Irving, *The Rise and Fall of the Luftwaffe: The Life of Luftwaffe Marshal Erhard Milch* (London: Weidenfeld & Nicolson, 1972), discusses the German air force records in the British Museum.

These critical remarks about the content of the Alexandria records are not to imply that they had no value to the study of German-Spanish relations, 1936-1939. In the course of skimming hundreds of serials I found significant documents. The guides are indispensable, but titles of files are misleading, and there is no substitute for actual examination. Light is shed on the nature of the Four-Year Plan and Göring's role in it within certain files of the Miscellaneous German Records Collection (T-84). This collection also has a significant file on the "Canary Islands Expedition."

Chapter 4, with the precise economic data on the background for German-Spanish economic relations, was built on German Economics Ministry (T-71) files and other economic agencies filmed in the Miscellaneous Collection (T-84). Also, the Economic Warfare Section, Wi. Rü. Amt (Wirtschaft Rüstungs Amt), of the OKW (T-77) built up vast files of economic data that were very helpful throughout.

The SS Records T-175 on Marxism and communism were helpful for chapters 2 and 3.

The Berlin Document Center records were also filmed by the AHA, but unfortunately without frame numbers. Roll 999 of its collection T-580 gives a complete list.

THE MILITARY INSTITUTE AT FREIBURG (MFA)

The most valuable part of the MFA collection for this topic, from the point of view of an American, is for the air force records not available on microfilm in the United States. Some additional naval materials also not filmed can be found there. From the European point of view, the original OKW, OKH, OKM, and RLM (Reichsluftministerium) records can all be seen there. My citations (e.g., MFA/ L, Militärgeschichtliches Forschungsamt/Luftminis-terium) have been changed to RL/BA MA, Reichsluftministerium/Bun-desarchiv Militärische Amt.

The so-called Milch diary is really an appointments calendar, and from the context many of the entries seem to have been one day behind. He may have written about the previous day's experience early in the morning.

SPANISH DOCUMENTS

In general, Spain's archives are in a state of underdevelopment when compared to Great Britain's or even West Germany's. Four different Spanish archives are important:

(1) Servicio Histórico Militar, Madrid, houses the official operational records of General Franco. By Spanish standards they have a well-organized index, but there is no substitute for looking at entire bundles. The index looks good in theory, and the archivists would like to give the researcher only a specific file. But the files for Germany contain only the most routine formal correspondence, while the real German story is buried throughout all the bundles—which are indexed under aviation, trucks, cannon, et. Therefore, the researcher has to go through the four major sections—Administration, Intelligence, Operations, and Supply—to see the picture as a whole. Unfortunately, because of time restrictions, I worked in only 72 bundles out of a possible 682 just for the Headquarters (CGG). There are also field units and captured Republican army records in the military archive. A history and guide to the archive has been published by anonymous editors, "Archivos del Servicio Histórico Militar: El de la Guerra de Liberación," *Revista de Historia Militar* 24 (1968): 161-70.

(2) Jefatura Nacional de Adquisiciones is a second group of most important military and economic records, consisting of about 100 bundles out of a total of 222 bundles of documents, mostly individual bills of sale and requests kept by the Nationalist army's office of supply. They became the property of the Dirección General de Adquisiciones, also called during the civil war the Jefatura Nacional de Adquisiciones (JNA). The 222 bundles cover the period 1936 to 1950. The records are found in the Archivo Histórico National, Madrid. Catalogue no. 66 gives a brief, inadequate description. Franco created the Jefatura on 26 February 1938 as a subsection of the vice presidency, then under General Count Francisco Gómez-Jordana. Although the basic collection begins in the spring of 1938, the Jefatura inherited some scattered files that cover the period from the fall of 1936 to February 1938 from Nicolás Franco, general secretary to the chief of state and older brother of the generalissimo.

For purposes of this book, the bundles may be classified into nine sections:

1. Pedidos de Alemania (HISMA-ROWAK) (labeled A):   13 bundles
2. Pedidos de la Comandancia (MC) bills,
     General de Artilleria:_   13 bundles

3. Pedidos de la Intendencia M) bills:	6 bundles
4. Pedidos del Ministerio del Aire (MA) bills:	3 bundles
5. Pedidos de Marina (MB):	2 bundles
6. Pedidos de Italia (I):	2 bundles
7. Pedidos de Portugal (P) bills:	1 bundle
8. Other military operational sections, such as transport, health, and tires:	16 bundles
9. Other correspondence, bills, budgets, and charts, mostly with private manufacturers:	50 bundles

The Franco regime accumulated the rest of the hundred-odd bundles of documents in the period 1940-1950.

The system of labeling all bills apparently began with the German section in March 1937 (see bundle 1, file A869), but only after June and July 1937 are the records systematic. The basis of the numbering system is by delivery date rather than by order date.

Bundle 167 shows the origin of the Germn bills A section. It is doubtful that archivists will ever discover all the records from July 1936 to July 1937. Beginning with bill A709 on 29 July 1937 (see also bundle 186), the numbers of the list of purchases from Germany are complete to the end of the war. Another key document explaining the system can be found in bundle 204, file 1.

One year later, Franco's supply office organized the other sections on a systematic basis. For example, the first two orders received for the navy were given the numbers MB 200 and MB 201. Numbers 1 to 200 seem to have been left blank in each subsection of the Jefatura—artillery, tires, etc.—for the records of order from the period July 1936 to July 1938 that they hoped would turn up.

Unfortunately, the archivists' labeling of the bundles from 1 to 222 does not reflect an entirely chronological or topical ordering of the documents. The bundle numbers used in my endnotes are the archival numbers in catalogue 66. Bundles 202, 203, and 204 consist of important index materials to the whole record group and should be looked at first by future researchers.

(3) The Ministerio Asúntos Exteriores records are officially open through 1945. The records for the period 1914 to 1931 seem to be complete but are not well organized, despite the fact that the files show evidence of being reorganized three times. For guides see James W. Cortada, "Spanish Foreign Office Archives," Society for Historians of American Foreign Relations Newsletter 4 (Sept. 1973): 2-4; Cortada, "Libraries and Archives of Madrid," Journal of Library History 9 (Apr. 1974): 176-88; and Robert H. Whealey, "Opportunities and Disappointments in the Spanish Foreign Ministry Archives," Archives 12 (Autumn 1975): 68-73. More comprehensive guides are needed.

As of 1977-1978 (the last time I was in Spain), the records up to 1945 were available but did not seem complete. Rather they appear to have been the political director's most routine files. During 1937, the day-to-day head for foreign relations was Miguel Angel de Muguiro, secretary of exterior relations. His office forwarded economic questions raised by the Germans to the relevant authorities in the Junta Técnica within a day or two of receipt. There the delay might be considerable. The Germans would send inquiries about every two months reminding the Spaniards of the original inquiry.

The reorganization of the Spanish government in the spring of 1938 did away with the Junta Técnica in favor of traditional ministries. The work done by de Muguiro was taken over by E.E. de Monteros, subsecretary of the foreign ministry. He handled most routine business rather than Count Jordana, who was also second in command to Franco for nonmilitary administrative matters. In 1939 de Muguiro was serving as Nationalist minister to Hungary.

The 1938 reorganization resulted in the misplacement of some files and delays in handling inquiries. Also in 1938 the German embassy moved to San Sebastián, where the other diplomatic representatives to the Nationalists were located. This meant a delay of up to a week between the date letters were dispatched and the time they were received by the Foreign Ministry in Burgos.

(4) The Archivo General Alcalá de Henares is a relatively new archive, eventually to be centralized to accept documents from all the major ministries. The archive was begun in the 1970s. The Foreign Ministry section has deposited twelve boxes of records from the Spanish Republic's procurement agency, CAMPSA-Gentibus, which shed light on aid by the Soviets and others to the Republic. There are also two additional bundles of Gentibus records in the JNA documents (see above, point 2.)

SPANISH NEWSPAPERS

The Hemeroteca Muncipal in Madrid is excellent for newspapers and magazines of the 1930s.

UNPUBLISHED ITALIAN DOCUMENTS

The National Archives has a fragmentary collection of Italian documents on microfilm, T-586. Roll 1 gives the complete list. They were captured by the U.S. army when invading Italy and were filmed by a joint American-British military intelligence unit during World War II. A published catalogue is available. These records are extremely diverse in nature, including fragments from several Italian ministries for the years 1920-1943. Only two groups of documents shed light on Spain: the files of the Duce's secretary and the minister of popular culture. They contain some interesting material on Italian-French-Spanish relations in 1939. There is nothing on Spain in the unpublished "Lisbon Papers" that has not been published in *Ciano's Diplomatic Papers*. The "Akten Sammelstelle Sud," in the World War II Branch of the National Archives, is good for the Italian army's campaigns in the 1940s, but of little interest for Spain in the 1930s. The complex story of Italian archives is explained in great detail in Howard McCaw Smyth, *Secrets of the Fascist Era: How Uncle Sam Obtained Some of the Top-Level Documents of Mussolini's Period* (Carbondale, Ill.: Southern Illinois Univ. Press, 1975), and also in a chapter in Robert Wolfe's *Captured German Records. The Fascist Era* contains a valuable appendix and a comment (p. 17) that lists by document certain entries in *Ciano's Diplomatic Papers (L'Europa verso la catastrofe)* which are incomplete or inaccurate and should be checked with archives. None of these documents was used in this book.

Ismael Saz and Javier Tusell edited a collection of 402 Italian Foreign Ministry documents: *Fascistas en España: La intervención en la Guerra Civil a través de los telegramas de le missione militare Italiana en Spagna 15 Diciembre 1936-31 Marzo 1937* (Madrid: Consejo Superior de Investigaciónes Cientificas Escuela España de História y Arqueologia en Roma, 1981). These include mostly military reports to Rome from General Roatta.

OMGUS RECORDS

Records from the U.S. military occupation of Germany are in the National Archives at the branch in Suitland, Maryland. They were partially released in 1972, and the screening was completed in 1979. I used most of the records in 1977 when shipping lists were available. By 1981 many were reboxed. The researcher must hunt in Spanish style through many boxes, although the shipping list (SL) serves as a rough guide. Some minor files were still classified as of 1981.

In 1945, at the end of World War II, the U.S. government was interested in Operation Safehaven, rounding up German assets in Spain. Important interrogations were held in Germany and Madrid in 1944-1948. The collection reveals much about economics and ties in with U.S. State Department records on Operation Safehaven. See memo, n.s., Madrid, to U.S. State Department, 4 Oct. 1945, shipping list, box 64, part 2/3, file "External Assets Spain," for a description of the Safehaven project and its personnel. For the origin of Safehaven, stemming from the Bretton Woods conference of February 1944, see Herron Adams, Foreign Exchange Control, London, to Allan Fischer, Foreign Exchange & Blockade Branch, U.S. Control Committee, Financial Division, Frankfurt, 24 July 1945, shipping list, box 66, part 3/3, file "Safehaven Negotiations"; also *FRUS*, 1944, 2: 213-51, (1945), 2: 852-925.

BRITISH AND U.S. RECORDS

The Foreign Office papers and cabinet records at the Public Record Office
are so well organized in contrast to German, Spanish, and Italian that little
comment is necessary. FO/371 stands for the complete documents with
minutes by Foreign Office officials. Copies of the most important documents can be seen in the series of "Confidential Prints." A specific fact or
question can be traced through the register books (index books) to an exact
telegram within minutes. U.S. State Department records from before World
War II are also well catalogued and easy to work with.

INTERVIEWS

Some interviews are of little value because researchers have not done
enough basic homework. I had the opportunity to interview three Germans
involved in this story: Commander Helmuth Heye of the OKM; Erhard
Milch, state secretary for the Luftwaffe; and Helmuth Wohlthat, ministerial
director. I did not learn much from my interview with then Admiral Heye
because my research was still in a formative stage in 1960. Heye was on the
NATO staff and none too eager to discuss the Spanish Civil War with me.

My interviews with Wohlthat in 1970 and 1971 were of an entirely dif-
ferent character. I talked with him three times, about four hours each time.
By then I had done sufficient research to have well formulated questions.
Wohlthat was entirely removed from politics and was willing to talk history.

I met Milch through Wohlthat in 1971 for another four-hour session.
Minutes of these interviews have been turned over to the Southworth
Collection of the University of California, San Diego, to Ohio University,
and to the Oral History Collection of Columbia University. Both Wohlthat
and Milch reveal incidental details about German policy that have nothing to
do with this book but that other scholars may find interesting.

Published Historiography of Germano-Spanish Relations

There are no comprehensive works in English dealing with the German
intervention, but there are six accounts of the German role in the Spanish
Civil War and all were written by Germans. None of them use any Spanish
or U.S. documents. Only one has used the Foreign Office records. Manfred
Merkes, *Die deutsche Politik gegenüber dem spanischen Bürgerkrieg,
1936-1939*, Bonner Historische Forschungen, 2nd ed. (Bonn: Ludwig
Rohrscheid Verlag, 1967), has an excellent summary of the military aspects
of German intervention and a good bibliography. His account is judicious
and technically competent, but he presents a conservative case most favorable for German intervention without justifying Hitler or nazism. He sticks
so close to the documentary record that his work at times becomes a

justification for the German bureaucracy, making it seem independent of the Führer, whom in fact it loyally served. Unlike Anglo-American writers, Merkes does not regret the demise of the Second Spanish Republic, nor is he concerned with the relationship of the Spanish Civil War to the outbreak of World War II. His goal is to ensure that Anglo-American writers do not exaggerate the extent of Germany's military intervention in a limited, sideshow war.

Military historian Merkes is correct about the "sideshow war," but, in terms of diplomatic history, my work disagrees in pointing out the importance of the Spanish Civil War to the balance of power. His interpretation of Hitler and communism differs markedly from mine. In the first place, on social grounds he has a conservative bias that he identifies as "anti-communism." He uses the term "communism" as a label both for social unrest in Spain and for the foreign policy of the Soviet Union. This makes his entire work unclear. Despite his ample use of footnotes and exhaustive lists of sources, his encyclopedic approach to footnoting does not help pinpoint for the reader exactly who was saying what. In short, he set out on an ambitious project in which the text is too short for the quantity of materials available.

A second account of German-Spanish diplomatic relations during the civil war has been written by the East German scholar Marion Einhorn, *Die ökonomischen Hintergründe der faschistischen deutschen Intervention in Spanien, 1936-1939,* Deutsche Akademie der Wissenschaften zu Berlin, Schriften des Instituts für Geschichte Reihe 1: Allgemeine und Deutsche Geschichte, Band 15 (Berlin: Akademie Verlag, 1962). Despite its Communist bias, it is well documented, particularly on the economic questions. Some of these documents are unavailable in the West.

One collection used from the Deutsches Wirtschaftsinstitut in East Berlin contains corporate files from a vast variety of private German firms. A detailed examination of Einhorn's footnotes shows that many Foreign Ministry documents available in Washington on microfilm can also be found in the Deutsches Zentralarchiv Potsdam. In fact, it would appear that all but a small percentage of the Foreign Ministry documents at Potsdam are duplicated in the U.S. National Archives. Einhorn's material about the conspiracy before July 1936 (see above chap. 1, pp. 00-00) can be dismissed as propaganda. Both Einhorn and Merkes have deficiencies, yet taken together their strengths complement each other.

Hans-Henning Abendroth, *Hitler in der spanischen Arena: Die deutsch–spanischen Beziehungen im Spannungsfeld der europäischen Interessenpolitik vom Ausbruch des Bürgerkrieges bis zum Ausbruch des Weltkrieges, 1936-1939* (Paderborn: Ferdinand Schöningh, 1973), is much closer to my theme than either Merkes or Einhorn. But when the reader compares the tables of contents of our works, the differences become clear. My emphasis is more on Hitler's policy toward Spain in relation to his general European policy, whereas Abendroth emphasizes more the arena, i.e., events in Spain. His chapters 2, 6, and 12 cover themes similar to mine, but he has more to say about the Non-Intervention Committee and the other Great Powers and is, therefore, closer to Dante Puzzo (1962) and Patricia Van der Esch (1951). Both of these general diplomatic accounts are obsolete.

Abendroth differs from Merkes in that he uses considerable records from the British Foreign Office. Unlike Einhorn and myself, Abendroth plays down the role of economic factors. Like Merkes, Abendroth is a social conservative who partly justifies German intervention as serving the "cause of anti-communism," but he is less conservative and more critical of the German bureaucracy than is Merkes.

Abendroth has kept up with the literature by adding two more articles: "Die deutsche Intervention im spanischen Bürgerkrieg," *Vierteljahreshefte für Zeitgeschichte* 30 (Jan. 1982): 117-29; and "Deutschland, Frankreich und der spanische Bürgerkrieg, 1936-1939," in Klaus Hilderbrand, Ferdinand Werner, and Klaus Manfrass, eds., *Deutschland und Frankreich, 1936-1939 [Francia Beihefte]* 10 (Munich: Artemis Verlag, 1981): 453-74 The first article stresses the importance of anti-communism in the mentality of Hitler, but Abendroth does not define the term. The second, written on the occasion of a conference, devotes half its space to Germany. That side of the article basically reconfirms his earlier book. Hitler's antipathy toward and fear of communism are discussed on pp. 461-63, and Abendroth concludes, "Behind the defensive façade hid the aggressor." A weak France was essential for Hitler's planned conquest in the East, Abendroth also claims (p. 464). In short, he reconfirms the liberalism of Bullock and Weinberg.

Abendroth, *Mittelmann zwischen Franco und Hitler: Johannes Bernhardt erinnert 1936* (Marktheidenfeld: Willy Schleunung GmbH, 1978), is a booklet written in cooperation with Johannes Bernhardt and his wife, who read the text in 1976. It supplements and complements Angel Viñas, *La Alemania nazi y el 18 de Julio: Antecedentes de la intervención alemana en la guerra española* (Madrid, 1974, 1977), although Abendroth did not consult Viñas (see 2nd ed., p. 321).

In *Der spanische Bürgerkrieg in der Internationalen Politik, 1936-1939* (Munich: Nymphenburger Verlagshandlung, 1976), Wolfgang Schieder and Christof Dipper edit thirteen essays, most of which are reprints of authors such as Einhorn. Schieder writes an introduction and an essay on German intervention. Half the book focuses on German-Italian relations, the other half on the USSR. What is notable about Schieder's introduction and essay is that he is a West German who finally escapes from the "anti-communist" viewpoint. The civil war is not communism vs. fascism, but rather anarchism vs. militarism (p. 12). Schieder and I disagree, however, as to Hitler's motives. He sees improvisation and nihilism (pp. 19, 168); I see the clever propagandist during the civil war and the shrewd diplomat who, until 1939, had a keen sense of timing and insight into the fears of his rivals: Baldwin, Chamberlain, Mussolini, Franco, Stalin, Blum, Bonnet, Delbos, and Daladier.

Otfried Dankelmann, *Franco zwischen Hitler und den Westmächten* (Berlin: VEB Deutscher Verlag der Wissenschaften, 1970), and Wilfried von Oven, *Hitler und der spanische Bürgerkrieg: Mission und Schicksal der Legion Condor* (Tübingen: Grabert Verlag, 1978), are both popular, broad accounts.

The only scholarly work in Spanish that comes close to the theme of this book is Viñas, *La Alemania nazi y el 18 de julio,* first and second editions. The scholarship of this Spaniard meets the best of the British, American, and German writers. Viñas writes about the same subject I have covered in chapter 1 and the second section of chapter 2. He also includes a chapter about German economic policy from 1931 to 25 July 1936. Basically his book ends where mine begins—on 25 July. His title is somewhat misleading, but the eighteenth of July—the date of the uprising—makes sense for a Spanish audience. This is one of those few books in which scholars will want to check both editions. The first edition (1974) has 558 pages, and the second (1977) has 476 pages. The bibliographies are very different. The second is more readable, but much valuable material was also cut.

Two monographs in English handle specialized aspects of the topic: Glenn T. Harper, *German Economic Policy in Spain during the Spanish Civil War, 1936-1939* (The Hague: Mouton, 1967); and Raymond Proctor (a former U.S. Air Force officer), *Hitler's Luftwaffe in the Spanish Civil War* (Westport, Conn.: Greenwood Press, 1983). Proctor consulted an outstanding list of German official Legion Condor histories and war diaries located in Freiburg. This book is good tactical military history, although it is too much of an apology for the German Luftwaffe and shows too little concern for its victims. It takes the view of history that technocrats have common sense and politicians are foolish.

There are three books that take up where this study ends and concentrate on Hitler's futile attempt to get Franco to enter the war against Britain in 1940. Donald S. Detwiler, *Hitler, Franco and Gibraltar: Die Frage des spanischen Eintritts in den Zweiten Weltkrieg* (Wiesbaden: Franz Steiner Verlag, 1962), concentrates on the diplomatic side. Charles B. Burdick, *Military Strategy and Spain in World War II* (Syracuse, N.Y.: Syracuse Univ. Press, 1968), concentrates on the military side and has an excellent bibliography. Klaus-Jorg Rühl, *Spanien im Zweiten Weltkrieg: Franco, die Falange und das 'Dritte Reich'* (Hamburg: Hoffman & Campe, 1975), is the most comprehensive of these books. Denis Smyth, "Reflex Reaction: Germany and the Onset of the Spanish Civil War," in Paul Preston, ed., *Revolution and War in Spain, 1931-1939* (New York: Harper, 1984), 243-65, is an essay of interpretation. Here, "onset" means to December 1936. He handles well Hitler's use of "communism" to influence British conservative opinion. Insofar as he uses German sources, he follows Abendroth and ignores Merkes entirely. He also plays down the Italian factor.

Bibliography of Published Books, Dissertations, and Articles

Abendroth, Hans-Henning. *Hitler in der spanischen Arena: Die deutsch-spanischen Beziehungen im Spannungsfeld der europäischeninteressen Politik vom Ausbruch des Bürgerkrieges bis zum Ausbruch des Weltkrieges 1936-1939.* Paderborn: Ferdinand Schöningh, 1973.

————. *Mittelsmann Zwischen Franco und Hitler: Johannes Bernhardt erinnert 1936.* Marktheidenfeld: Willy Schleunung G.m.b.H., 1978.

Abshagen, Karl Heinz. *Canaris.* Trans. Alan Houghton Brodrick. London: Hutchinson, 1956.

Academia Nauk CCCP. *Solidarnost narodov s ispanskoi respublukoi 1936-1939.* Moscow: Izdatelstvo Nauka, 1972.

Adamthwaite, Anthony. *France and the Coming of the Second World War.* London: Frank Cass, 1977.

Alcazar de Velasco, Angel. *Memorias de un agente secreto.* Barcelona: Plaza & Janes, S.A., 1979.

Alcofar Nassaes, José Luis. *La Marina italiana en la Guerra de España.* Madrid: Editorial Enros, 1975.

Alvarez del Vayo, Julio. *Freedom's Battle.* Trans. Eileen E. Brooke. New York: Knopf, 1940.

Arrarás, Joaquín. *Francisco Franco.* Trans. Manuel Espinosa. 9th ed. London: Bles, 1938.

————, ed. *Historia de la Cruzada española.* Vol. 38. Madrid: Ediciones Españolas, 1940.

Askew, William C. "Italian Intervention in Spain: The Agreements of March 31, 1934 with the Spanish Monarchist Parties." *Journal of Modern History* 24 (June 1952): 181-83.

Astorkia, Madeline. "L'Aviation et la Guerre d'Espagne: la cinquième arme face aux exigences de la guerre moderne." In *Deutschland und Frankreich 1936-1939,* ed. Klaus Hinderbrand and Karl Ferdinand Warner. Munich: Artemis, 1981.

Avery, David. *Not on Queen Victoria's Birthday: The Story of the Rio Tinto Mines.* London: Collins, 1974.

Aviv, Aviva and Isaac. "The Madrid Working Class, the Spanish Socialist Party and the Collapse of the Second Republic (1934-1936)." *Journal of Contemporary History* 16 (April 1981): 229-50.

Azcárate y Flores, Pablo D. *Mi embajada en Londres durante la guerra civil española.* Barcelona: Ariel, 1976.

Bamler, Rudolf. "Die Rolle des deutschen Militärischen Geheimdienstes bei der Vorbereitung und Provozierung des Zweiten Weltkrieges." *Arbeitsgemeinschaft ehemaliger Offiziere Mitteilungsblatt.* Vol. 2: 3-6. East Berlin: Kongress Verlag, 1958.

Barrett, Michael B., ed. *Proceedings of the Citadel Symposium on Hitler and the National Socialist Era, 24-25 April 1980.* Charleston, S.C.: Citadel Foundation, 1982.

Bartz, Karl. *The Downfall of the German Secret Service.* Trans. Edward Fitzgerald. London: W. Kimber, 1956.

Beck, Clarence. "A Study of German Involvement in Spain, 1936-1939." Ph.D. diss., Univ. of New Mexico, 1972.

Bertrán y Musitu, José. *Experiencias de los Servicios de Información del Nordeste de España (SIFNE) durante la guerra: una teoría técnica y una escuela sobre información general.* Madrid: Espasa Calpe, S.A., 1940.

Bird, Keith W. *German Naval History: A Guide to the Literature.* New York: Garland Reference Library of Social Science, 1985.

Birkenhead, Earl of. *The Life of Lord Halifax.* London: Hamish Hamilton, 1965.

Blinkhorn, Martin. *Carlism and the Crisis in Spain, 1931-1939.* Cambridge: Cambridge Univ. Press, 1975.

Bolín, Luís A. *Spain: The Vital Years.* Foreword, Sir Arthur Bryant. London: Cassell, 1967.

Bolloten, Burnett. *The Grand Camouflage: The Communist Conspiracy in the Spanish Civil War.* New York: Praeger, 1961.

———. *The Spanish Revolution: The Left and the Struggle for Power during the Civil War.* Chapel Hill: Univ. of North Carolina Press, 1979, 1986.

Bottai, Giuseppi. *Diario 1935-1944.* Milan: Giordano Bruno Guerri, 1982.

Bowers, Claude. *My Mission to Spain: Watching the Rehearsal for World War II.* New York: Simon & Schuster, 1954.

Brenan, Gerald. *The Spanish Labyrinth: An Account of the Social and Political Background of the Civil War.* 2nd ed. Cambridge: Cambridge Univ. Press, 1950.

Brissaud, André. *Canaris: The Biography of Admiral Canaris, Chief of German Military Intelligence in the Second World War.* Trans. and ed. Ian Colvin. London: Weidenfeld, 1973.

Broué, Pierre, and Emile Témime. *La Revolution et la Guerre d'Espagne.* Paris: Les Editions de Minuit, 1961; English translation, Boston: MIT Press, 1972.

Buchheit, Gert. *Der deutsche Geheimdienst: Geschichte der militärischen Abwehr.* Munich: Cist, 1966.

Buckley, Henry. *Life and Death of the Spanish Republic.* London: Hamish Hamilton, 1940.

Bullock, Alan L.C. *Hitler: A Study in Tyranny.* Rev. ed. New York: Harper, 1962.

Burdick, Charles B. *Germany's Military Strategy and Spain in World War II.* Syracuse, N.Y.: Syracuse Univ. Press, 1968.

Butler, J.R.M. *Lord Lothian.* New York: Macmillan, 1960.

Cannistraro, Philip V., and Wynot, Edward D., Jr. "On the Dynamics of Anti-Communism as a Function of Fascist Foreign Policy, 1933-1943." *Politico* 38 (Dec. 1973): 645-81.

Cantalupo, Roberto. *Fu la Spagna: Ambasciata pressor Franco*. Verona: Arnaldo Mondadori, 1948.

Carew-Hunt, Robert. "Willi Muenzenberg." *International Communism*. St. Antony Papers, no. 9, Carbondale: Southern Illinois Univ. Press, 1960.

Carlson, Verner R. "The Hossbach Memorandum." *Military Review* 63 (Aug. 1983): 14-30.

Carlton, David. *Anthony Eden: A Biography*. London: Allen Lane, 1981.

————. "Eden, Blum, and the Origins of Non-Intervention." *Journal of Contemporary History* 6 (July 1971): 40-54.

Carr, Raymond. *The Spanish Tragedy: The Civil War in Perspective*. London: Weidenfeld & Nicholson, 1977.

Cassels, Alan. "Mussolini and German Nationalism, 1922-25." *Journal of Modern History* 35 (June 1963): 137-57.

————. *Mussolini's Early Diplomacy*. Princeton: Princeton Univ. Press, 1970.

Castelles, Andreu. *Las Brigadas Internacionales de la guerra de España* [Coleccion Horas de España]. Barcelona: Ariel, 1974.

Cattell, David. *Communism and the Spanish Civil War*. Berkeley: Univ. of California Press, 1956.

Ceplair, Larry. *Under the Shadow of War: Fascism, Anti-Fascism and Marxists, 1918-1939*. New York: Columbia Univ. Press, 1987.

Cervera-Valderrama, Admiral Juan. *Memorias de guerra: Mi labor en el estado Mayor de la armada afecto al cuartel general del generalísimo durante la Guerra de Liberación Nacional 1936-1939*. Madrid: Editora Nacional, 1968.

Channon, Sir Henry. *'Chips': The Diaries of Sir Henry Channon*. Ed. Robert Rhodes James. London: Weidenfeld & Nicolson, 1967.

Churchill, Winston S. *Winston S. Churchill, 1922-1939: The Prophet of Truth*. Vol. 5. Ed. Martin Gilbert. Boston: Houghton Mifflin, 1977.

Ciano, Galeazzo. *The Ciano Diaries, 1939-1943*. Ed. Hugh Gibson. Garden City, N.Y.: Doubleday, 1946.

————. *Ciano's Hidden Diary, 1937-1938*. Trans. and annotated Andreas Mayer. Introduction, Malcolm Muggeridge: E.P. Dutton, 1953.

Cierva, Ricardo de la. *Historia ilustrada de la guerra civil española*. Barcelona: Ediciones Danae, 1970.

Colodny, Robert G. *The Struggle for Madrid: The Central Epic of the Spanish Conflict*. New York: Paine-Whitman, 1958.

Colton, Joel. *Léon Blum: Humanist in Politics*. New York: Knopf, 1966.

Colvin, Ian G. *Master Spy: The Incredible Story of Admiral Wilhelm Canaris, Who While Hitler's Chief of Intelligence Was a Secret Ally of the British*. New York: McGraw-Hill, 1951.

Cooper, Norman. "The Church: From Crusade to Christianity." In *Spain in Crisis*, 48-81, ed. Paul Preston. New York: Barnes & Noble, 1976.

Cornford, John. *John Conford: A Memoir*. Ed. Pat Sloan. London: Johnathan Cape, 1938.

Cot, Pierre. "Ce qui fut la 'Non-Intervention' relachée." *Le Monde*, 21 Nov. 1975.

————. *Triumph of Treason*. Trans. Sybille Crane and Milton Crane. New York: Ziff-Davis, 1944.

Coverdale, John F. *Italian Intervention in the Spanish Civil War.* Princeton: Princeton Univ. Press, 1975.

———. "Italian Intervention in the Spanish Civil War, July 1936-March 1937." Ph.D. diss., Univ. of Wisconsin, 1971.

Cowling, Maurice. *The Impact of Hitler: British Politics and British Policy, 1933-1940.* (Cambridge: Cambridge Univ. Press, 1975.

De Felice, Renzo. *Mussolini il Duce.* Vol. 2: *Lo Stato Totalitario 1936-1940.* Turin: Giulio Einaudi Editore, 1981.

Detwiler, Donald S. *Hitler, Franco und Gibraltar: Die Frage des spanischen Eintritts in den zweiten Weltkrieg.* Wiesbaden: Franz Steiner Verlag, 1962.

———. "The Origins of the Second World War" [review article]. *Air University Review* 21 (July-Aug. 1969): 94-101.

Eden, Sir Anthony. *The Memoirs of Anthony Eden, Earl of Avon: Facing the Dictators.* Boston: Houghton Mifflin, 1962.

Edwards, Jill. *The British Government and the Spanish Civil War, 1936-1939.* Forward, Hugh Thomas. London: Macmillan, 1979.

Ehrt, Adolf. *Der Weltbolschewismus: Ein internationales Gemeinschaftswerk über die bolschewistische Wühlarbeit und Umsturzversuche der Komintern in allen Ländern.* Leipzig: Nibelungen Verlag G.m.b.H., 1936. [The author worked for the Anti-Komintern Section of the German Propaganda Ministry.]

Einhorn, Marion. *Die ökonomischen Hintergrunde der faschistischen deutschen Intervention in Spanien 1936-1939.* Deutsche Akademie der Wissenschaften zu Berlin Schriften des Instituts für Geschichte Reihe 1: Allgemeine und Deutscher Geschichte, vol. 15. East Berlin: Akademie Verlag, 1962.

Ellwood, Sheelagh M. "Falange Española, 1933-9 from Fascism to Francoism." In *Spain in Conflict, 1931-1939: Democracy and Its Enemies,* ed. Martin Blinkhorn, 206-23. London: Sage Publications, 1986.

Escobar, José Ignacio [Marques de Valdeiglesias]. *Así empezó.* Madrid: G. del Toro, 1974.

Feistmann, Rudolf. "Franco's Nazi Advisor." *Living Age* 352 (June 1937): 327-30.

Feldt, Rainer Hans-Joachim. "An Account of the Activities of the Condor Legion during the Spanish Civil War." M.A. diss., California State Univ., Fullerton, 1981.

Flanner, Janet. *Men and Monuments.* New York: Harper, 1957.

Fleming, Shannon E. "A Firm Bulwark for the Defence of Western Civilization: The Nationalists' Uses of the Moroccan Protectorate during the Spanish Civil War." Paper, AHA Conference, Chicago, Dec. 1986.

Foard, Douglas W. "The Forgotten Falangist: Ernesto Gimenez Caballero." *Journal of Contemporary History* 10 (Jan. 1975): 3-18.

Foltz, Charles, Jr. *The Masquerade in Spain.* Boston: Houghton Mifflin, 1948.

Foss, William, and Gerahty, Cecil. *The Spanish Arena.* Preface, Duke of Alba. London: John Gifford, 1938.

Franco Salgado-Araujo, Francisco. *Mis conversaciones privadas con Franco.* Barcelona: Editorial Planeta, 1976.

———. *Mi vida junto a Franco.* Barcelona: Editorial Planeta, 1977.

Frank, Willard C., Jr. "Naval Operations in the Spanish Civil War, 1936-1939." *Naval War College Review* 37 (Jan.-Feb. 1984): 24-55.

———. "Sea Power, Politics, and the Onset of the Spanish Civil War." Ph.D. diss., Univ. of Pittsburgh, 1969.

————. "The Soviet Navy and the Spanish Civil War." *Proceedings of the Conference on War and Diplomacy, 1976.* Ed. David H. White. Charleston, S.C.: Citadel, 1976.

————. "The Spanish Civil War and the Coming of the Second World War." *International History Review* 9 (Aug. 1987): 368-409.

Friedlander, Robert. "Great Power Politics and Spain's Civil War." *Historian* 90 (Jan. 1975): 103-12.

————. "The July 1936 Military Rebellion in Spain: Background and Beginnings." Ph.D. diss., Northwestern Univ., 1963.

Funke, Manfred. *Sanktionen und Kanonen.* Düsseldorf: Droste Verlag, 1970.

Gallagher, M.D. "Léon Blum and the Spanish Civil War." *Journal of Contemporary History* 6 (July 1971): 56-64.

Galland, Adolf. *The First and Last: The Rise and Fall of the German Fighter Forces, 1938-1945.* Trans. Mervyn Savill. London: Ballantine, 1954.

Gárate Górdoba, José María. *La guerra de las Españas: Brevia historia de la guerra del 36.* Barcelona: Biblioteca Universal Caralt, 1976.

Garriga, Ramón. *La Legión Condor.* Madrid: G. del Toro, 1975.

————. *Las relaciones secretas entre Franco y Hitler.* Buenos Aires: Jorge Alvarez Editor, 1965.

Gemzell, Carl-Axel. *Raeder, Hitler und Skandinavien: Der Kampf für einen Maritimen Operationsplan.* Lund, Sweden: CWK Gleercup, 1965.

George, Margaret. *The Warped Vision: British Foreign Policy, 1933-1939.* Pittsburgh: Univ. of Pittsburgh Press, 1965.

Geyer, Michael. "National Socialist Germany: The Politics of Information." In Ernest R. May, ed., *Knowing One's Enemies: Intelligence Assessment before the Two World Wars.* Princeton: Princeton Univ. Press, 1985.

Gilbert, Martin, and Gott, Richard. *The Appeasers.* Boston: Houghton Mifflin, 1963.

Gil-Robles y Quinones, José María. *No fué posible la paz.* Buenos Aires: Editorial Sud America, 1968.

Gisevius, Hans. *To the Bitter End.* Trans. Richard Winston and Clara Winston. Boston: Houghton Mifflin, 1947.

Greene, Nathanael. *Crisis and Decline: The French Socialists and the Popular Front Era.* Ithaca: Cornell Univ. Press, 1969.

Greton, Peter. "The Nyon Conference—The Naval Aspect." *English Historical Review* 90 (Jan. 1975): 103-12.

Groscurth, Helmuth. *Tagebücher eines Abwehroffiziers 1938-1940: Mit weiteren Dokumenten zur Militäropposition gegen Hitler.* Ed. Helmut Krausnick and Harold C. Deutsch, with the assistance of Hildegard von Kotze. Stuttgart: Deutsche Verlags-Anstalt, 1970.

Gross, Babette. *Willi Münzenberg: A Political Biography.* Trans. Marian Jackson. East Lansing: Michigan State Univ. Press, 1974.

Gruber, Helmut. "Willi Münzenberg: Propagandist for and against the Comintern." *International Review of Social History* 10, pt. 2 (1965): 188-210.

Guariglia, Raffaele. *Ricordi, 1922-46.* Naples: Edizioni scienfiche italiane, 1950.

Guarnieri, Felice. *Battaglie economiche fra le due grandi guerre.* 2 vols. Milan: Garzanti, 1953.

Guderian, Heinz. *Panzer Leader.* Trans. Constantine Fitzgibbon. New York: Dutton, 1952.

Harper, Glenn T. *German Economic Policy in Spain during the Spanish Civil War, 1936-1939.* The Hague: Mouton, 1967.

Hart, B.H. Liddell. *The German Generals Talk.* New York: Morrow, 1948.

———. *Memoirs.* New York: Dutton, 1952.

Harvey, Charles E. "Politics and Pyrites during the Spanish Civil War." *Economic History Review* 31 (February 1978): 89-104.

Harvey, John, ed. *The Diplomatic Diaries of Oliver Harvey, 1937-1940.* London: Collins, 1970.

Haslam, Jonathan. "The Comintern and the Origins of the Popular Front." *Historical Journal* 22 (Sept. 1979): 673-91.

———. *The Soviet Union and the Struggle for Collective Security in Europe, 1933-1939.* New York: St. Martin's Press, 1984.

Hauser, Oswald. "England und Hitler, 1936-1939." In *Geschichte und Gegenwart: Festschrift für Karl Dietrich Erdmann,* ed. Hartmut Boockmann, Kurt Jürgensen, and Gerhard Stolteberg. Neumünster: Karl Wachholtz Verlag, 1980.

Henke, Joseph. *England in Hitlers politischem Kalkül 1935-1939.* Boppard: Harald Boldt, 1973.

Henrikson, Göran. "Das Nürnberger Dokument 386-PS (das 'Hossbach-Protokoll')." In *Probleme Deutscher Zeitgeschichte,* ed. Göran Rystad and Sven Tägil. Stockholm: Läronedelsförlagen, 1971.

Hernández, Jesús. *La grande Trahison.* Trans. Pierre Berthelin. Paris: Fasquelle, 1953.

Hesse, Fritz. *Hitler and the English.* Ed. and trans. F.A. Voight. London: Allan Wingate, 1954.

Hiden, John, and Farquharson, John. *Explaining Hitler's Germany: Historians and the Third Reich.* Totowa, N.J.: Barnes & Noble, 1983.

Hills, George. *Franco: The Man and His Nation.* London: Robert Hale, 1967.

Hitler, Adolf. *Mein Kampf.* Complete and unabridged. Editorial sponsors, Sidney B. Fay et al. New York: Reynal & Hitchcock, 1939.

———. *On National Socialism and World Relations* [speech, 30 Jan. 1937]. Berlin: Müller & Sohn, 1937.

———. *The Speeches of Adolf Hitler: April 1922-August 1939.* Ed. and trans. Norman H. Baynes. 2 vols. London: Oxford Univ. Press, 1942.

Homze, Edward L. *Arming the Luftwaffe: The Reich Air Ministry and the German Aircraft Industry, 1919-1939.* Lincoln: Univ. of Nebraska Press, 1976.

———. *German Military Aviation: A Guide to the Literature.* New York: Garland, 1984.

Horton, Albert C. "Germany and the Spanish Civil War." Ph.D. diss., Columbia Univ., 1966.

Iklé, Frank. *German-Japanese Relations, 1936-1940.* New York: Bookman, 1956.

Irving, David, ed. [Unofficial documents] *The Rise and Fall of the Luftwaffe: The Life of Luftwaffe Marshal Erhard Milch.* London: Weidenfeld & Nicholson, 1973.

Jackson, Gabriel. *The Spanish Republic and the Civil War, 1931-1939.* Princeton: Princeton Univ. Press, 1965.

Jacobsen, Jans-Adolf. *Nationalsozialistische Aussenpolitik, 1933-1938.* Frankfurt: Alfred Metzner Verlag, 1968.

Jellinek, Frank. *The Civil War in Spain.* London: Gollancz, 1938.

Joll, James. "The Making of the Popular Front." In *Decline of the Third Republic,* ed. Joll. St. Antony Papers, no. 5. London: Chatto & Windus, 1959.

Jones, Thomas. *A Diary with Letters, 1931-1950.* Oxford: Clarendon Press, 1954.

Kahn, David. "The Forschungsamt: Nazi Germany's Most Secret Communications Agency." *Cryptologia* 2 (Jan. 1978): 12-19.

————. *Hitler's Spies: German Military Intelligence in World War II.* London: Hodder & Stoughton, 1978.

Kesselring, Albert. *The Memoirs of Field Marshal Kesselring.* London: William Kimber, 1953.

Kleinfeld, Gerald R., and Tambs, Lewis A. *Hitler's Spanish Legion: The Blue Division in Russia.* Carbondale: Southern Illinois Univ. Press, 1979.

Knox, MacGregor. "Conquest, Foreign and Domestic in Fascist Italy and Nazi Germany." *Journal of Modern History* 56 (March 1984): 1-57.

Kordt, Erich. *Nicht aus den Akten.* Stuttgart: Deutsche Verlags-Anstalt, 1950.

Krausnick, Helmut. "Canaris." *Neue deutsche Biographie* 3: 116-18. Berlin: Puncker & Humbolt, 1957.

Kritvitsky, Walther. *In Stalin's Secret Service.* New York: Harper, 1939.

Kühne, Horst. *Revolutionäre Militärpolitik 1936-39: Militärpolitische Aspekte des nationalrevolutionären Kriegs in Spanien.* East Berlin: Deutscher Verlag, 1969.

Kuusisto, Seppo. *Alfred Rosenberg in der nationalsozialistichen Aussenpolitik 1933-39.* Helsinki: Soumen historiallinen Seura, 1984.

Lacouture, Jean. *André Malraux.* Trans. Alan Sheridan. New York: Pantheon, 1975.

Last, Jef. *The Spanish Tragedy.* London: Routledge, 1939.

Laureau, Patrick. "L'Aviation Sovietique en Espagne en 1936 L'Echelon Precurseur." *Mélanges de la Casa de Velázquez* 21 (Paris: Defusion de Boccard, 1985): 309-29.

Lee, Asher. *The German Air Force.* Forward, Carl Spaatz. London: Duckworth, 1946.

Levy, Louis. *The Truth about France.* Trans. W. Pickles. London: Penguin, 1941.

Lewis, S.J. *Forgotten Legions: German Army Infantry Policy, 1918-1941.* New York: Praeger, 1986.

Lewy, Guenter. *The Catholic Church and Nazi Germany.* New York: McGraw Hill, 1964.

Linz, Juan. "Political Space and Fascism as a Late Comer." In *Who Were the Fascists? Social Roots of European Fascism,* ed. Stein U. Larsen, et al., 153-89. New York: Columbia Univ. Press, 1981.

————. "Some Notes toward a Comparative Study of Fascism in Sociological Historical Perspective." In *Fascism: A Readers Guide: Analyses, Interpretations, Bibliography,* ed. Walter Z. Laqueur, 3-121. Berkeley: Univ. of California Press, 1976.

Loveday, Arthur F. *World War in Spain.* London: John Murray, 1939.

Low, Mary, and Brea, Juan. *Red Spanish Notebook: The First Six Months of the Revolution and the Civil War.* London: Secker & Warburg, 1937.

Ludecke, Kurt G.W. *I Knew Hitler: The Story of a Nazi Who Escaped the Blood Purge.* London: Jerrolds, 1938.

Macdonald, Nancy. *Homage to the Spanish Exiles.* New York: Human Sciences Press, March 1987.

Madariaga, Salvador de. *Spain: A Modern History.* New York: Praeger, 1953.

Magistrati, Massimo. *L'Italia a Berlino, 1937-1939*. Verona: Arnaldo Mondadori, 1956.

Maíz, B. Félix. *Alzamiento en España: De un diario de la conspiración*. Pamplona: Gómez, 1952.

———. *Mola: Aquel Hombre*. Barcelona: Editorial Planeta, 1976.

Malraux, André. *Man's Hope*. Trans. Stuart Gilbert and Alastair MacDonald. New York: Random House, 1938.

Manne, Robert. "The British Decision for Alliance with Russia, May 1939." *Journal of Contemporary History* 9 (July 1974): 3-26.

Manvell, Roger, and Fraenkel, Heinrich. *The Canaris Conspiracy: The Secret Resistance to Hitler in the Germany Army*. New York: McKay, 1969.

Margina Barrio, Antonio. "El Vaticano contra la cruzada: El Cardenal Gomá: El fracaso diplomático del Marqués de Magaz." *Historia 16* 3, no. 22 (Feb. 1978): 39-52.

Mason, T.W. "Some Origins of the Second World War." *Past & Present* 29 (Dec. 1964): 67-87.

Matsuoka, Yosuke. *Die Bedeutung des Deutsch-Japanischen Abkommens gegen die Kommunistische Internationale*. Tokyo: Nippon Dempo Tsushin-sha, n.d. [1939-40?].

May, Ernest R., ed. *Knowing One's Enemies: Intelligence Assessment before the Two World Wars*. Princeton: Princeton Univ. Press, 1985.

McKale, Donald M. *The Swastika outside Germany*. Kent, Oh.: Kent State Univ. Press, 1977.

Meaker, Gerald H. *The Revolutionary Left in Spain, 1914-1923*. Stanford: Stanford Univ. Press, 1974.

Meier-Dörnberg, Wilhelm. *Die Ölversorgung der Kriegsmarine 1935 bis 1945*. Freiburg: Verlag Rombach, 1973.

Meir, Michaelis. "La prima missione del principe d'Assia presso Mussolini Agosto '36." *Nuova Rivista Storica* 55 (May-Aug. 1971): 367-70.

———. "World Power Status or World Dominion? A Survey of Literature on Hitler's Plan of World Dominion, 1937-1970." *Historical Journal* 15 (June 1972): 331-60.

Merkes, Manfred. *Die deutsche Politik gegenüber dem spanischen Bürgerkrieg 1936-1939*. Bonner Historische Forschungen, 2nd ed. Bonn: Ludwig Röhrscheid, 1969.

Micaud, Charles A. *The French Right and Nazi Germany*. Durham: Duke Univ. Press, 1943.

Michalka, Wolfgang. *Ribbentrop und die deutsche Weltpolitik 1933-1940: Aussenpolitische Konzeptionen und Entscheidungsprozesse im Dritten Reich*. Munich: Wilhelm Fink Verlag, 1980.

Miksche, Ferdinand Otto. *Attack: A Study of Blitzkrieg Tactics*. New York: Random House, 1942.

———. *Paratroops*. New York: Random House, 1943.

Milton, Sybil. "The Spanish Republican Refugees in France, 1938-41." Paper at conference on "World War II—The 50th Anniversary: 1936–The Spanish Civil War." Siena College, New York, June 1986.

Mola-Vidal, Emilio. *Memorias*. 2nd ed. Barcelona: Editorial Planeta, 1977. [1st ed., 1932]

Moreno, Francisco. *La Guerra en el Mar: Hombres, Barcos y Honra.* Barcelona: Editorial A.H.R., 1959.

Morley, James W., ed. *Deterrent Diplomacy: Japan, Germany, and the USSR (1935-1940).* Trans. Hans H. Baerwald. New York: Columbia Univ. Press, 1977.

Murray, Williamson. *Luftwaffe.* Baltimore, Md.: Nautical & Aviation Publication Co., 1984.

O'Duffy, Eoin. *Crusade in Spain.* Dublin: Robert Hale, 1938.

Ohata, L., and Tokushiro, F. "The Anti-Comintern Pact, 1935-1939." In *Deterrent Diplomacy,* ed. James Morley. New York: Columbia Univ. Press, 1977.

Papeleux, Léon. *L'Amiral Canaris entre Franco et Hitler: Le Rôle de Canaris dans les relations germano-espagnoles (1915-1944).* Paris: Casterman, 1977.

Paris Equilaz, Higinio. *España en la economía mundial.* Madrid: Diana Artes Gráficas, 1947.

Payne, Stanley G. "The Army, the Republic and the Outbreak of the Civil War." In Raymond Carr, ed., *The Republic and the Civil War in Spain,* 79-106. New York: St. Martins, 1971.

—————. *Falange: History of Spanish Fascism.* Stanford: Stanford Univ. Press, 1961.

—————. *Fascism: Comparison and Definition.* Madison: Univ. of Wisconsin Press, 1980.

—————. "Fascism and Right Authoritarianism in the Iberian World—The Last Twenty Years." *Journal of Contemporary History* 21 (April 1986): 163-77.

—————. *The Franco Regime, 1936-1975.* Madison: Univ. of Wisconsin Press, 1987.

—————. *Politics and the Military in Modern Spain.* Palo Alto: Stanford Univ. Press, 1967.

—————. "Spain." In Hans Rogger and Eugene Weber, eds., *The European Right: A Historical Profile.* Berkeley: Univ. of California Press, 1965.

—————. *The Spanish Revolution.* New York: Norton, 1970.

Pertinax [André Géraud]. *The Gravediggers of France.* Garden City, N.Y.: Doubleday, 1944.

Petersen, Jens. *Hitler-Mussolini: Die Entstehung der Achse Berlin-Rom 1933-1936.* Tübingen: Max Niemeyer Verlag, 1973.

Pike, David Wingeate. *Conjecture, Propaganda, and Deceit and the Spanish Civil War: The International Crisis over Spain, 1936-1939, As Seen in the French Press.* Stanford: California Institute of International Studies, 1968.

—————. "Franco and the Axis Stigma." *Journal of Contemporary History* 17 (July 1982): 369-407.

Preston, Paul. *The Coming of the Spanish Civil War: Reform, Reaction and Revolution in the Second Republic, 1931-1936.* New York: Harper & Row, 1978.

—————. *Revolution and War in Spain, 1931-1939.* New York: Methuen, 1984.

—————, ed. *Spain in Crisis: The Evolution and Decline of the Franco Regime.* New York: Barnes & Noble, 1976.

Primo de Rivera, José Antonio. "El interrogatorio de José Antonio," ed. Ricardo de la Cierva. *Historia y Vida,* no. 88 (July 1975): 50-63.

Proctor, Raymond L. *Agony of a Neutral: Spanish-German Wartime Relations and the "Blue Division."* Moscow, Ida.: Idaho Research Foundation, 1974.

—————. "Condor Legion." In *Historical Dictionary of the Spanish Civil Wars,* ed. James W. Cortada. Westport, Conn.: Greenwood, 1982.

———. *Hitler's Luftwaffe in the Spanish Civil War.* Westport, Conn.: Greenwood, 1983.

Rauschning, Hermann. *Hitler Speaks: A Series of Political Conversations with Adolf Hitler on His Real Aims.* London: Butterworth, 1939.

Rello, Salvador. *La aviación en la guerra en España.* Vol. 1. Madrid: San Martin, 1969.

Richardson, R. Dan. *Comintern Army: The International Brigades in the Spanish Civil War.* Lexington: Univ. Press of Kentucky, 1982.

Ridruejo, Dionisio. *Casi unas memorias: Con fuego y con raíces.* Prologue, Salvador de Madariaga. Barcelona: Editorial Planeta, 1976.

———. *Escrito en España.* Prologue, Ramón Serrano Súñer. 2nd ed. Madrid: Editorial G. del Toro, 1976. [1st ed., 1961]

Robertson, Esmonde M. *Mussolini as Empire Builder: Europe and Africa, 1932-1936.* New York: St. Martin's Press, 1977.

Robinson, Richard A.H. *The Origins of Franco's Spain: The Right, the Republic and Revolution, 1931-1936.* Pittsburgh, Pa.: Univ. of Pittsburgh Press, 1970.

Roskill, Stephen. *Naval Policy between the Wars.* Vol. 2: *The Period of Reluctant Rearmament, 1930-1939.* London: Collins, 1976.

Rosselli, Carlo. "The Diary of a Militiaman." In Frances Keene, ed. *Neither Liberty Nor Bread: The Meaning and Tragedy of Fascism.* New York: Harper, 1940.

Sáinz Rodríguez, Pedro. *Testimonio y recuerdos.* Barcelona: Editorial Planeta, 1978.

Salas Larrazábal, Jesús. *Air War over Spain.* Trans. Margaret A. Kelly. London: Allan, 1969.

———. *La intervención extranjera en la guerra de España.* Madrid: Editora Nacional, 1974.

Salas Larrozábal, Ramón. *Historia del Ejército Popular de la República.* 4 vols., vols. 1, 2, 4. Madrid: Editora Nacional, 1973.

Scheele, Alexander von. "Legion Condor." *Die Wehrmacht,* 7 June 1939, 4-8.

Schieder, Wolfgang, and Dipper, Christof, eds. *Der Spanische Bürgerkrieg in der Internationalen Politik 1936-1939.* Munich: Nymphenburger Verlagshandlung, 1976.

Schlabrendorff, Fabian von. *The Secret War against Hitler.* Trans. Hilda Simon. New York: Pitman, 1965.

Schleimann, Jorgen. "The Organizational Man: The Life and Work of Willi Münzenberg." *Survey,* no. 55 (Apr. 1965): 64-91.

Schmidt, Paul. *Hitler's Interpreter,* ed. R.H.C. Steed. London: Heinemann, 1950.

Schreiber, Gerhard. *Revisionismus und Weltmachtstreben: Marineführung und deutsch-italienische Beziehungen 1919 bis 1944.* Stuttgart: Deutsche Verlagsanstalt, 1978.

Schuschnigg, Kurt. *Austrian Requiem.* Trans. Franz von Hilderbrand. New York: Putnam, 1946.

Schwoerer, Lois G. "Lord Halifax's Visit to Germany: November 1937." *Historian* 32 (May 1970): 353-75.

Serrano Suñer, Ramón. *Entre Hendaya y Gibraltar: Noticia y reflexión, frente a una leyenda, sobre nuestra política en dos guerras.* 2nd ed. Madrid: Ediciones y publicaciones españolas, S.A., 1947.

———. *Entre el silencio y la propaganda: La historia como fué memoria.* Barcelona: Editorial Planeta, 1977.

Sipols, V., and Pankroskova, M. "Preparation of the Munich Deal: Britain's Road to Munich." 5 parts. *International Affairs* (Moscow), nos. 4, 6, 7, 10 (Apr.-Nov. 1973): 78 ff.

Slaughter, Margaret J. "Italian Antifascism: The Italian Volunteers in the Spanish Civil War." Ph.D. diss., Univ. of New Mexico, 1973.

Sommer, Theo. *Deutschland und Japan Zwischen den Mächten 1935-1940: Vom Antikominternpakt zum Dreimachte Pakt.* Tübingen: J.C.B. Mohr, 1962.

Southworth, Herbert R. "Conspiración contra la República." *Historia 16·3* (June 1978): 41-57.

————. *Guernica! Guernica! A Study of Journalism, Diplomacy, Propaganda and History.* Berkeley: Univ. of California Press, 1977.

Speer, Albert. *Spandau: The Secret Diaries.* Trans. Richard Winston and Clara Winston. New York: Macmillan, 1976.

Stein, Louis. *Beyond Death and Exile: The Spanish Republicans in France, 1939-1955.* Cambridge, Mass.: Harvard Univ. Press, 1979.

Stone, Glyn. "Britain, Non-Intervention and the Spanish Civil War." *European Studies Review* 9 (Jan. 1979): 129-49.

Stratton, Roy A. "Germany's Secret Supply Service." *United States Naval Institute Proceedings* 79 (Oct. 1953): 1085-90.

Sywottek, Julia. *Mobilmachung für den totalen Krieg: Die propagandistische Vorbereitung der deutsche Bevölkerung auf den Zweiten Weltkrieg.* Opladen: West-deutscher Verlag, 1976.

Szembeck, Jan. *Journal, 1933-1939.* Trans. J. Rzewuska and T. Zaleski, prepared by Leon Noël. Paris: Plon, 1952.

Tabouis, Geneviève. *They Called Me Cassandra.* New York: Scribner, 1942.

Tanner, Stephen. "German Naval Intervention in the Spanish Civil War as Reflected by the German Records, 1936-1939." Ph.D. diss., American Univ., 1976.

Thomas, Georg. *Geschichte der deutschen Wehr-und Rüstungswirtschaft 1918-1943/45.* Ed. Wolfgang Birkenfeld. Boppard am Rhein: Harald Boldt Verlag, 1966.

Thomas, Hugh. *The Spanish Civil War.* 1st, 3rd, and 4th eds. New York: Harper, 1961, 1977, 1986.

Tiersky, Ronald. *French Communism, 1920-1972.* New York: Columbia Univ. Press, 1974.

Toscano, Mario. *The Origins of the Pact of Steel.* Baltimore: Johns Hopkins Univ. Press, 1967.

Treue, Wilhelm. "Hitlers Denkschrift zum Vierjahresplan 1936." *Vierteljahrshefte für Zeitgeschichte* 3 (Apr. 1955): 184-203.

Tussell, Javier. *Las elecciones de Frente Popular.* 2 vols. Madrid: Cuadernos Para el Díalogo, 1971.

————. *Franco y los católicos: La Política interior Española entre 1945 y 1947.* Madrid: Alianza Union, 1984.

Ulbricht, Walther. *Zur Geschichte der deutschen Arbeiterbewegung: Aus Reden und Aufsätzen.* 2 vols. Berlin: Dietz Verlag, 1954.

"USSR." In *Solidarnost narodov s ispanskoi respublukoi 1936-1939.* Ed. Academia Nauk CCCP. Moscow: Izdatelstvo Nauka, 1972.

Velarde Fuertes, Juan. "Un aspecto del asunto Montaña." *De Economia* 21 (March 1968): 131-55.

Vigón, General Jorge. *General Mola: El conspirador.* Barcelona: Ediciones A.H.R., 1957.

Viñas Martin, Angel. *La Alemania nazi y el 18 de Julio.: Antecedentes de la intervención alemana en la guerra española.* 1st ed. Madrid: Alianza Editorial, 1974.

———. *La Alemania nazi y el 18 de Julio:.* 2nd ed. Madrid: Alianza Editorial, 1977.

———. "Los espías nazis entran en la guerra civil." *Historia Internacional* no. 7 (Oct. 1975): 27-29.

———. *Guerra, Dinero, Dictadura: Ayuda fascista y autarquía en la España de Franco.* Barcelona: Editorial Crítica, 1984.

———. *El oro español en la Guerra Civil.* Madrid: Instituto de Estudios Fiscales Ministerio de Hacienda, 1976.

———. *El oro de Moscú: Alfa y omega de un mito franquista.* 2nd ed. Barcelona: Ediciones Grijalbo, 1979.

———, et al. *Política comercial exterior en España (1931-1975).* Vol. 1. Madrid: Banco Exterior de España, 1979.

Waite, Robert. *The Psychopathic God: Adolf Hitler.* New York: Basic Books, 1977.

Watt, D.C. "Appeasement: The Rise of a Revisionist School?" *Political Quarterly* 36 (April-June 1965): 191-213.

Weber, Eugen. *Action Française.* Stanford: Stanford Univ. Press, 1962.

Weinberg, Gerhard. "Die geheimen Abkommen zum Anti-Komintern Pakt." *Vierteljahreshefte für Zeitgeschichte* 2 (Apr. 1954): 193-201.

———. *The Foreign Policy of Hitler's Germany.* Vol. 1: *Diplomatic Revolution in Europe, 1933-36.* Vol. 2: *Starting of World War II, 1937-39.* Chicago: Univ. of Chicago Press, 1970, 1980.

[Weizsäcker, Ernst von]. *Die Weizsäcker-Papiere 1933-1950.* Ed. Leonidas E. Hill. Berlin: Propyläean, n.d. [1975].

Westmann, K. "Juni 1937—Die Provokation des leichten Kreuzers 'Leipzig.' " *Marinewesen* 7 (1968): 747-52.

Whealey, Robert. H. "Anglo-American Oil Confronts Spanish Nationalism, 1927-31: A Study of Economic Imperialism." *Diplomatic History* 12 (Spring 1988): 111-26.

———. "La diplomacia española del petróleo: De junio de 1927 a abril de 1931." In *Cuadernos Economicos de ICE* no. 10, 511-31. Madrid: Información Comercial Española, Ministerio de Comercio y Turismo, 1979.

———. "Economic Influence of the Great Powers in the Spanish Civil War: From the Popular Front to the Second World War." *International History Review* 5 (May 1983): 229-54.

———. "Foreign Intervention in the Spanish Civil War." In *The Republic and the Civil War in Spain,* ed. Raymond Carr, 213-34. New York: St. Martin's Press, 1971.

———. "Franco." In *Historical Dictionary of the Spanish Civil War,* ed. James Cortada. Westport, Conn.: Greenwood, 1982.

———. "German-Spanish Relations, January-August 1939: The Failure of Germany to Conclude Economic and Military Agreements with Spain." Ph.D. diss., Univ. of Michigan, 1963.

———. "How Franco Financed His War—Reconsidered." *Journal of Contempo-*

rary History 12 (Jan. 1977): 133-52. Second and expanded edition in *Spain in Conflict 1931-1939: Democracy and Its Enemies,* ed. Martin Blinkhorn, 244-63. London: Sage, 1986.

———. "Mussolini's Ideological Diplomacy: An Unpublished Document." *Journal of Modern History* 39 (Dec. 1967): 432-37.

———. "Nazi Economic Imperialism: Spain, 1936-1939." In *Proceedings of the Citadel Symposium on Hitler and the National Socialist Era, 24-25 April 1980,* ed. Michael B. Barrett. Charleston, S.C.: Citadel Foundation, 1982.

———. "Opportunities and Disappointments in the Spanish Foreign Ministry Archives." *Archives* 12 (Autumn 1975): 68-73.

Wheeler-Bennett, John. *King George VI: His Life and Reign.* New York: St. Martin's, 1958.

Wilberg, Hellmuth. "Auf Geheimen Befehl." *Der Adler.* Heft 8, Sonderheft Legion Condor an die Front, 1 June 1939, 8-10.

Windell, George. "Leon Blum and the Crisis over Spain, 1936." *Historian* 24 (Aug. 1962): 423-49.

Wiskemann, Elizabeth. *The Rome-Berlin Axis.* New York: Oxford Univ. Press, 1949.

Young, A.P., ed. [Unofficial documents.] *The X Documents.* Ed. Arthur Primrose Young. London: André Deutsch, 1974.

Young, Robert J. "French Military Intelligence and Nazi Germany, 1938-1939." In Ernest R. May, ed., *Knowing One's Enemies: Intelligence Assessment before the Two World Wars.* Princeton: Princeton Univ. Press, 1985.

Zeman, Z.A.B. *Nazi Propaganda.* London: Oxford Univ. Press for Wiener Library, 1964.

Zuerl, Walter. *Pour-le-Mérite Flieger: Heldentaten und Erlebnisse unserer Kriegsflieger.* Foreword, Gen. Friedrich Christiansen. Munich: Curt Pechstein Verlag, 1938.

Index